IP MULTICAST WITH APPLICATIONS TO IPTV AND MOBILE DVB-H

IP MULTICAST WITH APPLICATIONS TO IPTV AND MOBILE DVB-H

Daniel Minoli

WILEY-INTERSCIENCE

A JOHN WILEY & SONS, INC., PUBLICATION

Library of Congress Cataloging-in-Publication Data

Minoli, Daniel, 1952-
   IP multicast with applications to IPTV and mobile DVB-H / Daniel Minoli.
      p. cm.
   Includes bibliographical references and index.
   ISBN 978-0-470-25815-6 (cloth)
1.   Webcasting.   2.   Internet television.   3.   Digital video.   I.   Title.
   TK5105.887M578 2008
   006.7–dc22

                               2007038116

For Anna and the kids.
And for my parents Gino and Angela

Also thanking
Mike Neen

CONTENTS

PREFACE

This book updates early-release published work undertaken by the author in the early-to-mid-1990s on the topic of video-for-telcos ("telco TV"), video-over-packet, video-over-DLS, and video-over-ATM contained in the book *Video Dialtone Technology: Digital Video over ADSL, HFC, FTTC, and ATM*, McGraw-Hill, 1995, and based on extensive hands-on work on broadband communications and digital video/digital imaging. At this juncture, the focus of this book (and for this industry) is completely on commercial-quality video over IP, IPTV.

Of late there has been renewed interest in IP multicast protocols and technologies because of the desire by traditional telephone companies to deliver entertainment-level video services over their network using next-generation infrastructures based on IP networking, by the cell phone companies for video streams to hand held telephone sets and personal digital assistants (PDAs), and by the traditional TV broadcast companies seeking to enter the same mobile video market. Critical factors in multicasting include bandwidth efficiency and delivery tree topology optimization.

IP multicast technology is stable and relatively easy to implement, particularly for architecturally simple (yet large) networks. A lot of the basic IP multicast mechanisms were developed in the mid-to-late 1980s, with other basic work undertaken in the 1980s. A number of recent functional enhancements have been added. From a commercial deployment perspective, IP multicast is now where IP was in the mid-1990s: poised to take off and experience widespread deployment. Examples of applications requiring one-to-many or many-to-many communications include but are not limited to digital entertainment video and audio distribution, multisite corporate videoconferencing, broad distribution financial data, stock quotes and news bulletins, database replication, software distribution, and content caching (for example, Web site caching).

The text literature on IP multicast is limited and somewhat dated, particularly in reference to IPTV applications. This compact text is intended for practitioners that seek a quick practical review of the topic with emphasis on the major and most-often used aspects of the technology. Given its focus on IPTV and DVB-H it can also be used by technology integrators and service providers that wish to enter this field.

Following an introductory discussion in Chapter 1, Chapter 2 covers multicast addressing for payload distribution. Chapter 3 focuses on multicast payload forwarding. Chapter 4 covers the important topic of dynamic host registration using the Internet Group Management Protocol. Chapter 5 looks at multicast routing in sparse-mode environments and the broadly used PIM-SM. Chapter 6 discusses CBT. Chapter 7 looks at multicast routing for dense-mode protocols and PIM-DM in particular. Chapter 8 examines DVMRP and MOSPF. The next chapter, Chapter 9, covers IP multicasting in IPv6 environments. Chapter 10 looks at Multicast Listener Discovery (MLD) snooping switches. Finally, Chapters 11 and 12 give examples in the IPTV and (mobile) DVB-H environments, respectively. Portions of the presentation are pivoted off and summarized from fundamental RFCs; other key sections are developed here for the first time, based on the author's multidecade experience in digital video. The reference RFCs and protocols are placed in the proper context of a commercial-grade infrastructure for the delivery of robust, entertainment-quality linear and nonlinear video programming.

Telephone carriers (telcos), cell phone companies, traditional TV broadcasters, cable TV companies, equipment manufacturers, content providers, content aggregators, satellite companies, venture capitalists, and colleges and technical schools can make use of this text. The text can be used for a college course on IP multicast and/or IPTV. There is now a global interest by all the telcos in Europe, Asia, and North America to enter the IPTV and DVB-H market in order to replace revenues that have eroded to cable TV companies and wireless providers. Nearly all the traditional telcos worldwide are looking into these technologies at this juncture. Telcos need to compete with cable companies and IPTV and DVB-H is the way to do it. In fact, even the cable TV companies themselves are looking into upgrading their ATM technology to IP. This book is a brand-new look at the IP multicast space.

ABOUT THE AUTHOR

Daniel Minoli has many years of technical hands-on and managerial experience (including budget and/or PL responsibility) in networking, telecom, video, enterprise architecture, and security for global best-in-class carriers and financial companies. He has worked at AIG, ARPA think tanks, Bell Telephone Laboratories, ITT, Prudential Securities, Bell Communications Research (now Telcordia), AT&T, Capital One Financial, and SES AMERICOM, where he is director of terrestrial systems engineering. Previously, he also played a founding role in the launching of two companies through the high-tech incubator Leading Edge Networks Inc., which he ran in the early 2000s; Global Wireless Services, a provider of secure broadband hotspot mobile Internet and hotspot VoIP services; and InfoPort Communications Group, an optical and Gigabit Ethernet metropolitan carrier supporting Data Center/SAN/channel extension and Grid Computing network access services.

For several years he has been Session-, Tutorial-, or overall Technical Program Chair for the IEEE ENTNET (Enterprise Networking) conference. ENTNET focuses on enterprise networking requirements for large financial firms and other corporate institutions.

At SES AMERICOM, Mr. Minoli has been responsible for engineering satellite-based IPTV and DVB-H systems. This included overall engineering design, deployment, and operation of SD/HD encoding, inner/outer AES encryption, Conditional Access Systems, video middleware, Set Top boxes, Headends, and related terrestrial connectivity. At Bellcore/Telcordia, he did extensive work on broadband; on video-on-demand for the RBOCs (then known as Video Dialtone); on multimedia over ISDN/ATM; and on distance learning (satellite) networks. At DVI he deployed (satellite-based) distance-learning system for William Patterson College. At Stevens Institute of Technology (Adjunct), he taught about a dozen graduate courses on digital video. At AT&T, he deployed large broadband networks also to support video applications, for example, video over ATM. At Capital One, he was involved with the deployment of corporate Video-on-demand over the IP-based intranet. As a consultant he handled the technology-assessment function of several high-tech companies seeking funding, developing multimedia, digital video, physical layer switching, VSATs, telemedicine, Java-based CTI, VoFR & VPNs, HDTV, optical chips, H.323 gateways, nanofabrication/ (Quantum Cascade Lasers), wireless, and TMN mediation.

Mr. Minoli has also written columns for *ComputerWorld, NetworkWorld*, and *Network Computing* (1985–2006). He has taught at New York University (Information Technology Institute), Rutgers University, Stevens Institute of Technology, and

Monmouth University (1984–2006). Also, he was a Technology Analyst At-Large, for Gartner/DataPro (1985–2001); based on extensive hand-on work at financial firms and carriers, he tracked technologies and wrote around 50 CTO/CIO-level technical/ architectural scans in the area of telephony and data systems, including topics on security, disaster recovery, IT outsourcing, network management, LANs, WANs (ATM and MPLS), wireless (LAN and public hotspot), VoIP, network design/economics, carrier networks (such as metro Ethernet and CWDM/DWDM), and e-commerce. Over the years, he has advised Venture Capitals for investments of $150M in a dozen high-tech companies. He has acted as Expert Witness in a (won) $11B lawsuit regarding a VoIP-based wireless Air-to-Ground communication system, and has been involved as a technical expert in a number of patent infringement proceedings.

1

INTRODUCTION TO IP MULTICAST

1.1 INTRODUCTION

Although "not much" new has occurred in the "science" of the Internet Protocol (IP) multicast space in the past few years, there is now keen interest in this technology because of the desire by traditional telephone companies to deliver entertainment-level video services over their networks using next-generation infrastructures based on IP networking and by the cell phone companies to deliver video streams to handheld telephone sets and Personal Digital Assistants (PDAs). A critical factor in multicasting is bandwidth efficiency in the transport network. IP multicast, defined originally in RFC 988 (Request for Comments) (1986) and then further refined in RFC 1054 (1988), RFC 1112 (1989), RFC 2236 (1977), RFC 3376 (2002), and RFC 4604 (2006), among others, is the basic mechanism for these now-emerging applications. The technology is stable and relatively well understood, particularly for architecturally simple (yet large) networks.

Even in spite of the opening statement above, enhancements to IP multicast have actually occurred in the recent past, including the issuing of Internet Group Management Protocol (IGMP), Version 3 (October 2002); the issuing of Multicast Listener Discovery

(MLD), Version 2 for IP, Version 6 (IPv6) (June 2004); the issuing of Source-Specific Multicast (SSM) for IP (August 2006); and the publication of new considerations for IGMP and MLD snooping switches (May 2006). Work is also underway to develop new protocols and architectures to enable better deployment of IP over Moving Pictures Expert Group 2 (MPEG-2) transport and provide easier interworking with IP networks.

From a commercial deployment perspective, IP multicast is now where IP was in the mid-1990s: poised to take off and experience widespread deployment. Examples of applications requiring one-to-many or many-to-many communications include, but are not limited to, digital entertainment video and audio distribution, multisite corporate videoconferencing, broad-distribution financial data, grid computing, stock quotes and news bulletins distribution, database replication, software distribution, and content caching (e.g., Web site caching).

This book provides a concise guide to the IP multicast technology and its applications. It is an updated survey of the field with the underlying focus on IP-based Television (IPTV)[1] (also known in some quarters as telco TV) and Digital Video Broadcast— Handheld (DVB-H) applications.

IPTV deals with approaches, technologies, and protocols to deliver commercial-grade Standard-Definition (SD) and High-Definition (HD) entertainment-quality real-time linear and on-demand video content over IP-based networks, while meeting all prerequisite Quality of Service (QoS), Quality of Experience (QoE), Conditional Access (CA) (security), blackout management (for sporting events), Emergency Alert System (EAS), closed captions, parental controls, Nielsen rating collection, secondary audio channel, picture-in-picture, and guide data requirements of the content providers and/or regulatory entities. Typically, IPTV makes use of Moving Pictures Expert Group 4 (MPEG-4) encoding to deliver 200–300 SD channels and 20–40 HD channels; viewers need to be able to switch channels within 2 s or less; also, the need exists to support multi-set-top boxes/multiprogramming (say 2–4) within a single domicile. IPTV is not to be confused with simple delivery of video over an IP network (including video streaming), which has been possible for over two decades; IPTV supports all business, billing, provisioning, and content protection requirements that are associated with commercial video distribution. IP-based service needs to be comparable to that received over cable TV or direct broadcast satellite. In addition to TV sets, the content may also be delivered to a personal computer. MPEG-4, which operates at 2.5 Mbps for SD video and 8–11 Mbps for HD video, is critical to telco-based video delivery over a copper-based plant because of the bandwidth limitations of that plant, particularly when multiple simultaneous streams need to be delivered to a domicile; MPEG-2 would typically require a higher bit rate for the same perceived video quality. IP multicast is typically employed to support IPTV.[2]

---

[1] Some also use the expansion "IPTV (Internet TV)," e.g., CHA 200701. We retain the more general perspective of IPTV as TV (video, video on demand, etc.) distributed over any kind of IP-based network (including possibly the Internet).

[2] While some have advanced Peer-to-Peer (P2P) models for IPTV (e.g., see CHA 200701), nearly all the commercial deployment to date is based on the classical client–server model; this is the model discussed in this book.

Properly, DVB-H is a protocol. More broadly, DVB-H deals with approaches and technologies to deliver commercial-grade, medium-quality, real-time linear and on-demand video content to handheld, battery-powered devices such as mobile telephones and PDAs. IP multicast is also typically employed to support DVB-H.

1.2 WHY MULTICAST PROTOCOLS ARE WANTED/NEEDED

There are three types of communication between systems in an IP network:

- Unicast—here one system communicates directly to another system
- Broadcast—here one system communicates to all systems
- Multicast—here one system communicates to a select group of other systems

In traditional IP networks, a packet is typically sent by a source to a single destination (unicast); alternatively, the packet can be sent to all devices on the network (broadcast). There are business- and multimedia-entertainment applications that require a multicast transmission mechanism to enable bandwidth-efficient communication between groups of devices where information is transmitted to a single multicast address and received by any device that wishes to obtain such information. In traditional IP networks, it is not possible to generate a *single transmission* of data when this data is destined for a (large) group of remote devices. There are classes of applications that require distribution of information to a defined (but possibly dynamic) set of users. IP multicast, an extension to IP, is required to properly address these communication needs. As the term implies, IP multicast has been developed to support efficient communication between a source and multiple remote destinations.

Multicast applications include, among others, datacasting, distribution of real-time financial data, entertainment digital television over an IP network (commercial-grade IPTV), Internet radio, multipoint video conferencing, distance learning, streaming media applications, and corporate communications. Other applications include distributed interactive simulation, grid computing [MIN200401], and distributed video gaming (where most receivers are also senders). IP multicast protocols and underlying technologies enable efficient distribution of data, voice, and video streams to a large population of users, ranging from hundreds to thousands to millions of users. IP multicast technology enjoys intrinsic scalability, which is critical for these types of applications.

As an example in the IPTV arena, with the current trend toward the delivery of High-Definition TV (HDTV) signals, each requiring in the 12-Mbps range, and the consumers' desire for a large number of channels (200–300 being typical), there has to be an efficient mechanism of delivering a signal of 1–2 Gbps[3] in aggregate to a large number of remote

---

[3] Currently a typical digital TV package may consist of 200–250 SD signals each operating at 3 Mbps and 30–40 HD signals each operating at 12 Mbps; this equates to about 1 Gbps; as more HDTV signals are added, the bandwidth will reach in the range of 2 Gbps.

users. If a source had to deliver one Gbps of signal to, say, one million receivers by transmitting all of this bandwidth across the core network, it would require a petabit–per-second network fabric; this is not currently possible. On the contrary, if the source could send the 1 Gbps of traffic to (say) 50 remote distribution points (e.g., headends), each of which then makes use of a local distribution network to reach 20,000 subscribers, the core network needs to support 50 Gbps only, which is possible with proper design. For these kinds of reasons, IP multicast is seen as a bandwidth-conserving technology that optimizes traffic management by simultaneously delivering a stream of information to a large population of recipients, including corporate enterprise users and residential customers. See Figure 1.1 for a pictorial example.

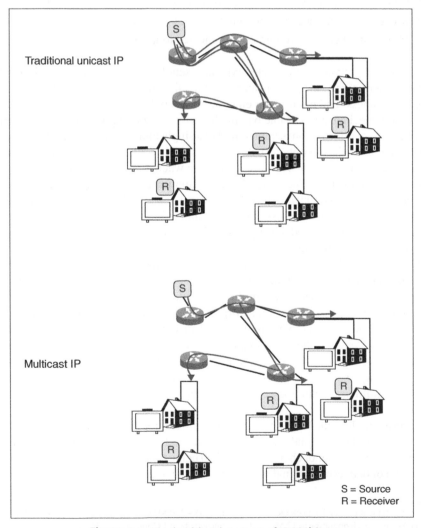

Figure 1.1. Bandwidth Advantage of IP Multicast

One important design principle of IP multicast is to allow receiver-initiated attachment (joins) to information streams, thus supporting a distributed informatics model. A second important principle is the ability to support optimal pruning such that the distribution of the content is streamlined by pushing replication as close to the receiver as possible. These principles enable bandwidth-efficient use of underlying network infrastructure.

The issue of security in multicast environments is addressed via conditional access systems that provide per-program[4] encryption (typically, but not always, symmetric encryption) (also known as inner encryption) or aggregate IP-level encryption (again typically, but not always, symmetric encryption) (also known as outer encryption).

1.3 BASIC MULTICAST PROTOCOLS AND CONCEPTS

Multicast communication is based on the construct of a group of receivers (hosts) that have an interest in receiving a particular stream of information, be it voice, video, or data. There are no physical or geographical constraints, or boundaries, to belong to a group, as long as the hosts have (broadband) network connectivity. The connectivity of the receivers can be heterogeneous in nature, in terms of bandwidth and connecting infrastructure (e.g., receivers connected over the Internet), or homogenous (e.g., IPTV or DVB-H users). Hosts that are desirous of receiving data intended for a particular group join the group using a group management protocol: hosts/receivers must become explicit members of the group to receive the data stream, but such membership may be ephemeral and/or dynamic. Groups of IP hosts that have joined the group and wish to receive traffic sent to this specific group are identified by multicast addresses, as discussed below.

Multicast transmission mechanisms for multipoint distribution are available at both the data link layer (layer 2) and the network layer (layer 3). Of late, the focus has been on layer 3 IP-level systems. There are local-area network (LAN)–level approaches to multicast, but typical contemporary business applications (e.g., IPTV) require a reach of a campus or, even more likely, a wide-area environment.

Deering's work in the late 1980s defined the IP multicast service model, and he invented algorithms that allow hosts to arbitrarily join and leave a multicast group [RFC1054, RFC1112, RFC2201].

Multicast transmission at layer 3 involves several mechanisms, as we discuss next. Below, we briefly outline key concepts; all of the material introduced below will be discussed in detail in appropriate chapters in the text.

Addressing for Payload—To communicate with a group of receivers (hosts), one needs a layer 3 address; also, there must be a mechanism of mapping the layer 3 address onto layer 2 multicast addresses of the underlying LAN. Ethernet multicast

---

[4] A program in this context equates to a video channel, more specifically to an MPEG-2/4 transport stream with a given Program ID (PID) (this topic is revisited in Chapters 2 and 11).

addresses have a hex "01" in the first byte of the six-octet destination address. The Internet Assigned Numbers Authority (IANA) manages the assignment of IP addresses at layer 3, and it has assigned the (original) Class D address space to be used for IP multicast. A Class D address consists of 1110 as the higher order bits in the first octet, followed by a 28-bit group address. A 1110-0000 address in the first byte starts at 224 in the dotted decimal notation; a typical address might be 224.10.10.1, and so on. All IP multicast group addresses belong to the range 224.0.0.0–239.255.255.255. In addition, all IPv6 hosts are required to support multicasting. The mapping of IP multicast addresses to Ethernet addresses takes the lower 23 bits of the Class D address and maps them into a block of Ethernet addresses that have been allocated for multicast.

Dynamic Host Registration—There must be a mechanism that informs the network that a host (receiver) is a member of a particular group (otherwise, the network would have to flood rather than multicast the transmissions for each group). For IP networks, the IGMP serves this purpose.

Multicast Payload Forwarding—Typical IP multicast applications make use of User Datagram Protocol (UDP) at the transport layer and IP at the network layer. UDP is the "best effort delivery" protocol with no guarantee of delivery; it also lacks the congestion management mechanism [such as those utilized in Transmission Control Protocol (TCP)]. Real-time applications such as commercial live video distribution do not (and cannot) make use of a retransmission mechanism (such as the one utilized in TCP). In some cases, portions of the network may be simplex (such as a satellite link), practically precluding end-to-end retransmission. Hence, the risk exists for audio and video broadcasts to suffer content degradation due to packet loss. To minimize lost packets, one must provision adequate bandwidth and/or keep the distribution networks simple and with as few hops as possible. IP QoS (*diffserv*), the Real-Time Transport Protocol (RTP), and 802.1p at layer 2 are often utilized to manage QoS. [To minimize in-packet bit corruption, Forward Error Correction (FEC) mechanisms may be used—a state-of-the-art mechanism can improve Bit Error Rates (BERs) by an impressive four or five orders of magnitude.]

Multicast Routing—A multicast network requires a mechanism to build distribution trees that define a unique forwarding path between the subnet of the content source and each subnet containing members of the multicast group, specifically, receivers. A principle utilized in the construction of distribution trees is to guarantee that at most one copy of each packet is forwarded on each branch of the tree. This is implemented by ascertaining that there is sufficient real-time topological information at the multicast router of the source host for constructing a spanning tree rooted at said multicast router (or other appropriate router) and providing connectivity to the local multicast routers of each receiving host. A multicast router forwards multicast packets to two types of devices: downstream-dependent routers and receivers (hosts) that are members of a particular multicast group. See Table 1.1 for a list of some key multicast-related protocols.

Multicast routing protocols belong to one of two categories: Dense-Mode (DM) protocols and Sparse-Mode (SM) protocols.

TABLE 1.1. Multicast Protocols At a Glance

Protocol	Function
IGMP	Client [receiver, Set-Top Box (STB), PC] to router signaling
Protocol Independent Multicast (PIM) Distance Vector Multicast Routing Protocol (DVMRP) Core-Based Tree (CBT) Multicast Open Shortcut Path First (MOSPF)	Router to router topology (multicast route) management
Multiprotocol BGP (MBGP) Multicast Source Discovery Protocol (MSDP)	Large-scale router to router
GLOP Multicast Address Dynamic Client Allocation Protocol (MADCAP) Multicast Address Set Claim Protocol (MASC)	Multicast address allocation
Cisco Group Management Protocol (CGMP) GARP Multicast Registration Protocol (GMRP) IGMP snooping Router-Port Group Management Protocol (RGMP)	Router to switch (Cisco specific)

- DM protocols are designed on the assumption that the majority of routers in the network will need to distribute multicast traffic for each multicast group. DM protocols build distribution trees by initially flooding the entire network and then pruning out the (presumably small number of) paths without active receivers. The DM protocols are used in LAN environments, where bandwidth considerations are less important but can also be used in wide-area networks (WANs) in special cases (e.g., where the backbone is a one-hop broadcast medium such as a satellite beam with wide geographic illumination, e.g., in some IPTV applications).
- SM protocols are designed on the assumption that only few routers in the network will need to distribute multicast traffic for each multicast group. SM protocols start out with an empty distribution tree and add drop-off branches only upon explicit requests from receivers to join the distribution. SM protocols are generally used in WAN environments, where bandwidth considerations are important.

For IP multicast, there are several multicast routing protocols that can be employed to acquire real-time topological and membership information for active groups. Routing protocols that may be utilized include the PIM, the DVMRP, the MOSPF, and CBTs. Multicast routing protocols build distribution trees by examining the routing forwarding table that contains unicast reachability information. PIM and CBT use the unicast forwarding table of the router. Other protocols use their specific unicast reachability routing tables; for example, DVMRP uses its distance vector routing protocol to determine how to create source-based distribution trees, whereas MOSPF utilizes its link-state table to create source-based distribution trees. MOSPF, DVMRP, and PIM DM are DM routing protocols, whereas CBT and PIM SM are SM routing protocols. PIM is currently the most widely used protocol.

Specifically, PIM Version 2 (PIMv2) is a protocol that provides intradomain multicast forwarding for all underlying unicast routing protocols [e.g., Open Shortest Path First (OSPF) or BGP], independent from the intrinsic unicast protocol. Two modes exist: PIM SM and PIM DM.[5]

PIM DM (defined in RFC 3973, January 2005) is a multicast routing protocol that uses the underlying unicast routing information base to flood multicast datagrams to all multicast routers. Prune messages are used to prevent future messages from propagating to routers without group membership information [RFC3973]. PIM DM attempts to send multicast data to all potential receivers (flooding) and relies upon their self--pruning (removal from the group) to achieve distribution. In PIM DM, multicast traffic is initially flooded to all segments of the network. Routers that have no downstream neighbors or directly connected receivers prune back the unwanted traffic. PIM DM assumes most receivers (hosts, PCs, TV viewers, cellular phone handsets) wish to receive the multicast; therefore the protocol forwards the multicast datagrams everywhere, and then routers prune the distribution tree where it is not needed. PIM is now being utilized for IPTV applications; typically DM is used in the backbone; however, SM could also be utilized in some applications or portions of the overall network.

In SM PIM, only network segments with active receivers that have explicitly requested multicast data are forwarded the traffic. PIM SM relies on an explicit joining request before attempting to send multicast data to receivers of a multicast group. In a PIM SM network, sources must send their traffic to a Rendezvous Point (RP); this traffic is in turn forwarded to receivers on a shared distribution tree. SM works by routers sending PIM Join messages to start the multicast feed being sent across links. The assumption in SM is that relatively few users need the multicast information and therefore PIM SM starts with no flooding of multicast. In short order, router-to-router PIM Join messages cause the multicast stream to be forwarded across links to where it is needed. This is the current standard for Internet Service Providers (ISPs) supporting Internet multicast [WEL200101].

An RP (described in RFC 2362) acts as the meeting place for sources and receivers of multicast data. It is required only in networks running PIM SM and is needed only to start new sessions with sources and receivers. In a PIM SM network, sources send their traffic to the RP; this traffic is in turn forwarded to receivers downstream on a shared distribution

---

[5] PIM bidirectional (PIM bidir) (a variant of PIM) allows data flow both up and down the same distribution tree. PIM bidir uses only shared tree forwarding, thereby reducing the creation of "state" information.

tree. A Designated Router (DR) is the router on a subnet that is selected to control multicast routes for the members on its directly attached subnet. The receiver sends an IGMP Join message (see below) to this designated multicast router.[6] IP multicast traffic transmitted from the multicast source is distributed over the tree, via the designated router, to the receiver's subnet. When the designated router of the receiver learns about the source, it sends a PIM Join message directly to the source's router, creating a source-based distribution tree, from the source to the receiver. This source tree does not include the RP unless the RP is located within the shortest path between the source and receiver.

Auto-RP is a mechanism where a PIM router learns the set of group-to-RP mappings required for PIM SM. Auto-RP automates the distribution of group-to-RP mappings. To make auto-RP work, a router must be designated as an RP mapping agent that receives the RP announcement messages from the RPs and arbitrates conflicts. Bootstrap Router (BSR) is another mechanism with which a PIM router learns the set of group-to-RP mappings required for PIM SM. BSR operates similarly to Auto-RP: it uses candidate routers for the RP function and for relaying the RP information for a group. RP information is distributed through BSR messages that are carried within PIM messages. PIM messages are link-local multicast messages that travel from PIM router to PIM router. Each method for configuring an RP has its strengths, weaknesses, and complexity. Auto-RP is typically used in a conventional IP multicast network given that it is straightforward to configure, well tested, and stable.

IGMP (Versions 1, 2, and 3) is the protocol used by IP Version 4 (IPv4) hosts to communicate multicast group membership states to multicast routers. IGMP is used to dynamically register individual hosts/receivers on a particular local subnet (e.g., LAN) to a multicast group. IGMPv1 defined the basic mechanism. It supports a Membership Query (MQ) message and a Membership Report (MR) message. Most implementations at press time employed IGMPv2; Version 2 adds Leave Group (LG) messages. Version 3 adds source awareness allowing the inclusion or exclusion of sources. IGMP allows group membership lists to be dynamically maintained. The host (user) sends an IGMP "report," or join, to the router to be included in the group. Periodically, the router sends a "query" to learn which hosts (users) are still part of a group. If a host wishes to continue its group membership, it responds to the query with a "report." If the host does not send a "report," the router prunes the group list to delete this host; this eliminates unnecessary network transmissions. With IGMPv2, a host may send a "leave group" message to alert the router that it is no longer participating in a multicast group; this allows the router to prune the group list to delete this host before the next query is scheduled, thereby minimizing the time period during which unneeded transmissions are forwarded to the network.

---

[6] This is different from the router-to-router PIM Join message just described; this message is from a receiver to its gateway multicast router.

Other basic multicast protocols/mechanisms include the following:

- IGMP snooping is a method by which a switch can constrain multicast packets to only those ports that have requested the stream IGMP.
- MLDv2 is a protocol that allows a host to inform its neighboring routers of its desire to receive IPv6 multicast transmissions; it is similar to (and based on) IGMPv3 used in the IPv4 context.
- STUB multicast routing is a mechanism that allows IGMP messages to be forwarded through a non-PIM-enabled router toward a PIM-enabled router.
- PIM SSM is a multicast protocol where forwarding uses only source-based forwarding trees. IGMPv3 is used to support SSM. SSM mapping is a mapping that allows SSM routing to occur without IGMPv3 being present. SSM mapping uses statically configured tables or dynamic Domain Name System (DNS) discovery of the source address for a SSM channel.
- MSDP is a protocol that allows multiple PIM SM domains to share information about active sources. The protocol announces active sources to MSDP peers.
- MPBGP is a protocol that defines multiprotocol extensions to the BGP, the unicast interdomain protocol that supports multicast-specific routing information. MPBGP augments BGP to enable multicast routing policy and connect multicast topologies within and between BGP autonomous systems. It carries multiple instances of routes for unicast routing as well as multicast routing.
- Pragmatic General Multicast (PGM) is a reliable multicast transport protocol for applications that require ordered, duplicate-free multicast data delivery. The protocol guarantees that a receiver in a multicast group receives all data packets from direct transmissions or via retransmissions of lost packets. PGM can detect unrecoverable data packet loss.
- RGMP is a protocol that constrains IP multicast on switches that have only routers attached.

Some of these protocols (but not all) are covered in the chapters.

Figure 1.2 illustrates where some of these protocols apply in the context of a typical multicast network.

It should be noted that the design and turnup of IP multicast networks is fairly complex. This is because by its very nature IP multicast traffic is "blasted all over the map"; hence, a simple design mistake (or oversight) will push traffic to many interfaces and easily flood and swamp router and switch interfaces.[7]

---

[7] This statement is based on some 100-h weeks spent by the author configuring IPTV networks while endeavoring to meet established business deadlines.

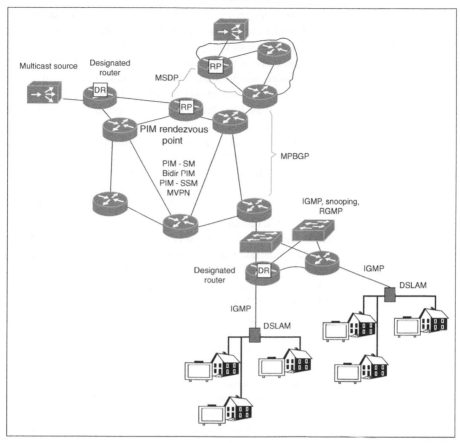

Figure 1.2. Multicast Protocols Usage in a Typical Multicast Network

1.4 IPTV AND DVB-H APPLICATIONS

While IP multicast has been around for a number of years, it is now finding fertile commercial applications in the IPTV and DVB-H arenas. Applications such as datacasting (e.g., stock market or other financial data) tend to make use of large multihop networks; pruning is often employed and nodal store-and-forward approaches are totally acceptable. Applications such as video are very sensitive to end-to-end delay, jitter, and (uncorrectable) packet loss; QoS considerations are critical. These networks tend to have fewer hops, and pruning may be somewhat trivially implemented by making use of a simplified network topology.

IPTV services enable advanced content viewing and navigation by consumers; the technology is rapidly emerging and becoming commercially available. IPTV services enable traditional carriers to deliver SD and HD video to their customers in support of their triple/quadruple play strategies. With the significant erosion in revenues from traditional voice services on wireline-originated calls (both in terms of depressed pricing and a shift to voice over IP (VoIP) over broadband Internet services delivered over cable TV infrastructure) and with the transition of many customers from wireline to wireless services, the traditional telephone carriers find themselves in need of generating new revenues by seeking to deliver video services to their customers. Traditional phone carriers find themselves challenged in the voice arena (by VoIP and other providers); their Internet services are also challenged in the broadband Internet access arena (by cable TV companies); and their video services are nascent and challenged by a lack of deployed technology. Multimedia (and new media) services are a way to improve telco revenues (e.g., but not limited to, [MIN198601], [MIN199301], [MIN199401], [MIN199402], [MIN199403], [MIN199404], [MIN199501], [MIN199502], [MIN199503], [MIN199504], [MIN199505], [MIN199601], [MIN199602], [MIN199603], [MIN199701], [MIN199702], [MIN199801], [MIN199802], [MIN199803], [MIN199804], [MIN200001], [MIN200301]).

There was a recognition in the mid-1990s that a video strategy was important, and considerable technical work was undertaken under the Federal Communications Commission (FCC's) Video Dialtone Initiative. That effort was described by this author in the well-received book *Video Dialtone Technology: Digital Video over ADSL, HFC, FTTC, and ATM*, McGraw-Hill, 1995 [MIN199501]. In 1992, various telcos filed applications with the FCC for a service called "video dialtone" that would have allowed phone companies to use their networks to compete with cable television distributors. By 1995, according to FCC reports, 24 applications were completed representing 43 different cities/states to be upgraded. As far back as 1997, 9.7 million homes should have received this service. These upgrades were supposed to handle 500+ channels on average. Table 1.2 is a compilation of telco commitments filed with the FCC [KUS200601]. Unfortunately, none of these plans led to actual TV services.

The problem was that the emphasis by the telcos for local delivery was totally pivoted on Digital Subscriber Line (DSL). DSL had a bandwidth range of around 1.5 Mbps when using mid-1990s technology. Consequently, the use of MPEG-1 encoding techniques operating at 1.5 Mbps limited the domicile access to a single stream of video into a home at any point in time, which was a market nonstarter [MIN200001]. In addition, the Asynchronous Transfer Mode (ATM) core infrastructure turned out to be expensive. Now a decade later, in the mid-to-late 2000s, the recognition has emerged that an IP infrastructure (with IP multicast) is the best mechanism for distribution of entertainment video by the telcos, aiming at a 200–300-channel pool and typically with up to three simultaneous streams of video traffic per domicile based on efficient, yet high-quality, MPEG-4 standards (e.g., see [MIN200301]). The current delivery model is state-of-the-art DSL services and possibly Very High Data Rate DSL (VDSL)/ VDSL2 (see Table 1.3, [DSL200701]) in the near term and Fiber To The Home (FTTH) in the longer term. Tier 2 and tier 3 telcos may rely on VDSL/VDSL2 for the next few years, while at least some tier 1 telcos (e.g., Verizon FiOS) may move to in short order, or already use, FTTH technologies. Figures 1.3 and 1.4 illustrate a simplified IPTV application from an infrastructure perspective.

Some of the areas that require consideration and technical support to develop and deploy IPTV systems include the following, among many others:

TABLE 1.2. Video Dialtone Applications by the Phone Companies According to the FCC First Video Report, 1994

Date	Telephone Company	Location	Homes	Type of Proposal
10/21/92	Bell Atlantic-VA	Arlington, VA	2,000	Technical/market
10/30/92	NYNEX	New York, NY	2,500	Technical
11/16/92	New Jersey Bell	Florham Park, NJ	11,700	Permanent
12/15/92	New Jersey Bell	Dover Township, NJ	38,000	Permanent
04/27/93	SNET	West Hartford, CT	1,600	Technical/market
06/18/93	Rochester Telephone	Rochester, NY	350	Technical/market
06/22/93	US WEST	Omaha, NE	60,000	Technical/market
12/15/93	SNET	Hartford & Stamford, CT	150,000	Technical/market
12/16/93	Bell Atlantic	MD & VA	300,000	Permanent
12/20/93	Pacific Bell	Orange Co., CA	210,000	Permanent
		So. San Francisco Bay, CA	490,000	Permanent
		Los Angeles, CA	360,000	Permanent
		San Diego, CA	250,000	Permanent
01/10/94	US West	Denver, CO	330,000	Permanent
01/24/94	US West	Portland, OR	132,000	Permanent
		Minneapolis/St. Paul, MN	292,000	Permanent
01/31/94	Ameritech	Detroit, MI	232,000	Permanent
		Columbus & Cleveland, OH	262,000	Permanent
		Indianapolis, IN	115,000	Permanent
		Chicago, IL	501,000	Permanent
		Milwaukee, WI	146,000	Permanent
03/16/94	US West	Boise, ID	90,000	Permanent
		Salt Lake City, UT	160,000	Permanent
04/13/94	Puerto Rico Tel. Co.	Puerto Rico	250	Technical
05/23/94	GTE - Contel of Va.	Manassas, VA	109,000	Permanent
	GTE Florida Inc.	Pinella and Pasco Co., FL	476,000	Permanent
	GTE California Inc.	Ventura Co., CA	122,000	Permanent
	GTE Hawaiian Tel.	Honolulu, HW	334,000	Permanent
06/16/94	Bell Atlantic	Wash. DC LATA	1,200,000	Permanent
		Baltimore, MD; northern NJ; DE; Philadelphia, PA; Pittsburgh, PA; and S.E.VA	2,000,000	Permanent
06/27/94	BellSouth	Chamblee & DeKalb, GA	12,000	Technical/market
07/08/94	NYNEX	RI	63,000	Permanent
		MA	334,000	Permanent
09/09/94	Carolina Tel. & Tel.	Wake Forest, NC	1,000	Technical/market
04/28/95	SNET	CT	1,000,000	Permanent

- Content aggregation
- Content encoding [e.g., Advanced Video Coding (AVC)/H.264/MPEG-4 Part 10, MPEG-2, SD, HD, Serial Digital Interface (SDI), Asynchronous Serial Interface (ASI), layer 1 switching/routing]
- Audio management

TABLE 1.3. Typical DSL Technologies That May be Used in Current-Day IPTV While Waiting for FTTH

DSL	A technology that exploits unused frequencies on copper telephone lines to transmit traffic typically at multimegabit speeds. DSL can allow voice and high-speed data to be sent simultaneously over the same line. Because the service is "always available," end users do not need to dial in or wait for call setup. Variations include ADSL, G.lite ADSL (or simply G.lite), VDSL [International Telecommunications Union (ITU) G.993.1], and VDSL2 (ITU G.993.2). The standard forms of ADSL [ITU G.992.3 and G.992.5 and American National Standards Institute (ANSI) T1.413-Issue 2] are all built upon the same technical foundation, Discrete Multitone (DMT). The suite of ADSL standards facilitates interoperability between all standard forms of ADSL.
ADSL (Full-Rate Asymmetric DSL)	Access technology that offers differing upload and download speeds and can be configured to deliver up to 6 mbps (6000 kbps) from the network to the customer. ADSL enables voice and high-speed data to be sent simultaneously over the existing telephone line. This type of DSL is the most predominant in commercial use for business and residential customers around the world. Good for general Internet access and for applications where downstream speed is most important, such as video on demand. ITU-T recommendation G.992.1 and ANSI standard T1.413-1998 specify full-rate ADSL. ITU recommendation G.992.3 specifies ADSL2, which provides advanced diagnostics, power saving functions, PSD shaping, and better performance than G.992.1. ITU recommendation G.992.5 specifies ADSL2Plus, which provides the benefits of ADSL2Plus twice the bandwidth so that bit rates as high as 20 Mbps downstream can be achieved on relatively short lines.
G.lite ADSL (or simply G.lite)	A standard that was specifically developed to meet the plug-and-play requirements of the consumer market segment. G.lite is a medium-bandwidth version of ADSL that allows Internet access at up to 1.5 Mbps downstream and up to 500 kbps upstream. G.lite is an ITU standard (ITU G.992.2). G.lite has seen comparatively little use, but it did introduce the valuable concept of splitterless installation.
RADSL (Rate Adaptive DSL)	A nonstandard version of ADSL. Note that standard ADSL also permits the ADSL modem to adapt speeds of data transfer.
VDSL	A standard for up to 26 Mbps over distances up to 50 m on short loops such as from fiber to the curb. In most cases, VDSL lines are served from neighborhood cabinets that link to a central office via optical fiber. It is useful for "campus" environments—universities and business parks, for example. VDSL is currently being introduced in market trials to deliver video services over existing phone lines. VDSL can also be configured in symmetric mode.
VDSL2 (Second-Generation VDSL)	ITU recommendation G.993.2 specifies eight profiles that address a range of applications including up to 100-Mbps symmetric transmission on loops about 100 m long (using a bandwidth of 30 MHz), symmetric bit rates in the 10–30-Mbps range on intermediate-length loops (using a bandwidth

TABLE 1.3. (*Continued*)

	of 12 MHz), and asymmetric operation with downstream rates in the range of 10–40 Mbps on loops of lengths ranging from 3 km to 1 km (using a bandwidth of 8.5 MHz). VDSL2 includes most of the advanced feature from ADSL2. The rate/reach performance of VDSL2 is better than VDSL.
Symmetric flavors DSL	Symmetric variations of DSL that include SDSL, SHDSL, HDSL, HDSL2, and IDSL. The equal speeds make symmetric DSLs useful for LAN access, video conferencing, and locations hosting Web sites.
SDSL (Symmetric DSL)	A vendor-proprietary version of symmetric DSL that may include bit rates to and from the customer ranging from 128 kbps to 2.32 Mbps. SDSL is an umbrella term for a number of supplier-specific implementations over a single copper pair providing variable rates of symmetric service. SDSL uses 2 Binary, 1 Quaternary (2B1Q).
SHDSL	A state-of-the-art, industry standard symmetric DSL, SHDSL equipment conforms to ITU recommendation G.991.2, also known as G.shdsl, approved by the ITU-T in 2001. SHDSL achieves 20% better loop reach than older versions of symmetric DSL and it causes much less cross talk into other transmission systems in the same cable. SHDSL systems may operate at many bit rates, from 192 kbps to 5.7 Mbps, thereby maximizing the bit rate for each customer. G.shdsl specifies operation via one pair of wires, or for operation on longer loops, two pairs of wire may be used. For example, with two pairs of wire, 1.2 Mbps can be sent over 20,000 ft of American Wire Gage (AWG) 26 wire. SHDSL is best suited to data-only applications that need high upstream bit rates. Though SHDSL does not carry voice like ADSL, new voice-over-DSL techniques may be used to convey digitized voice and data via SHDSL. SHDSL is being deployed primarily for business customers.
HDSL (High-Data-Rate DSL)	A DSL variety created in the late 1980s that delivers symmetric service at speeds up to 2.3 Mbps in both directions. Available at 1.5 or 2.3 Mbps, this symmetric fixed-rate application does not provide standard telephone service over the same line and is already standardized through the ETSI (European Telecommunications Standards Institute) and ITU. Seen as an economical replacement for T1 or E1, it uses one, two, or three twisted copper pairs.
HDSL2 (Second-Generation HDSL)	A variant of DSL that delivers 1.5-Mbps service each way, supporting voice, data, and video using either ATM, private-line service, or frame relay over a single copper pair. This ATIS standard (T1.418) supports a fixed 1.5-Mbps rate both up and downstream. HDSL2 does not provide standard voice telephone service on the same wire pair. HSDL2 differs from HDSL in that HDSL2 uses one pair of wires to convey 1.5 Mbps whereas ANSI HDSL uses two wire pairs.

(*continued*)

TABLE 1.3. (*Continued*)

HDSL4	A high-data-rate DSL that is virtually the same as HDSL2 except it achieves about 30% greater distance than HDSL or HDSL2 by using two pairs of wire (thus, four conductors), whereas HDSL2 uses one pair of wires.
IDSL (Integrated Services Digital Network DSL)	A form of DSL that supports symmetric data rates of up to 144 kbps using existing phone lines. Has the ability to deliver services through a DLC (Digital Loop Carrier: a remote device often placed in newer neighborhoods to simplify the distribution of cable and wiring from the phone company). While DLCs provide a means of simplifying the delivery of traditional voice services to newer neighborhoods, they also provide a unique challenge in delivering DSL into those same neighborhoods. IDSL addresses this market along with ADSL and G.lite as they are implemented directly into those DLCs. IDSL differs from its relative ISDN (Integrated Services Digital Network) in that it is an "always-available" service, but capable of using the same terminal adapter, or modem, as for ISDN.

Courtesy: DSL Forum.

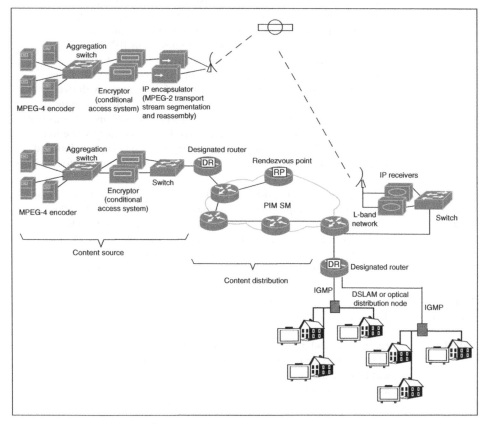

Figure 1.3. Simplified IPTV Application

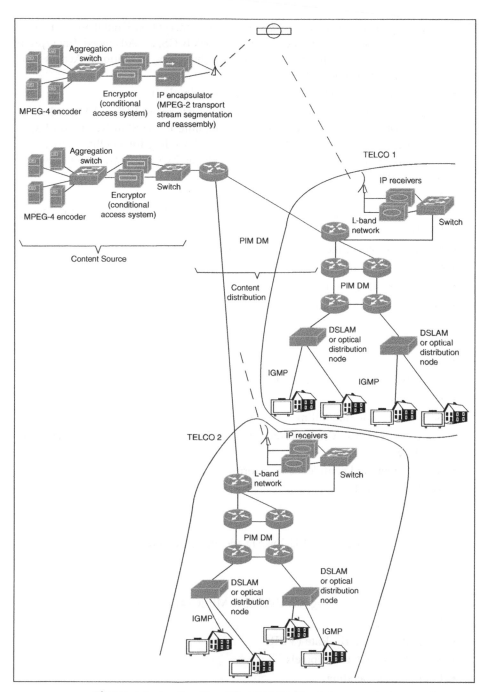

Figure 1.4. Another Simplified IPTV Multicast Arrangement

- Digital rights management/conditional access: encryption Digital Video Broadcasting Common Scrambling Algorithm (DVB-CSA), Advanced Encryption Standard (AES); key management schemes [basically, Conditional-Access System (CAS)]; transport rights
- Encapsulation (MPEG-2 transport stream distribution)
- Backbone distribution, for example, satellite or terrestrial Digital Video Broadcasting Satellite, Version 2 (DVB-S2), Quadrature Phase Shift Keying (Q-PSK), 8-point Phase Shift Keying (8-PSK), FEC, turbocoding for satellite—(Synchronous Optical Network/Synchronous Digital Hierarchy/Optical Transport Network) SONET/SDH/OTN for terrestrial
- Metro-level distribution
- Last-mile distribution, LAN/WAN/optics, (Gigabit Ethernet) GbE, DSL/FTTH
- Multicast protocol mechanisms (IP multicast)
- QoS, Backbone distribution
- QoS, metro-level distribution
- QoS, last-mile distribution
- QoS, channel surfing
- STB/middleware
- QoE
- EPG (Electronic Program Guide)
- Blackouts
- Service provisioning/billing, service management
- Advanced video services, Personal Digital Recorder (PDR), Video on Demand (VoD), etc.
- Management and confidence monitoring
- Triple play/quadruple play

In reference to encoding, typical H.264 SD encoder parameters are as follows:
   Video

- Advanced Video Coding (AVC)/H.264/(MPEG-4, Part 10)
- Main profile/level 3
- Capped Variable Bit Rate (VBR)
- 352×480 to 720×480 pixels
- Look-ahead encoding
- Closed captioning
- Picture-in-picture

Audio

- MPEG-1, layer II
- Dolby AC3
- AAC-HE (Advanced Audio Coding—High Efficiency)

A CAS is a system by which electronic transmission of digital media (e.g., satellite television signals) is limited only to subscribed clients:

- Signal is encrypted and is unavailable for unauthorized reception
- STB is required in the customer premises to receive and decrypt the signal

The *DVB Project* (see below) has developed specifications for digital television systems which are turned into standards by international bodies such as ETSI and CENELEC (Comite Europeen de Normalisation Electrotechnique—European Committee for Electrotechnical Standardization). For Digital Rights Management (DRM) it developed, DVB-CA defines a DVB-CSA and a Common Interface (DVB-CI) for accessing scrambled content:

- DVB system providers develop their proprietary conditional access systems within these specifications
- DVB transports include metadata called Service Information (DVB-SI) that links the various elementary streams into coherent programs and provides human-readable descriptions for electronic program guides

This topic will be reexamined in Chapter 11. Next, we briefly discuss DVB-H applications.

DVB-H is a technical development activity by the *DVB Project Office* organization [DVB200701] targeting handheld, battery-powered devices such as mobile telephones, PDAs, and so on. It addresses the requirements for reliable, high-speed, high-data-rate reception for a number of mobile applications, including real-time video to handheld devices. DVB-H systems typically make use of IP multicast. DVB-H is generating significant interest in the broadcast and telecommunications worlds, and DVB-H services are expected to start at this time. Industry proponents expect to see 300 million DVB-H-capable handsets to be deployed by 2009. The DVB-H protocols are being standardized through ETSI.

Digital Video Broadcasting (DVB) is a consortium of over 300 companies in the fields of broadcasting and manufacturing that work cooperatively to establish common international standards for digital broadcasting. DVB-generated standards have become the leading international standards, commonly referred to as "DVB," and the accepted choice for technologies that enable an efficient, cost-effective, higher quality, and interoperable digital broadcasting. The DVB standards for digital television have been adopted in the United Kingdom, across mainland Europe, in the Middle East, in South America, and in Australasia.

DVB-H is based on DVB-T, a standard for digital transmission of terrestrial over-the-air TV signals. When DVB-T was first published in 1997, it was not designed to target mobile receivers. However, DVB-T mobile services have been launched in a number of countries. Indeed, with the advent of diversity antenna receivers, services that target fixed reception can now largely be received on the move as well. DVB-T is deployed in more than 50 countries. Yet, a new standard was sought, namely DVB-H.

Despite the success of mobile DVB-T reception, the major concern with any handheld device is that of battery life. The current and projected power consumption of DVB-T front ends is too high to support handheld receivers that are expected to last from one to several days on a single charge. The other major requirements for DVB-H were an ability to receive 15 Mbps in an 8-MHz channel and in a wide-area Single-Frequency Network (SFN) at high speed. These requirements were drawn up after much debate and with an eye on emerging convergence devices providing video services and other broadcast data services to second- and not quite third-generation (2.5G) and 3G handheld devices. Furthermore, all this should be possible while maintaining maximum compatibility with existing DVB-T networks and systems. Figure 1.5 depicts a block-level view of a DVB-H network.

In order to meet these requirements, the newly developed DVB-H specification includes the capabilities discussed next.

Time Slicing. Rather than continuous data transmission as in DVB-T, DVB-H employs a mechanism where bursts of data are received at a time—the so-called IP datacast carousel. This means that the receiver is inactive for much of the time and can thus, by means of clever control signaling, be "switched off." The result is a power saving of about 90% and more in some cases.

4K Mode. With the addition of a 4K mode with 3409 active carriers, DVB-H benefits from the compromise between the high-speed small-area SFN capability of 2K DVB-T and the lower speed but larger area SFN of 8K DVB-T. In addition, with the aid of enhanced in-depth interleavers in the 2K and 4K modes, DVB-H has even better immunity to ignition interference.

Multiprotocol Encapsulation–Forward Error Correction (MPE–FEC). The addition of an optional, multiplexer-level, forward error correction scheme means that DVB-H

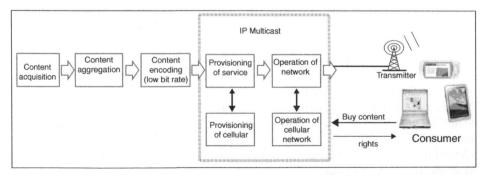

Figure 1.5. Block-Level View of a DVB-H Network

transmissions can be even more robust. This is advantageous when considering the hostile environments and poor (but fashionable) antenna designs typical of handheld receivers.

Like DVB-T, DVB-H can be used in 6-, 7-, and 8-MHz channel environments. However, a 5-MHz option is also specified for use in nonbroadcast environments. A key initial requirement, and a significant feature of DVB-H, is that it can coexist with DVB-T in the same multiplex. Thus, an operator can choose to have two DVB-T services and one DVB-H service in the same overall DVB-T multiplex.

Broadcasting is an efficient way of reaching many users with a single (configurable) service. DVB-H combines broadcasting with a set of measures to ensure that the target receivers can operate from a battery and on the move and is thus an ideal companion to 3G telecommunications, offering symmetric and asymmetric bidirectional multimedia services.

DVB-H trials have taken place in recent years in Germany, Finland, and the United States (Las Vegas). Such trials help frequency planning and improve understanding of the complex issue of interoperability with telecommunications networks and services.

This topic will be reexamined in Chapter 12.

1.5   COURSE OF INVESTIGATION

Following this introductory discussion, Chapter 2 covers multicast addressing for payload distribution. Chapter 3 focuses on multicast payload forwarding. Chapter 4 covers the important topic of dynamic host registration using the IGMP. Chapter 5 looks at multicast routing in SM environments and the broadly used PIM SM. Chapter 6 discusses CBT. Chapter 7 looks at multicast routing for DM protocols and PIM DM in particular. Chapter 8 examines DVMRP and MOSPF. Chapter 9 covers IP multicasting in IPv6 environments. Chapter 10 looks at MLD snooping switches. Finally, Chapters 11 and 12 give examples in the IPTV and (mobile) DVB-H environments, respectively.

APPENDIX 1.A: MULTICAST IETF REQUEST FOR COMMENTS

The following are the key RFCs that define multicast operation:

- RFC 988, Host Extensions for IP Multicasting, S. E. Deering, July 1986. (obsoletes RFC 966) (obsoleted by RFC 1054, RFC 1112).
- RFC 1054, Host Extensions for IP Multicasting, S. E. Deering, May 1988 (obsoletes RFC 0988) (obsoleted by RFC 1112).
- RFC 1075, Distance Vector Multicast Routing Protocol, D. Waitzman, C. Partridge, S. Deering, November 1988.
- RFC 1112, Host Extensions for IP Multicasting, S. E. Deering, August 1989 (obsoletes RFC 0988, RFC1054) (Updated by RFC 2236) (also STD0005) (status: standard).
- RFC 1469, IP Multicast over Token-Ring Local Area Networks, T. Pusateri, June 1993 (status: historic).
- RFC 1584, Multicast Extensions to OSPF, J. Moy, March 1994.

- RFC 2117, Protocol Independent Multicast-Sparse-Mode (PIM SM): Protocol Specification, D. Farinacci, A. Helmy, et al., June 1997 (obsoleted by RFC 2362).
- RFC 2201, Core Based Trees (CBT) Multicast Routing Architecture, A. Ballardie, September 1997.
- RFC 2236, Internet Group Management Protocol, Version 2, W. Fenner, November 1997 (status: standard).
- RFC 2337, Intra-LIS IP Multicast among Routers over ATM using Sparse-Mode PIM, D. Farinacci, D. Meyer, Y. Rekhter. April 1998 (status: experimental).
- RFC 2362, Protocol Independent Multicast-Sparse-Mode (PIM SM): Protocol Specification, D. Estrin, D. Farinacci, et al., June 1998.
- RFC 2365, Administratively Scoped IP Multicast, D. Meyer. July 1998 (also BCP0023) (status: best current practice).
- RFC 2366, Definitions of Managed Objects for Multicast over UNI 3.0/3.1based ATM Networks, C. Chung, M. Greene, July 1998 (obsoleted by RFC 2417) (status: proposed standard).
- RFC 2432, Terminology for IP Multicast Benchmarking. K. Dubray, October 1998. (status: informational).
- RFC 2490, A Simulation Model for IP Multicast with RSVP, M. Pullen, R.Malghan, L. Lavu, G. Duan, J. Ma, H. Nah, January 1999 (status: informational).
- RFC 2588, IP Multicast and Firewalls, R. Finlayson, May 1999 (status: informational).
- RFC 2710, Multicast Listener Discovery (MLD) for IPv6, S. Deering, W. Fenner, W., B. Haberman, October 1999.
- RFC 2730, Multicast Address Dynamic Client Allocation Protocol (MADCAP), S. Hanna, B. Patel, M. Shah, December 1999.
- RFC 2909, The Multicast Address-Set Claim (MASC) Protocol, P. Radoslavov, D. Estrin, et al., September 2000.
- RFC 3170, IP Multicast Applications: Challenges and Solutions, B. Quinn, K. Almeroth. September 2001 (status: informational).
- RFC 3228, IANA Considerations for IPv4 Internet Group Management Protocol (IGMP), B. Fenner, February 2002 (also BCP0057) (status: best current practice).
- RFC 3232, J. Reynolds, Editor, Assigned Numbers: RFC 1700 is replaced by an on-line database, January 2002, obsoletes RFC 1700 (status: informational).
- RFC 3353, Overview of IP Multicast in a Multi-Protocol Label Switching (MPLS) Environment, D. Ooms, B. Sales, W. Livens, A. Acharya, F. Griffoul, F. Ansari, August 2002 (status: informational).
- RFC 3376, Internet Group Management Protocol, Version 3, B. Cain, S. Deering, I. Kouvelas, B. Fenner, A. Thyagarajan, October 2002 (obsoletes RFC 2236) (updated by RFC 4604) (status: proposed standard).
- RFC 3678, Socket Interface Extensions for Multicast Source Filters, D. Thaler, B. Fenner, B. Quinn, January 2004.

- RFC 3754, IP Multicast in Differentiated Services (DS) Networks, R. Bless, K. Wehrle, April 2004 (status: informational).
- RFC 3810, Multicast Listener Discovery Version 2 (MLDv2) for IPv6, R. Vida, L. Costa, June 2004.
- RFC 3918, Methodology for IP Multicast Benchmarking, D. Stopp, B. Hickman, October 2004 (status: informational).
- RFC 3973, Protocol Independent Multicast–Dense-Mode (PIM–DM): Protocol Specification (Revised), A. Adams, J. Nicholas, W. Siadak, January 2005, (status: experimental).
- RFC 4541, Considerations for Internet Group Management Protocol (IGMP) and Multicast Listener Discovery (MLD) Snooping Switches, M. Christensen, K. Kimball, F. Solensky, May 2006 (status: informational).
- RFC 4604, Using Internet Group Management Protocol Version 3 (IGMPv3) and Multicast Listener Discovery Protocol Version 2 (MLDv2) for Source-Specific Multicast, H. Holbrook, B. Cain, B. Haberman, August 2006 (updates RFC 3376, RFC 3810) (status: proposed standard).
- RFC 4605, Internet Group Management Protocol (IGMP)/Multicast Listener Discovery (MLD)-Based Multicast Forwarding ("IGMP/MLD Proxying"), B. Fenner, H. He, B. Haberman, H. Sandick, August 2006 (status: proposed standard).
- RFC 4607, Source-Specific Multicast for IP, H. Holbrook, B. Cain, August 2006.

APPENDIX 1.B: MULTICAST BIBLIOGRAPHY

The following is a (partial) listing of textbooks on the topic. Most were written several years ago.

- Thomas Albert Maufer, *Deploying IP Multicast in the Enterprise*, Pearson Education, December 1997.
- Dave R. Kosiur, *IP Multicasting: The Complete Guide to Interactive Corporate Networks*, John Wiley & Sons, April 1998.
- C. Kenneth Miller, *Multicast Networking and Applications*, Pearson Education, October 1998.
- Paul Sanjoy, *Multicasting on the Internet and Its Applications*, Springer-Verlag, New York, June 1998.
- Beau Williamson, Jay D. Zorn, and Glen Zorn, *Developing IP Multicast Networks*, Volume I, Pearson Education, October 1999.

REFERENCES

[CHA200701] S. H. G. Chan, N. L. S. daFonseca, Peer-to-Peer Streaming, *IEEE Magazine*, June 2007, page 84.

[DSL200701] DSL Forum, Fremont, CA, http://www.dslforum.org.

[DVB200701] The DVB Project Office, Peter MacAvock, Executive Director, DVB-H White Paper, http://www.dvb.org, Grand Saconnex, Geneva, Switzerland.

[KUS200601] B. Kushnick, New Networks Institute, Telecom & Broadband Research for the Public Interest, www.newnetworks.com.

[MIN198601] D. Minoli, Putting Video on Desktops, *Computerworld*, October 1986, page 35.

[MIN199301] D. Minoli, Digital Video Compression: Getting Images across a Net, *Network Computing*, July 1993, page 146.

[MIN199401] D. Minoli, Designing Corporate Networks to Carry Multimedia, ICA Summer Program, University of Colorado, Boulder, CO, 1994.

[MIN199402] D. Minoli, Support of Corporate Multimedia over ATM, United Technologies Engineering Coordination Activities Eng. Ops. Subcom. for Computer Maintenance, Springfield, MA, April 1994.

[MIN199403] D. Minoli, Video Dialtone and Digital Video over ATM, Mt. Jade Science & Technology, Newark, NJ, December 1994.

[MIN199404] D. Minoli, *Distributed Multimedia through Broadband Communication Services* (co-authored), Artech House, 1994.

[MIN199501] D. Minoli, *Video Dialtone Technology: Digital Video over ADSL, HFC, FTTC, and ATM*, McGraw-Hill, New York, 1995.

[MIN199502] D. Minoli, An Assessment of Digital Video and Video Dialtone Technology, Regulation, Services, and Competitive Markets, DataPro Market Report on Convergence Strategies & Technologies, April 1995.

[MIN199503] D. Minoli, 1995: The Year of Video in Enterprise Nets, *Network World*, December 5, 1994, page 21.

[MIN199504] D. Minoli, Video Compression Schemes, DataPro Market Report on Convergence Strategies & Technologies, May 1995.

[MIN199505] D. Minoli, WilTel/Vyvx Video Services, Datapro Report CNS, June 1995.

[MIN199601] D. Minoli, Voice, Video, and Multimedia over ATM, CMA Spring Session, New York, June 1996.

[MIN199602] D. Minoli, Keynote Speech: Network Issues in Convergence; IEEE Convergence of Networks and Services, New York, November 1996.

[MIN199603] D. Minoli, *Distance Learning: Technology and Applications*, Artech House, 1996.

[MIN199701] D. Minoli, Convergence of Networking Technologies, 1997 Conference on Emerging Technologies, Nashville, TN, January 1997.

[MIN199702] D. Minoli, *Video Dialtone Technology*, Publishing House of Electronics Industry, 1997 (Chinese translation).

[MIN199801] D. Minoli, Integrating Circuit and Packet Switching: Achieving QOS in Public IP Networks, Institute for International Research, Orlando, FL, December 1998.

[MIN199802] D. Minoli, *IP Applications with ATM* (co-authored), McGraw-Hill, 1998.

[MIN199803] D. Minoli, *High-Speed Internet Access with ADSL*, Fall Condex, Miami Beach, FL, September 1998.

[MIN199804] D. Minoli, Designing ATM and IP Backbones, Interop 1998, Las Vegas, NV, May 1998.

[MIN200001] D. Minoli, Digital Video Technologies, video section in K. Terplan and P. Morreale, Editors. *The Telecommunications Handbook*, IEEE Press, 2000.

[MIN200301] D. Minoli, *Telecommunications Technology Handbook*, 2nd ed., Artech House, Norwood, MA, 2003.

[MIN200401] D. Minoli, *A Networking Approach to Grid Computing*, Wiley, New York, 2006.

[RFC988] RFC 988, Host Extensions for IP Multicasting, S. E. Deering, July 1986.

[RFC1054] RFC 1054, Host Extensions for IP Multicasting, S. E. Deering, May 1988.

[RFC1112] RFC 1112, Host Extensions for IP Multicasting, S. E. Deering, August 1989.

[RFC2201] RFC 2201, Core Based Trees (CBT) Multicast Routing Architecture, A. Ballardie, September 1997.

[RFC3973] RFC 3973, Protocol Independent Multicast–Dense-Mode (PIM–DM): Protocol Specification (Revised), A. Adams, J. Nicholas, W. Siadak, January 2005.

[WEL200101] P. J. Welcher, The Protocols of IP Multicast, White Paper, Chesapeake NetCraftsmen, Arnold, MD.

2

MULTICAST ADDRESSING
FOR PAYLOAD

Multicast communication is predicated on the need to send the same content to multiple destinations simultaneously. The group or groups of recipients are generally dynamic in nature and the join and dejoin (leave) rate may be high; furthermore, the implementation time for a given join/dejoin action is expected to occur in 1–2 s (consider the typical example of viewers changing TV channels on their remote control device).

Underpinning this ability to sustain multipoint communication is the addressing scheme. There is a desire in multicast environments to have distributed control of the user groups. The implication is that the source should not have to know and specifically address each intended recipient individually, thereby having to maintain large central tables of current users. Therefore, it follows that a mechanism needs to be available to accomplish this distribution in an efficient manner. This is accomplished via the use of multicast IP addresses and the multicast Media Access Control MAC addresses. This topic is discussed in this chapter.

2.1 IP MULTICAST ADDRESSES

Multicast addresses define, in effect, the group of hosts that participate in the shared reception of the content intended for that group. One can think of this by analogy with a

IP Multicast with Applications to IPTV and Mobile DVB-H   by Daniel Minoli
Copyright © 2008 John Wiley & Sons, Inc.

local TV station or local radio station. When a user "tunes" the TV to, say, Channel 7 (WABC TV in New York City), the user joins the set of viewers (receivers) that receive the content produced and distributed by WABC TV. When a user then changes channel and "tunes" the TV to, say, Channel 4 (WNBC TV in New York City), the user joins the set of viewers (receivers) that receive the content produced and distributed by WNBC TV. In IP multicast the analogous activity is accomplished by using IP multicast addresses. The various content providers stream IP packets that have their own source address and a multicast address as the destination address. For example, WABC TV in New York City could generate programming with the address 239.10.10.1, WNBC TV in New York City could generate programming with the address 239.10.10.2, and so on.

RFC 1112 specifies the extensions required of a host implementation of IP to support multicasting. The IANA controls the assignment of IP multicast addresses. IANA has allocated what has been known as the Class D address space to be utilized for IP multicast. IP multicast group addresses are in the range 224.0.0.0–239.255.255.255. See Figure 2.1. For each multicast address, there exists a set of zero or more hosts (receivers) that look for packets transmitted to that address. This set of devices is called a host group. A source (host) that sends packets to a specific group does not need to be a member of the group and the host typically does not even know the current members in the group [PAR200601]. As noted above, the source address for multicast IP packets is always the unicast source address.

There are two types of host groups [PAR200601]:

- Permanent host groups: Applications that are part of this type of group have an IP address permanently assigned by the IANA. A permanent group continues to exist even if it has no members. Membership in this type of host group is not permanent: a host (receiver) can join or leave the group as desired. An application can use DNS to obtain the IP address assigned to a permanent host group using the domain

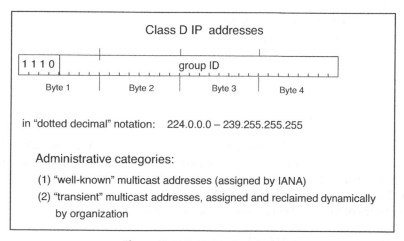

Figure 2.1. IP Multicast Address

mcast.net. The application can determine the permanent group from an address by using a pointer query in the domain 224.in-addr.arpa.

- Transient host groups: Any group that is not permanent as just described is by definition transient. The group is available for dynamic assignment as needed. Transient groups cease to exist when the number of members drops to zero.

As described above, some IP multicast addresses have been reserved for specific functions. Addresses in the range 224.0.0.0–224.0.0.255 are reserved to be used by network protocols on a local network segment. Network protocols make use of these addresses for automatic router discovery and to communicate routing information (e.g., OSPF uses 224.0.0.5 and 224.0.0.6 to exchange link-state information). IP packets with these addresses are not forwarded by a router; they remain local on a particular LAN segment [they have a Time-to-Live (TTL) parameter set to 1; even if the TTL is different from 1, they still are not forwarded by the router]. These addresses are also known as link-local addresses.

The statically assigned link-local scope is 224.0.0.0/24. The list of IP addresses assigned to permanent host groups is included in RFC 3232. From November 1977 through October 1994, the IANA periodically published tables of the IP parameter assignments in RFCs entitled, "Assigned Numbers." The most current of these assigned number RFCs had standard status and carried the designation: STD 2, RFC 1700. At this time, RFC 1700 has been obsoleted by RFC 3232. Since 1994, this sequence of RFCs has been replaced by an online database accessible through the IANA Web page (www.iana.org).

Some well known link-local addresses are the following:

- 224.0.0.1: All systems on this subnet
- 224.0.0.2: All routers on this subnet
- 224.0.0.4: DVMRP routers
- 224.0.0.5: OSPF routers
- 224.0.0.6: OSPF designated routers
- 224.0.0.12: DHCP server/relay agent
- 224.0.0.13: All PIM routers
- 224.0.0.22: All IGMPv3-capable multicast routers
- 224.0.0.102: HSRP
- 224.0.0.253: Teredo

The addresses from 224.0.1.0 to 238.255.255.255 are known as globally scoped addresses. These addresses are used to transmit multicast information across the Internet and between organizations. Some of these addresses have been reserved for specific uses such as Network Time Protocol (NTP) (224.0.1.1).

Examples of globally scoped address ranges are as follows:

- 224.1.0.0–224.1.255.255: ST multicast groups
- 224.2.0.0–224.2.127.253: Multimedia conference calls

- 224.2.127.254: SAPv1 announcements
- 224.2.128.0–224.2.255.255: SAP dynamic assignments
- 224.252.0.0–224.255.255.255: DIS transient groups
- 232.0.0.0–232.255.255.255: VMTP transient groups

At a more granular level, examples of globally scoped addresses are as follows:

- 224.0.12.000–224.0.12.063: Microsoft and MSNBC
- 224.0.13.000–224.0.13.255: WorldCom Broadcast Services
- 224.0.15.000–224.0.15.255: Agilent Technologies
- 224.0.16.000–224.0.16.255: XingNet
- 224.0.17.000–224.0.17.031: Mercantile & Commodity Exchange
- 224.0.18.000–224.0.18.255: Dow Jones
- 224.0.19.000–224.0.19.063: Walt Disney Company
- 224.0.19.064–224.0.19.095: Cal Multicast
- 224.0.19.096–224.0.19.127: SIAC Market Service
- 224.0.25.0–224.0.28.255: CME Market Data
- 224.0.29.0–224.0.30.255: Deutsche Boerse
- 224.0.252.0–224.0.252.255: KPN Broadcast Services
- 224.0.253.000–224.0.253.255: KPN Broadcast Services
- 224.0.254.000–224.0.254.255: Intelsat IPTV
- 224.0.255.000–224.0.255.255: Intelsat IPTV

Some of these globally scoped addresses have been assigned recently, for example:

- 224.0.25.0–224.0.28.255, CME Market Data: assigned March 22, 2007
- 224.0.254.000–224.0.254.255, Intelsat IPTV: assigned March 31, 2006
- 224.0.23.52, Amex Market Data: assigned August 11, 2006
- 224.4.4.0–224.4.0.254, London Stock Exchange: assigned March 31, 2006

2.1.1 Limited Scope Addresses

The addresses from 239.0.0.0 to 239.255.255.255 are called limited scope addresses (also known as administratively scoped addresses). RFC 2365 defines these addresses to be limited to a local group or organization. Routers are required to be configured with packet filters to prevent multicast traffic in this address range from flowing outside of an Autonomous System (AS); these are similar to the 10.x.x.x or 192.x.x.x ranges for traditional intranets.

Within an AS the limited scope address space can be subdivided so that local multicast boundaries can be defined. This also allows for address reuse between these subdomains.

RFC 2365 defines two limited scopes of interest: the IPv4 Local Scope and IPv4 Organization Local Scope.

The IPv4 Local Scope—239.255.0.0/16 239.255.0.0/16 is defined to be the IPv4 Local Scope. The local scope is the minimal enclosing scope and hence is not further divisible. Although the exact extent of a local scope is site dependent, locally scoped regions must obey certain topological constraints. In particular, a local scope must not span any other scope boundary. Further, a local scope must be completely contained within or equal to any larger scope. In the event that scope regions overlap in area, the area of overlap must be in its own local scope. This implies that any scope boundary is also a boundary for the local scope. The IPv4 Local Scope space grows "downward." As such, the IPv4 Local Scope may grow downward from 239.255.0.0/16 into the reserved ranges 239.254.0.0/16 and 239.253.0.0/16. However, these ranges should not be utilized until the 239.255.0.0/16 space is no longer sufficient.

The IPv4 organization Local Scope—239.192.0.0/14 239.192.0.0/14 is defined to be the IPv4 organization Local Scope and is the space from which an organization should allocate subranges when defining scopes for private use. The ranges 239.0.0.0/ 10, 239.64.0.0/10, and 239.128.0.0/10 are unassigned and available for expansion of this space. These ranges should be left unassigned until the 239.192.0.0/14 space is no longer sufficient. This is to allow for the possibility that future revisions may define additional scopes on a scale larger than organizations.

2.1.2   GLOP Addressing

RFC 2770 recommended that the 233.0.0.0/8 address range be reserved for statically defined addresses by organizations that already have an AS number reserved. The AS number of the domain is embedded into the second and third octets of the 233.0.0.0/8 range. GLOP is a mechanism that allocates multicast addresses to ASs (GLOP is neither an acronym nor an abbreviation).

For example, if an organization had AS 5662 assigned to it, written in binary, left padded with 0s, one gets 0001-0110-0001-1110 (hex 161E). Mapping the high-order octet to the second octet of the address, and the low-order octet to the third octet, one gets 233.22.30.0 As another example, if an organization had AS 62010, it is written as 1111-0010-0011-1010 (hex F23A). Looking at the two octets F2 and 3A one gets 242 and 58 in decimal. This gives a subnet of 233.242.58.0 that would be globally reserved for the organization that has this AS assigned to it.

2.1.3   Generic IPv4 Addressing

In IPv4 a host address is a 32-bit value that contains the network and host number fields. Traditionally (formerly) there have been five classes of Internet addresses: the class defined the size of the network and host fields. See Figure 2.2.

Internet addresses are commonly displayed in *dotted decimal notation* format XXX.XXX.XXX.XXX. Addresses can also be shown in hex form or in binary

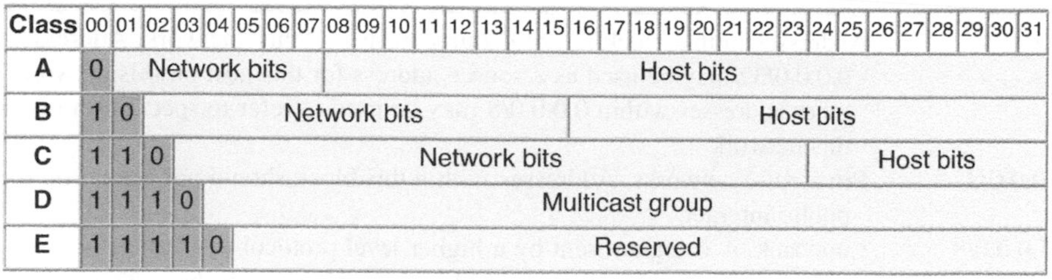

Class	00	01	02	03	04	05	06	07	08	09	10	11	12	13	14	15	16	17	18	19	20	21	22	23	24	25	26	27	28	29	30	31
A	0	Network bits															Host bits															
B	1	0	Network bits																		Host bits											
C	1	1	0	Network bits																					Host bits							
D	1	1	1	0	Multicast group																											
E	1	1	1	1	0	Reserved																										

Figure 2.2. Traditional IPv4 Address Classes

form. Consider, for example, 192.168.8.4. In binary form that would be 11000000|10101000|00001000|00000100; in hex form that would be C0-A8-08-04.

Table 2.1 depicts some key address allocations in the various classes (Class D is what is of interest in multicast, as already noted) [NET200701].

2.2   LAYER 2 MULTICAST ADDRESSES

During normal operation as defined in the Institute of Electrical and Electronics Engineers (IEEE) 802.3 LAN specifications, a Network Interface Card (NIC) connected to a physical LAN accepts only

- frames destined for that card as defined by the destination MAC address and the burned-in MAC address on the NIC or
- the broadcast MAC address (the broadcast address is 0xFFFF.FFFF.FFFF).

It follows that some mechanism has to be defined so that multiple hosts could receive the same packet and still be able to differentiate between multicast groups. In the IEEE 802.3 standard, bit 0 of the first octet is used to indicate a broadcast and/or multicast frame, as shown in Figure 2.3. This broadcast/multicast bit denotes that the frame is intended for an arbitrary group of hosts or all hosts on the network. IP multicast utilizes this capability to transmit IP packets to a group of hosts on a LAN segment.

2.2.1   Ethernet MAC Address Mapping

The IANA owns a block of Ethernet MAC addresses that can be allocated for multicast addresses: 0100.5E00.0000–0100.5E7F.FFFF. With this approach, 23 bits in the Ethernet address are made to correspond to the IP multicast group address. A mapping is used that places the lower 23 bits of the IP multicast group address into these available 23 bits in the Ethernet address (shown in Figure 2.4; also see Figure 2.5 for a specific example; Figure 2.6 depicts the full Ethernet frame for reference). However, because the upper five bits of the IP multicast address are dropped, the resulting address is not unique. Specifically, 32 different multicast group IDs map to the same Ethernet address. This predicament has to be kept in mind when designing a system.

TABLE 2.1. IPv4 Address Block Allocation

Block	Description
0.0.0.0/8	Addresses in this block refer to source hosts on "this" network. Address 0.0.0.0/32 may be used as a source address for this host on this network; other addresses within 0.0.0.0/8 may be used to refer to specified hosts on this network.
10.0.0.0/8	Private-use networks. Addresses within this block should not appear on the public Internet.
127.0.0.0/8	Loopback. A datagram sent by a higher level protocol to an address anywhere within this block should loop back inside the host. This is ordinarily implemented using only 127.0.0.1/32 for loopback, but no addresses within this block should ever appear on any network anywhere.
128.0.0.0/16	This block, corresponding to the numerically lowest of the former Class B addresses, was initially and is still reserved by the IANA. Given the present classless nature of the IP address space, the basis for the reservation no longer applies and addresses in this block are subject to future allocation to a Regional Internet Registry for assignment in the normal manner.
169.254.0.0/16	Link local. It is allocated for communication between hosts on a single link. Hosts obtain these addresses by autoconfiguration, such as when a Dynamic Host Configuration Protocol (DHCP) server may not be found.
172.16.0.0/12	Private-use networks. Addresses within this block should not appear on the public Internet.
191.255.0.0/16	This block, corresponding to the numerically highest of the former Class B addresses, was initially and is still reserved by the IANA. Given the present classless nature of the IP address space, the basis for the reservation no longer applies and addresses in this block are subject to future allocation to a Regional Internet Registry for assignment in the normal manner.
192.0.0.0/24	This block, corresponding to the numerically lowest of the former Class C addresses, was initially and is still reserved by the IANA. Given the present classless nature of the IP address space, the basis for the reservation no longer applies and addresses in this block are subject to future allocation to a Regional Internet Registry for assignment in the normal manner.
192.0.2.0/24	Test-Net. It is often used in conjunction with domain names example.com or example.net in vendor and protocol documentation. Addresses within this block should not appear on the public Internet.
192.88.99.0/24	6 to 4 relay anycast.
192.168.0.0/16	Private-use networks. Addresses within this block should not appear on the public Internet.
223.255.255.0/24	This block, corresponding to the numerically highest of the former Class C addresses, was initially and is still reserved by the IANA. Given the present classless nature of the IP address space, the basis for the reservation no longer applies and addresses in this block are subject to future allocation to a Regional Internet Registry for assignment in the normal manner.
224.0.0.0/4	Multicast. Formerly known as the Class D address space, it is allocated for use in IPv4 multicast address assignments.
240.0.0.0/4	This block, formerly known as the Class E address space, is reserved. The "limited broadcast" destination address 255.255.255.255 should never be forwarded outside the (sub-)net of the source. The remainder of this space is reserved for future use.

Courtesy: Network Sorcery, Inc.

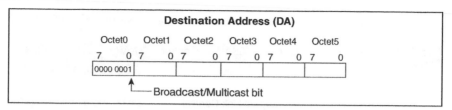

Figure 2.3. IEEE 802.3 MAC Address Format

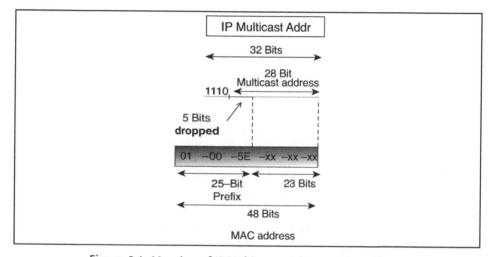

Figure 2.4. Mapping of IP Multicast to Ethernet MAC Address

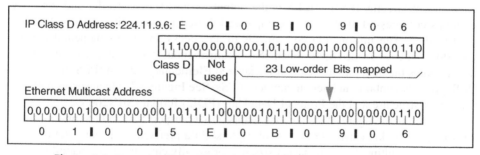

Figure 2.5. Example of Mapping of IP Multicast to Ethernet MAC Address

2.3 MPEG-LAYER ADDRESSES

In the video arena there is an additional "address" (channel indicator) that is often used. This is the Packet Identifier (PID[1]). The topic is introduced briefly here and revisited in Chapter 11. Operators typically maintain tables that show both the multicast IP address

[1]Some also call this the Program ID.

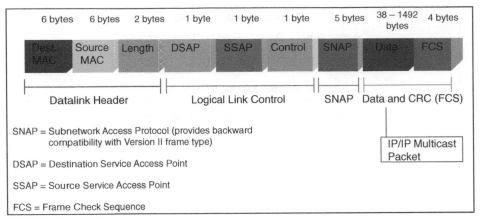

Figure 2.6. Full Ethernet Frame

and the PID as a way to manage the content delivery. The video portion of the IPTV system is defined by key documents such as (but not limited to):

- MPEG-2 Transport Stream Specifications—ISO/IEC 13818-1
- DVB-SI Specification—ETSI EN 300 468

The MPEG-2 and/or MPEG-4 standard defines three layers: audio, video, and systems. The systems layer supports synchronization and interleaving of multiple compressed streams, buffer initialization and management, and time identification. The audio and the video layers define the syntax and semantics of the corresponding Elementary Streams (ESs). An ES is the output of an MPEG encoder and typically contains compressed digital video, compressed digital audio, digital data, and digital control data. The information corresponds to an access unit (a fundamental unit of encoding), such as a video frame. Each ES is in turn an input to an MPEG-2 processor that accumulates the data into a stream of Packetized Elementary Stream (PES) packets. A PES typically contains an integral number of ESs. See Figure 2.7, which shows both the multiplex structure and the Protocol Data Unit (PDU) format [MIN200801].

As seen in the figure, PESs are then mapped to Transport Stream (TS) unit(s). Each MPEG-2 TS packet carries 184 octets of payload data prefixed by a four-octet (32-bit) header (the resulting 188-byte packet size was originally chosen for compatibility with ATM systems). These packets are the basic unit of data in a TS. They consist of a sync byte (0×47), followed by flags and a 13-bit PID. This is followed by other (some optional) transport fields; the rest of the packet consists of the payload. DVB specifications for transmission add 16 bytes of Reed–Solomon forward error correction to create a packet that is 204 bytes long. See Figure 2.8.

As noted, the PID is a 13-bit field that is used to uniquely identify the stream to which the packet belongs (e.g., PES packets corresponding to an ES) generated by the multiplexer. The PID allows the receiver to differentiate the stream to which each received packet belongs; effectively, it allows the receiver to accept or reject PES packets

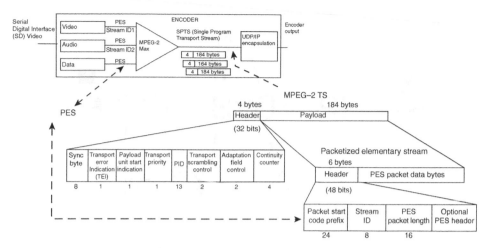

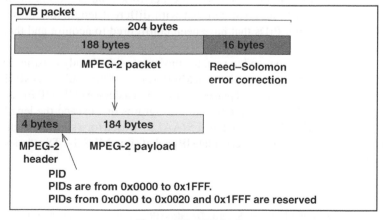

Figure 2.7. PES and TS Multiplexing

at a high level without burdening the receiver with extensive processing. Often one sends only one PES (or a part of single PES) in a TS packet (in some cases, however, a given PES packet may span several TS packets so that the majority of TS packets contain continuation data in their payloads). MPEG TS are typically encapsulated in the User Datagram Protocol (UDP) and then in IP.

Note: traditional approaches make use of the PID to identify content; in IPTV applications, the IP multicast address is used to identify the content. Also, the latest IPTV systems make use of MPEG-4-coded PESs.

Ultimately, an IPTV stream consists of packets of fixed size, each of which carries a stream-identifying number called a PID. These MPEG packets are aggregated into an IP packet; the IP packet is transmitted using IP multicast methods. Each PID contains specific video, audio, or data information. To display a channel of IPTV digital television, the

Figure 2.8. DVB Packet

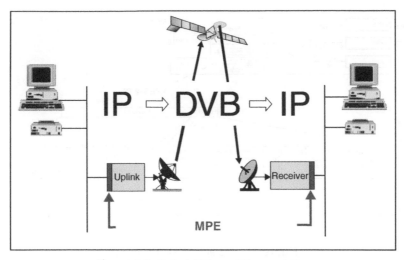

Figure 2.9. Pictorial View of Encapsulation

DVB-based application configures the driver in the receiver to pass up to it the packets with a set of specific PIDs, for example, PID 121 containing video and PID 131 containing audio (these packets are then sent to the MPEG decoder, either hardware or software based). So, in conclusion, a receiver or demultiplexer extracts elementary streams from the TS in part by looking for packets identified by the same PID.

Programs are groups of one or more PID streams that are related to each other. For example, a TS used in IPTV could contain five programs to represent five video channels. Assume that each channel consists of one video stream, one or two audio streams, and metadata. A receiver wishing to tune to a particular "channel" has to decode the payload of the PIDs associated with its program. It can discard the contents of all other PIDs.

DVB embodies the concept of "virtual channels" in analogous fashion as ATM. Virtual channels are identified by PIDs and are also colloquially known as "PIDs." DVB packets are transmitted over the satellite network (one can think of the DVB packets as being similar to an ATM cell, but with different length and format). The receiver looks for specific PIDs that have been configured to acquire and then inject into the telco network.

For satellite transmission, and to remain consistent with already existing MPEG-2 technology,[2] TSs are further encapsulated in Multiprotocol Encapsulation (MPE—RFC 3016) and then segmented again and placed into TSs via a device called IP Encapsulator (IPE); see Figure 2.9. MPE is used to transmit datagrams that exceed the length of the DVB "cell," just like ATM Adaptation Layer 5 (AAL5) is used for a similar function in an ATM context. MPE allows one to encapsulate IP packets into MPEG-2 TSs ("packets," or "cells"). See Figure 2.10.

---

[2]Existing receivers [specifically, Integrated Receiver Decoders (IRDs)] are based on hardware that works by de-enveloping MPEG-2 TSs; hence, the MPEG-4-encoded PESs are mapped to TSs at the source.

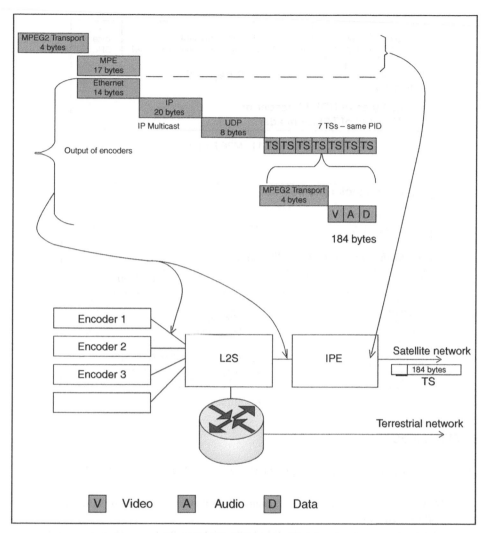

Figure 2.10. IPE Protocol Stack

IPEs handle statistical multiplexing and facilitate coexistence. IPE receives IP packets from an Ethernet connection and encapsulates packets using MPE and then maps these streams into an MPEG-2 TS. Once the device has encapsulated the data, the IPE forwards the data packets to a satellite link.

Note: IPEs are usually not employed if the output of the layer 2 switch is connected to a router for transmission over a terrestrial network; in this case the head end is responsible for proper downstream enveloping and distribution of the traffic to the ultimate consumer. The MPE packet has the format shown in Figure 2.11. Figure 2.12 shows the encapsulation process.

This topic is revisited in Chapter 11.

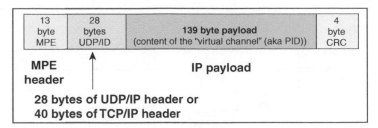

Figure 2.11. MPE Packet

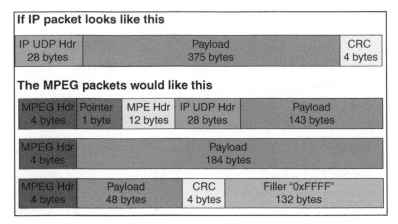

Figure 2.12. Encapsulation Process

REFERENCES

[MIN200801] D. Minoli, K. Iniewski, C. McCrosky, *Data Networks—VLSI and Optical Fibre*, Wiley, New York, 2008.

[NET200701] Network Sorcery, Inc., Technical Information, San Diego, CA, http://www. networksorcery.com.

[PAR200601] P. Lydia, L. Wei, et al., TCP/IP Tutorial and Technical Overview, IBM Press, Redbook Abstract, IBM Form Number GG24-3376-07, 2006.

[RFC1112] RFC 1112, Host Extensions for IP Multicasting, S.E. Deering, August 1989 (obsoletes RFC 0988, RFC1054) (updated by RFC 2236) (also STD0005) (status: standard).

[RFC2365] RFC 2365, Administratively Scoped IP Multicast, D. Meyer, University of Oregon, July1998.

[RFC2770] RFC 2770, GLOP Addressing in 233/8, D. Meyer, P. Lothberg, February 2000.

[RFC3232] RFC 3232, Assigned Numbers: RFC 1700 is Replaced by an Online Database, J. Reynolds, Editor, January 2002 (obsoletes RFC 1700) (status: informational).

3

MULTICAST PAYLOAD FORWARDING

This chapter looks at the mechanisms used in IP multicast to transmit payload information to receivers. It covers multicasting on a LAN segment and, more importantly, over a multihop routed infrastructure. Multicasting on the local subnetwork does not require a multicast router or the use of a multicast routing algorithm: on a shared-media subnet a source host, which does not necessarily have to be a group member, just transmits a multicast data packet; the packet is received by any member hosts connected to the medium. But for multicasts to extend beyond the local subnetwork, the subnet must be attached to a multicast-capable router, which itself is attached to other multicast-capable routers. This requires three mechanism: (i) the ability to build distribution trees; (ii) the presence of a multicast routing protocol (e.g., PIM); and (iii) the presence of a group management protocol at the edges that enables the subnet's multicast router (or routers) to monitor group membership presence on its directly attached links, such that if multicast data arrives, the router knows over which of its links to send a copy of the packet. This chapter focuses on the first mechanism and chapters that follow focus on other mechanisms.

IP Multicast with Applications to IPTV and Mobile DVB-H by Daniel Minoli
Copyright © 2008 John Wiley & Sons, Inc.

3.1 MULTICASTING ON A LAN SEGMENT

The transmission process at the source builds a datagram stream with a specified destination IP multicast address, as defined in Chapter 2. The source network driver encapsulates the datagram with an Ethernet frame that includes the source Ethernet address and a(n appropriate) destination Ethernet address. The process then sends the packet to the destination. In unicast IP traffic forwarding, the encapsulation of the IP multicast packet into an Ethernet frame with the MAC address of the receiving device makes use of the Address Resolution Protocol (ARP). As discussed in the previous chapter, a static mapping has been defined to "create" the destination MAC address (a multicast Ethernet address.) As noted in Chapter 2, in an Ethernet network, multi-casting is supported by setting the high-order octet of the data link address to 0×01. The 32-bit multicast IP address is mapped to an Ethernet address by placing the low-order 23 bits of the Class D address into the low-order 23 bits of the IANA-reserved address block. Because the high-order 5 bits of the IP multicast group are not utilized, 32 different IP-level multicast groups are mapped to the same Ethernet address. Figure 3.1 illustrates one example. The destination process informs its network device drivers that it wishes to receive datagrams destined for a given IP multicast address. The device driver enables reception of packets for that IP multicast address.

Because of the nonunique IP-to-Ethernet address mapping, filtering by the device driver is required. This is accomplished by checking the destination address in the IP header before passing the packet to the IP layer. This ensures the receiving process does not receive unneeded datagrams. Hosts that are not participating in a host group are not listening for the multicast address; here, multicast packets are filtered by lower layer network interface hardware [PAR200601].

3.2 MULTICASTING BETWEEN NETWORK SEGMENTS

Multicast routing protocols have been developed to transmit packets across a routed network while at the same time seeking to avoid routing loops. There are two functions required to support multicast transmission across a routed network:

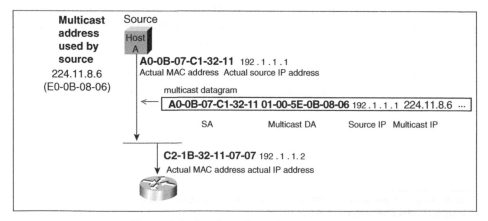

Figure 3.1. Creation of a Multicast Datagram

- Determining multicast participants: a capability for determining if a multicast datagram needs to be forwarded on a specific network. The IGMP [RFC3376] supports this capability.
- Determining multicast scope: the TTL field in a multicast datagram is used to determine the scope of a transmission. The value contained in this field is decremented at each router that is traversed.

When a host or multicast-capable router receives a datagram, datagram processing depends on both the destination IP address and the TTL value:

If TTL $= 0$, the datagram is restricted to the source host.

If TTL $= 1$, the datagram reaches all users/hosts on the subnet that are members of the group. Multicast routers decrement the value to zero. (Note that no Time Exceeded error messages are sent to the source, unlike the case for unicast datagrams where error messages are, in fact, sent.)

If TTL > 1, the datagram reaches all users/hosts on the subnet that are members of the group. The action performed by multicast routers depends on the group address, as follows [PAR200601]:

- Addresses inside the 224.0.0.0–224.0.0.255 block: Multicast routers do not forward datagrams with destination addresses in this range since this set of addresses is intended for single-hop multicast applications. However, even though multicast-capable router do not forward these datagrams, a host must still report membership in a group within this range; the report is used to inform other hosts on the subnet that the reporting host is a member of the group.
- Addresses outside the 224.0.0.0–224.0.0.255 block: These datagrams are forwarded by the multicast-capable router but the TTL value is decremented by 1 at each stage.

This mechanism allows a host to locate the nearest user/host seeking a specific multicast address. The source host sends out a datagram with a TTL value of 1 (same subnet) and waits for a reply. If no reply is received, the source host resends the datagram with a TTL value of 2. If no reply is received, the host continues to increment the TTL value until the nearest user is found.

3.3 MULTICAST DISTRIBUTION TREES

Multicast-capable routers create logical distribution trees that control the path that IP multicast traffic takes through the network in order to deliver traffic to all receivers. Mechanisms exist for creating and for maintaining (e.g., pruning) the distribution trees. Different multicast algorithms (e.g., PIM, CBT, DVMRP) use different techniques for establishing the distribution tree. One can classify algorithms into source-based tree algorithms and shared-tree algorithms. Different algorithms have different scaling characteristics, and the characteristics of the resulting trees differ too, for example, from an end-to-end delay perspective.

Members of multicast groups can join or leave (dejoin) at any point in time, therefore, the distribution trees must be dynamically updated. When all the active receivers on a particular branch stop requesting the traffic for a particular multicast group, the multicast-capable routers prune that branch from the distribution tree and stop forwarding traffic along that branch. If a receiver on that branch becomes active and requests the multicast traffic, the multicast-capable router will dynamically modify the distribution tree and start forwarding traffic again [CIS200701]. Note that IP multicast does not require senders to be group members of that group.

The two basic types of multicast distribution trees are *source trees* [also known as Shortest Path Trees (SPTs) or source-based trees] and *shared trees* (also known as share-based trees). Messages are replicated only where the tree branches. Both SPTs and shared trees are loop-free topologies.

The simplest form of a multicast distribution tree is the *source tree*. A source tree has its root at the multicast source and has branches forming a spanning tree over the network to the receivers. The tree makes use of the shortest path through the network and so a separate SPT may exist for each individual source sending to each group. The notation of (S,G) is utilized to describe an SPT where S is the IP address of the source and G is the multicast group address. Figure 3.2 depicts an example of an SPT for group 239.1.1.1 rooted at the source, host A, and connecting three receivers, hosts B, C, and D. Using the (S,G) notation, the SPT is (92.1.1.1, 239.1.1.1).

SPTs achieve, by definition, the optimal path topology between the source and the receivers in terms of the number of hops, resulting in the minimum amount of network latency for distributing multicast traffic. However, the multicast-capable routers are required to maintain path information for each source. In large networks,

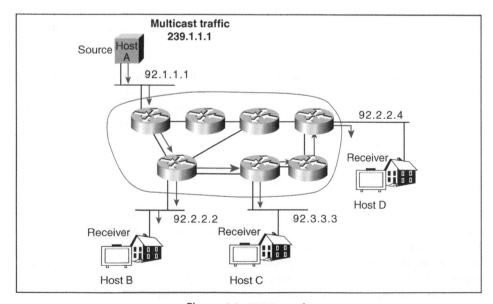

Figure 3.2. SPT Example

with either many sources and/or many groups, this state information can overtax the routers, particularly for memory resources needed to store the multicast routing table. Note that Deering's multicast algorithms [RFC988, RFC1054, RFC1112] build source-rooted delivery trees, with one delivery tree per sender subnetwork [RFC2201].

Figure 3.3 depicts a simple IPTV example; in this example the SPT is employed to efficiently distribute video to remote users. Figure 3.4 shows the real-time pruning that takes place.

Shared trees use a single common root placed at a selected point in the network. This shared root is called a Rendezvous Point (RP) (also called *core* or *center*). Figure 3.5 shows a shared tree for the group 239.1.1.1 along with the shared root. When making use of a shared tree, sources send their traffic to the root (RP) and then the traffic is forwarded along the shared tree to reach all active receivers. In this example, multicast traffic from sources 1 and 2 travels to the router at the shared root and then along the shared tree to the three receivers, hosts B, C, and D. All sources in the multicast group use the common shared tree. The notation (*, G) is used to represent the tree. In this case, "*" is a wildcard that means all sources. The shared tree shown in Figure 3.5 is written as (*, 239.1.1.1).

Shared trees require the minimum amount of state information in each router, thereby minimizing the memory requirements for the routers and the mechanisms to keep the state information up to date. However, the paths between the source and receivers may not be the optimal paths in terms of hops and, consequently, latency. This

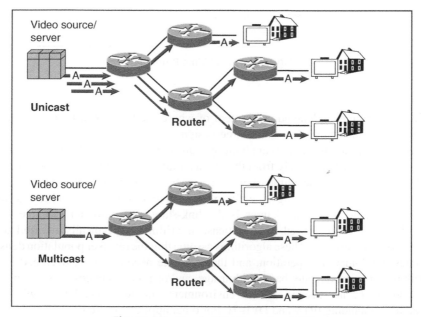

Figure 3.3. Simple IPTV Example of SPT

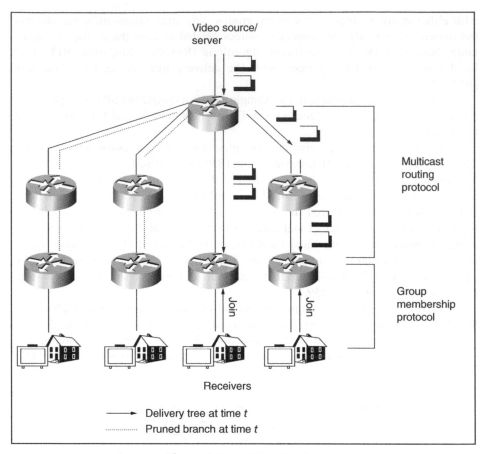

Figure 3.4. Real-Time Pruning

predicament requires a detailed assessment of where the RP should be located in the network when implementing a shared-tree design.

Source-based multicast trees are built by a distance-vector-based algorithm, which may be implemented separately from the unicast routing algorithm (as is the case with DVMRP); alternatively, the multicast tree may also be built using the information present in the underlying unicast routing table (for example, with PIM DM). The other algorithm used for building source-based trees is the link-state algorithm (an example being M-OSPF). Most source-based tree multicast algorithms are typically referred to as "dense-mode" algorithms. These algorithms assume that the receiver population densely populates the domain of operation, and therefore the accompanying overhead in the algorithms (in terms of state, bandwidth usage, and/or processing costs) is acceptable. This tends to be the case in a local environment and for a number of wide-area applications, including IPTV and DVB-H. For other applications (e.g., grid computing, datacasting), group membership tends to be sparsely distributed throughout the

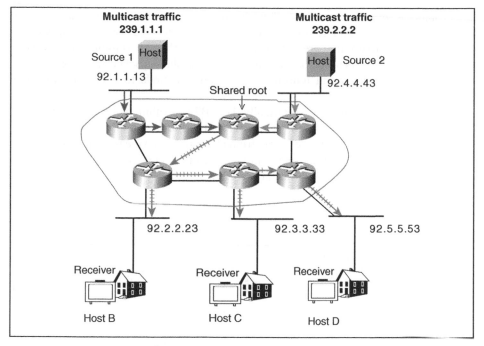

Figure 3.5. Shared Distribution Tree

institutional network, carrier network, or Internet; with these applications there may be "pockets" of denseness, but at the global level, wide-area groups tend to be sparsely distributed [RFC2201].

A shared-tree architecture offers an improvement in scalability over source tree architectures by a factor of the number of active sources. Source trees scale $O(S \times G)$, since a distinct delivery tree is built per active source. Shared trees eliminate the source S scaling factor; all sources use the same shared tree, therefore, a shared tree scales $O(G)$. The implication of this is that applications with many active senders, such as distributed interactive simulation applications and distributed video gaming (where most receivers are also senders), have significantly less impact on underlying multicast routing if shared trees are used [RFC2201]. Notice that in IPTV the source is typically unique because the source (call it a supersource) itself aggregates many content channels (from various providers, e.g., 200 providers) into a single IP multicast stream in order to apply a consistent coding scheme (e.g., convert from MPEG-2 to MPEG-4, convert from analog to digital MPEG-4, convert from component video to MPEG-4 video) and to apply a consistent conditional access (digital rights management) discipline.

For general applications (such as but not limited to datacasting and grid computing), shared trees incur significant bandwidth and state savings compared with source trees. The first reason for this is that the tree only spans a group's receivers (including links/routers leading to receivers)—there is no cost to routers/links in other parts of the network. The second reason for this is that routers between a nonmember sender and the delivery tree are not incurring any overhead pertaining to multicast, and indeed, these routers need not even be multicast capable—packets from nonmember senders are encapsulated and transmitted in a unicast mode to a core on the tree [RFC2201].

Some multicast algorithms, specifically the CBT algorithm, make use of a CBT. A CBT is a "bidirectional shared tree" where the routing state is "bidirectional," namely, packets can flow both down the tree away from the core and up the tree toward the core, depending on the location of the source in the network, and the tree is "shared" by all sources to the group. Figure 3.6 illustrates a CBT.

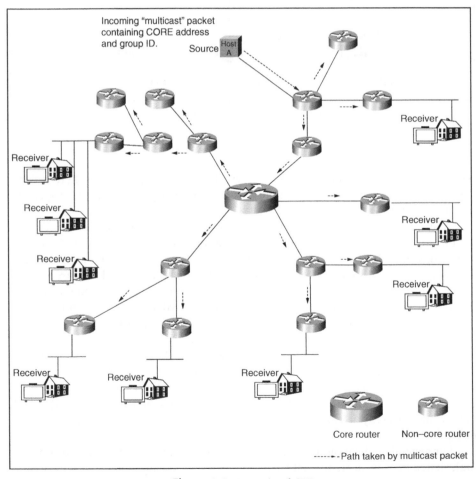

Figure 3.6. Example of CBT

3.4 MULTICAST FORWARDING: REVERSE PATH FORWARDING

The basic approach in unicast routing is forwarding information toward the *receiver*. In multicast routing, the source needs to send traffic to a dynamic group of hosts, as represented by a multicast group address. The basic approach in multicast routing is forwarding multicast traffic *away from the source*; this approach is called Reverse Path Forwarding (RPF).

In traditional unicast routing, traffic is relayed through the network along a single path from the source to the destination. The router uses its routing table to determine how to forward the traffic toward that destination, specifically to determine the outgoing router link that a datagram should utilize. The table is indexed on destination addresses since a unicast router is generally only concerned with the destination address on a datagram that needs forwarding.[1] After the interface is selected, the router forward a single copy of the unicast datagram out that interface in the direction of the destination.

RPF enables multicast-capable routers to correctly forward multicast traffic along the distribution tree and avoid loops. A multicast-capable router must keep track of which direction is toward the source (upstream) and which direction(s) is (are) toward the receiver (downstream). A multicast-capable router only forward a multicast packet if it is received on the upstream interface. When there are multiple downstream paths, the router replicates the packet and forwards it along the appropriate downstream paths.

RPF employs the existing unicast routing table to determine the upstream and downstream neighbors. When a multicast packet arrives at a router, the router will perform an RPF check on the packet, namely, determine if it has been received on the upstream interface. If the RPF check is successful, the packet is forwarded; otherwise the packet is dropped.

For traffic flowing along a source tree, the RPF check procedure works as follows [CIS200701]:

Step 1. Router looks up the source address in the unicast routing table to determine if it has arrived on the interface that is on the reverse path back to the source.

Step 2. If the packet has arrived on the interface leading back to the source, the RPF check is successful and the packet will be forwarded.

Step 3. If the RPF check in 2 fails, the packet is dropped.

Figure 3.7 shows examples of RPF checks. If a multicast packet from source 152.11.5.6 is received on interface Serial 0 (S0), a check of the multicast route table shows that this packet should be dropped. If the multicast packet, on the contrary, arrived on S1, then the RPF check passes and the packet is forwarded according to the interface defined in the unicast routing table (could be S2, as an example.)

Note: the RPF algorithm builds a tree for each source in a multicast group.

---

[1] A router is generally not concerned about the source address except in special cases.

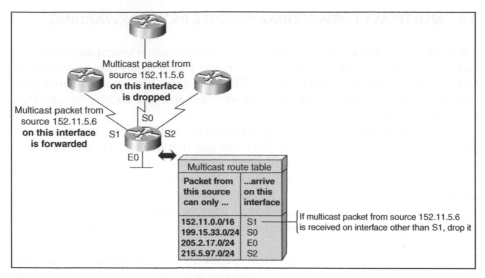

Figure 3.7. RPF Check

3.5 MULTICAST FORWARDING: CENTER-BASED TREE ALGORITHM

The CBT algorithm defines another method to determine (near) optimum paths to support multicast groups. (The disadvantage of the CBT algorithm is that it could in theory build a suboptimal path for some sources and receivers.) This algorithm builds a delivery tree for each multicast group, but the tree is identical for all sources. Each router maintains a single tree for the entire group. The algorithm operates by making use of the following steps [PAR200601, RFC2189, RFC2201]:

1. A fixed *center point* in the network is chosen.
2. Each receiver sends a Join request directed toward the center point. This is accomplished using an IGMP membership report for that group (as discussed in more detail in Chapter 4).
3. The request is processed by all intermediate routers located between the multicast receiver and the center point. If the router receiving the request is already a member of the tree, it marks one more interface as belonging to the group. If this is the first Join request, the router forwards the request one step further toward the source.
4. Multicast packets from a source are forwarded toward the center point until they reach a router belonging to the tree. At this stage, the packets are forwarded using the multicast processing of the CBT.

Chapter 6 provides additional details on CBT.

3.6 IMPLEMENTING IP MULTICAST IN A NETWORK

Wide-area multicast applications (for example, IPTV, DVB-H, datacasting) require datagrams to traverse multiple subnet boundaries and router hops. Support for IP multicast requires multicast-ready network elements such as routers and layer 2 switches; also, it requires multicast-ready clients (as potential receivers) and servers (as potential multicast sources).

Users (*Hosts*): Server and client hosts must have an IP stack supporting multicast, as specified in Internet RFC 1112, *inter alia*; this enables hosts to send and receive multicast data. TCP/IP stacks are now generally multicast enabled. Servers and clients run applications that support IP multicast delivery, such as audio broadcast, video broadcast, or videoconferencing. In addition to the usual unicast and broadcast capability, NICs on all receiving hosts must be configured to monitor multicast packets.

Network Infrastructure: A high-performance backbone is required to support multicast services. Such backbone should support switched Ethernet connections from the backbone to the sources and the receivers. An end-to-end layer 2/layer 3 switched network from source to receiver [for example, using Multiprotocol Label Switching (MPLS)] may also be desirable; the switched infrastructure can provide adequate bandwidth to allow unicast and multimedia applications to coexist within the subnet. A well-tuned traditional IP backbone can also be used.

The most appropriate layer 2 switches for multicast have a switch architecture that allows multicast traffic to be forwarded to a large number of attached group members without overloading the switch fabric. Layer 2 switches also need some degree of multicast awareness (for example, IGMP snooping) to avoid flooding multicasts to all switch ports. Multicast control in layer 2 switches can be accomplished in a number of ways [CIS200701]:

- VLANs can be defined to correspond to the boundaries of the multicast group. This is a simple approach; however, this approach does not support dynamic changes to group membership and adds to the administrative burden of unicast VLANs.
- Layer 2 switches can snoop IGMP queries and reports to learn the port mappings of multicast group members. This allows the switch to dynamically track group membership. But snooping every multicast data and control packet consumes a lot of switch processing capacity and therefore can degrade forwarding performance and increase latency.
- Taking advantage of the Generic Attribute Registration Protocol (GARP) (IEEE 802.1p) will allow the end system to communicate directly with the switch to join a 802.1p group corresponding to a multicast group. This shifts much of the responsibility for multicast group configuration from layer 3 to layer 2, which may be most appropriate in large, flat, switched networks.

In reference to layer 3 infrastructure equipment, most modern routers (or more specifically, router software) include support for IP multicast. Intermediate routers and/

or layer 3 switches between senders and receivers must be IP multicast enabled; at the very least, the ingress and egress routers to the backbone should be multicast routers. If the intervening backbone routers lack support for IP multicast, IP tunneling (encapsulating multicast packets within unicast packets) may be used as an interim measure to link multicast routers. The choice of multicast routing protocol among PIM, DVMRP, MOSPF, and CBT should be based on the characteristics of the multicast application being deployed as well as the "density" and geographical location of receiving hosts [CIS200701].

REFERENCES

[CIS200701] Cisco Systems, Internet Protocol (IP) Multicast Technology Overview, White Paper, Cisco Systems, San Jose, CA.

[PAR200601] L. Parziale, W. Liu, et al., TCP/IP Tutorial and Technical Overview, IBM Press, Redbook Abstract, IBM Form Number GG24-3376-07, 2006.

[RFC2189] RFC 2189, Core Based Trees (CBT Version 2) Multicast Routing—Protocol Specification, A. Ballardie, September 1997.

[RFC2201] RFC 2201, Core Based Trees (CBT) Multicast Routing Architecture, A. Ballardie, September 1997.

4

DYNAMIC HOST REGISTRATION—INTERNET GROUP MANAGEMENT PROTOCOL

This chapter covers the important topic of dynamic host registration. In a multicast environment, group membership information is exchanged between a receiver (host) and the nearest multicast router. The IGMP is used by host receivers to join or leave a multicast host group. Hosts establish group memberships by sending IGMP messages to their local multicast router. Multicast-enabled routers monitor for IGMP messages to maintain forwarding tables for the various interfaces on the router. Multicast-enabled routers periodically send out queries to discover which groups are active or inactive on a given subnet.

IGMP is used by IPv4-based receivers to report their IP multicast group memberships to neighboring multicast routers: it defines the signaling communication occurring between receiving hosts and their local multicast router. IGMP2, now widely deployed, is defined by RFC 2236 (November 1997).

The latest version at press time was Version 3, defined in RFC 3376 (IGMPv3, October 2002); RFC 3376 subsumes and obsoletes RFC 2236 (IGMPv2). IGMPv3 supports receivers that explicitly signal sources from which they wish to receive traffic. Specifically, IGMPv3 is employed by hosts to signal channel access in SSM. For SSM to work, IGMPv3 must be available in last-hop routers and receiver host operating system

IP Multicast with Applications to IPTV and Mobile DVB-H by Daniel Minoli
Copyright © 2008 John Wiley & Sons, Inc.

network stacks and be used by the applications running on those receiver hosts. Benefits of SSM include:

- Optimized access bandwidth utilization—Receivers are able to request traffic only from explicitly known sources, relieving the typically congested access link from unnecessary traffic, especially in cases where the access is DSL based (as covered briefly in Chapter 1).
- Risk reduction—Eliminates denial-of-service attacks from unknown sources.

This chapter provides an overview of IGMP. Appendix 4.A provides a formal description of IGMPv2. Appendix 4.B covers basic operation of IGMP snooping switches. Appendix 4.C provides a basic description of commercial router configuration for IGMP operation.

4.1   IGMP MESSAGES

In Version 1 (defined in RFC 1112), there are two types of IGMP messages: MQ and MR. In a Version 1 implementation, receivers interested in joining a particular multicast group generate MRs, which contain reference to that multicast address (group). The router, in turn, builds a forwarding table entry and routinely forwards the multicast packets to the interface(s) that support the subnet where registered hosts reside. The router periodically sends out an IGMP MQ to verify that at least one host on the subnet is still interested in receiving traffic directed to that group. When there is no reply to the three consecutive IGMP MQs, the router times out the group and stops forwarding traffic directed toward that group.

The basic IGMPv2 (defined in RFC 2236) message types are MQ, MR,[1] and Leave Group (LG). MQs can be generic (general MQ) or specific (group-specific MQ). In the discussion below, the querier is the sender of a Query message—the querier is a multicast router.

IGMPv2 works in a similar fashion as Version 1 but with the addition of the LG message. With the LG mechanism, receivers/hosts can explicitly communicate their intention to depart from the group to the local multicast router. The use of LGs reduces the traffic on subnets, especially if there is a lot of join/change/leave activity. Upon receiving an LG message the router issues a group-specific query to determine if there are any remaining hosts on that subnet that are in need of receiving the traffic. If there are no replies, the router times out the group and stops forwarding the traffic.

The IGMP messages for IGMPv2 are shown in Figure 4.1. The message comprises an eight-octet structure. During transmission, IGMP messages are encapsulated in IP datagrams; to indicate that an IGMP packet is being carried, the IP header contains a protocol number of 2. For reference, Figure 4.2 shows the format of an IP datagram along

---

[1]There are Versions 1, 2 MRs

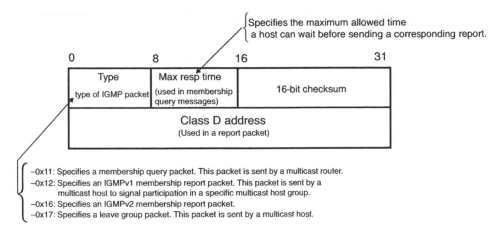

Figure 4.1. IGMPv2 Message Format

with a short list of protocol types, of which IGMP is one of many. An IGMPv2 PDU consists of a 20-byte IP header and 8 bytes of IGMP.

The Type field identifies the type of IGMP packet.

- A MQ packet has a type of 0×11. This message is sent by a multicast-enabled router. An MQ packet is sent by a multicast router either to learn which groups have members on an attached network (also known as general query) or to learn if a particular group has any members on an attached network (also known as group-specific query).
- An IGMPv1 membership report packet has a type of 0×12. This message is sent by a multicast receiver (host) to indicate a request for participation in a specific multicast receiver (host) group.
- An IGMPv2 membership report packet has a type of 0×16. This is the Join message (MR).
- An LG packet has a type of 0×17. This message is sent by a multicast receiver (host) to indicate a request for disassociation from a group.

The *Max Response Time* field is employed in membership query messages and it specifies the maximum time a host can wait before sending a corresponding report. This parameter allows routers to optimize the leave latency and the time between the last receiver (host) leaves a group and the time the routing protocol is notified that there are no more active members in that group. The maximum response time is measured in tenths of a second.

The *Checksum* field contains a 16-bit checksum for the message. The checksum is the 16-bit one's complement of the one's complement sum of the whole IGMP message (the entire IP payload). For computing the checksum, the Checksum field is set to zero.

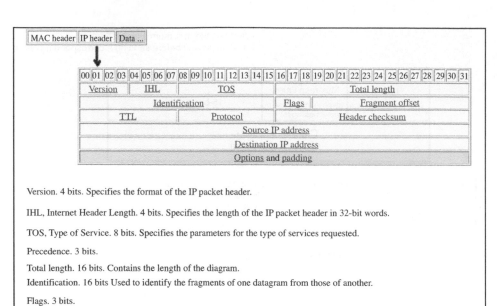

| MAC header | IP header | Data ... |

00	01	02	03	04	05	06	07	08	09	10	11	12	13	14	15	16	17	18	19	20	21	22	23	24	25	26	27	28	29	30	31
Version				IHL				TOS								Total length															
Identification																Flags			Fragment offset												
TTL								Protocol								Header checksum															
Source IP address																															
Destination IP address																															
Options and padding																															

Version. 4 bits. Specifies the format of the IP packet header.

IHL, Internet Header Length. 4 bits. Specifies the length of the IP packet header in 32-bit words.

TOS, Type of Service. 8 bits. Specifies the parameters for the type of services requested.

Precedence. 3 bits.

Total length. 16 bits. Contains the length of the diagram.

Identification. 16 bits Used to identify the fragments of one datagram from those of another.

Flags. 3 bits.

Fragment offset. 13 bits. Used to direct the reassembly of a fragmented datagram.

TTL Time-to-Live. 8 bits. A timer field used to track the lifetime of the datagram.
When the TTL field is decremented down to zero, the datagram is discarded

Protocol. 8. bits. This field specifies the encapsulated protocol

Value	Protocol
0	**HOPOPT.**IPv6 Hop-by-Hop Option.
1	**ICMP.**Internet Control Message Protocol
2	**IGAP.**IGMP for user Authentication Protocol **IGMP.**Internet Group Management Protocol. **RGMP.**Router-port Group Management Protocol.
3	**GGP.**Gateway to Gateway Protocol.
4	**IP in IP encapsulation**
5	**ST.**Internet Stream Protocol.
6	**TCP.**Transmission Control Protocol.
7	**UCL.CBT**
8	**EGP.**Exterior Gateway Protocol.
9	**IGRP.**Interior Gateway Routing Protocol.

Electera
Electera

Header checksum. 16 bits. A 16-bit one's complement checksum of the IP header and IP options

Source IP address. 32 bits. IP address of the sender.

Destination IP address. 32 bits. IP address of the intended receiver.
This also includes multicast addresses (see Chapter 2).

Options. Variable length.

Figure 4.2. IP Packet Format

The *Class D Address* field contains a valid multicast group address and is used in a report packet.

Note: In IPv4, multicasting and IGMP support are optional. However, IGMP functions are integrated directly into IPv6, implying that all IPv6 hosts are required to support multicasting.

4.2 IGMPv3 MESSAGES

In the recent past, the IGMPv2 message format has been extended in IGMPv3. Version 3 allows receivers to subscribe to or exclude a specific *set* of sources within a multicast group, rather than just an individual source (this is called, as noted, source-specific multicast). With this feature, IGMPv 3 adds support for "source filtering," that is, the ability for a system to report interest in receiving packets sent to a particular multicast address *only* from specific source addresses or from *all but* specific source addresses. That information may be used by multicast routing protocols to avoid delivering multicast packets from specific sources to (sub)networks where there are no interested receivers [RFC3376]. IGMPv3 is not widely implemented as of press time.

"Source filtering" enables a multicast receiver (host) to signal to a multicast-enabled router that groups the host that wants to receive multicast traffic from (that is, signal membership to a multicast host group) and from which source(s) this traffic is expected. This membership information allows a multicast-enabled router to forward traffic from only those sources from which receivers requested the traffic. "Source filtering" supports an atomic leave/join; this helps recovery from lost "leave" messages and simplifies some of the error recovery scenarios. This capability also halves the message traffic, as now only a single message is needed to "leave" one stream and "join" another.

Receivers signal membership to a multicast host group in the following two modes [CIS200701]:

- INCLUDE mode—In this mode, the receiver announces membership to a host group and provides a list of IP addresses (the INCLUDE list) from which it wishes to receive traffic.
- EXCLUDE mode—In this mode, the receiver announces membership to a host group and provides a list of IP addresses (the EXCLUDE list) from which it does not wish to receive traffic. This indicates that the host wants to receive traffic only from other sources whose IP addresses are not listed in the EXCLUDE list.

To support this capability the membership query packet (type of 0×11) has been changed; in addition, a new packet type of 0×22 has been added. Note that all IGMPv3 implementations must still support packet types 0×12, 0×16, and 0×17.

In IGMPv3 there are the following three variants of the Query message:

1. A "general query" is sent by a multicast router to learn the complete multicast reception state of the neighboring interfaces (that is, the interfaces attached to the network on which the query is transmitted). In a general query, both the Group Address field and the Number of Sources field are zero (see below).
2. A "group-specific query" is sent by a multicast router to learn the reception state, with respect to a *single* multicast address, of the neighboring interfaces. In a group-specific query, the Group Address field contains the multicast address of interest, and the Number of Sources field contains zero (see below).

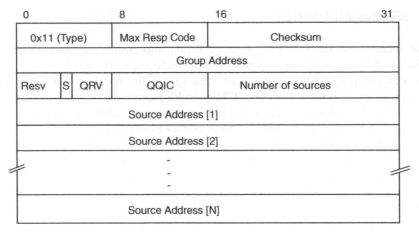

Figure 4.3. IGMPv3 Membership Query Message

3. A "group-and-source-specific query" is sent by a multicast router to learn if any neighboring interface desires reception of packets sent to a specified multicast address from any of the specified list of sources. In a group-and-source-specific query, the Group Address field contains the multicast address of interest, and the Source Address fields contain the source address(es) of interest.

The IGMPv3 membership query packet 0×11 message includes a field that specifies the number of sources being covered by the request along with a list of Class D addresses. See Figure 4.3.

The Type field remains unchanged.

The *Max Response Code* field has been modified and it distinguishes between a maximum response *code* and a maximum response *time*. The Max Resp Code field specifies the maximum time allowed before sending a responding report. The actual time allowed, called the Max Resp Time, is represented in units of 1/10 s and is derived from the maximum response code. Here is how that is done—when the maximum response code is less than 128, the value of the maximum response time equates to the value of the maximum response code. When the maximum response code is greater than 128, the maximum response time is calculated as follows.

If Max Resp Code $\geq$ 128, Max Resp Code represents a floating-point value where the coding is

```
 0  1  2  3  4  5  6  7
+-+-+-+-+-+-+-+-+
|1|  exp  |  mant  |
+-+-+-+-+-+-+-+-+
```

mant = mantissa
exp = exponent

Max Resp Time = (mant | 0×10) $\ll$ (exp + 3)

(l is the Boolean or function; e.g., 0010|10000 = 10010) (note that the *exp* calculation uses a binary representation of decimal 3, namely 11) "≪" is the bitwise left shift operator. It defines the shift bits of a number to the left by a certain number of places and zero is used for filling.

For example, 2147483646 ≪ 1 leads to the following: the 32-bit binary representation of 2147483646 is 10000000000000000000000000000010. If its leftmost bit is removed and a zero is filled at the rightmost position, the result is 00000000000000000000000000000100, which is equal to 4 in decimal representation. Consider the example of 18 ≪ 6: the 11-bit binary representation is 00000010010. If its leftmost 6 bits are removed and six zeros are filled at the rightmost positions, the result is 10010000000 or decimal 1152. Now we are ready to apply the formula.

As an example, assume that the value of the maximum response code is decimal 178. The bit string representation of this is 10110010. From this, the fields of the maximum response code are

- Byte $0 = 1$
- $exp = 011$
- $mant = 0010$

The subsequent calculations are

- $(mant|0 \times 10) = (0010|10000) = 10010$
- $exp + 11 = 011 + 11 = 110$ (basically, $3 + 3 = 6$ in base 10, or 110 in base 2)

Now,

- $10010 \ll exp + 11 = 10010 \ll 110 = 10010000000$
- Binary $10010000000 = $ decimal 1152

Therefore, when the maximum response code is decimal 178, the maximum response time is 1152 tenths of a second.

Small values of Max Resp Time allow IGMPv3 routers to tune the "leave latency" (the time between the moment the last host leaves a group and the moment the routing protocol is notified that there are no more members). Larger values allow tuning of the burstiness of IGMP traffic on a network.

The *Checksum* field contains a 16-bit checksum and remains unchanged from Version 2.

The *Group Address* field contains the Class D address and is the same as Version 2. The Group Address field is set to zero when sending a general query, and set to the IP multicast address being queried when sending a group-specific query or a group-and-source-specific query.

The *Resv* field is reserved and is set to zero on transmission and is ignored on reception.

The *S Flag* field is used as follows: when set to 1, this field indicates that any receiving multicast routers should suppress the timer updates normally performed upon receiving a query.

The *QRV* field (Querier's Robustness Variable) carries a parameter that is used in tuning timer values for expected packet loss. The higher the value of the QRV, the more tolerant the environment is for lost packets. One needs to keep in mind, however, that increasing the QRV also increases the delay in detecting a problem. If nonzero, the QRV field contains the [Robustness Variable] value used by the querier (that is, the sender of the query, a multicast router). If the querier's [Robustness Variable] exceeds 7, the maximum value of the QRV field, the QRV is set to zero. Routers adopt the QRV value from the most recently received query as their own [Robustness Variable] value, unless that most recently received QRV was zero, in which case the receivers use the default [Robustness Variable] value.

The *QQIC* field (Querier's Query Interval Code) carries a value specifying the query interval, in seconds, used by the originator of this query. In other words, QQIC specifies the [Query Interval] used by the querier. The actual interval, called the Querier's Query Interval (QQI), is represented in units of seconds and is derived from the QQIV. Multicast routers that are not the current querier adopt the QQI value from the most recently received query as their own [Query Interval] value, unless that most recently received QQI was zero, in which case the receiving routers use the default [Query Interval] value. The calculations to convert this code into the actual interval time are the same used for the maximum response code discussed above.

Number of Sources field indicates how many source addresses are contained within the Query message. This number is zero in a general query or a group-specific query and nonzero in a group-and-source-specific query. This number is limited by the Maximum Transfer Unit (MTU) of the network over which the query is transmitted. For example, on an Ethernet with an MTU of 1500 octets, the IP header including the Router Alert option consumes 24 octets, and the IGMP fields, including the Number of Sources (N) field, consume 12 octets, leaving 1464 octets for source addresses, which limits the number of source addresses to 366 (1464/4).

Source Addresses: This list of fields identifies *N* IP unicast addresses, where the value *N* corresponds to the Number or Sources field.

As noted earlier, IGMPv3 adds a new type of 0×22 to support the IGMPv3 MR; see Figure 4.4 for the format of Version 3 reports. MRs are sent by IP systems to report (to neighboring routers) the current multicast reception state, or changes in the multicast reception state, of their interfaces. Notice how each group record is assembled in the MR message.

The *Record Type* field indicates whether the group record type is a *current-state, filter-mode-change,* or *source-list-change* record. *Current-state* records (MODE_IS_INCLUDE, MODE_IS_EXCLUDE) are records sent by a system in response to a query received on an interface and report the current reception of that interface. *Filter-mode-change* records (CHANGE_TO_INCLUDE_MODE, CHANGE_TO_EXCLUDE_MODE) are records sent by a system when an interface's state changes for a particular multicast address. *Source-list-change* records (ALLOW_NEW_SOURCES, BLOCK_OLD_SOURCES) are records sent by a system when an interface wishes

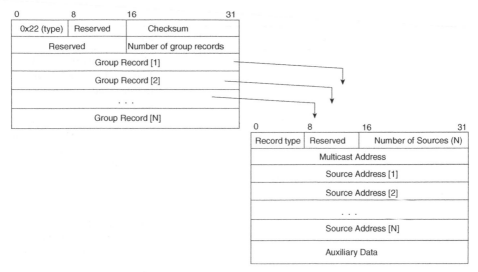

Figure 4.4. Membership Report Message

to alter the list of source addresses without altering its state. See Table 4.1 for more details.

Version 3 reports are sent with an IP destination address of 224.0.0.22, to which all IGMPv3-capable multicast routers listen. A system that is operating in Version 1 or 2 compatibility modes sends Version 1 or 2 reports to the multicast group specified in the Group Address field of the report. In addition, a system must accept and process any Version 1 or 2 report whose IP Destination Address field contains *any* of the addresses (unicast or multicast) assigned to the interface on which the report arrives [RFC3376].

Note: Because of its higher complexity, IGMPv3 is not universally supported by all the receiver hosts or the receiver applications as of press time; IGMPv2 is more common, especially in IPTV applications.[2]

Note: All routers on a subnet must be configured for the same version of IGMP.

Note: One must be careful when using IGMPv3 with switches that support and are enabled for IGMP snooping, because, as seen above, IGMPv3 messages are different from the messages used in IGMPv1 and IGMPv2. If a switch does not recognize IGMPv3 messages, then hosts will not correctly receive traffic if IGMPv3 is being used. In this case, either IGMP snooping may be disabled on the switch or the router may be configured for IGMPv2 on the interface (which would remove the ability to use SSM for host applications that cannot support Version 3) [CIS200701].

Note: IGMPv3 has no confirming reply: like IGMPv2, messages must be sent twice to guard against loss, and there is no mechanism to return an error code to the client.

Note: One limitation of IGMPv3 in the context of telco networks and IPTV is as follows [ITU200201]: An IGMPv2 PDU fits in a single ATM cell (20-byte IP header, 8 bytes of IGMP). The source filtering capability of the IGMP requires at least 52 bytes

---

[2]Some vendors have developed IGMP Version 3 lite (IGMPv3 lite).

TABLE 4.1. Record Types

Record Type	Mode	Function
Current-state record type	MODE_IS_INCLUDE	Indicates that the interface has a filter mode of INCLUDE for the specified multicast addresses.
	MODE_IS_EXCLUDE	Indicates that the interface has a filter mode of EXCLUDE for the specified multicast addresses.
Filter-mode-change record type	CHANGE_TO_INCLUDE_ MODE	Indicates that the interface has changed to the INCLUDE filter mode for the specified multicast addresses.
	CHANGE_TO_EXCLUDE_ MODE	Indicates that the interface has changed to the EXCLUDE filter mode for the specified multicast addresses.
Source-list-change record type	ALLOW_NEW_SOURCES	Indicates that the interface has changed such that it wants to receive messages from additional sources. If the filter is an INCLUDE filter, the specified multicast addresses is added. If it is an EXCLUDE filter, the specified multicast addresses is removed.
	BLOCK_OLD_SOURCES	Indicates that the interface has changed such that it no longer wants to receive messages from additional sources. If the filter is an INCLUDE filter, the specified multicast addresses is removed. If it is an EXCLUDE filter, the specified multicast addresses is added.

and, in turn, two ATM cells (20-byte IP header, 8 bytes of IGMP header, 12 bytes for the first group record, and 12 bytes for the second group record). This doubles both the ATM bandwidth and buffer memory required to process channel zapping messages. In turn, this requires a more complicated ATM Segmentation and Reassembly (SAR) and increases the amount of software processing in the multicast signaling termination function within the access network.

Note: IGMP, as we have seen, allows an IPv4 host to communicate IP multicast group membership information to its neighboring routers; IGMPv3 provides the ability for a host to selectively request or filter traffic from individual sources within a multicast group. The protocol MLD defined in RFC 2710 offers similar functionality for IPv6 hosts. MLDv2 provides the analogous source filtering functionality of IGMPv3 for IPv6 [RFC4604]. This topic is revisited in Chapter 10.

4.3 IGMP OPERATION

IGMP is an asymmetric protocol, specifying separate behaviors for group members— that is, hosts that wish to receive multicast packets and multicast routers. As discussed, it is used by IP hosts to report their multicast group memberships to routers. (Note that a multicast router that is also a group member performs both parts of IGMP, receiving and responding to its own IGMP message transmissions as well as those of its neighbors.)

Host Operations   To receive multicast datagrams, a host must join a group. To join a group, the host sends an IGMP membership report packet through an attached interface. The report is addressed to the desired multicast group. As noted above, in IGMPv3, a host can specify a list of multicast addresses from which it wishes to receive messages and/or it can specify a list of multicast addresses from which it does *not* wish to receive messages. A host can modify these lists to add or remove multicast addresses; this can be done using the filter-mode-change and source-list-change records discussed above.

Multicast Router Operations   Multicast routers listen to all multicast addresses to detect membership reports. When a receiver (host) signals to join a group, the multicast router on the subnet receives the membership report packet and creates an entry in the *local group database*. This database tracks the group membership of the router's directly attached networks. The information in the local group database is used to forward multicast datagrams. When the multicast-enabled router receives a datagram, it is forwarded to each interface containing hosts belonging to the group. To verify group membership, multicast routers regularly send (every 125 s) an IGMP Query message to the all hosts' multicast addresses. Each receiver (host) that still wishes to be a member of a group sends a reply; to avoid traffic bursts, replies to query messages are sent using a random delay. Because routers do not track the number of hosts in each group, any receiver (host) that detects another device claiming membership cancels any pending membership replies. If no hosts claim membership within the specified interval, the multicast router assumes that no hosts on that network are members of the group [PAR200601].

In summary [ITU200201]:

- A multicast router keeps a list of multicast group memberships and a timer for each membership; querier routers periodically send a general MQ to solicit membership information. Hosts respond to this general MQ to report their membership status for each multicast group. Group-specific MQs may also be sent, for example, when a router needs to check whether there are more members of a group for which an LG message has been received. If no MRs are received for a certain multicast group during a predefined period of time, the router assumes that there are no more members and stops forwarding traffic for that group.

- When a host joins a multicast group, it sends an unsolicited MR for that group. To cover the possibility of the initial MR being lost or damaged, RFC 2236 recommends that it be repeated once or twice after short delays [Unsolicited Report Interval]. When a host leaves a multicast group, it sends an LG message.
- When a querier receives an LG message, it sends group-specific MQs to the group being left. If no MRs are received in response to these MQs, the router assumes that there are no more members and stops forwarding traffic for that group.

Switches Using IGMP Snooping   The flooding of a network segment with multi-cast packets, when in fact there might not be any nodes on that segment that wish to receive these packets, can saturate an interface link, even when operating at 10/100/1000 Gbps, and/or saturate the buffers on the NIC. IGMP snooping utilizes a router to send out IGMP Query messages to identify potentially interested receivers. Membership reports are returned to the router, which builds a mapping table of the group and associates forwarding filters for the member port. If no router is available, some switches can take on the query function. IGMPv2 allows only one active querier on the network. RFC 4541 provides mechanisms to allow switches to "snoop" on IGMP traffic. With these mechanisms, switches can analyze the data contained within the IGMP header and determine if the traffic needs to be forwarded to every segment to which the switch is connected. This reduces the amount of unnecessary multicast traffic flooding to locally attached networks that have no active receivers.

See Appendix 4.A for additional information on IGMP operation.

Figure 4.5 illustrates the process at a macrolevel; here receivers seek to access a video multicast from an IPTV source. The basic steps are as follows [CIS200701]:

1. The receiver sends an IGMP Join message to its (designated) multicast router. As noted above, an IGMPv2 MR packet has a type of 0×16; this is the Join message (MR). The destination MAC address maps to the Class D address of the group being joined, rather being the MAC address of the router, as covered in Chapter 2. The body of the IGMP datagram also includes the Class D group address, as shown in Figure 4.1, and is encapsulated in an IP datagram, as shown in Figure 4.2.

2. The router logs the Join message and utilizes PIM or another multicast routing protocol to add this segment to the multicast distribution tree, as discussed in Chapter 3. The action of the router must be fairly quick (typically less than 2 s and preferably around 1 s) because the join may be the action generated by a user's STB driving the TV monitor when the viewer hits the change channel button on his or her remote control device.

3. IP multicast traffic transmitted from the source is now distributed via the designated router to the client's subnet. The destination MAC address corresponds to the Class D address of group. In this example, and as is typical of satellite-based IPTV systems, the "backbone" network is basically a single hop to the telco's headend—in theory the backbone can be more complex (as in the multirouter examples shown in Chapter 3), but then QoS considerations must be rigorously kept in mind for high-quality entertainment video.

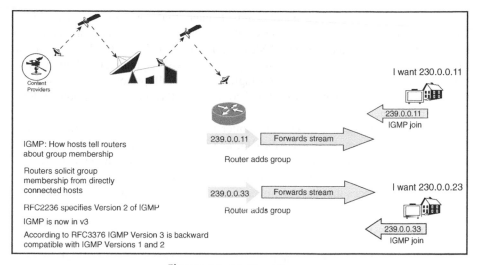

IGMP: How hosts tell routers about group membership

Routers solicit group membership from directly connected hosts

RFC2236 specifies Version 2 of IGMP

IGMP is now in v3

According to RFC3376 IGMP Version 3 is backward compatible with IGMP Versions 1 and 2

Figure 4.5. Multicast Process

4. The switch receives the multicast packet and examines its forwarding table. If no entry exists for the MAC address, the packet is flooded to all ports within the broadcast domain. If an entry does exist in the switch table, the packet will be forwarded only to the designated ports.

5. With IGMPv2, the client can cease group membership by sending an IGMP leave to the router. With IGMPv1, the client remains a member of the group until it fails to send a Join message in response to a query from the router. Multicast routers also periodically send an IGMP query to the "all multicast hosts" group or to a specific multicast group on the subnet to determine which groups are still active within the subnet. As noted above, each host delays its response to a query by a small random period and will then respond only if no other host in the group has already reported. This mechanism prevents many hosts from congesting the network with simultaneous reports.

APPENDIX 4.A: PROTOCOL DETAILS FOR IGMPv2

4.A.1   Overview[3]

IGMP is used by IP hosts to report their multicast group memberships to any immediately neighboring multicast routers. This appendix describes the use of IGMP between hosts

---

[3]This section is based on RFC 2236 Copyright (C) The Internet Society (1997). All rights reserved. This document and translations of it may be copied and furnished to others, and derivative works that comment on or otherwise explain it or assist in its implementation may be prepared, copied, published, and distributed, in whole or in part, without restriction of any kind, provided that the copyright notice and this paragraph are included on all such copies and derivative works.

and routers to determine group membership. Routers that are members of multicast groups are expected to behave as hosts as well as routers and may even respond to their own queries. Like the Internet Control Message Protocol (ICMP), IGMP is an integral part of IP. It is required to be implemented by all hosts wishing to receive IP multicasts. IGMP messages are encapsulated in IP datagrams, with an IP protocol number of 2. All IGMP messages are sent with IP TTL 1 and contain the IP Router Alert option per RFC 2113 in their IP header.

In the discussion below, timer and counter names appear in square brackets. The term "interface" is sometimes used in the RFC 2113 to mean "the primary interface on an attached network;" if a router has multiple physical interfaces on a single network, this protocol need only run on one of them. Hosts, on the other hand, need to perform their actions on all interfaces that have memberships associated with them.

4.A.2   Protocol Description

Multicast routers use IGMP to learn which groups have members on each of their attached physical networks. A multicast router keeps a list of multicast group memberships for each attached network and a timer for each membership. "Multicast group membership" means the presence of at least one member of a multicast group on a given attached network and not a list of all of the members.

With respect to each of its attached networks, a multicast router may assume one of the two roles—querier or nonquerier. A querier is the sender of the query. There is normally only one querier per physical network. All multicast routers start up as a querier on each attached network. If a multicast router receives a Query message from a router with a lower IP address, it must become a nonquerier on that network. If a router has not heard a Query message from another router for [Other Querier Present Interval], it resumes the role of querier. Routers periodically [Query Interval] send a general query on each attached network for which this router is the querier, to solicit membership information. On startup, a router is expected to send [Startup Query Count] general queries spaced closely together [Startup Query Interval] in order to quickly and reliably determine membership information. A general query is addressed to the all-systems multicast group (224.0.0.1), has a group address field of 0, and has Max Response Time of [Query Response Interval].

When a host receives a general query, it sets delay timers for each group (excluding the all-systems group) of which it is a member on the interface from which it received the query. Each timer is set to a different random value, using the highest clock granularity available on the host, selected from the range (0, Max Response Time] with Max Response Time as specified in the query packet. When a host receives a group-specific query, it sets a delay timer to a random value selected from the range (0, Max Response Time] as above for the group being queried if it is a member on the interface from which it received the query. If a timer for the group is already running, it is reset to the random value only if the requested Max Response Time is less than the remaining value of the running timer. When a group's timer expires, the host multicasts a Version 2 MR to the group, with IP TTL of 1. If the host receives another host's report (Version 1 or 2) while it has a timer running, it stops its timer for the specified group and does not send a report in order to suppress duplicate reports.

When a router receives a report, it adds the group being reported to the list of multicast group memberships on the network on which it received the report and sets the timer for the membership to the [Group Membership Interval]. Repeated reports refresh the timer. If no reports are received for a particular group before this timer has expired, the router assumes that the group has no local members and that it need not forward remotely originated multicasts for that group onto the attached network.

When a host joins a multicast group, it is expected to immediately transmit an unsolicited Version 2 MR for that group, in case it is the first member of that group on the network. To cover the possibility of the initial MR being lost or damaged, it is recommended that it be repeated once or twice after short delays [Unsolicited Report Interval]. (A simple way to accomplish this is to send the initial Version 2 MR and then act as if a group-specific query was received for that group and set a timer appropriately.)

When a host leaves a multicast group, if it was the last host to reply to a query with an MR for that group, it should send a Leave Group message to the all-routers multicast group (224.0.0.2). If it was not the last host to reply to a query, it may send nothing as there must be another member on the subnet. This is an optimization to reduce traffic; a host without sufficient storage to retain status information as to whether it was the last host to reply may always send a Leave Group message when it leaves a group. Routers should accept a Leave Group message addressed to the group being left in order to accommodate implementations of an earlier version of this standard. Leave Group messages are addressed to the all-routers group because other group members do not need to know that a host has left the group, but it does no harm to address the message to the group.

When a querier receives a Leave Group message for a group that has group members on the reception interface, it sends [Last Member Query Count] group-specific queries every [Last Member Query Interval] to the group being left. These group-specific queries have their Max Response Time set to [Last Member Query Interval]. If no reports are received after the response time of the last query expires, the routers assume that the group has no local members, as above. Any querier-to-nonquerier transition is ignored during this time; the same router keeps sending the group-specific queries.

Nonqueriers must ignore Leave Group messages, and queriers should ignore Leave Group messages for which there are no group members on the reception interface.

When a nonquerier receives a Group-Specific Query message, if its existing group membership timer is greater than [Last Member Query Count] times the Max Response Time specified in the message, it sets its group membership timer to that value.

4.A.3   Receiver (Host) State Diagram

Host behavior is more formally specified by the state transition diagram shown in Figure 4.1A. A host may be in one of the following three possible states with respect to any single IP multicast group on any single network interface:

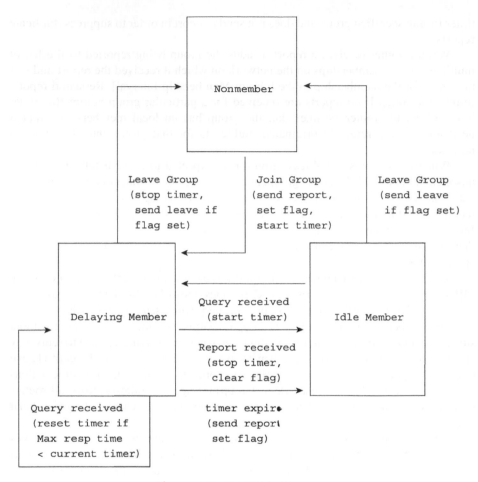

Figure 4.A1. Host State Diagram

- "nonmember" state, when the host does not belong to the group on the interface. This is the initial state for all memberships on all network interfaces; it requires no storage in the host.
- "Delaying member" state, when the host belongs to the group on the interface and has a report delay timer running for that membership.
- "Idle Member" state, when the host belongs to the group on the interface and does not have a report delay timer running for that membership.

The following five significant events can cause IGMP state transitions:

- "Join group" occurs when the host decides to join the group on the interface. It may occur only in the Nonmember state.

- "Leave group" occurs when the host decides to leave the group on the interface. It may occur only in the Delaying Member and Idle Member states.
- "Query received" occurs when the host receives either a valid General Membership Query message or a valid Group-Specific Membership Query message. To be valid, the Query message must be at least eight octets long and have a correct IGMP checksum. The group address in the IGMP header must either be zero (a general query) or a valid multicast group address (a group-specific query). A general query applies to all memberships on the interface from which the query is received. A group-specific query applies to membership in a single group on the interface from which the query is received. Queries are ignored for memberships in the Nonmember state.
- "Report received" occurs when the host receives a valid IGMP MR message (Version 1 or 2). To be valid, the Report message must be at least eight octets long and have a correct IGMP checksum. An MR applies only to the membership in the group identified by the MR, on the interface from which the MR is received. It is ignored for memberships in the Nonmember or Idle Member state.
- "Timer expired" occurs when the report delay timer for the group on the interface expires. It may occur only in the Delaying Member state.

All other events, such as receiving invalid IGMP messages or IGMP messages other than Query or Report, are ignored in all states.

There are seven possible actions that may be taken in response to the above events as follows:

- "Send report" for the group on the interface. The type of report is determined by the state of the interface. The Report message is sent to the group being reported.
- "Send leave" for the group on the interface. If the interface state says the querier is running IGMPv1, this action should be skipped. If the flag saying we were the last host to report is cleared, this action may be skipped. The Leave message is sent to the all-routers group (224.0.0.2).
- "Set flag" that we were the last host to send a report for this group.
- "Clear flag" since we were not the last host to send a report for this group.
- "Start timer" for the group on the interface, using a delay value chosen uniformly from the interval (0, Max Response Time], where Max Response Time is specified in the query. If this is an unsolicited report, the timer is set to a delay value chosen uniformly from the interval (0, [Unsolicited Report Interval]].
- "Reset timer" for the group on the interface to a new value, using a delay value chosen uniformly from the interval (0, Max Response Time], as described in "start timer."
- "Stop timer" for the group on the interface.

In the following state diagrams (Figures 4A.2–4A.4), each state transition arc is labeled with the event that causes the transition and, in parentheses, any actions taken

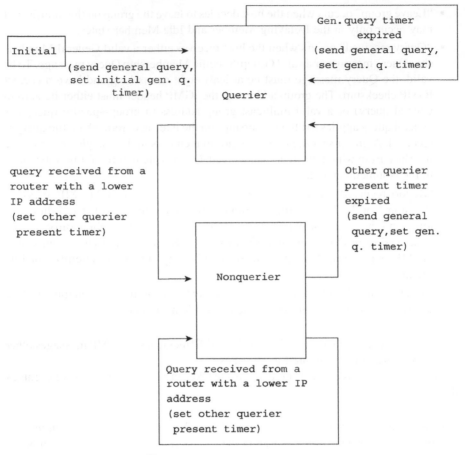

Figure 4.A2. Router State Diagram

during the transition. Note that the transition is always triggered by the event; even if the action is conditional, the transition still occurs.

The all-systems group (address 224.0.0.1) is handled as a special case. The host starts in the Idle Member state for that group on every interface, never transitions to another state, and never sends a report for that group.

In addition, a host may be in one of two possible states with respect to any single network interface:

- "No IGMPv1 Router Present," when the host has not heard an IGMPv1 style query for the [Version 1 Router Present Timeout]. This is the initial state.
- "IGMPv1 Router Present," when the host has heard an IGMPv1 style query within the [Version 1 Router Present Timeout].

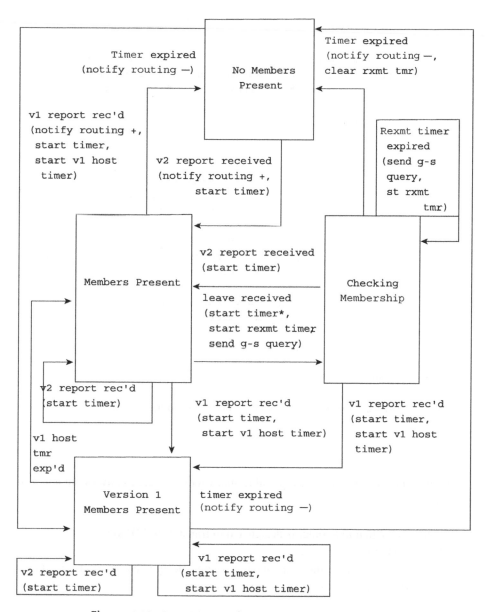

Figure 4.A3. State Diagram for a Router in Nonquerier State

4.A.4 Router State Diagram

Router behavior is more formally specified by the state transition diagram shown in Figure 4A.2.

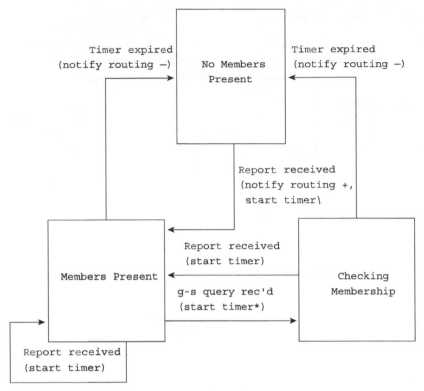

Figure 4.A4. State Diagram for a Router in Nonquerier State

A router may be in one of two possible states with respect to any single attached network:

- "Querier," when this router is designated to transmit IGMP membership queries on this network.
- "Nonquerier," when there is another router designated to transmit IGMP membership queries on this network.

The following three events can cause the router to change states:

- "Query timer expired" occurs when the timer set for query transmission expires.
- "Query received from a router with a lower IP address" occurs when an IGMP membership query is received from a router on the same network with a lower IP address.

- "Other querier present timer expired" occurs when the timer set to note the presence of another querier with a lower IP address on the network expires.

There are three actions that may be taken in response to the above events:

- "Start general query timer" for the attached network.
- "Start other querier present timer" for the attached network [Other Querier Present Interval].
- "Send general query" on the attached network. The general query is sent to the all-systems group (224.0.0.1) and has a Max Response Time of [Query Response Interval].

A router should start in the Initial state on all attached networks and immediately move to the querier state.

In addition, to keep track of which groups have members, a router may be in one of the four possible states with respect to any single IP multicast group on any single attached network:

- "No Members Present" state, when there are no hosts on the network which have sent reports for this multicast group. This is the initial state for all groups on the router; it requires no storage in the router.
- "Members Present" state, when there is a host on the network that has sent an MR for this multicast group.
- "Version 1 Members Present" state, when there is an IGMPv1 host on the network which has sent a Version 1 MR for this multicast group.
- "Checking Membership" state, when the router has received a Leave Group message but has not yet heard an MR for the multicast group.

There are six significant events that can cause router state transitions:

- "v2 report received" occurs when the router receives a Version 2 MR for the group on the interface. To be valid, the Report message must be at least eight octets long and must have a correct IGMP checksum.
- "v1 report received" occurs when the router receives a Version 1 MR for the group on the interface. The same validity requirements apply.
- "Leave received" occurs when the router receives an IGMP Group Leave message for the group on the interface. To be valid, the Leave message must be at least eight octets long and must have a correct IGMP checksum.
- "Timer expired" occurs when the timer set for a group membership expires.
- "Retransmit timer expired" occurs when the timer set to retransmit a group-specific membership query expires.
- "v1 host timer expired" occurs when the timer set to note the presence of Version 1 hosts as group members expires.

There are six possible actions that may be taken in response to the above events:

- "Start timer" for the group membership on the interface—also resets the timer to its initial value [Group Membership Interval] if the timer is currently running.
- "Start timer*" for the group membership on the interface—this alternate action sets the timer to [Last Member Query Interval] × [Last Member Query Count] if this router is a querier or the [Max Response Time] in the packet × [Last Member Query Count] if this router is a nonquerier.
- "Start retransmit timer" for the group membership on the interface [Last Member Query Interval].
- "Start v1 host timer" for the group membership on the interface, also resets the timer to its initial value [Group Membership Interval] if the timer is currently running.
- "Send group-specific query" for the group on the attached network. The group-specific query is sent to the group being queried and has a Max Response Time of [Last Member Query Interval].
- "Notify routing +," notifies the routing protocol that there are members of this group on this connected network.
- "Notify routing −," notifies the routing protocol that there are no longer any members of this group on this connected network.

The state diagram for a router in the Querier state is shown in Figure 4A.3.

The state diagram for a router in the Nonquerier state is similar, but nonqueriers do not send any messages and are only driven by message reception; see Figure 4A.4. Note that nonqueriers do not care whether a MR message is Version 1 or 2.

APPENDIX 4.B: IGMP SNOOPING SWITCHES

This appendix describes the concept of IGMP snooping. It is summarized from and based on concepts discussed in [RFC4541].

The IEEE bridge standard [IEEE Std. 802.1D-2004, IEEE Standard for Local and Metropolitan Area Networks, Media Access Control (MAC) Bridges] specifies how LAN packets are "bridged" (switched) between LAN segments. Traditionally, when processing a packet whose destination MAC address is a multicast address, the switch forwards, a copy of the packet into each of the remaining network interfaces that are in the forwarding state; the spanning tree algorithm ensures that the application of this rule at every switch in the network makes the packet accessible to all nodes connected to the network. In recent years, however, vendors have introduced products described as "IGMP snooping switches." IGMP snooping switches utilize information in the upper level protocol headers as factors to be considered in processing at the lower levels. This is in contrast to the normal switch behavior where multicast traffic is typically forwarded on all interfaces. IGMP snooping switches filter packets addressed to unrequested group addresses because, in a generic multicast environment, signifi-cant bandwidth can be wasted by flooding all ports [RFC4541]. Note that the IGMP snooping function applies only to IPv4 multicasts. For IPv6, MLD must be used instead.

IGMP snooping functionality: Forwarding rules

1. A snooping switch forwards IGMP MRs to only those ports where multicast routers are attached. In other words, a snooping switch does not forward IGMP MRs to ports on which only hosts (receivers) are attached. An administrative control may be provided to override this restriction, allowing the Report messages to be flooded to other ports. This is the main IGMP snooping functionality for the control path.

   Sending MRs to other hosts can result in unintentionally preventing a host from joining a specific multicast group. When an IGMPv1 or IGMPv2 host receives a MR for a group address that it intends to join, the host will suppress its own MR for the same group. This join or message suppression is a requirement for IGMPv1 and IGMPv2 hosts. However, if a switch does not receive a MR from the host, it will not forward multicast data to it. This is not a problem in an IGMPv3—only in the network because there is no suppression of IGMP MRs. The administrative control allows IGMP MR messages to be processed by network monitoring equipment such as packet analyzers or port replicators.

   The switch supporting IGMP snooping must maintain a list of multicast routers and the ports on which they are attached. This list can be constructed in any combination of the following ways:

   (a) This list is built by the snooping switch sending Multicast Router Solicitation messages as described in IGMP multicast router discovery. It may also snoop Multicast Router Advertisement messages sent by and to other nodes.
   (b) The arrival port for IGMP queries (sent by multicast routers) where the source address is not 0.0.0.0. The 0.0.0.0 address represents a special case where the switch is proxying IGMP queries for faster network convergence but is not itself the querier. The switch does not use its own IP address (even if it has one) because this would cause the queries to be seen as coming from a newly elected querier. The 0.0.0.0 address is used to indicate that the query packets are not from a multicast router.
   (c) Ports explicitly configured by management to be IGMP-forwarding ports, in addition to or instead of any of the above methods to detect router ports.

2. IGMP networks may also include devices that implement "proxy reporting," in which reports received from downstream hosts are summarized and used to build internal membership states. Such proxy-reporting devices may use the all-zeros IP source address when forwarding any summarized reports upstream. For this reason, IGMP MRs received by the snooping switch must not be rejected because the source IP address is set to 0.0.0.0.

3. The switch that supports IGMP snooping must flood all unrecognized IGMP messages to all other ports and must not attempt to make use of any information beyond the end of the network layer header. In addition, earlier versions of IGMP should interpret IGMP fields as defined for their versions and must not alter these fields when forwarding the message. When generating new messages, a given IGMP version should set fields to the appropriate values for its own version. If any fields are reserved or otherwise undefined for a given IGMP version, the fields should be ignored when parsing the message and must be set to zeros when new messages are generated by implementations of that IGMP version. An exception may occur if the switch is performing a spoofing function and is aware of the settings for new or reserved fields that would be required to correctly spoof for a different IGMP version.

4. An IGMP snooping switch is typically aware of link-layer topology changes caused by a spanning tree operation. When a port is enabled or disabled by a spanning tree, a general query may be sent on all active nonrouter ports to reduce network convergence time. Nonquerier switches should be aware of whether the querier is in IGMPv3 mode. If so, the switch does not spoof any general queries unless it is able to send an IGMPv3 query that adheres to the most recent information sent by the true querier. In no case should a switch introduce a spoofed IGMPv2 query into an IGMPv3 network, as this may create excessive network disruption. If the switch is not the querier, it should use the "all-zeros" IP source address in these proxy queries (even though some hosts may elect to not process queries with a 0.0.0.0 IP source address). When such proxy queries are received, they must not be included in the querier election process.

5. The snooping switch must not rely exclusively on the appearance of IGMP Group Leave announcements to determine when entries should be removed from the forwarding table. It should implement a membership timeout mechanism, such as the router-side functionality of the IGMP, as described in the IGMP and MLD specifications, on all its nonrouter ports. This timeout value should be configurable.

IGMP snooping functionality: Data forwarding rules

1. Packets with a destination IP address outside 224.0.0.X, which are not IGMP, will be forwarded according to group-based port membership tables and must also be forwarded on router ports. This is the main IGMP snooping functionality for the data path. One approach that an implementation could take would be to maintain separate membership and multicast router tables in software and then "merge" these tables into a forwarding cache.

2. Packets with a Destination IP (DIP) address in the 224.0.0.X range, which are not IGMP, must be forwarded on all ports. Many host systems do not send join IP multicast addresses in this range before sending or listening to IP multicast packets. Furthermore, since the 224.0.0.X address range is defined as link local (not to be routed), it seems unnecessary to keep the state for each address in this

range. Additionally, some routers operate in the 224.0.0.X address range without issuing IGMP joins, and these applications would break if the switch were to prune them due to not having seen a Join Group message from the router.

3. An unregistered packet is defined as an IPv4 multicast packet with a destination address that does not match any of the groups announced in earlier IGMP MRs. If a switch receives an unregistered packet, it must forward that packet on all ports to which an IGMP router is attached. A switch may default to forwarding unregistered packets on all ports. Switches that do not forward unregistered packets to all ports must include a configuration option to force the flooding of unregistered packets on specified ports.

   In an environment where IGMPv3 hosts are mixed with snooping switches that do not yet support IGMPv3, the switch's failure to flood unregistered streams could prevent Version 3 hosts from receiving their traffic. Alternatively, in environments where the snooping switch supports all of the IGMP versions that are present, flooding unregistered streams may cause IGMP hosts to be overwhelmed by multicast traffic, even to the point of not receiving queries and failing to issue new MRs for their own groups.

   Snooping switches must at least recognize and process IGMPv3 join reports, even if this processing is limited to the behavior for IGMPv2 joins, that is, is done without considering any additional "include source" or "exclude source" filtering. When IGMPv3 joins are not recognized, a snooping switch may incorrectly prune off the unregistered data streams for the groups (as noted above); alternatively, it may fail to add in forwarding to any new IGMPv3 hosts if the group has previously been joined as IGMPv2 (because the data stream is seen as already having been registered).

4. All non-IPv4 multicast packets should continue to be flooded out to all remaining ports in the forwarding state as per normal IEEE bridging operations. This recommendation is a result of the fact that groups made up of IPv4 hosts and IPv6 hosts are completely separate and distinct groups. As a result, information gleaned from the topology among members of an IPv4 group would not be applicable when forming the topology among members of an IPv6 group.

5. IGMP snooping switches may maintain forwarding tables based on either MAC addresses or IP addresses. If a switch supports both types of forwarding tables, then the default behavior should be to use IP addresses. IP-address-based forwarding is preferred because the mapping between IP multicast addresses and link-layer multicast addresses is ambiguous. In the case of Ethernet, there is a multiplicity of 1 Ethernet address to 32 IP addresses.

6. Switches which rely on information in the IP header should verify that the IP header checksum is correct. If the checksum fails, the information in the packet must not be incorporated into the forwarding table. Further, the packet should be discarded.

7. When IGMPv3 "include source" and "exclude source" MRs are received on shared segments, the switch needs to forward the superset of all received MRs on to the shared segment. Forwarding of traffic from a particular source S to a group G

must happen if at least one host on the shared segment reports an IGMPv3 membership of the type INCLUDE(G, S list 1) or EXCLUDE(G, S list 2), where S is an element of S list 1 and not an element of S list 2. The practical implementation of the (G,S1,S2, . . .)-based data forwarding tables are not within the scope of this document. However, one possibility is to maintain two (G,S) forwarding lists— one for the INCLUDE filter where a match of a specific (G,S) is required before forwarding will happen and one for the EXCLUDE filter where a match of a specific (G,S) will result in no forwarding.

APPENDIX 4.C: EXAMPLE OF ROUTER CONFIGURATIONS

This appendix contains an illustrative example. To configure IGMPv3 on a Cisco Systems router, one can use the following commands beginning in global configuration mode:

	Command	Purpose
Step 1	Router(config)# interface *type number*	Selects an interface that is connected to hosts on which IGMPv3 can be enabled.
Step 2	Router(config-if)# ip pim {sparse-mode | sparse-dense-mode}	Enables PIM on an interface. One must use either sparse mode or sparse–dense mode.
Step 3	Router(config-if)# ip igmp version 3	Enables IGMPv3 on this interface. The default version of IGMP is set to Version 2.

To verify that IGMPv3 is configured properly, one can use the following show commands:

- show ip igmp groups
- show ip mroute

Related commands include the following:

ip igmp query-max-response-time	Configures the maximum response time advertised in IGMP queries.
ip igmp query-timeout	Configures the timeout time before the router takes over as the querier for the interface, after the previous querier has stopped querying.
show ip igmp groups	Displays the multicast groups that are directly connected to the router and that were learned through IGMP.
show ip igmp interface	Displays multicast-related information about an interface.

The following configuration example shows how to configure a Cisco Systems router (running IGMPv3) for SSM:
ip multicast-routing
!
interface Ethernet3/1
ip address 172.21.200.203 255.255.255.0
ip pim sparse-dense-mode
ip igmp Version 3
!
interface Ethernet3/2
ip address 131.108.1.2 255.255.255.0
ip pim sparse-dense-mode
ip igmp version 3
!
ip pim ssm default

REFERENCES

[CIS200701] Cisco Systems, Internet Protocol (IP) Multicast Technology Overview, White Paper, Cisco Systems, Inc., San Jose, CA.

[ITU200201] ITU-T FS-VDSL Telecommunication Standardization Sector of ITU, Full-Service VDSL Focus Group, Channel Change Protocol, Version 1.00, November 29 2002.

[PAR200601] L. Parziale, W. Liu, et al., TCP/IP Tutorial and Technical Overview, IBM Press, Redbook Abstract, IBM Form Number GG24-3376-07, 2006.

[RFC2236] RFC 2236, Internet Group Management Protocol, Version 2, W. Fenner, November 1997.

[RFC3376] RFC 3376, Internet Group Management Protocol, Version 3, B. Cain, S. Deering, I. Kouvelas, B. Fenner, A. Thyagarajan, October 2002.

[RFC4541] RFC 4541, Considerations for Internet Group Management Protocol (IGMP) and Multicast Listener Discovery (MLD) Snooping Switches, M. Christensen, K. Kimball, F. Solensky, May 2006. (status: informational).

[RFC4604] RFC4604, Using Internet Group Management Protocol, Version 3 (IGMPv3) and Multicast Listener Discovery Protocol, Version 2 (MLDv2) for Source-Specific Multicast, H. Holbrook, B. Cain, B. Haberman, August 2006.

5

MULTICAST ROUTING—
SPARSE-MODE PROTOCOLS:
PROTOCOL INDEPENDENT
MULTICAST

In Chapter 3, we discussed multicast forwarding algorithms and how they are used to establish efficient (multicast) paths in the network. A number of multicast routing protocols have been developed over the years that implement and support these algorithms. The next few chapters describe these protocols. This chapter opens the discussion by examining the Protocol Independent Multicast (PIM). PIM has two modes of operation: PIM DM, specified in RFC 3973, and PIM SM, specified in RFC 2362. This chapter focuses on the SM (DM is covered in Chapter 7). PIM does not send and/or receive multicast routing updates between routers as is the case in IP routing: instead of building up a completely separate multicast routing table, PIM uses the unicast routing information to support the multicast forwarding function. At the same time, it is independent of IP routing, namely, it can make use of any underlying unicast routing protocols utilized to manage the unicast routing table, including EIGRP, OSPF, BGP, or even static routes. Specifically, PIM uses the unicast routing table to perform the RPF check function. PIM is implemented by the leading router manufacturers, particularly by Cisco Systems, and is widely deployed. A preliminary overview in Section 5.1 is followed by a more detailed description of the protocol in Section 5.2.

IP Multicast with Applications to IPTV and Mobile DVB-H   by Daniel Minoli
Copyright © 2008 John Wiley & Sons, Inc.

5.1   INTRODUCTION TO PIM

Multicast routing algorithms aim at accomplishing the following:

- Forward information only to members of the group
- Optimize the path from source to destinations in terms of number of hops and bandwidth used on each hop
- Establish and maintain loop-free routes
- Provide scalable mechanisms in terms of the number of receivers and groups.

A number of algorithms have been developed over the years. The RPF algorithm discussed in Chapter 3 uses a multicast delivery tree to enable the forwarding of packets from the source to each member in the multicast group. With RPF, packets are replicated only at the furthest branches in the delivery tree where connectivity is still possible. See Figure 5.1.

To identify the routers that require connectivity to support receiver membership to individual groups, distribution trees are established and updated dynamically. Using this process, duplicate packets that may be generated by network loops are discarded along the way. A *reverse path table* is used at each nodal router to maintain a map between every known source and the optimal(ly preferred) interface required to reach that source. When a nodal router needs to forward multicast packets along, it does so based on the following rule: if the packet arrived over the interface used to transmit data back to the source, the packet is forwarded through every appropriate downstream interface; otherwise, if the

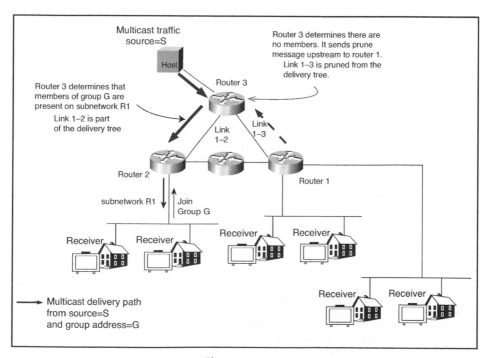

Figure 5.1.   RPF

packet arrived through a suboptimal path, it is discarded. RPF has the following characteristics:

- Traffic follows the shortest path from the source to each destination.
- A different tree is computed for each source node.
- Packet delivery is distributed over multiple network links.

PIM is a broadly deployed multicast routing protocol. Since PIM is independent of any underlying unicast routing protocol, it interoperates with all the existing unicast routing protocols. Dense mode and sparse mode refer to the density of group members within an area. In a random sampling, a group is considered dense if the probability of finding at least one group member within the sample is high. A group is considered sparse if the probability of finding group members within the sample is low [PAR200601].

PIM DM uses a *push* mechanism to flood multicast traffic to every edge router in the network. This method for delivering data to the receivers is often resource intensive, but if there are active receivers on every subnet in the network it can, in fact, be an efficient mechanism. An approach to commercial-grade/large-population linear-content IPTV, especially in the core network—which may in fact be maintained by a different provider than the ultimate (distribution) telc—is to use PIM DM within the core tier (and possibly also at the edge distribution tier). However, if the population of active users is significantly less than the total population, SM may be the better approach. PIM DM can only support source trees—(S,G) entries; it cannot be used to build a shared distribution tree (see Chapter 3). PIM DM initially floods multicast traffic throughout the network, but routers that do not have any downstream neighbors prune back the unwanted traffic. This process repeats every 3 min. The flood-and-prune mechanism is the technique used by the routers to accumulate their state information—by receiving data streams that contain the source and group information downstream routers can build up their multicast forwarding table [CIS200701]. PIM DM is revisited in Chapter 7.

PIM SM [RFC2362] uses a *pull* mechanism to deliver multicast traffic. Only subnetworks (network segments) that have active receivers that have explicitly requested the information via IGMP joins are forwarded to the traffic. PIM SM makes use of a shared tree to distribute the information to active sources.[1] The PIM SM protocol shared tree algorithm actually uses a variant of the center-based tree algorithm (both shared tree and center-based tree were discussed in Chapter 3.) PIM SM makes use of a RP.

DM is typically used when senders and receivers are in close geographic/topological proximity to one another, when there are few senders and many receivers, when the volume of multicast traffic is high, and when the stream of multicast traffic is constant [CIS200701]. This is generally the case for IPTV/DVB-H applications. Sparse multicast

---

[1]While the traffic can remain on the shared tree, on a Cisco Systems router the default behavior is to switch over to an optimized source distribution tree. Here, the traffic starts to flow down the shared tree and then routers along the path determine if there is a better path to the source. If a better path exists, the designated router (router closest to the receiver) sends a "Join" message toward the source and then reroute to the traffic along this path. If the shared tree is not an optimal path between the source and the receiver, the routers will dynamically create a source tree and stop traffic from flowing down the shared tree. Network administrators can force traffic to stay on the shared tree by using a configuration option (ip pim spt-threshold infinity) [CIS200701].

is typically used when there are few receivers in a group, when senders and receivers are separated by point-to-point WAN links, and when the type of traffic is intermittent. This is generally the case for datacasting applications. Note that modern PIM routers are able to simultaneously support DM for some multipoint groups and SM for others. SM PIM is optimized for environments where there are many multipoint data streams and each data stream is required by a relatively small number of subnets. PIM SM postulates that no hosts want the multicast traffic unless they specifically ask for it. PIM provides the ability to switch between SM and DM and also permits both modes to be used within the same group.

As noted, PIM SM works by defining an RP. An RP is the point in the network where multicast sources connect to multicast receivers. When a sender wishes to send data, it first sends it to the RP, and when a receiver wishes to receive data, it registers with the RP. After the data stream begins to flow from sender to RP to receiver, the routers in the path optimize the path automatically to remove any unnecessary hops.

Senders register their requests with the RP and in so doing join a tree rooted at the RP. The RP is similar to the center point used in the center-based tree algorithm. Initially, traffic from the sender flows through the RP to reach each receiver. The benefit of a SM protocol is that multicast data is blocked from a network segment unless a receiver specifically signals to receive the data. This reduces the amount of traffic traversing the network for those cases where indeed there are just a few receivers on the network at any given point in time (as noted, this is not generally the model for IPTV or DVB-H). This approach also implies that no pruning information is maintained for routers without active receivers; pruning information is maintained only in routers connected to the multicast delivery tree. In typical implementations (especially in enterprise networks), the RP is administratively configured; sources register with the RP and then data is forwarded down the shared tree to the receivers.[2]

Given the membership requirements of typical multicast (datacasting) applications over the Internet, PIM SM is currently the most popular multicast routing protocol in use (PIM SM scales well to a network of any size). The reason is that a multicast source connected over the Internet may have a (relatively) small set of potential receivers that are distributed all over the globe. PIM SM makes good sense. On the contrary, current IPTV/DVB-H applications are delivered over private networks (the Internet is not generally used because of QoS considerations) and tend to be concentrated to a geographic area [market served by a telco, such as a city, county, or DMA (Demographic Marketing Area)].

There are a number of protocols for multicast routing within an AS that predate PIM, which are discussed in the chapters that follow, but PIM is the most widely

---

[2] Cisco has implemented an alternative to choosing just DM or just SM on a router interface. This is called sparse–dense mode. This was necessitated by a change in the paradigm for forwarding multicast traffic via PIM that became apparent during its development. It turned out that it was more efficient to choose sparse or dense on a per-group basis rather than a per-router interface basis. Sparse–dense mode facilitates this ability. Network administrators can also configure sparse–dense mode. This configuration option allows individual groups to be run in either sparse or dense mode depending on whether RP information is available for that group. If the router learns RP information for a particular group, it will be treated as SM, otherwise that group will be treated as DM [CIS200701].

implemented protocol. DVMRP is an interior gateway protocol used to build per-source, per-group multicast delivery trees within an AS; it does not route unicast datagrams, hence, any router that must handle both multicast and unicast datagrams must support two separate routing mechanisms. MOSPF requires OSPF as unicast routing protocol, but it is known to be complex and not to scale well. The CBT protocol is a network layer multicast routing protocol that builds and maintains a shared-delivery tree for a multicast group. The sending and receiving of multicast data by hosts on a subnetwork conforms to the traditional IP multicast service model. CBT is a multicast routing architecture that builds a single delivery tree per group that is shared by all of the group's senders and receivers. Most multicast algorithms build one multicast tree per sender (subnetwork), the tree being rooted at the sender's subnetwork. The primary advantage of the shared tree approach is that it typically offers more favorable scaling characteristics than all other multicast algorithms. All multicast routing protocols make use of IGMP, which as we have seen in Chapter 4 operates between hosts and multicast router(s) belonging to the same subnetwork. IGMP enables the subnet's multicast router(s) to monitor group membership presence on its directly attached links, so that if multicast data arrive, it knows over which of its links to send a copy of the packet [RFC2201].

One of the most critical processes in PIM SM is the creation of the multicast distribution tree. Basic tree mechanisms were discussed in Chapter 3. The mechanism entails creating a shared, RP-centered, distribution tree that reaches all group members. When a data source first sends to a group, its DR unicasts Register messages to the RP with the source's data packets encapsulated within. If the data rate is high, the RP can send source-specific Join/Prune messages back toward the source and the source's data packets will follow the resulting forwarding state and travel unencapsulated to the RP. Whether they arrive encapsulated or natively, the RP forward the source's deencapsulated data packets down the RP-centered distribution tree toward group members. If the data rate warrants it, routers with local receivers can join a source-specific, shortest path distribution tree and then prune this source's packets off of the shared RP-centered tree. For low-data-rate sources, neither the RP nor the last-hop routers need join a source-specific shortest path tree and data packets can be delivered via the shared RP-tree [RFC2117].

The process to build the reverse path tree is as follows (more details are provided in the next section):

Step 1: A multicast router that has active receivers sends periodic PIM Join messages to a group-specific RP. Each multicast router along the path, with the RP being on the upstream, generates and issues PIM Join requests to the RP. This process builds a group-specific multicast delivery reverse path tree rooted at the RP. Figure 5.2 depicts this operation. Note that the PIM Join requests follow a reverse path from the receiver to the RP, building out the reverse path tree.

Step 2: The multicast router supporting the source initially encapsulates each multicast packet in a register message sent to the RP. The RP deencapsulates these unicast messages and forwards the packets to the set of downstream receivers, as depicted in Figure 5.3.

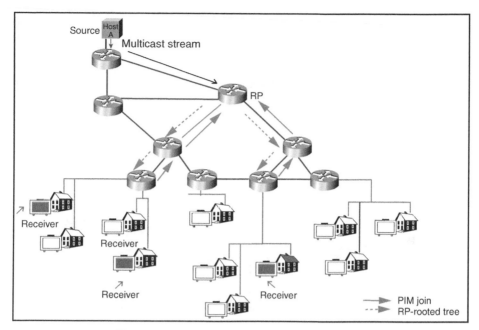

Figure 5.2. RP-Rooted Reverse Path Delivery Tree

Step 3: The RP-based tree may need optimization. At this juncture the router supporting the source can create a *source-based* multicast delivery tree (e.g., see Figure 5.4).

Step 4: When the downstream router starts to receive multicast packets through both the RP-based delivery tree and the source-based delivery tree, it generates PIM Prune messages, which are sent upstream toward the RP. See Figure 5.5. This causes the RP to prune this branch of the tree. When this process is complete, multicast data from the source is forwarded only through the source-based delivery tree.

Figure 5.6 depicts the basic format of a PIM message. Section 5.2 provides additional details on this topic; casual readers may focus only on the first few sections that follow—more advanced readers may want to go through the entire section.

5.2 PIM SM DETAILS

This section (based on RFC 2362[3]) describes in some detail PIM SM, which as we have seen is a protocol that can be used for efficiently routing to multicast groups

---

[3]Copyright (C) The Internet Society (1998). All rights reserved. This document and translations of it may be copied and furnished to others, and derivative works that comment on or otherwise explain it or assist in its implementation may be prepared, copied, published, and distributed, in whole or in part, without restriction of any kind, provided that the copyright notice and this paragraph are included on all such copies and derivative works.

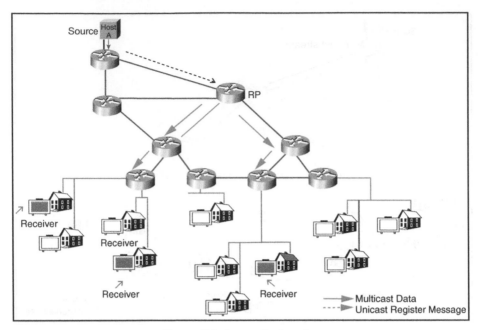

Figure 5.3. Source Registration

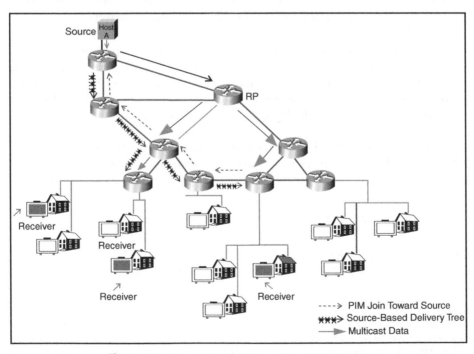

Figure 5.4. Source-Based Delivery Tree Optimization

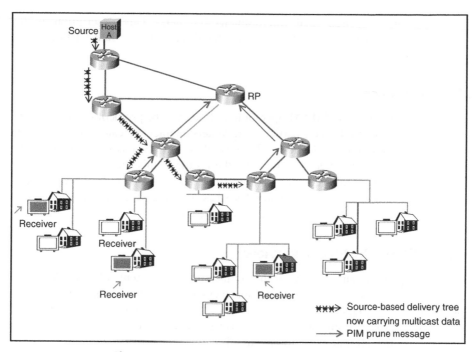

Figure 5.5. Pruning of the RP-Based Delivery Tree

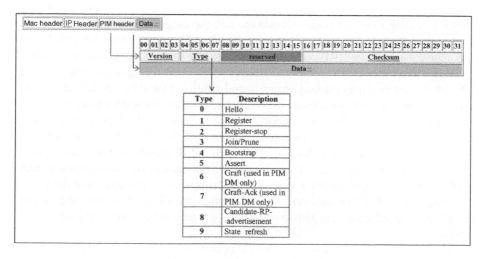

Figure 5.6. PIM Message Format

that may span wide-area (and interdomain) internets. This description is for informative value only; developers should refer directly to the latest RFC/release of the protocol.

5.2.1 Approach

Section 5.2.2 summarizes PIM SM operation; it describes the protocol from a network perspective, specifically, how the participating routers interact to create and maintain the multicast distribution tree. Section 5.2.3 describes PIM SM operations from the perspective of a single router implementing the protocol; this section constitutes the main body of the protocol specification. It is organized according to PIM SM message type; for each message type, the section describes its contents, its generation, and its processing. Section 5.2.4 provides packet format details.

5.2.2 PIM SM Protocol Overview

This section provides an overview of the architectural components of PIM SM.

A router receives explicit PIM Join/Prune messages from those neighboring routers that have downstream group members. The router then forwards data packets addressed to a multicast group G only onto those interfaces on which explicit joins have been received. Note that all routers mentioned in this description are assumed to be PIM SM capable, unless otherwise specified.

A DR sends periodic Join/Prune messages toward a group-specific RP for each group for which it has active members. Each router along the path toward the RP builds a wildcard (any source) state for the group and sends Join/Prune messages on toward the RP. The term *route entry* refers to the state maintained in a router to represent the distribution tree. A route entry may include such fields as the source address, the group address, the incoming interface from which packets are accepted, the list of outgoing interfaces to which packets are sent, timers, flag bits, and so on. The wildcard route entry's incoming interface points toward the RP; the outgoing interfaces point to the neighboring downstream routers that have sent Join/Prune messages toward the RP. This state creates a shared, RP-centered distribution tree that reaches all group members.

When a data source first sends to a group, its DR unicasts Register messages to the RP with the source's data packets encapsulated within. If the data rate is high, the RP can send source-specific Join/Prune messages back toward the source and the source's data packets will follow the resulting forwarding state and travel unencapsulated to the RP. Whether they arrive encapsulated or natively, the RP forward the source's deencapsulated data packets down the RP-centered distribution tree toward group members. If the data rate warrants it, routers with local receivers can join a source-specific, shortest path distribution tree and prune this source's packets off of the shared RP-centered tree. For low-data-rate sources, neither the RP nor last-hop routers need join a source-specific shortest path tree and data packets can be delivered via the shared RP-tree.

The following sections describe PIM SM operation in more detail, in particular the control messages and the actions they trigger.

5.2.2.1   Local Hosts Joining a Group. In order to join a multicast group G, a host conveys its membership information through IGMP (as discussed in Chapter 4). From this point on, one refers to such a host as a receiver R (or member) of the group G.

When a DR gets a membership indication from IGMP for a new group G, the DR looks up the associated RP. The DR creates a wildcard multicast route entry for the group, referred to here as an (*,G) entry; if there is no more specific match for a particular source, the packet will be forwarded according to this entry. The RP address is included in a special field in the route entry and is included in periodic upstream Join/Prune messages. The outgoing interface is set to that included in the IGMP membership indication for the new member. The incoming interface is set to the interface used to send unicast packets to the RP.

When there are no longer directly connected members for the group, IGMP notifies the DR. If the DR has neither local members nor downstream receivers, the (*,G) state is deleted.

5.2.2.2   Establishing the RP-Rooted Shared Tree. Triggered by the (*,G) state, the DR creates a Join/Prune message with the RP address in its join list and the Wildcard bit (WC-bit) and RP-Tree bit (RPT-bit) set to 1. The WC-bit indicates that any source may match and be forwarded according to this entry if there is no longer a match; the RPT-bit indicates that this join is being sent up the shared RP-tree. The prune list is left empty. When the RPT-bit is set to 1, it indicates that the join is associated with the shared RP-tree and therefore the Join/Prune message is propagated along the RP-tree. When the WC-bit is set to 1, it indicates that the address is an RP and the downstream receivers expect to receive packets from all sources via this (shared tree) path. The term RPT-bit is used to refer to both the RPT-bit flags associated with route entries and the RPT-bit included in each encoded address in a Join/Prune message.

Each upstream router creates or updates its multicast route entry for (*,G) when it receives a Join/Prune with the RPT-bit and WC-bit set. The interface on which the Join/Prune message arrived is added to the list of outgoing interfaces (oifs) for (*,G). Based on this entry, each upstream router between the receiver and the RP sends a Join/Prune message in which the join list includes the RP. The packet payload contains Multicast-Address = G, Join = RP, WC-bit, RPT-bit, Prune = NULL.

5.2.2.3   Hosts Sending to a Group. When a host starts sending multicast data packets to a group, initially, its DR must deliver each packet to the RP for distribution down the RP-tree. The sender's DR initially encapsulates each data packet in a Register message and unicasts it to the RP for that group. The RP decapsulates each Register message and forwards the enclosed data packet natively to downstream members on the shared RP-tree.

If the data rate of the source warrants the use of a source-specific SPT, the RP may construct a new multicast route entry that is specific to the source, hereafter referred to as (S,G) state, and send periodic Join/Prune messages toward the source. Note that over time the rules for when to switch can be modified without global coordination. When and if the RP does switch to the SPT, the routers between the source and the RP build and maintain the (S,G) state in response to these messages and send (S,G) messages upstream toward the source.

The source's DR must stop encapsulating data packets in registers when (and so long as) it receives Register-Stop messages from the RP. The RP triggers Register-Stop messages in response to registers if the RP has no downstream receivers for the group (or for that particular source) or if the RP has already joined the (S,G) tree and is receiving the data packets natively. Each source's DR maintains, per (S,G), a register-suppression timer. The register-suppression timer is started by the Register-Stop message; upon expiration, the source's DR resumes sending data packets to the RP, encapsulated in Register messages.

A router with directly connected members first joins the shared RP-tree. The router can switch to a source's shortest path tree (SP-tree) after receiving packets from that source over the shared RP-tree. The recommended policy is to initiate the switch to the SP-tree after receiving a significant number of data packets during a specified time interval from a particular source. To realize this policy, the router can monitor data packets from sources for which it has no source-specific multicast route entry and initiate such an entry when the data rate exceeds the configured threshold.

When an (S,G) entry is activated (and periodically so long as the state exists), a Join/Prune message is sent upstream toward the source S, with S in the join list. The payload contains Multicast-Address=G, Join=S, Prune=NULL. When the (S,G) entry is created, the outgoing interface list is copied from (*,G), that is, all local shared tree branches are replicated in the new SP-tree. In this way, when a data packet from S arrives and matches on this entry, all receivers will continue to receive the source's packets along this path. (In more complicated scenarios, other entries in the router have to be considered.) Note that the (S,G) state must be maintained in each last-hop router that is responsible for initiating and maintaining an SP-tree. Even when (*,G) and (S,G) overlap, both states are needed to trigger the source-specific Join/Prune messages. The (S,G) state is kept alive by data packets arriving from that source. A timer, [Entry-Timer], is set for the (S,G) entry and this timer is restarted whenever data packets for (S,G) are forwarded out at least one oif or registers are sent. When the entry timer expires, the state is deleted. The last-hop router is the router that delivers the packets to their ultimate end-system destination. This is the router that monitors if there is group membership and joins or prunes the appropriate distribution trees in response. In general, the last-hop router is the DR for the LAN. However, under various conditions described later, a parallel router connected to the same LAN may take over as the last-hop router in place of the DR.

Only the RP and routers with local members can initiate switching to the sp-tree; intermediate routers do not. Consequently, last-hop routers create an (S,G) state in response to data packets from the source S, whereas intermediate routers only create an (S,G) state in response to Join/Prune messages from downstream that have S in the join list.

The (S,G) entry is initialized with the SPT-bit cleared, indicating that the SP-tree branch from S has not yet been set up completely, and the router can still accept packets from S that arrive on the (*,G) entry's indicated incoming interface (iif). Each PIM multicast entry has an associated incoming interface on which packets are expected to arrive.

When a router with an (S,G) entry and a cleared SPT-bit starts to receive packets from the new source S on the iif for the (S,G) entry, and that iif differs from the (*,G) entry's iif, the router sets the SPT-bit and sends a Join/Prune message toward the RP, indicating that the router no longer wants to receive packets from S via the shared RP-tree. The Join/Prune message sent toward the RP includes S in the prune list, with the RPT-bit set indicating that S's packets must not be forwarded down this branch of the shared tree. If the router receiving the Join/Prune message has an (S,G) state (with or without the route entry's RPT-bit flag set), it deletes the arriving interface from the (S,G) oif list. If the router has only a (*,G) state, it creates an entry with the RPT-bit flag set to 1. For brevity, one refers to an (S,G) entry that has the RPT-bit flag set to 1 as an (S,G)RPT-bit entry. This notational distinction is useful to point out the different actions taken for (S,G) entries depending on the setting of the RPT-bit flag. Note that a router can have no more than one active (S,G) entry for any particular S and G at any particular time; whether the RPT-bit flag is set or not. In other words, a router never has both an (S,G) and an (S,G)RPT-bit entry for the same S and G at the same time. The Join/Prune message payload contains Multicast-Address = G, Join = NULL, Prune = S, RPT-bit.

A new receiver may join an existing RP-tree on which a source-specific prune state has been established (e.g., because downstream receivers have switched to SP-trees). In this case, the prune state must be eradicated upstream of the new receiver to bring all sources' data packets down to the new receiver. Therefore, when an (*,G) join arrives at a router that has any (S,G)RPT-bit entries (i.e., entries that cause the router to send source-specific prunes toward the RP), these entries must be updated upstream of the router so as to bring all sources' packets down to the new member. To accomplish this, each router that receives an (*,G) Join/Prune message updates all the existing (S,G)RPT-bit entries. The router may also trigger an (*,G) Join/Prune message upstream to cause the same updating of RPT-bit settings upstream and pull down all active sources' packets. If the arriving (*,G) join has some sources included in its prune list, then the corresponding (S,G) RPT-bit entries are left unchanged (i.e., the RPT-bit remains set and no oif is added).

5.2.2.4 Steady State Maintenance of Distribution Tree (i.e., Router State).
In the steady state, each router sends periodic Join/Prune messages for each active PIM route entry; the Join/Prune messages are sent to the neighbor indicated in the corresponding entry. These messages are sent periodically to capture state, topology, and membership changes. A Join/Prune message is also sent on an event-triggered basis each time a new route entry is established for some new source (note that some damping function may be applied, for example, a short delay to allow for merging of new join information). Join/Prune messages do not elicit any form of explicit acknowledgment; routers recover from lost packets using the periodic refresh mechanism.

5.2.2.5 Obtaining RP Information.
To obtain the RP information, all routers within a PIM domain collect Bootstrap messages. Bootstrap messages are sent hop by hop within the domain; the domain's Bootstrap Router (BSR) is responsible for originating the Bootstrap messages. Bootstrap messages are used to carry out a dynamic BSR election when needed and to distribute RP information in the steady state.

A domain in this context is a contiguous set of routers that implement all PIM and is configured to operate within a common boundary defined by PIM Multicast Border Routers (PMBRs). PMBRs connect each PIM domain to the rest of the Internet.

Routers use a set of available RPs (called the RP-set) distributed in Bootstrap messages to get the proper group-to-RP mapping. The following paragraphs summarize the mechanism; details of the mechanism may be found in RFC 2362. A (small) set of routers, within a domain, is configured as Candidate BSRs (C-BSRs) and, through a simple election mechanism, a single BSR is selected for that domain. A set of routers within a domain is also configured as Candidate RPs (C-RPs); typically, these will be the same routers that are configured as C-BSRs. C-RPs periodically unicast C-RP-Advertisement messages (C-RP-Advs) to the BSR of that domain. C-RP-Advs include the address of the advertising C-RP, as well as an optional group address and a Mask Length field, indicating the group prefix(es) for which the candidacy is advertised. The BSR then includes a set of these C-RPs (the RP-set), along with the corresponding group prefixes, in Bootstrap messages it periodically originates. Bootstrap messages are distributed hop-by-hop throughout the domain.

Routers receive and store Bootstrap messages originated by the BSR. When a DR gets a membership indication from IGMP for (or a data packet from) a directly connected host, for a group for which it has no entry, the DR uses a hash function to map the group address to one of the C-RPs whose group prefix includes the group. The DR then sends a Join/Prune message toward (or unicasts registers to) that RP.

The Bootstrap message indicates liveness of the RPs included therein. If an RP is included in the message, then it is tagged as "up" at the routers, while RPs not included in the message are removed from the list of RPs over which the hash algorithm acts. Each router continues to use the contents of the most recently received Bootstrap message until it receives a new Bootstrap message.

If a PIM domain partitions, each area separated from the old BSR will elect its own BSR, which will distribute an RP-set containing RPs that are reachable within that partition. When the partition heals, another election will occur automatically and only one of the BSRs will continue to send out Bootstrap messages. As is expected at the time of a partition or healing, some disruption in packet delivery may occur. This time will be on the order of the region's round-trip time and the bootstrap router timeout value.

5.2.2.6   Interoperation with Dense-Mode Protocols Such as DVMRP.   In order to interoperate with networks that run dense-mode, broadcast and prune, protocols, such as DVMRP, all packets generated within a PIM SM region must be pulled out to that region's PMBRs and injected (i.e., broadcast) into the DVMRP network. A PMBR is a router that sits at the boundary of a PIM SM domain and interoperates with other types of multicast routers such as those that run DVMRP. Generally, a PMBR would speak both protocols and implement interoperability functions not required by regular PIM routers. To support interoperability, a special entry type, referred to as (*,*,RP), must be supported by all PIM routers. For this reason, one includes details about (*,*,RP) entry handling in this general PIM specification.

A data packet will match on an (*,*,RP) entry if there is no more specific entry [such as (S,G) or (*,G)], and the destination group address in the packet maps to the RP listed in the (*,*,RP) entry. In this sense, an (*,*,RP) entry represents an aggregation of all the groups that hash to that RP. PMBRs initialize the (*,*,RP) state for each RP in the domain's RP-set. The (*,*,RP) state causes the PMBRs to send (*,*,RP) Join/Prune messages toward each of the active RPs in the domain. As a result, distribution trees are built that carry all data packets originated within the PIM domain (and sent to the RPs) down to the PMBRs.

PMBRs are also responsible for delivering externally generated packets to routers within the PIM domain. To do so, PMBRs initially encapsulate externally originated packets (i.e., received on DVMRP interfaces) in Register messages and unicast them to the corresponding RP within the PIM domain. The Register message has a bit indicating that it was originated by a border router and the RP caches the originating PMBR's address in the route entry so that duplicate registers from other PMBRs can be declined with a Register-Stop message.

All PIM routers must be capable of supporting the (*,*,RP) state and interpreting associated Join/Prune messages.

5.2.2.7 *Multicast Data Packet Processing.*

Data packets are processed in a manner similar to other multicast schemes. A router first performs the longest match on the source and group address in the data packet. An (S,G) entry is matched first if one exists; an (*,G) entry is matched otherwise. If neither state exists, then an (*,*,RP) entry match is attempted as follows: the router hashes on G to identify the RP for group G and looks for an (*,*,RP) entry that has this RP address associated with it. If none of the above exists, then the packet is dropped. If a state is matched, the router compares the interface on which the packet arrived to the incoming interface field in the matched route entry. If the iif check fails, the packet is dropped; otherwise the packet is forwarded to all interfaces listed in the outgoing interface list.

Some special actions are needed to deliver packets continuously while switching from the shared to the SP-tree. In particular, when an (S,G) entry is matched, incoming packets are forwarded as follows:

1. If the SPT-bit is set, then:
   (a) If the incoming interface is the same as a matching (S,G) iif, the packet is forwarded to the oif list of (S,G).
   (b) If the incoming interface is different than a matching (S,G) iif, the packet is discarded.
2. If the SPT-bit is cleared, then:
   (a) If the incoming interface is the same as a matching (S,G) iif, the packet is forwarded to the oif list of (S,G). In addition, the SPT-bit is set for that entry if the incoming interface differs from the incoming interface of the (*,G) or (*,*,RP) entry.
   (b) If the incoming interface is different than a matching (S,G) iif, the incoming interface is tested against a matching (*,G) or (*,*,RP) entry. If the iif is the

same as one of those, the packet is forwarded to the oif list of the matching entry.

(c) Otherwise, the iif does not match any entry for G and the packet is discarded.

Data packets never trigger prunes. However, data packets may trigger actions that in turn trigger prunes.

5.2.2.8 Operation Over Multiaccess Networks.

This section describes a few additional protocol mechanisms needed to operate PIM over multiaccess networks: DR election, Assert messages to resolve parallel paths, and the join/prune-suppression timer to suppress redundant joins on multiaccess networks.

Designated Router Election. When there are multiple routers connected to a multiaccess network, one of them must be chosen to operate as the DR at any point in time. The DR is responsible for sending triggered Join/Prune and Register messages toward the RP.

A simple DR election mechanism is used for both SM and traditional IP multicast routing. Neighboring routers send Hello messages to each other. The sender with the largest network layer address assumes the role of DR. Each router connected to the multiaccess LAN sends the hellos periodically in order to adapt to changes in router status.

Parallel Paths to a Source or the RP—Assert Process. If a router receives a multicast datagram on a multiaccess LAN from a source whose corresponding (S,G) outgoing interface list includes the interface to that LAN, the packet must be a duplicate. In this case, a single forwarder must be elected. Using Assert messages addressed to "224.0.0.13" (ALL-PIM-ROUTERS group) on the LAN, upstream routers can resolve which one will act as the forwarder. Downstream routers listen to the asserts so they know which one was elected and therefore where to send subsequent joins. Typically, this is the same as the downstream router's RPF neighbor; but there are circumstances where this might not be the case, for example, when using multiple unicast routing protocols on that LAN. The RPF neighbor for a particular source (or RP) is the next-hop router to which packets are forwarded en route to that source (or RP) and therefore is considered a good path via which to accept packets from that source.

The upstream router elected is the one that has the shortest distance to the source. Therefore, when a packet is received on an outgoing interface, a router sends an assert message on the multiaccess LAN indicating what metric it uses to reach the source of the data packet. The router with the smallest numerical metric (with ties broken by highest address) will become the forwarder. All other upstream routers will delete the interface from their outgoing interface list. The downstream routers also do the comparison in case the forwarder is different than the RPF neighbor.

Associated with the metric is a metric preference value. This is provided to deal with the case where the upstream routers may run different unicast routing protocols. The numerically smaller metric preference is always preferred. The metric preference is treated as the high-order part of assert metric comparison. Therefore, a metric value can be compared with another metric value provided both metric preferences are the same. A metric preference can be assigned per unicast routing protocol and needs to be consistent for all routers on the multiaccess network.

Asserts are also needed for (*,G) entries since an RP-tree and an SP-tree for the same group may both cross the same multiaccess network. When an assert is sent for a (*,G) entry, the first bit in the metric preference (RPT-bit) is always set to 1 to indicate that this path corresponds to the RP-tree and that the match must be done on (*,G) if it exists. Furthermore, the RPT-bit is always cleared for metric preferences that refer to SP-tree entries; this causes an SP-tree path to always look better than an RP-tree path. When the SP-tree and RP-tree cross the same LAN, this mechanism eliminates the duplicates that would otherwise be carried over the LAN.

In case the packet or the Assert message matches on oif for the (*,*,RP) entry, a (*,G) entry is created, and asserts take place as if the matching state were (*,G).

The DR may lose the (*,G) assert process to another router on the LAN if there are multiple paths to the RP through the LAN. From then on, the DR is no longer the last-hop router for local receivers and removes the LAN from its (*,G) oif list. The winning router becomes the last-hop router and is responsible for sending (*,G) Join messages to the RP.

Join/Prune Suppression. Join/prune suppression may be used on multiaccess LANs to reduce duplicate control message overhead; it is not required for correct performance of the protocol. If a Join/Prune message arrives and matches on the incoming interface for an existing (S,G), (*,G), or (*,*,RP) route entry, and the holdtime included in the Join/Prune message is greater than the recipient's own [Join/Prune-Holdtime] (with ties resolved in favor of the higher network layer address), a timer (the join/prune-suppression timer) in the recipient's route entry may be started to suppress further Join/Prune messages. After this timer expires, the recipient triggers a Join/Prune message and resumes sending periodic join/prunes for this entry. The join/prune-suppression timer should be restarted each time a Join/Prune message is received with a higher holdtime.

5.2.2.9 Unicast Routing Changes.
When unicast routing changes, an RPF check is done on all active (S,G), (*,G), and (*,*,RP) entries, and all affected expected incoming interfaces are updated. In particular, if the new incoming interface appears in the outgoing interface list, it is deleted from the outgoing interface list. The previous incoming interface may be added to the outgoing interface list by a subsequent join/prune from downstream. Join/Prune messages received on the current incoming interface are ignored. Join/Prune messages received on new interfaces or on existing outgoing interfaces are not ignored. Other outgoing interfaces are left as is until they are explicitly pruned by downstream routers or are timed out due to lack of appropriate Join/Prune messages. If the router has an (S,G) entry with the SPT-bit set, and the updated iif(S,G) does not differ from iif(*,G) or iif(*,*,RP), then the router resets the SPT-bit.

The router must send a Join/Prune message with S in the join list out to any new incoming interfaces to inform upstream routers that it expects multicast datagrams over the interface. It may also send a Join/Prune message with S in the prune list out to the old incoming interface, if the link is operational, to inform upstream routers that this part of the distribution tree is going away.

5.2.3 Detailed Protocol Description

This section describes the protocol operations from the perspective of an individual router implementation. In particular, for each message type, the section describes how it is generated and processed.

5.2.3.1 Hello. Hello messages are sent so neighboring routers can discover each other.

SENDING HELLOS. Hello messages are sent periodically between PIM neighbors, every [Hello-Period] seconds. This informs routers what interfaces have PIM neighbors. Hello messages are multicast using address 224.0.0.13 (ALL-PIM-ROUTERS group). The packet includes a holdtime, set to [Hello-Holdtime], for neighbors to keep the information valid. Hellos are sent on all types of communication links.

RECEIVING HELLOS. When a router receives a Hello message, it stores the network layer address for that neighbor, sets its neighbor timer for the hello sender to the holdtime included in the hello, and determines the DR for that interface. The highest addressed system is elected DR. Each hello received causes the DR's address to be updated.

When a router that is the active DR receives a hello from a new neighbor (i.e., from an address that is not yet in the DR's neighbor table), the DR unicasts its most recent RP-set information to the new neighbor.

TIMING OUT NEIGHBOR ENTRIES. A periodic process is run to time out PIM neighbors that have not sent hellos. If the DR has gone down, a new DR is chosen by scanning all neighbors on the interface and selecting the new DR to be the one with the highest network layer address. If an interface has gone down, the router may optionally time out all PIM neighbors associated with the interface.

5.2.3.2 Join/Prune. Join/Prune messages are sent to join or prune a branch off of the multicast distribution tree. A single message contains both a join and prune list, either one of which may be null. Each list contains a set of source addresses, indicating the source-specific trees or shared tree that the router wants to join or prune.

SENDING JOIN/PRUNE MESSAGES. Join/Prune messages are merged such that a message sent to a particular upstream neighbor N includes all of the current joined and pruned sources that are reached via N; according to unicast routing Join/Prune messages are multicast to all routers on multiaccess networks with the target address set to the next hop router toward S or RP. Join/Prune messages are sent every [Join/Prune-Period] seconds. One can introduce mechanisms to rate limit this control traffic on a hop-by-hop basis, in order to avoid excessive overhead on small links. In addition, certain events cause triggered Join/Prune messages to be sent.

Periodic Join/Prune Messages. A router sends a periodic Join/Prune message to each distinct RPF neighbor associated with each (S,G), (*,G), and (*,*,RP) entry. Join/Prune messages are only sent if the RPF neighbor is a PIM neighbor. A periodic Join/Prune message sent to a particular RPF neighbor is constructed as follows:

1. Each router determines the RP for a (*,G) entry by using the hash function described. The RP address (with RPT- and WC-bits set) is included in the join list of a periodic Join/Prune message under the following conditions:
   (a) The Join/Prune message is being sent to the RPF neighbor toward the RP for an active (*,G) or (*,*,RP) entry, and
   (b) The outgoing interface list in the (*,G) or (*,*,RP) entry is non-NULL, or the router is the DR on the same interface as the RPF neighbor.
2. A particular source address, S, is included in the join list with the RPT and WC-bits cleared under the following conditions:
   (a) The Join/Prune message is being sent to the RPF neighbor toward S,
   (b) There exists an active (S,G) entry with the RPT-bit flag cleared, and
   (c) The oif list in the (S,G) entry is not null.
3. A particular source address, S, is included in the prune list with the RPT and WC bits cleared under the following conditions:
   (a) The Join/Prune message is being sent to the RPF neighbor toward S,
   (b) There exists an active (S,G) entry with the RPT-bit flag cleared, and
   (c) The oif list in the (S,G) entry is null.
4. A particular source address, S, is included in the prune list with the RPT-bit set and the WC-bit cleared under the following conditions:
   (a) The Join/Prune message is being sent to the RPF neighbor toward the RP and there exists an (S,G) entry with the RPT-bit flag set and null oif list, or
   (b) The Join/Prune message is being sent to the RPF neighbor toward the RP, there exists an (S,G) entry with the RPT-bit flag cleared and SPT-bit set, and the incoming interface toward S is different than the incoming interface toward the RP, or
   (c) The Join/Prune message is being sent to the RPF neighbor toward the RP, and there exists an (*,G) entry and (S,G) entry for a directly connected source.
5. The RP address (with RPT- and WC-bits set) is included in the prune list if
   (a) The Join/Prune message is being sent to the RPF neighbor toward the RP and there exists a (*,G) entry with a null oif list.

Triggered Join/Prune Messages. In addition to periodic messages, the following events will trigger Join/Prune messages if, as a result, (a) a new entry is created or (b) the oif list changes from null to nonnull or nonnull to null. The contents of triggered messages are the same as the periodic, described above.

1. Receipt of an indication from IGMP that the state of directly connected membership has changed (i.e., new members have just joined "membership indication" or all members have left), for a group G, may cause the last-hop router to build or modify the corresponding (*,G) state. When IGMP indicates

that there are no longer directly connected members, the oif is removed from the oif list if the oif timer is not running. A Join/Prune message is triggered if and only if (a) a new entry is created or (b) the oif list changes from null to nonnull or nonnull to null, as follows:

(a) If the receiving router does not have a route entry for G, the router creates a (*,G) entry, copies the oif list from the corresponding (*,*,RP) entry (if it exists), and includes the interface included in the IGMP membership indication in the oif list; as always, the router never includes the entry's iif in the oif list. The router sends a Join/Prune message toward the RP with the RP address and RPT- and WC-bits set in the join list. Or,

(b) If an (S,G)RPT-bit or (*,G) entry already exists, the interface included in the IGMP membership indication is added to the oif list (if it was not included already).

2. Receipt of a Join/Prune message for (S,G), (*,G), or (*,*,RP) will cause building or modifying the corresponding state, and subsequent triggering of upstream Join/Prune messages, in the following cases:

(a) When there is no current route entry, the RP address included in the Join/Prune message is checked against the local RP-set information. If it matches, an entry will be created and the new entry will in turn trigger an upstream Join/Prune message. If the router has no RP-set information, it may discard the message or optionally use the RP address included in the message.

(b) When the outgoing interface list of an (S,G) RPT-bit entry becomes null, the triggered Join/Prune message will contain S in the prune list.

(c) When there exists an (S,G)RPT-bit with null oif list and a (*,G) Join/Prune message is received, the arriving interface is added to the oif list and a (*,G) Join/Prune message is triggered upstream.

(d) When there exists a (*,G) with null oif list and a (*,*,RP) Join/Prune message is received, the receiving interface is added to the oif list and a (*,*,RP) Join/Prune message is triggered upstream.

3. Receipt of a packet that matches an (S,G) entry whose SPT-bit is cleared triggers the following if the packet arrived on the correct incoming interface and there is a (*,G) or (*,*,RP) entry with a different incoming interface: (a) the router sets the SPT-bit on the (S,G) entry and (b) the router sends a Join/Prune message toward the RP with S in the prune list and the RPT-bit set.

4. Receipt of a packet at the DR from a directly connected source S, on the subnet containing the address S, triggers a Join/Prune message toward the RP with S in the prune list and the RPT-bit set under the following conditions: (a) there is no matching (S,G) state and (b) there exists a (*,G) or (*,*,RP) for which the DR is not the RP.

5. When a Join/Prune message is received for a group G, the prune list is checked. If the prune list contains a source or RP for which the receiving router has a corresponding active (S,G), (*,G) or (*,*,RP) entry, and whose iif is that on which the join/prune was received, then a join for (S,G), (*,G), or (*,*,RP) is triggered to

override the prune, respectively. (This is necessary in the case of parallel downstream routers connected to a multiaccess network.)

6. When the RP fails, the RP will not be included in the Bootstrap messages sent to all routers in that domain. This triggers the DRs to send (*,G) Join/Prune messages toward the new RP for the group, as determined by the RP-set and the hash function. As described earlier, PMBRs trigger (*,*,RP) joins toward each RP in the RP-set.

7. When an entry's join/prune-suppression timer expires, a Join/Prune message is triggered upstream corresponding to that entry, even if the outgoing interface has not transitioned between null and nonnull states.

8. When the RPF neighbor changes (whether due to an assert or changes in unicast routing), the router sets a random delay timer (the random-delay-join timer) whose expiration triggers sending a Join/Prune message for the asserted route entry to the assert winner (if the join/prune-suppression timer has expired).

One does not trigger prunes onto interfaces based on data packets. Data packets that arrive on the wrong incoming interface are silently dropped. However, on point-to-point interfaces, triggered prunes may be sent as an optimization.

It is possible that a Join/Prune message constructed according to the preceding rules could exceed the MTU of a network. In this case, the message can undergo semantic fragmentation, whereby information corresponding to different groups can be sent in different messages. However, if a Join/Prune message must be fragmented, the complete prune list corresponding to a group G must be included in the same Join/Prune message as the associated RP-tree join for G. If such semantic fragmentation is not possible, IP fragmentation should be used between the two neighboring hops.

RECEIVING JOIN/PRUNE MESSAGES. When a router receives a Join/Prune message, it processes it as follows:

The receiver of the join/prune notes the interface on which the PIM message arrived, call it I. The receiver then checks to see if the Join/Prune message was addressed to the receiving router itself (i.e., the router's address appears in the Unicast Upstream Neighbor Router field of the Join/Prune message). (If the router is connected to a multiaccess LAN, the message could be intended for a different router.) If the join/prune is for this router, the following actions are taken.

For each group address, G, in the Join/Prune message, the associated join list is processed as follows. One refers to each address in the join list as Sj; Sj refers to the RP if the RPT-bit and WC-bit are both set. For each Sj in the join list of the Join/Prune message:

1. If an address, Sj, in the join list of the Join/Prune message has the RPT-bit and WC-bit set, then Sj is the RP address used by the downstream router(s) and the following actions are taken:

   (a) If Sj is not the same as the receiving router's RP mapping for G, the receiving router may ignore the Join/Prune message with respect to that group entry. If the router does not have any RP-set information, it may use the address Sj included in the Join/Prune message as the RP for the group.

(b) If Sj is the same as the receiving router's RP mapping for G, the receiving router adds I to the outgoing interface list of the (*,G) route entry [if there is no (*,G) entry, the router creates one first] and sets the Oif-timer for that interface to the holdtime specified in the Join/Prune message. In addition, the oif-deletion delay for that interface is set to one-third the holdtime specified in the Join/Prune message. If a (*,*,RP) entry exists, for the RP associated with G, then the oif list of the newly created (*,G) entry is copied from that (*,*,RP) entry.

(c) For each (Si,G) entry associated with group G: (i) if Si is not included in the prune list, (ii) if I is not on the same subnet as the address Si, and (iii) if I is not the iif, then interface I is added to the oif list and the oif timer for that interface in each affected entry is increased (never decreased) to the Holdtime included in the Join/Prune message. In addition, if the oif timer for that interface is increased, the oif deletion delay for that interface is set to one-third the holdtime specified in the Join/Prune message.

If the group address in the Join/Prune message is "*," then every (*,G) and (S,G) entry, whose group address hashes to the RP indicated in the (*,*,RP) join/prune message, is updated accordingly. A "*" in the group field of the join/prune is represented by a group address 224.0.0.0 and a group mask length of 4, indicating a (*,*,RP) join.

(d) If the (Si,G) entry has its RPT-bit flag set to 1, and its oif list is the same as the (*,G) oif list, then the (Si,G)RPT-bit entry is deleted,

(e) The incoming interface is set to the interface used to send unicast packets to the RP in the (*,G) route entry, that is, RPF interface toward the RP.

2. For each address, Sj, in the join list whose RPT-bit and WC-bit are not set, and for which there is no existing (Sj,G) route entry, the router initiates one. The router creates an (S,G) entry and copies all outgoing interfaces from the (S,G) RPT-bit entry, if it exists. If there is no (S,G) entry, the oif list is copied from the (*,G) entry; and if there is no (*,G) entry, the oif list is copied from the (*,*,RP) entry, if it exists. In all cases, the iif of the (S,G) entry is always excluded from the oif list.

(a) The outgoing interface for (Sj,G) is set to I. The incoming interface for (Sj,G) is set to the interface used to send unicast packets to Sj (i.e., the RPF neighbor).

(b) If the interface used to reach Sj is the same as I, this represents an error (or a unicast routing change) and the join/prune must not be processed.

3. For each address, Sj, in the join list of the Join/Prune message, for which there is an existing (Sj,G) route entry:

(a) If the RPT-bit is not set for Sj listed in the Join/Prune message, but the RPT-bit flag is set on the existing (Sj,G) entry, the router clears the RPT-bit flag on the (Sj,G) entry, sets the incoming interface to point toward Sj for that

(Sj,G) entry, and sends a Join/Prune message corresponding to that entry through the new incoming interface.

(b) If I is not the same as the existing incoming interface, the router adds I to the list of outgoing interfaces.

(c) The oif timer for I is increased (never decreased) to the holdtime included in the Join/Prune message. In addition, if the oif timer for that interface is increased, the oif-deletion delay for that interface is set to one-third the holdtime specified in the Join/Prune message.

(d) The (Sj,G) entry's SPT-bit is cleared until data comes down the shortest path tree.

For each group address G, in the Join/Prune message, the associated prune list is processed as follows. One refers to each address in the prune list as Sp; Sp refers to the RP if the RPT-bit and WC-bit are both set. For each Sp in the prune list of the Join/Prune message:

1. For each address, Sp, in the prune list whose RPT-bit and WC-bit are cleared:

   (a) If there is an existing (Sp,G) route entry, the router lowers the entry's oif timer for I to its oif-deletion delay, allowing for other downstream routers on a multiaccess LAN to override the prune. However, on point-to-point links, the oif timer is expired immediately.

   (b) If the router has a current (*,G), or (*,*,RP), route entry, and if the existing (Sp,G) entry has its RPT-bit flag set to 1, then this (Sp,G)RPT-bit entry is maintained (not deleted) even if its outgoing interface list is null.

2. For each address, Sp, in the prune list whose RPT-bit is set and whose WC-bit is cleared:

   (a) If there is an existing (Sp G) route entry, the router lowers the entry's oif timer for I to its oif-deletion delay, allowing for other downstream routers on a multiaccess LAN to override the prune. However, on point-to-point links, the oif timer is expired immediately.

   (b) If the router has a current (*,G), or (*,*,RP), route entry, and if the existing (Sp,G) entry has its RPT-bit flag set to 1, then this (Sp,G)RPT-bit entry is not deleted, and the entry timer is restarted, even if its outgoing interface list is null.

   (c) If (*,G), or corresponding (*,*,RP), state exists, but there is no (Sp,G) entry, an (Sp,G)RPT-bit entry is created. The outgoing interface list is copied from the (*,G), or (*,*,RP), entry, with the interface I on which the prune was received deleted. Packets from the pruned source Sp match on this state and are not forwarded toward the pruned receivers.

   (d) If there exists an (Sp,G) entry, with or without the RPT-bit set, the oif timer for I is expired, and the entry timer is restarted.

3. For each address, Sp, in the prune list whose RPT-bit and WC-bit are both set:

   (a) If there is an existing (*,G) entry, with Sp as the RP for G, the router lowers the entry's oif timer for I to its oif-deletion delay, allowing for other downstream routers on a multiaccess LAN to override the prune. However, on point-to-point links, the oif timer is expired immediately.

(b) If the corresponding (*,*,RP) state exists, but there is no (*,G) entry, an (*,G) entry is created. The outgoing interface list is copied from the (*,*,RP) entry, with the interface I on which the prune was received deleted.

For any new (S,G), (*,G), or (*,*,RP) entry created by an incoming Join/Prune message, the SPT-bit is cleared (and if a join/prune-suppression timer is used, it is left off).

If the entry has a join/prune-suppression timer associated with it, and if the received join/prune does not indicate the router as its target, then the receiving router examines the join and prune lists to see if any addresses in the list "completely match" the existing (S,G), (*,G), or (*,*,RP) state for which the receiving router currently schedules Join/Prune messages. An element on the join or prune list "completely matches" a route entry only if both the addresses and RPT-bit flag are the same. If the incoming Join/Prune message completely matches an existing (S,G), (*,G), or (*,*,RP) entry and the join/prune arrived on the iif for that entry, then the router compares the holdtime included in the Join/Prune message, to its own [Join/Prune-Holdtime]. If its own [Join/Prune-Holdtime] is lower, the join/prune-suppression timer is started at the [Join/Prune-Suppression-Timeout]. If the [Join/Prune-Holdtime] is equal, the tie is resolved in favor of the Join/Prune Message originator that has the higher network layer address. When the join/prune timer expires, the router triggers a Join/Prune message for the corresponding entry(ies).

5.2.3.3 Register and Register-Stop.
When a source first starts sending to a group, its packets are encapsulated in Register messages and sent to the RP. If the data rate warrants source-specific paths, the RP sets up a source-specific state and starts sending (S,G) Join/Prune messages toward the source, with S in the join list.

SENDING REGISTERS AND RECEIVING REGISTER-STOPS. Register messages are sent as follows:

1. When a DR receives a packet from a directly connected source S on the subnet containing the address, S:

   (a) If there is no corresponding (S,G) entry, the router has RP-set information, and the DR is not the RP for G, the DR creates an (S,G) entry with the register-suppression timer turned off and the RP address set according to the hash function mapping for the corresponding group. The oif list is copied from the existing (*,G) or (*,*,RP) entries, if they exist. The iif of the (S,G) entry is always excluded from the oif list. If there exists a (*,G) or (*,*,RP) entry, the DR sends a Join/Prune message toward the RP with S in the prune list and the RPT-bit set.

   (b) If there is an (S,G) entry in existence, the DR simply restarts the corresponding entry timer.

   When a PMBR (e.g., a router that connects the PIM SM region to a dense-mode region running DVMRP or PIM DM) receives a packet from a source in the dense-mode region, the router treats the packet as if it were from a directly connected source. A separate document will describe the details of interoperability.

2. If the new or previously existing (S,G) entry's register-suppression timer is not running, the data packet is encapsulated in a Register message and unicast to the RP for that group. The data packet is also forwarded according to the (S,G) state in the DR if the oif list is not null since a receiver may join the SP-tree while the DR is still registering to the RP.

3. If the (S,G) entry's register-suppression timer is running, the data packet is not sent in a Register message, it is just forwarded according to the (S,G) oif list.

When the DR receives a Register-Stop message, it restarts the register-suppression timer in the corresponding (S,G) entry(ies) at [Register-Suppression-Timeout] seconds. If there is data to be registered, the DR may send a null register (a Register message with a zero-length data portion in the inner packet) to the RP [Probe-Time] seconds before the register-suppression timer expires to avoid sending occasional bursts of traffic to an RP unnecessarily.

RECEIVING REGISTER MESSAGES AND SENDING REGISTER-STOPS. When a router (i.e., the RP) receives a Register message, the router does the following:

1. Decapsulates the data packet and checks for a corresponding (S,G) entry.

    (a) If an (S,G) entry with a cleared (0) SPT-bit exists, and the received register does not have the null-register bit set to 1, the packet is forwarded, and the SPT-bit is left cleared (0). If the SPT-bit is 1, the packet is dropped, and Register-Stop messages are triggered. Register-stops should be rate limited (in an implementation-specific manner) so that not more than a few are sent per round-trip time. This prevents a high-data-rate stream of packets from triggering a large number of Register-Stop messages between the time that the first packet is received and the time when the source receives the first register-stop.

    (b) If there is no (S,G) entry, but there is a (*,G) entry, and the received register does not have the null-register bit set to 1, the packet is forwarded according to the (*,G) entry.

    (c) If there is an (*,*,RP) entry but no (*,G) entry, and the register received does not have the null-register bit set to 1, a (*,G) or (S,G) entry is created and the oif list is copied from the (*,*,RP) entry to the new entry. The packet is forwarded according to the created entry.

    (d) If there is no G or (*,*,RP) entry corresponding to G, the packet is dropped, and a register-stop is triggered.

    (e) A "border bit" is added to the Register message to facilitate interoperability mechanisms. PMBRs set this bit when registering for external sources. If the "border bit" is set in the register, the RP does the following:

        i. If there is no matching (S,G) state, but there exists a (*,G) or (*,*,RP) entry, the RP creates an (S,G) entry, with a "PMBR" field. This field holds the source of the register (i.e., the outer network layer address of the register packet). The RP triggers an (S,G) join towards the source of the data packet and clears the SPT-bit for the (S,G) entry. If the received register is not a "null register," the packet is forwarded according to the created state. Else:

ii. If the "PMBR" field for the corresponding (S,G) entry matches the source of the register packet and the received register is not a "null register," the de-encapsulated packet is forwarded to the oif list of that entry. Else:

iii. If the "PMBR" field for the corresponding (S,G) entry matches the source of the register packet, the deencapsulated packet is forwarded to the oif list of that entry. Else:

iv. The packet is dropped, and a register-stop is triggered toward the source of the register.

The (S,G) entry timer is restarted by registers arriving from that source to that group.

2. If the matching (S,G) or (*,G) state contains a null oif list, the RP unicasts a Register-Stop message to the source of the Register message; in the latter case, the Source Address field, within the Register-Stop message, is set to the wildcard value (all 0's). This message is not processed by intermediate routers, hence, no (S,G) state is constructed between the RP and the source.

3. If the Register message arrival rate warrants it and there is no existing (S,G) entry, the RP sets up an (S,G) route entry with the outgoing interface list, excluding iif (S,G), copied from the (*,G) outgoing interface list, and its SPT-bit is initialized to 0. If a (*,G) entry does not exist, but there exists a (*,*,RP) entry with the RP corresponding to G, the oif list for (S,G) is copied—excluding the iif—from that (*,*,RP) entry.

A timer [Entry-Timer] is set for the (S,G) entry and this timer is restarted by receipt of data packets for (S,G). The (S,G) entry causes the RP to send a Join/Prune message for the indicated group toward the source of the Register message.

If the (S,G) oif list becomes null, Join/Prune messages will not be sent toward the source S.

5.2.3.4 Multicast Data Packet Forwarding. Processing a multicast data packet involves the following steps:

1. Look up the route state based on the longest match of the source address and an exact match of the destination address in the data packet. If neither S nor G find the longest match entry, and the RP for the packet's destination group address has a corresponding (*,*,RP) entry, then the longest match does not require an exact match on the destination group address. In summary, the longest match is performed in the following order: (1) (S,G), (2) (*,G). If neither is matched, then a lookup is performed on (*,*,RP) entries.

2. If the packet arrived on the interface found in the matching entry's iif field and the oif list is not null:

   (a) Forward the packet to the oif list for that entry, excluding the subnet containing S, and restart the entry timer if the matching entry is (S,G). Optionally, the (S,G) entry timer may be restarted by periodic checking of the matching packet count.

   (b) If the entry is an (S,G) entry with a cleared SPT-bit, and a (*,G) or associated (*,*,RP) also exists whose incoming interface is different than that for (S,G), set the SPT-bit for the (S,G) entry and trigger an (S,G) RPT-bit prune toward the RP.

   (c) If the source of the packet is a directly connected host and the router is the DR on the receiving interface, check the register-suppression timer associated with the (S,G) entry. If it is not running, then the router encapsulates the data packet in a Register message and sends it to the RP.

   This covers the common case of a packet arriving on the RPF interface to the source or RP and being forwarded to all joined branches. It also detects when packets arrive on the SP-tree and triggers their pruning from the RP-tree. If it is the DR for the source, it sends data packets encapsulated in registers to the RPs.

3. If the packet matches to an entry but did not arrive on the interface found in the entry's iif field, check the SPT-bit of the entry. If the SPT-bit is set, drop the packet. If the SPT-bit is cleared, then look up the (*,G), or (*,*,RP), entry for G. If the packet arrived on the iif found in (*,G), or the corresponding (*,*,RP), forward the packet to the oif list of the matching entry. This covers the case when a data packet matches an (S,G) entry for which the SP-tree has not yet been completely established upstream.

4. If the packet does not match any entry but the source of the data packet is a local, directly connected host and the router is the DR on a multiaccess LAN and has RP-set information, the DR uses the hash function to determine the RP associated with the destination group G. The DR creates an (S,G) entry, with the register-suppression timer not running, encapsulates the data packet in a Register message, and unicasts it to the RP.

5. If the packet does not match any entry and it is not a local host or the router is not the DR, drop the packet.

DATA TRIGGERED SWITCH TO SP-TREE. Different criteria can be applied to trigger switching over from the RP-based shared tree to source-specific SP-trees.

One proposal is to do so based on data rate. For example, when a (*,G), or corresponding (*,*,RP), entry is created, a data rate counter may be initiated at the last-hop routers. The counter is incremented with every data packet received for directly connected members of an SM group if the longest match is (*,G) or (*,*,RP). If and when the data rate for the group exceeds a certain configured threshold (t1), the router initiates "source-specific" data rate counters for the following data packets. Then, each counter for a source is incremented when packets matching on (*,G), or (*,*,RP), are received from that source. If the data rate from the particular source exceeds a configured threshold (t2), an (S,G) entry is created and a Join/Prune message is sent toward the source. If the RPF interface for (S,G) is not the same as that for (*,G) or (*,*,RP), then the SPT-bit is cleared in the (S,G) entry.

Other configured rules may be enforced to cause or prevent establishment of the (S,G) state.

5.2.3.5 Assert. asserts are used to resolve which of the parallel routers connected to a multiaccess LAN is responsible for forwarding packets onto the LAN.

SENDING ASSERTS. The following assert rules are provided when a multicast packet is received on an outgoing multiaccess interface "I" of an existing active (S,G), (*,G), or (*,*,RP) entry.

1. Do unicast routing table lookup on source address from data packet, and send assert on interface "I" for source address in data packet; include metric preference of routing protocol and metric from routing table lookup.
2. If route is not found, use metric preference of 0x7fffffff and metric 0xffffffff.

When an assert is sent for a (*,G) entry, the first bit in the metric preference (the RPT-bit) is set to 1, indicating the data packet is routed down the RP-tree.

Asserts should be rate limited in an implementation-specific manner.

RECEIVING ASSERTS. When an assert is received, the router performs the longest match on the source and group address in the Assert message, only active entries—that have packet forwarding state—are matched. The router checks the first bit of the metric preference (RPT-bit).

1. If the RPT-bit is set, the router first does a match on (*,G), or (*,*,RP), entries; if no matching entry is found, it ignores the assert.
2. If the RPT-bit is not set in the assert, the router first does a match on (S,G) entries; if no matching entry is found, the router matches (*,G) or (*,*,RP) entries.

Receiving Asserts on an Entry's Outgoing Interface. If the interface that received the Assert message is in the oif list of the matched entry, then this assert is processed by this router as follows:

1. If the assert's RPT-bit is set and the matching entry is (*,*,RP), the router creates a (*,G) entry. If the assert's RPT-bit is cleared and the matching entry is (*,G), or (*,*,RP), the router creates an (S,G)RPT-bit entry. Otherwise, no new entry is created in response to the assert.
2. The router then compares the metric values received in the assert with the metric values associated with the matched entry. The RPT-bit and metric preference (in that order) are treated as the high-order part of an assert metric comparison. If the value in the assert is less than the router's value (with ties broken by the IP

address, where the higher network layer address wins), delete the interface from the entry. When the deletion occurs for a (*,G) or (*,*,RP) entry, the interface is also deleted from any associated (S,G)RPT-bit or (*,G) entries, respectively. The entry timer for the affected entries is restarted.

3. If the router has won the election, the router keeps the interface in its outgoing interface list. It acts as the forwarder for the LAN.

The winning router sends an Assert message containing its own metric to that outgoing interface. This will cause other routers on the LAN to prune that interface from their route entries. The winning router sets the RPT-bit in the Assert message if a (*,G) or (S,G)RPT-bit entry was matched.

Receiving Asserts on an Entry's Incoming Interface. If the assert arrived on the incoming interface of an existing (S,G), (*,G), or (*,*,RP) entry, the assert is processed as follows. If the Assert message does not match the entry exactly, it is ignored; that is, the longest match is not used in this case. If the Assert message does match exactly, then:

1. Downstream routers will select the upstream router with the smallest metric preference and metric as their RPF neighbor. If two metrics are the same, the highest network layer address is chosen to break the tie. This is important so that downstream routers send subsequent joins/prunes (in SM) to the correct neighbor. An assert timer is initiated when changing the RPF neighbor to the assert winner. When the timer expires, the router resets its RPF neighbor according to its unicast routing tables to capture network dynamics and router failures.

2. If the downstream routers have downstream members, and if the assert caused the RPF neighbor to change, the downstream routers must trigger a Join/Prune message to inform the upstream router that packets are to be forwarded on the multiaccess network.

5.2.3.6 Candidate-RP-Advertisements and Bootstrap Messages.
C-RP-Advs are periodic PIM messages unicast to the BSR by those routers that are configured as C-RPs.

Bootstrap messages are periodic PIM messages originated by the BSR within a domain and forwarded hop by hop to distribute the current RP-set to all routers in that domain.

The Bootstrap messages also support a simple mechanism by which the C-BSR with the highest BSR priority and address (referred to as the preferred BSR) is elected as the BSR for the domain. The RFC recommends that each router configured as a C-RP also be configured as a C-BSR. Sections below entitled "Receiving C-RP-Advs and Originating Bootstrap" and "Receiving and Forwarding Bootstrap" describe the combined function of Bootstrap messages as the vehicle for BSR election and RP-set distribution.

SENDING C-RP-ADVS. C-RPs periodically unicast C-RP-Advs to the BSR for that domain. The interval for sending these messages is subject to local configuration at the C-RP.

C-RP-Advs carry Group Address and Group Mask fields. This enables the advertising router to limit the advertisement to certain prefixes or scopes of groups. The advertising router may enforce this scope acceptance when receiving registers or Join/Prune messages. C-RPs should send C-RP-Adv messages with the Priority field set to 0.

RECEIVING C-RP-ADVS AND ORIGINATING BOOTSTRAP. Upon receiving a C-RP-Adv, a router does the following:

1. If the router is not the elected BSR, it ignores the message. Else:
2. The BSR adds the RP address to its local pool of candidate RPs, according to the associated group prefix(es) in the C-RP-Adv message. The holdtime in the C-RP-Adv message is also stored with the corresponding RP, to be included later in the Bootstrap message. The BSR may apply a local policy to limit the number of C-RPs included in the Bootstrap message. The BSR may override the prefix indicated in a C-RP-Adv unless the Priority field is not zero.

The BSR keeps an RP timer per RP in its local RP-set. The RP timer is initialized to the holdtime in the RP's C-RP-Adv. When the timer expires, the corresponding RP is removed from the RP set. The RP timer is restarted by the C-RP-Advs from the corresponding RP.

The BSR also uses its bootstrap timer to periodically send Bootstrap messages. In particular, when the bootstrap timer expires, the BSR originates a Bootstrap message on each of its PIM interfaces. To reduce the Bootstrap message overhead during partition healing, the BSR should set a random time (as a function of the priority and address) after which the Bootstrap message is originated only if no other preferred Bootstrap message is received. The message is sent with a TTL of 1 to the "ALL-PIM-ROUTERS" group. In steady state, the BSR originates Bootstrap messages periodically. At startup, the bootstrap timer is initialized to [Bootstrap-Timeout], causing the first Bootstrap message to be originated only when and if the timer expires. For timer details, see the next section, "Receiving and Forwarding Bootstrap." A DR unicasts a Bootstrap message to each new PIM neighbor, that is, after the DR receives the neighbor's Hello message (it does so even if the new neighbor becomes the DR).

The Bootstrap message is subdivided into sets of Group-Prefix,RP-Count,RP-addresses. For each RP address, the corresponding holdtime is included in the RP-Holdtime field. The format of the Bootstrap message allows "semantic fragmentation" if the length of the original Bootstrap message exceeds the packet maximum boundaries (see Section 5.2.4). However, the RFC recommends against configuring a large number of routers as C-RPs to reduce the semantic fragmentation required.

RECEIVING AND FORWARDING BOOTSTRAP. Each router keeps a bootstrap timer initialized to [Bootstrap-Timeout] at startup.

When a router receives a Bootstrap message sent to the "ALL-PIM-ROUTERS" group, it performs the following:

1. If the message was not sent by the RPF neighbor toward the BSR address included, the message is dropped. Else:
2. If the included BSR is not preferred over and not equal to the currently active BSR:
   (a) If the bootstrap timer has not yet expired or if the receiving router is a C-BSR, then the Bootstrap message is dropped. Else:
   (b) If the bootstrap timer has expired and the receiving router is not a C-BSR, the receiving router stores the RP-set and BSR address and priority found in the message and restarts the timer by setting it to [Bootstrap-Timeout]. The Bootstrap message is then forwarded out of all PIM interfaces, excluding the one over which the message arrived, to the "ALL-PIM-ROUTERS" group, with a TTL of 1.
3. If the Bootstrap message includes a BSR address that is preferred over or equal to the currently active BSR, the router restarts its bootstrap timer at [Bootstrap-Timeout] seconds and stores the BSR address and RP-set information.

   The Bootstrap message is then forwarded out of all PIM interfaces, excluding the one over which the message arrived, to the "ALL-PIM- ROUTERS" group, with a TTL of 1.
4. If the receiving router has no current RP-set information and the bootstrap was unicast to it from a directly connected neighbor, the router stores the information as its new RP-set. This covers the startup condition when a newly booted router obtains the RP-set and BSR address from its DR.

When a router receives a new RP-set, it checks if each of the RPs referred to by the existing state [i.e., by (*,G), (*,*,RP), or (S,G)RPT-bit entries] is in the new RP-set. If an RP is not in the new RP-set, that RP is considered unreachable and the hash algorithm (see below) is reperformed for each group with locally active state that previously hashed to that RP. This will cause those groups to be distributed among the remaining RPs. When the new RP-set contains a new RP, the value of the new RP is calculated for each group covered by that C-RP's group prefix. Any group for which the new RP's value is greater than the previously active RP's value is switched over to the new RP.

5.2.3.7 Hash Function.
The hash function is used by all routers within a domain to map a group to one of the C-RPs from the RP-set. For a particular group G, the hash function uses only those C-RPs whose group prefix covers G. The algorithm takes as input the group address and the addresses of the candidate RPs and gives as output one RP address to be used.

The protocol requires that all routers hash to the same RP within a domain (except for transients). The following hash function must be used in each router:

1. For RP addresses in the RP-set whose group prefix covers G, select the RP with the highest priority (i.e., the lowest "priority" value), and compute a value

Value$(G,M,C(i)) = (1103515245 * ((1103515245 * (G\&M) + 12345)$ XOR C
$(i)) + 12345)$ mod 2^{31} where $C(i)$ is the RP address and M is a hash mask included
in Bootstrap messages. The hash mask allows a small number of consecutive
groups (e.g., 4) to always hash to the same RP. For instance, hierarchically
encoded data can be sent on consecutive group addresses to get the same delay
and fate-sharing characteristics.

For address families other than IPv4, a 32-bit digest to be used as $C(i)$ must first
be derived from the actual RP address. Such a digest method must be used
consistently throughout the PIM domain. For IPv6 addresses, the RFC recommends using the equivalent IPv4 address for an IPv4-compatible address and the
CRC-32 checksum of all other IPv6 addresses.

2. From the RPs with the highest priority (i.e., the lowest "priority" value), the
   candidate with the highest resulting value is then chosen as the RP for that group,
   and its identity and hash value are stored with the entry created.

Ties between RPs having the same hash value and priority are broken in advantage of
the highest address.

The hash function algorithm is invoked by a DR upon reception of a packet or IGMP
membership indication for a group for which the DR has no entry. It is invoked by any
router that has a (*,*,RP) state when a packet is received for which there is no
corresponding (S,G) or (*,G) entry. Furthermore, the hash function is invoked by all
routers upon receiving a (*,G) or (*,*,RP) Join/Prune message.

5.2.3.8 Processing Timer Events. This section enumerates all timers that have
been discussed or implied. Since some critical timer events are not associated with the
receipt or sending of messages, they are not fully covered by earlier sections.

Timers are implemented in an implementation-specific manner. For example, a
timer may count up or down or may simply expire at a specific time. Setting a timer to a
value T means that it will expire after T seconds.

TIMERS RELATED TO TREE MAINTENANCE. Each (S,G), (*,G), and (*,*,RP) route
entry has multiple timers associated with it: one for each interface in the outgoing interface
list, one for the multicast routing entry itself, and one optional join/prune-suppression
timer. Each (S,G) and (*,G) entry also has an assert timer and a random-delay-join
timer for use with asserts. In addition, DRs have a register-suppression timer for each
(S,G) entry and every router has a single join/prune timer. (A router may optionally keep
separate join/prune timers for different interfaces or route entries if different join/prune
periods are desired.)

- [Join/Prune-Timer]: This timer is used for periodically sending aggregate Join/
  Prune messages. To avoid synchronization among routers booting simultaneously, it
  is initially set to a random value between 1 and [Join/Prune-Period]. When it expires,
  the timer is immediately restarted to [Join/Prune-Period]. A Join/Prune message is
  then sent out to each interface. This timer should not be restarted by other events.

- [Join/Prune-Suppression-Timer (kept per route entry)]: A route entry's (optional) join/prune-suppression timer may be used to suppress duplicate joins from multiple downstream routers on the same LAN. When a Join message is received from a neighbor on the entry's incoming interface in which the included holdtime is higher than the router's own [Join/Prune-Holdtime] (with ties broken by a higher network layer address), the timer is set to [Join/Prune-Suppression-Timeout], with some random jitter introduced to avoid synchronization of triggered Join/Prune messages on expiration. (The random timeout value must be <1.5 * [Join/Prune-Period] to prevent losing data after two dropped join/prunes.) The timer is restarted every time a subsequent Join/Prune message (with higher holdtime/IP address) for the entry is received on its incoming interface. While the timer is running, Join/Prune messages for the entry are not sent. This timer is idle (not running) for point-to-point links.

- [Oif-Timer (kept per oif for each route entry)]: A timer for each oif of a route entry is used to time out that oif. Because some of the outgoing interfaces in an (S,G) entry are copied from the (*,G) outgoing interface list, they may not have explicit (S,G) Join messages from some of the downstream routers [i.e., where members are joining to the (*,G) tree only]. Thus, when an oif timer is restarted in a (*,G) entry, the oif timer is restarted for that interface in each existing (S,G) entry whose oif list contains that interface. The same rule applies to (*,G) and (S,G) entries when restarting an oif timer on a (*,*,RP) entry.

The following table shows its usage when first adding the oif to the entry's oif list, when it should be restarted (unless it is already higher), and when it should be decreased (unless it is already lower).

Set to included Holdtime	When adding oif off Join/Prune	Applies to (S,G) (*,G) (*,*,RP)
Increased (only) to included Holdtime	When received Join/Prune	Applies to (S,G) (*,G) (*,*,RP)
(*,*,RP) oif-timer value	(*,*,RP) oif-timer restarted	(S,G) (*,G)
(*,G) oif-timer value	(*,G) oif-timer restarted	(S,G)

When the timer expires, the oif is removed from the oif list if there are no directly connected members. When deleted, the oif is also removed in any associated (S,G) or (*,G) entries.

- [Entry-Timer (kept per route entry)]: A timer for each route entry is used to time out that entry. The following table summarizes its usage when first adding the oif to the entry's oiflist and when it should be restarted (unless it is already higher).

Set to	When created	Applies to (S,G)
[Data-Timeout]	off data packet	(S,G) (*,G) (*,*,RP)
included	created off	
Holdtime	Join/Prune	
Increased	When receiving	Applies to (S,G) no
(only) to	data packets	RPT-bit (S,G) RPT-bit
[Data-Timeout]	any oif-timer	(*,G) (*,*,RP)
oif-timer value	restarted	
[Assert-Timeout]	assert	(S,G) RPT-bit (*,G)
	received	w/null oif

When the timer expires, the route entry is deleted; if the entry is a (*,G) or (*,*,RP) entry, all associated (S,G)RPT-bit entries are also deleted.

- [Register-Suppression-Timer (kept per (S,G) route entry)]: An (S,G) route entry's register-suppression timer is used to suppress registers when the RP is receiving data packets natively. When a Register-Stop message for the entry is received from the RP, the timer is set to a random value in the range 0.5 × [Register-Suppression-Timeout] to 1.5 × [Register-Suppression-Timeout]. While the timer is running, registers for that entry will be suppressed. If null registers are used, a null register is sent [Probe-Time] seconds before the timer expires.
- [Assert-Timer (per (S,G) or (*,G) route entry)]: The assert timer for an (S,G) or (*, G) route entry is used for timing out asserts received. When an assert is received and the RPF neighbor is changed to the assert winner, the assert timer is set to [Assert-Timeout] and is restarted to this value every time a subsequent assert for the entry is received on its incoming interface. When the timer expires, the router resets its RPF neighbor according to its unicast routing table.
- [Random-Delay-Join-Timer (per (S,G) or (*,G) route entry)]: The random-delay-join timer for an (S,G) or (*,G) route entry is used to prevent synchronization among downstream routers on a LAN when their RPF neighbor changes. When the RPF neighbor changes, this timer is set to a random value between 0 and [Random-Delay-Join-Timeout] seconds. When the timer expires, a triggered Join/ Prune message is sent for the entry unless its join/prune-suppression timer is running.

TIMERS RELATED TO NEIGHBOR DISCOVERY

- [Hello-Timer]: This timer is used to periodically send Hello messages. To avoid synchronization among routers booting simultaneously, it is initially set to a random value between 1 and [Hello-Period]. When it expires, the timer is immediately restarted to [Hello-Period]. A Hello message is then sent out to each interface. This timer should not be restarted by other events.

- [Neighbor-Timer (kept per neighbor)]: A neighbor timer for each neighbor is used to time out the neighbor state. When a hello message is received from a new neighbor, the timer is initially set to the holdtime included in the Hello message (which is equal to the neighbor's value of [Hello-Holdtime]). Every time a subsequent hello is received from that neighbor, the timer is restarted to the holdtime in the hello. When the timer expires, the neighbor state is removed.

TIMERS RELATED TO RP INFORMATION

- [C-RP-Adv-Timer (C-RPs only)]: Routers configured as candidate RPs use this timer to periodically send C-RP-Adv messages. To avoid synchronization among routers booting simultaneously, the timer is initially set to a random value between 1 and [C-RP-Adv-Period]. When it expires, the timer is immediately restarted to [C-RP-Adv-Period]. A C-RP-Adv message is then sent to the elected BSR. This timer should not be restarted by other events.
- [RP-Timer (BSR only, kept per RP in RP-Set)]: The BSR uses a timer per RP in the RP-set to monitor liveness. When a C-RP is added to the RP-set, its timer is set to the holdtime included in the C-RP-Adv message from that C-RP (which is equal to the C-RP's value of [RP-Holdtime]). Every time a subsequent C-RP-Adv is received from that RP, its timer is restarted to the holdtime in the C-RP-Adv. When the timer expires, the RP is removed from the RP-set included in Bootstrap messages.
- [Bootstrap-Timer]: This timer is used by the BSR to periodically originate Bootstrap messages and by other routers to time out the BSR (see Section 3.6.3). This timer is initially set to [Bootstrap-Timeout]. A C-BSR restarts this timer to [Bootstrap-Timeout] upon receiving a Bootstrap message from a preferred router and originates a Bootstrap message and restarts the timer to [Bootstrap-Period] when it expires. Routers not configured as C-BSRs restart this timer to [Bootstrap-Timeout] upon receiving a Bootstrap message from the elected or a more preferred BSR and ignore Bootstrap messages from nonpreferred C-BSRs while it is running.

DEFAULT TIMER VALUES. Most of the default timeout values for state information are 3.5 times the refresh period. For example, hellos refresh the Neighbor state and the default hello timer period is 30 s, so a default neighbor timer duration of 105 s is included in the holdtime field of the hellos. In order to improve convergence, however, the default timeout value for information related to RP liveness and Bootstrap messages is 2.5 times the refresh period.

In this version of the spec, the RFC suggests particular numerical timer settings; it is possible to specify a mechanism for timer values to be scaled based upon observed network parameters.

- [Join/Prune-Period]: This is the interval between sending Join/Prune messages. Default: 60 s. This value may be set to take into account such things as the configured bandwidth and expected average number of multicast route entries for the attached network or link (e.g., the period would be longer for lower speed links or for routers in the center of the network that expect to have a larger number of entries). In addition, a router could modify this value (and corresponding [Join/Prune-Holdtime] value) if the number of route entries changes significantly (e.g., by an order of magnitude). For example, given a default minimum [Join/Prune-Period] value, if the number of route entries with a particular iif increases from N to $N*100$, the router could increase its [Join/Prune-Period] (and [Join/Prune-Holdtime]) for that interface by a factor of 10; and if/when the number of entries decreases back to N, the [Join/Prune-Period] (and [Join/Prune-Holdtime]) could be decreased to its previous value. If the [Join/Prune-Period] is modified, these changes should be made relatively infrequently and the router should continue to refresh at its previous [Join/Prune-Period] for at least [Join/Prune-Holdtime] in order to allow the upstream router to adapt.

- [Join-Prune Holdtime]: This is the holdtime specified in Join/Prune messages, and is used to time out oifs. This should be set to 3.5 * [Join/Prune-Period]. Default: 210 s.

- [Join/Prune-Suppression-Timeout]: This is the mean interval between receiving a join/prune with a higher holdtime (with ties broken by higher network layer address) and allowing duplicate join/prunes to be sent again. This should be set to approximately 1.25 * [Join/Prune-Period]. Default: 75 s.

- [Data-Timeout]: This is the time after which the (S,G) state for a silent source will be deleted. Default: 210 s.

- [Register-Suppression-Timeout]: This is the mean interval between receiving a register-stop and allowing registers to be sent again. A lower value means more frequent register bursts at RP, while a higher value means longer join latency for new receivers. Default: 60 s. (Note that if null registers are sent [Probe-Time] seconds before the timeout, register bursts are prevented, and [Register-Suppression-Timeout] may be lowered to decrease join latency.)

- [Probe-Time]: When null registers are used, this is the time between sending a null register and the register-suppression timer expiring unless it is restarted by receiving a register-stop. Thus, a null register would be sent when the register-suppression timer reaches this value. Default: 5 s.

- [Assert-Timeout]: This is the interval between the last time an assert is received and the time at which the assert is timed out. Default: 180 s.

- [Random-Delay-Join-Timeout]: This is the maximum interval between the time when the RPF neighbor changes and the time at which a triggered Join/Prune message is sent. Default: 4.5 s.

- [Hello-Period]: This is the interval between sending Hello messages. Default: 30 s.

- [Hello-Holdtime]: This is the holdtime specified in Hello messages, after which neighbors will time out their neighbor entries for the router. This should be set to 3.5 * [Hello-Period]. Default: 105 s.
- [C-RP-Adv-Period]: For C-RPs, this is the interval between sending C-RP-Adv messages. Default: 60 s.
- [RP-Holdtime]: For C-RPs, this is the holdtime specified in C-RP-Adv messages and is used by the BSR to time out RPs. This should be set to 2.5 * [C-RP-Adv-Period]. Default: 150 s.
- [Bootstrap-Period]: At the elected BSR, this is the interval between originating Bootstrap messages and should be equal to 60 s.
- [Bootstrap-Timeout]: This is the time after which the elected BSR will be assumed unreachable when Bootstrap messages are not received from it. This should be set to 2 * [Bootstrap-Period] + 10. Default: 130 s.

5.2.3.9 Summary of Flags Used.

Following is a summary of all the flags used in this scheme.

Bit	Used in	Definition
Border	Register	Register for external sources is coming from PIM multicast border router
Null	Register	Register sent as probe of RP, the encapsulated IP data packet should not be forwarded
RPT	Route entry	Entry represents state on the RP-tree
RPT	Join/prune	Join is associated with the shared tree and therefore the Join/Prune message is propagated along the RP-tree (source encoded is an RP address)
RPT	Assert	The data packet was routed down the shared tree; thus, the path indicated corresponds to the RP-tree
SPT	(S,G) entry	Packets have arrived on the iif toward S, and the iif is different from the (*,G) iif
WC	Join	The receiver expects to receive packets from all sources via this (shared tree) path. Thus, the join/prune applies to a (*,G) entry
WC	Route entry	Wildcard entry; if there is no more specific match for a particular source, packets will be forwarded according to this entry

Figure 5.7. Packet Format

5.2.4 Packet Formats

This section describes the details of the packet formats for PIM control messages. All PIM control messages have protocol number 103. Basically, PIM messages are either unicast (e.g., Register and Register-Stop) or multicast hop-by-hop to "ALL-PIM-ROUTERS" group "224.0.0.13" (e.g., Join/Prune, Assert). See Figure 5.7 (which is similar to Figure 5.6).

PIM Ver: PIM Version number is 2.

Type: Types for specific PIM messages. PIM types are as follows:

0 = Hello
1 = Register
2 = Register-Stop
3 = Join/Prune
4 = Bootstrap
5 = Assert
6 = Graft (used in PIM DM only)
7 = Graft-Ack (used in PIM DM only)
8 = Candidate-RP-Advertisement

Reserved. Set to zero; ignored upon receipt.

Checksum. The checksum is the 16-bit one's complement of the one's complement sum of the entire PIM message (excluding the data portion in the Register message). For computing the checksum, the Checksum field is zeroed.

5.2.4.1 Encoded Source and Group Address Formats

1. Encoded-Unicast Address: Takes the format shown in Figure 5.8.

Figure 5.8. Encoded-Unicast Address

Addr Family: The address family of the Unicast Address field of this address. Here is the address family numbers assigned by IANA:

Number	Description
0	Reserved
1	IP (IP Version 4)
2	IP6 (IP Version 6)
3	NSAP
4	HDLC (8-bit multidrop)
5	BBN 1822
6	802 (includes all 802 media plus Ethernet "canonical format")
7	E.163
8	E.164 (SMDS, frame relay, ATM)
9	F.69 (Telex)
10	X.121 (X.25, frame relay)
11	IPX
12	Appletalk
13	Decnet IV
14	Banyan Vines
15	E.164 with NSAP format subaddress

Encoding Type: The type of encoding used within a specific address family. The value "0" is reserved for this field and represents the native encoding of the address family.

Unicast Address: The unicast address as represented by the given address family and encoding type.

2. Encoded-Group Address: Takes the format of Figure 5.9.

Addr Family: Described above.
Encoding Type: Described above.
Reserved: Transmitted as zero. Ignored upon receipt.
Mask Length: The mask length is 8 bits. The value is the number of contiguous bits left justified used as a mask, which describes the address. It is less than or equal to the address length in bits for the given address family and encoding type. If the message is sent for a single group, then the mask length must equal the address length in bits for the

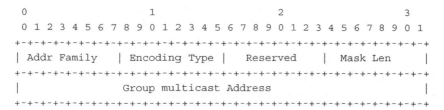

```
 0                   1                   2                   3
 0 1 2 3 4 5 6 7 8 9 0 1 2 3 4 5 6 7 8 9 0 1 2 3 4 5 6 7 8 9 0 1
+-+-+-+-+-+-+-+-+-+-+-+-+-+-+-+-+-+-+-+-+-+-+-+-+-+-+-+-+-+-+-+-+
| Addr Family   | Encoding Type |   Reserved    |  Mask Len     |
+-+-+-+-+-+-+-+-+-+-+-+-+-+-+-+-+-+-+-+-+-+-+-+-+-+-+-+-+-+-+-+-+
|                   Group multicast Address                     |
+-+-+-+-+-+-+-+-+-+-+-+-+-+-+-+-+-+-+-+-+-+-+-+-+-+-+-+-+-+-+-+-+
```

Figure 5.9. Encoded-Group Address

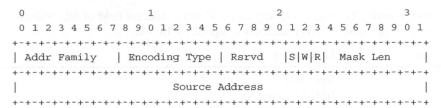

```
 0                   1                   2                   3
 0 1 2 3 4 5 6 7 8 9 0 1 2 3 4 5 6 7 8 9 0 1 2 3 4 5 6 7 8 9 0 1
+-+-+-+-+-+-+-+-+-+-+-+-+-+-+-+-+-+-+-+-+-+-+-+-+-+-+-+-+-+-+-+-+
| Addr Family   | Encoding Type | Rsrvd     |S|W|R|  Mask Len   |
+-+-+-+-+-+-+-+-+-+-+-+-+-+-+-+-+-+-+-+-+-+-+-+-+-+-+-+-+-+-+-+-+
|                          Source Address                       |
+-+-+-+-+-+-+-+-+-+-+-+-+-+-+-+-+-+-+-+-+-+-+-+-+-+-+-+-+-+-+-+-+
```

Figure 5.10. Encoded-Source Address

given address family and encoding type (for example, 32 for IPv4 native encoding and 128 for IPv6 native encoding).

The group multicast address contains the group address.

3. Encoded-Source Address: Takes the format of Figure 5.10.

Addr Family: Described above.

Encoding Type: Described above.

Reserved: Transmitted as zero, ignored on receipt.

S, W, R: see Section 5.2.4.5 for details.

Mask Length: Mask length is 8 bits. The value is the number of contiguous bits left justified used as a mask that describes the address. The mask length must be less than or equal to the address length in bits for the given address family and encoding type. If the message is sent for a single group, then the mask length must equal the address length in bits for the given address family and encoding type. In Version 2 of PIM, it is strongly recommended that this field be set to 32 for IPv4 native encoding.

Source Address: The source address.

5.2.4.2 Hello Message. This message is sent periodically by routers on all interfaces. See Figure 5.11.

PIM Version, Type, Reserved, Checksum: Described above.

OptionType: The type of the option given in the following OptionValue field.

OptionLength: The length of the OptionValue field in bytes.

OptionValue: A variable-length field carrying the value of the option.

The Option fields may contain the following values:

- OptionType = 1; OptionLength = 2; OptionValue = Holdtime; where Holdtime is the amount of time a receiver must keep the neighbor reachable in seconds. If the holdtime is set to "0xFFFF," the receiver of this message never times out the neighbor. This may be used with ISDN lines to avoid keeping the link up with periodic Hello messages. Furthermore, if the holdtime is set to "0," the information is timed out immediately.
- OptionType 2–16: Reserved
- The rest of the option types are defined in other documents.

In general, options may be ignored.

```
0                   1                   2                   3
0 1 2 3 4 5 6 7 8 9 0 1 2 3 4 5 6 7 8 9 0 1 2 3 4 5 6 7 8 9 0 1
+-+-+-+-+-+-+-+-+-+-+-+-+-+-+-+-+-+-+-+-+-+-+-+-+-+-+-+-+-+-+-+-+
|PIM Ver| Type  | Reserved      |           Checksum            |
+-+-+-+-+-+-+-+-+-+-+-+-+-+-+-+-+-+-+-+-+-+-+-+-+-+-+-+-+-+-+-+-+
|        OptionType             |          OptionLength         |
+-+-+-+-+-+-+-+-+-+-+-+-+-+-+-+-+-+-+-+-+-+-+-+-+-+-+-+-+-+-+-+-+
|                          OptionValue                          |
+-+-+-+-+-+-+-+-+-+-+-+-+-+-+-+-+-+-+-+-+-+-+-+-+-+-+-+-+-+-+-+++
|                               .                               |
|                               .                               |
|                               .                               |
+-+-+-+-+-+-+-+-+-+-+-+-+-+-+-+-+-+-+-+-+-+-+-+-+-+-+-+-+-+-+-+-+
|        OptionType             |          OptionLength         |
+-+-+-+-+-+-+-+-+-+-+-+-+-+-+-+-+-+-+-+-+-+-+-+-+-+-+-+-+-+-+-+-+
|                          OptionValue                          |
+-+-+-+-+-+-+-+-+-+-+-+-+-+-+-+-+-+-+-+-+-+-+-+-+-+-+-+-+-+-+-+++
```

Figure 5.11. Hello Message

5.2.4.3   Register Message. A Register message is sent by the DR or a PMBR to the RP when a multicast packet needs to be transmitted on the RP-tree. The source address is set to the address of the DR, the destination address to the RP's address. See Figure 5.12.

PIM Version, Type, reserved, and Checksum: Described above. Note that the checksum for registers is done only on the PIM header, excluding the data packet portion.

B — The Border Bit: If the router is a DR for a source that it is directly connected to, it sets the B bit to 0. If the router is a PMBR for a source in a directly connected cloud, it sets the *B* bit to 1.

N — The Null-Register Bit: Set to 1 by a DR that is probing the RP before expiring its local register-suppression timer. Set to 0 otherwise.

Multicast Data Packet: The original packet sent by the source.

For (S,G) null registers, the multicast data packet portion contains only a dummy header with S as the source address, G as the destination address, and a data length of zero.

```
0                   1                   2                   3
0 1 2 3 4 5 6 7 8 9 0 1 2 3 4 5 6 7 8 9 0 1 2 3 4 5 6 7 8 9 0 1
+-+-+-+-+-+-+-+-+-+-+-+-+-+-+-+-+-+-+-+-+-+-+-+-+-+-+-+-+-+-+-+-+
|PIM Ver| Type  | Reserved      |           Checksum            |
+-+-+-+-+-+-+-+-+-+-+-+-+-+-+-+-+-+-+-+-+-+-+-+-+-+-+-+-+-+-+-+-+
|B|N|                       Reserved                            |
+-+-+-+-+-+-+-+-+-+-+-+-+-+-+-+-+-+-+-+-+-+-+-+-+-+-+-+-+-+-+-+-+
|                                                               |
                        Multicast data packet
|                                                               |
+-+-+-+-+-+-+-+-+-+-+-+-+-+-+-+-+-+-+-+-+-+-+-+-+-+-+-+-+-+-+-+-+
```

Figure 5.12. Register Message

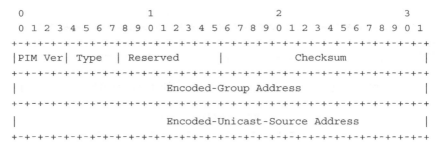

Figure 5.13. Register-Stop Message

5.2.4.4   Register-Stop Message.   A register-stop is unicast from the RP to the sender of the Register message. The source address is the address to which the register was addressed. The destination address is the source address of the register message. See Figure 5.13.

PIM Version, Type, Reserved, and Checksum: Described above.

Encoded-Group Address: Format described above. Note that for register-stops the Mask Length field contains full address length * 8 (e.g., 32 for IPv4 native encoding) if the message is sent for a single group.

Encoded-Unicast-Source Address: Host address of source from multicast data packet in register. The format for this address is given in the encoded-unicast address in Section 4.1. A special wildcard value (0s) can be used to indicate any source.

5.2.4.5   Join/Prune Message.   A Join/Prune message is sent by routers toward upstream sources and RPs. Joins are sent to build shared trees (RP-trees) or source trees (SPT). Prunes are sent to prune source trees when members leave groups as well as sources that do not use the shared tree. See Figure 5.14.

PIM Version, Type, Reserved, and Checksum: Described above.

Encoded-Unicast Upstream Neighbor Address: The address of the RPF or upstream neighbor. The format for this address is given in the encoded-unicast address in Section 5.2.4.1.

"Reserved" Transmitted as Zero: Ignored on receipt.

Holdtime: The amount of time a receiver must keep the join/prune state alive in seconds. If the holdtime is set to 0xffff, the receiver of this message never times out the oif. This may be used with ISDN lines to avoid keeping the link up with periodic Join/Prune messages. Furthermore, if the holdtime is set to 0, the information is timed out immediately.

Number of Groups: The number of multicast group sets contained in the message.

Encoded-Multicast Group Address: For format description see Section 5.2.4.1. A wildcard group in the (*,*,RP) join is represented by a 224.0.0.0 in the Group Address field and 4 in the Mask Length field. A (*,*,RP) join also has the WC-bit and the RPT-bit set.

```
 0                   1                   2                   3
 0 1 2 3 4 5 6 7 8 9 0 1 2 3 4 5 6 7 8 9 0 1 2 3 4 5 6 7 8 9 0 1
+-+-+-+-+-+-+-+-+-+-+-+-+-+-+-+-+-+-+-+-+-+-+-+-+-+-+-+-+-+-+-+-+
|PIM Ver| Type  | Reserved      |            Checksum           |
+-+-+-+-+-+-+-+-+-+-+-+-+-+-+-+-+-+-+-+-+-+-+-+-+-+-+-+-+-+-+-+-+
|              Encoded-Unicast-Upstream Neighbor Address        |
+-+-+-+-+-+-+-+-+-+-+-+-+-+-+-+-+-+-+-+-+-+-+-+-+-+-+-+-+-+-+-+-+
|  Reserved     | Num groups    |            Holdtime           |
+-+-+-+-+-+-+-+-+-+-+-+-+-+-+-+-+-+-+-+-+-+-+-+-+-+-+-+-+-+-+-+-+
|               Encoded-Multicast Group Address-1               |
+-+-+-+-+-+-+-+-+-+-+-+-+-+-+-+-+-+-+-+-+-+-+-+-+-+-+-+-+-+-+-+-+
|  Number of Joined  Sources    |  Number of Pruned Sources     |
+-+-+-+-+-+-+-+-+-+-+-+-+-+-+-+-+-+-+-+-+-+-+-+-+-+-+-+-+-+-+-+-+
|                 Encoded-Joined Source Address-1               |
+-+-+-+-+-+-+-+-+-+-+-+-+-+-+-+-+-+-+-+-+-+-+-+-+-+-+-+-+-+-+-+-+
|                             .                                 |
|                             .                                 |
+-+-+-+-+-+-+-+-+-+-+-+-+-+-+-+-+-+-+-+-+-+-+-+-+-+-+-+-+-+-+-+-+
|                 Encoded-Joined Source Address-n               |
+-+-+-+-+-+-+-+-+-+-+-+-+-+-+-+-+-+-+-+-+-+-+-+-+-+-+-+-+-+-+-+-+
|                 Encoded-Pruned Source Address-1               |
+-+-+-+-+-+-+-+-+-+-+-+-+-+-+-+-+-+-+-+-+-+-+-+-+-+-+-+-+-+-+-+-+
|                             .                                 |
|                             .                                 |
+-+-+-+-+-+-+-+-+-+-+-+-+-+-+-+-+-+-+-+-+-+-+-+-+-+-+-+-+-+-+-+-+
|                 Encoded-Pruned Source Address-n               |
+-+-+-+-+-+-+-+-+-+-+-+-+-+-+-+-+-+-+-+-+-+-+-+-+-+-+-+-+-+-+-+-+
|                             .                                 |
|                             .                                 |
|                             .                                 |
+-+-+-+-+-+-+-+-+-+-+-+-+-+-+-+-+-+-+-+-+-+-+-+-+-+-+-+-+-+-+-+-+
|               Encoded-Multicast Group Address-n               |
+-+-+-+-+-+-+-+-+-+-+-+-+-+-+-+-+-+-+-+-+-+-+-+-+-+-+-+-+-+-+-+-+
|  Number of Joined  Sources    |  Number of Pruned Sources     |
+-+-+-+-+-+-+-+-+-+-+-+-+-+-+-+-+-+-+-+-+-+-+-+-+-+-+-+-+-+-+-+-+
|                 Encoded-Joined Source Address-1               |
+-+-+-+-+-+-+-+-+-+-+-+-+-+-+-+-+-+-+-+-+-+-+-+-+-+-+-+-+-+-+-+-+
|                             .                                 |
|                             .                                 |
+-+-+-+-+-+-+-+-+-+-+-+-+-+-+-+-+-+-+-+-+-+-+-+-+-+-+-+-+-+-+-+-+
|                 Encoded-Joined Source Address-n               |
+-+-+-+-+-+-+-+-+-+-+-+-+-+-+-+-+-+-+-+-+-+-+-+-+-+-+-+-+-+-+-+-+
|                 Encoded-Pruned Source Address-1               |
+-+-+-+-+-+-+-+-+-+-+-+-+-+-+-+-+-+-+-+-+-+-+-+-+-+-+-+-+-+-+-+-+
|                             .                                 |
|                             .                                 |
+-+-+-+-+-+-+-+-+-+-+-+-+-+-+-+-+-+-+-+-+-+-+-+-+-+-+-+-+-+-+-+-+
|                 Encoded-Pruned Source Address-n               |
+-+-+-+-+-+-+-+-+-+-+-+-+-+-+-+-+-+-+-+-+-+-+-+-+-+-+-+-+-+-+-+-+
```

Figure 5.14. Join/Prune Message

Number of Joined Sources: Number of join source addresses listed for a given group.

Join Source Address 1 . . . n: This list contains the sources that the sending router will forward multicast datagrams for if received on the interface this message is sent on.

See Section 5.2.4.1. The field explanation for the encoded-source address format follows:

Reserved: Described above.

S—The Sparse bit is a 1-bit value, set to 1 for PIM SM. It is used for PIMv1 compatibility.

W—The WC-bit is a 1 bit value. If 1, the join or prune applies to the (*,G) or (*,*,RP) entry. If 0, the join or prune applies to the (S,G) entry where S is the source address. Joins and prunes sent toward the RP must have this bit set.

R—The RPT-bit is a 1-bit value. If 1, the information about (S,G) is sent toward the RP. If 0, the information must be sent toward S, where S is the source address.

Mask Length, Source Address: Described above.

Represented in the form of
<WC-bit><RPT-bit><Mask length><Source address>:

A source address could be a host IPv4 native encoding address:
<0><0><32><192.1.1.17>

A source address could be the RP's IP address:
<1><1><32><131.108.13.111>

A source address could be a subnet address to prune from the RP-tree:
<0><1><28><192.1.1.16>

A source address could be a general aggregate:
<0><0><16><192.1.0.0>

Number of Pruned Sources: Number of prune source addresses listed for a group.

Prune Source Address 1 ... n: This list contains the sources that the sending router does not want to forward multicast datagrams for when received on the interface this message is sent on. If the Join/Prune message boundary exceeds the maximum packet size, then the join and prune lists for the same group must be included in the same packet.

5.2.4.6 Bootstrap Message. The Bootstrap messages are multicast to the "ALL-PIM-ROUTERS" group, out to all interfaces having PIM neighbors (excluding the one over which the message was received). Bootstrap messages are sent with TTL value of 1. Bootstrap messages originate at the BSR and are forwarded by intermediate routers. If the original message exceeds the maximum packet size boundaries, the Bootstrap message is divided up into "semantic fragments."

The semantics of a single "fragment" is given in Figure 5.15.

PIM Version, Type, Reserved, and Checksum: Described above.

```
 0                   1                   2                   3
 0 1 2 3 4 5 6 7 8 9 0 1 2 3 4 5 6 7 8 9 0 1 2 3 4 5 6 7 8 9 0 1
+-+-+-+-+-+-+-+-+-+-+-+-+-+-+-+-+-+-+-+-+-+-+-+-+-+-+-+-+-+-+-+-+
|PIM Ver| Type  | Reserved      |             Checksum          |
+-+-+-+-+-+-+-+-+-+-+-+-+-+-+-+-+-+-+-+-+-+-+-+-+-+-+-+-+-+-+-+-+
|          Fragment Tag         | Hash Mask len | BSR-priority  |
+-+-+-+-+-+-+-+-+-+-+-+-+-+-+-+-+-+-+-+-+-+-+-+-+-+-+-+-+-+-+-+-+
|                  Encoded-Unicast-BSR-Address                  |
+-+-+-+-+-+-+-+-+-+-+-+-+-+-+-+-+-+-+-+-+-+-+-+-+-+-+-+-+-+-+-+-+
|                   Encoded-Group Address-1                     |
+-+-+-+-+-+-+-+-+-+-+-+-+-+-+-+-+-+-+-+-+-+-+-+-+-+-+-+-+-+-+-+-+
| RP-Count-1    | Frag RP-Cnt-1 |          Reserved             |
+-+-+-+-+-+-+-+-+-+-+-+-+-+-+-+-+-+-+-+-+-+-+-+-+-+-+-+-+-+-+-+-+
|                 Encoded-Unicast-RP-Address-1                  |
+-+-+-+-+-+-+-+-+-+-+-+-+-+-+-+-+-+-+-+-+-+-+-+-+-+-+-+-+-+-+-+-+
|          RP1-Holdtime         | RP1-Priority  |   Reserved    |
+-+-+-+-+-+-+-+-+-+-+-+-+-+-+-+-+-+-+-+-+-+-+-+-+-+-+-+-+-+-+-+-+
|                 Encoded-Unicast-RP-Address-2                  |
+-+-+-+-+-+-+-+-+-+-+-+-+-+-+-+-+-+-+-+-+-+-+-+-+-+-+-+-+-+-+-+-+
|          RP2-Holdtime         | RP2-Priority  |   Reserved    |
+-+-+-+-+-+-+-+-+-+-+-+-+-+-+-+-+-+-+-+-+-+-+-+-+-+-+-+-+-+-+-+-+
|                               .                               |
|                               .                               |
+-+-+-+-+-+-+-+-+-+-+-+-+-+-+-+-+-+-+-+-+-+-+-+-+-+-+-+-+-+-+-+-+
|                 Encoded-Unicast-RP-Address-m                  |
+-+-+-+-+-+-+-+-+-+-+-+-+-+-+-+-+-+-+-+-+-+-+-+-+-+-+-+-+-+-+-+-+
|          RPm-Holdtime         | RPm-Priority  |   Reserved    |
+-+-+-+-+-+-+-+-+-+-+-+-+-+-+-+-+-+-+-+-+-+-+-+-+-+-+-+-+-+-+-+-+
|                   Encoded-Group Address-2                     |
+-+-+-+-+-+-+-+-+-+-+-+-+-+-+-+-+-+-+-+-+-+-+-+-+-+-+-+-+-+-+-+-+
|                               .                               |
|                               .                               |
+-+-+-+-+-+-+-+-+-+-+-+-+-+-+-+-+-+-+-+-+-+-+-+-+-+-+-+-+-+-+-+-+
|                   Encoded-Group Address-n                     |
+-+-+-+-+-+-+-+-+-+-+-+-+-+-+-+-+-+-+-+-+-+-+-+-+-+-+-+-+-+-+-+-+
| RP-Count-n    | Frag RP-Cnt-n |          Reserved             |
+-+-+-+-+-+-+-+-+-+-+-+-+-+-+-+-+-+-+-+-+-+-+-+-+-+-+-+-+-+-+-+-+
|                 Encoded-Unicast-RP-Address-1                  |
+-+-+-+-+-+-+-+-+-+-+-+-+-+-+-+-+-+-+-+-+-+-+-+-+-+-+-+-+-+-+-+-+
|          RP1-Holdtime         | RP1-Priority  |   Reserved    |
+-+-+-+-+-+-+-+-+-+-+-+-+-+-+-+-+-+-+-+-+-+-+-+-+-+-+-+-+-+-+-+-+
|                 Encoded-Unicast-RP-Address-2                  |
+-+-+-+-+-+-+-+-+-+-+-+-+-+-+-+-+-+-+-+-+-+-+-+-+-+-+-+-+-+-+-+-+
|          RP2-Holdtime         | RP2-Priority  |   Reserved    |
+-+-+-+-+-+-+-+-+-+-+-+-+-+-+-+-+-+-+-+-+-+-+-+-+-+-+-+-+-+-+-+-+
|                               .                               |
|                               .                               |
|                               .                               |
+-+-+-+-+-+-+-+-+-+-+-+-+-+-+-+-+-+-+-+-+-+-+-+-+-+-+-+-+-+-+-+-+
|                 Encoded-Unicast-RP-Address-m                  |
+-+-+-+-+-+-+-+-+-+-+-+-+-+-+-+-+-+-+-+-+-+-+-+-+-+-+-+-+-+-+-+-+
|          RPm-Holdtime         | RPm-Priority  |   Reserved    |
+-+-+-+-+-+-+-+-+-+-+-+-+-+-+-+-+-+-+-+-+-+-+-+-+-+-+-+-+-+-+-+-+
```

Figure 5.15. Bootstrap Message

Fragment Tag: A randomly generated number, acts to distinguish the fragments belonging to different Bootstrap messages; fragments belonging to the same Bootstrap message carry the same fragment tag.

Hash Mask Length: The length (in bits) of the mask to use in the hash function. For IPv4 the RFC recommends a value of 30. For IPv6 the RFC recommends a value of 126.

BSR-Priority: Contains the BSR priority value of the included BSR. This field is considered as a high-order byte when comparing BSR addresses.

Encoded-Unicast-BSR Address: The address of the bootstrap router for the domain. The format for this address is given in the encoded-unicast address in Section 5.2.4.1.

"Encoded-Group Address 1 . . . n": The group prefix (address and mask) with which the C-RPs are associated. Format previously described.

RP-Count 1 . . . n: The number of C-RP addresses included in the whole Bootstrap message for the corresponding group prefix. A router does not replace its old RP-set for a given group prefix until/unless it receives RP-count addresses for that prefix; the addresses could be carried over several fragments. If only part of the RP-set for a given group prefix was received, the router discards it, without updating that specific group prefix's RP-set.

Frag RP-Cnt 1 . . . m: The number of C-RP addresses included in this fragment of the Bootstrap message for the corresponding group prefix. The Frag RP-Cnt field facilitates parsing of the RP-set for a given group prefix when carried over more than one fragment.

Encoded-Unicast-RP Address 1 . . . m: The address of the C-RPs for the corresponding group prefix. The format for this address is given in the encoded-unicast address in Section 4.1.

RP1 . . . m-Holdtime: The holdtime for the corresponding RP. This field is copied from the Holdtime field of the associated RP stored at the BSR.

RP1 . . . m-Priority: The "priority" of the corresponding RP and encoded-group address. This field is copied from the Priority field stored at the BSR when receiving a C-RP-Adv. The highest priority is 0 (i.e., the lower the value of the Priority field, the higher). Note that the priority is per RP per encoded-group address.

5.2.4.7   Assert Message.

The Assert message is sent when a multicast data packet is received on an outgoing interface corresponding to the (S,G) or (*,G) associated with the source. See Figure 5.16.

PIM Version, Type, Reserved, and Checksum: Described above.

Encoded-Group Address: The group address to which the data packet was addressed and which triggered the assert. Format previously described.

Encoded-Unicast-Source: Address source address from multicast datagram that triggered the assert packet to be sent. The format for this address is given in the encoded-unicast address in Section 4.1.

"R": RPT-bit is a 1-bit value. If the multicast datagram that triggered the assert packet is routed down the RP-tree, then the RPT-bit is 1; if the multicast datagram is routed down the SPT, it is 0.

Metric Preference: Preference value assigned to the unicast routing protocol that provided the route to the host address.

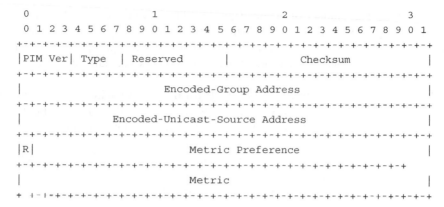

```
 0                   1                   2                   3
 0 1 2 3 4 5 6 7 8 9 0 1 2 3 4 5 6 7 8 9 0 1 2 3 4 5 6 7 8 9 0 1
+-+-+-+-+-+-+-+-+-+-+-+-+-+-+-+-+-+-+-+-+-+-+-+-+-+-+-+-+-+-+-+-+
|PIM Ver| Type  | Reserved      |            Checksum           |
+-+-+-+-+-+-+-+-+-+-+-+-+-+-+-+-+-+-+-+-+-+-+-+-+-+-+-+-+-+-+-+-+
|                      Encoded-Group Address                    |
+-+-+-+-+-+-+-+-+-+-+-+-+-+-+-+-+-+-+-+-+-+-+-+-+-+-+-+-+-+-+-+-+
|                  Encoded-Unicast-Source Address               |
+-+-+-+-+-+-+-+-+-+-+-+-+-+-+-+-+-+-+-+-+-+-+-+-+-+-+-+-+-+-+-+-+
|R|                    Metric Preference                        |
+-+-+-+-+-+-+-+-+-+-+-+-+-+-+-+-+-+-+-+-+-+-+-+-+-+-+-+-+-+-+-+-+
|                          Metric                               |
+-+-+-+-+-+-+-+-+-+-+-+-+-+-+-+-+-+-+-+-+-+-+-+-+-+-+-+-+-+-+-+-+
```

Figure 5.16. Assert Message

Metric: The unicast routing table metric. The metric is in units applicable to the unicast routing protocol used.

5.2.4.8 *Graft Message.* Used in dense mode.

5.2.4.9 *Graft-Ack Message.* Used in dense mode.

CANDIDATE-**RP**-ADVERTISEMENT. C-RP-Advs are periodically unicast from the C-RPs to the BSR. See Figure 5.17.
PIM Version, Type, Reserved, and Checksum: Described above.

```
 0                   1                   2                   3
 0 1 2 3 4 5 6 7 8 9 0 1 2 3 4 5 6 7 8 9 0 1 2 3 4 5 6 7 8 9 0 1
+-+-+-+-+-+-+-+-+-+-+-+-+-+-+-+-+-+-+-+-+-+-+-+-+-+-+-+-+-+-+-+-+
|PIM Ver| Type  | Reserved      |            Checksum           |
+-+-+-+-+-+-+-+-+-+-+-+-+-+-+-+-+-+-+-+-+-+-+-+-+-+-+-+-+-+-+-+-+
| Prefix-Cnt    | Priority      |            Holdtime           |
+-+-+-+-+-+-+-+-+-+-+-+-+-+-+-+-+-+-+-+-+-+-+-+-+-+-+-+-+-+-+-+-+
|                   Encoded-Unicast-RP-Address                  |
+-+-+-+-+-+-+-+-+-+-+-+-+-+-+-+-+-+-+-+-+-+-+-+-+-+-+-+-+-+-+-+-+
|                   Encoded-Group Address-1                     |
+-+-+-+-+-+-+-+-+-+-+-+-+-+-+-+-+-+-+-+-+-+-+-+-+-+-+-+-+-+-+-+-+
|                              .                                |
|                              .                                |
|                              .                                |
+-+-+-+-+-+-+-+-+-+-+-+-+-+-+-+-+-+-+-+-+-+-+-+-+-+-+-+-+-+-+-+-+
|                   Encoded-Group Address-n                     |
+-+-+-+-+-+-+-+-+-+-+-+-+-+-+-+-+-+-+-+-+-+-+-+-+-+-+-+-+-+-+-+-+
```

Figure 5.17. Candidate-RP-Advertisement

Prefix-Cnt: The number of encoded group addresses included in the message, indicating the group prefixes for which the C-RP is advertising. A Prefix-Cnt of 0 implies a prefix of 224.0.0.0 with mask length of 4, all multicast groups. If the C-RP is not configured with group prefix information, the C-RP puts a default value of 0 in this field.

Priority: The "priority" of the included RP for the corresponding encoded-group address (if any). highest priority is 0 (i.e., the lower the value of the Priority field, the higher the priority). This field is stored at the BSR upon receipt along with the RP address and corresponding encoded-group address.

Holdtime: The amount of time the advertisement is valid. This field allows advertisements to be aged out.

Encoded-Unicast-RP address: The address of the interface to advertise as a C-RP. The format for this address is given in the encoded-unicast address in Section 5.2.4.1.

IP Encoded-Group Address 1...*n*: The group prefixes for which the C-RP is advertising. Format previously described.

REFERENCES

[CIS200701] Cisco Systems, Internet Protocol (IP) Multicast Technology Overview, Cisco Systems, Inc., San Jose, CA.

[PAR200601] L. Parziale, W. Liu, et al., TCP/IP Tutorial and Technical Overview, IBM Press, Redbook Abstract, IBM Form Number GG24-3376-07, 2006.

[RFC2117] RFC 2117, Protocol Independent Multicast-Sparse Mode (PIM-SM): Protocol Specification, D. Farinacci, A. Helmy, et al., June 1997 (obsoleted by RFC 2362).

[RFC2201] RFC 2201, Core Based Trees (CBT) Multicast Routing Architecture, A. Ballardie, September 1997.

[RFC2362] RFC 2362, Protocol Independent Multicast-Sparse Mode (PIM-SM): Protocol Specification, D. Estrin, D. Farinacci, et al., June 1998.

[WEL200101] P. J. Welcher, The Protocols of IP Multicast, White Paper, Chesapeake NetCraftsmen, Arnold, MD.

6

MULTICAST ROUTING—SPARSE-MODE PROTOCOLS: CORE-BASED TREES

This chapter looks at multicast approaches that make use of Core-Based Trees (CBTs). The CBT protocol, defined in RFC 2201 and RFC 2189, is designed to build and maintain a shared multicast distribution tree that spans only networks and links that connect to active receivers. CBT is the earliest center-based tree protocol and it is the simplest. CBT was developed to address the issue of scalability: a shared tree architecture offers an improvement in scalability over source tree architectures by a factor of the number of active sources. Source trees scale $O(S \times G)$ because a distinct delivery tree is built per active source. Shared trees, on the contrary, eliminate the source (S) scaling factor; all sources use the same shared tree, and, therefore, shared trees scale $O(G)$. Core-based forwarding trees have a single node, for example, a router, known as the core of the tree, from which branches emanate; these branches are made up of other routers, known as noncore routers, that form a shortest path between a member host's directly attached router and the core. It should be noted that CBT's commercial deployment has been rather limited to this juncture. Three versions have evolved. But they are not backward compatible.[1]

[1]Version 2 of the CBT protocol specification differs significantly from the previous version. CBT Version 2 is not, and was not, intended to be backwards compatible with Version 1. The same is true for Version 3.

IP Multicast with Applications to IPTV and Mobile DVB-H   by Daniel Minoli
Copyright © 2008 John Wiley & Sons, Inc.

6.1 MOTIVATION

The Core-Based Tree Version 2 (CBTv2) network layer multicast routing protocol builds a shared multicast distribution tree per group. CBT is intended to support inter- and intradomain multicast routing. CBT may use a separate multicast routing table, or it may use that of underlying unicast routing, to establish paths between senders and receivers [RFC2189]. A CBT architecture is advantageous compared with the source-based architecture for the following reasons [BAL199301]:

   Scalability This is the fundamental premise for CBT. A core-based architecture allows the operator to significantly improve the overall scaling factor of $S \times G$ that one has in the source-based tree architecture to just G. This is the result of having just one multicast tree per group as opposed to one tree per (source, group) pair. Each router on the tree needs only store incident link information per group (i.e., per tree) as opposed to incident link information per (source, group) pair. This represents the minimum possible any router needs to store with respect to its membership of a particular group; routers not on the tree require no knowledge of the tree. CBT scales better than flood-and-prune protocols, particularly for sparse groups where only a small proportion of subnetworks have members because only routers on the distribution tree for a group keep forwarding a state for that group, and no router needs to keep information about any source [UCL200701]. Because CBT does not require a source-specific state, it is suited to applications that have many senders. Table 6.1, included in RFC 2189, compares for illustrative purposes the amount of state required by CBT and DVMRP for different group sizes with different numbers of active sources.

   Tree creation The formation of CBTs is receiver based; this means that no router resides on a tree for a particular group unless (i) that router itself is a member of that group or (ii) that router is on the path between a potential member and the tree, in which case that router must become part of the tree. Only one tree is ever created per group. This is of significant benefit to all routers on the

TABLE 6.1. Amount of State Required by CBT and DVMRP

No. of groups	10			100			1000		
Group size (# members)	20			40			60		
No. of srcs per group	10%	50%	100%	10%	50%	100%	10%	50%	100%
No. of DVMRP router entries	20K	100K	200K	4000K	2K	4K	6K	30K	60K
No. of CBT router entries	10			100			1000		

shortest path between a nonreceiver sender and the multicast tree since they incur no tree-building overhead.

Unicast routing separation CBT formation and multicast packet flow are decoupled from, but take full advantage of, underlying unicast routing, irrespective of which underlying unicast algorithm is being used. All of the multicast tree information can be derived solely from a router's existing unicast forwarding tables. These factors result in the CBT architecture being as robust as the underlying unicast routing algorithm (note that with respect to IP networks CBT requires no partition of the unicast address space). In this architecture there are two distinct routing phases:

- Unicast routing is used to route multicast packets to a multicast tree, allowing multicast groups and multicast packets to remain "invisible" to routers not on the tree. This is achieved by using the unicast address of the center (core) of the multicast spanning tree in the destination field of multicast packets originating off-tree.
- Once on the corresponding tree, multicast packets span the tree based on the packet's group identifier, or group-id (similar to a Class D IP address).

However, there are also weaknesses with one core-based multicast tree per group, including the following [BAL199301]:
- Core placement and shortest path trees. In practical implementations a manual "best guess" placement for the core router is used. However, CBTs may not provide the most optimal paths between members of a group; this is especially true for small, localized groups that have a nonlocal core. A dynamic core placement mechanism may have to be used. Without good core placement, CBTs can be inefficient; consequently, CBT has not been used as a global multicast routing protocol [UCL200701].
- The core as a point of failure. The most obvious point of vulnerability of a CBT is its core, whose failure can result in a tree becoming partitioned. Having multiple cores associated with each tree solves this problem (though at the cost of increased complexity).

Also, CBT never properly solved the problem of how to map a group address to the address of a core. In addition, good core placement is a hard problem.

6.2 BASIC OPERATION

In order to support multicast distribution, CBT builds a bidirectional shared tree. In a bidirectional shared tree the datagrams are able to flow both up the tree toward the core and down the tree away from the core, depending on the location of the source; the tree is shared by all sources to the group (note that SM PIM builds unidirectional shared

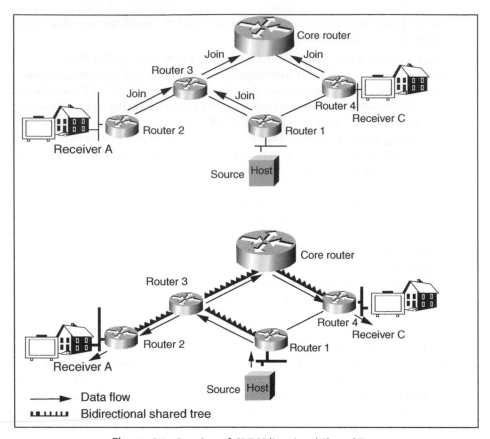

Figure 6.1. Creation of CBT Bidirectional Shared Tree

trees). When a receiver joins a multicast group, a multicast tree is built as follows (also see Figure 6.1): the receiver's local CBT router uses the multicast address to obtain the address of the core router for the group from its table. The local CBT router then sends a Join message for the group toward the core router. At each router on the way to the core router, forwarding state information is created for the group; additionally, an acknowledgment is sent back to the previous router.

After the bidirectional tree is built, if a sender (that happens to be a member of the group) needs to transmit multicast data to the group, the source's local router (router 1 in the example of Figure 6.1) forwards the packets to any of its neighbors that are on the multicast tree (router 3 in Figure 6.1). Each router that receives a packet forwards it out of all its interfaces that are on the tree except the one the packet came from (router 3 sends packets to router 2 and to the core router in Figure 6.1). It is conceivable that a sender's local router is not on the tree (recall that IP multicast does not require senders to a group to be members of the group). In this case, the datagram is forwarded to the next hop toward the core. At some point the datagram will either reach a router that is on the tree or reach the core; at that juncture the datagram is distributed along the multicast tree.

6.3   CBT COMPONENTS AND FUNCTIONS[2]

This section looks at CBT components and functions, as described in RFC 2201.

The CBT protocol is designed to build and maintain a shared multicast distribution tree that spans only those networks and links leading to the interested receivers. To achieve this, a host first expresses its interest in joining a group by multicasting an IGMP Host Membership Report (HMR) across its attached link. On receiving this report, a local CBT aware router invokes the tree joining process (unless it has already) by generating a JOIN_REQUEST message, which is sent to the next hop on the path toward the group's core router (how the local router discovers which core to join is discussed later). This Join message must be explicitly acknowledged (JOIN_ACK) either by the core router itself or by another router that is on the unicast path between the sending router and the core, which itself has already successfully joined the tree. Note that all CBT routers, similar to other multicast protocol routers, are expected to participate in IGMP for the purpose of monitoring directly attached group memberships and acting as IGMP querier when needed.

The Join message sets up a transient join state in the routers it traverses, and this state consists of <group, incoming interface, outgoing interface>. "Incoming interface" and "outgoing interface" may be "previous hop" and "next hop," respectively, if the corresponding links do not support multicast transmission. "Previous hop" is taken from the incoming control packet's IP source address, and "next hop" is gleaned from the routing table—the next hop to the specified core address. This transient state eventually times out unless it is "confirmed" with a join acknowledgment (JOIN_ACK) from upstream. The JOIN_ACK traverses the reverse path of the corresponding Join message, which is possible due to the presence of the transient join state. Once the acknowledgment reaches the router that originated the Join message, the new receiver can receive traffic sent to the group.

Loops cannot be created in a CBT because (i) there is only one active core per group and (ii) tree-building/maintenance scenarios that may lead to the creation of tree loops are avoided. For example, if a router's upstream neighbor becomes unreachable, the router immediately "flushes" all of its downstream branches, allowing them to individually rejoin if necessary. Transient unicast loops do not pose a threat because a new Join message that loops back on itself will never get acknowledged and thus eventually times out.

The state created in routers by the sending or receiving of a JOIN_ACK is bidirectional—data can flow either way along a tree "branch," and the state is group specific—it consists of the group address and a list of local interfaces over which Join messages for the group have previously been acknowledged. There is no concept of "incoming" or "outgoing" interfaces, though it is necessary to be able to distinguish the upstream interface from any downstream interfaces. In CBT, these interfaces are known as the "parent" and "child" interfaces, respectively.

With regards to the information contained in the multicast forwarding cache, on link types not supporting native multicast transmission an on-tree router must store the

---

[2]This section is based directly on RFC 2201.

address of a parent and any children. On links supporting multicast, however, parent and any child information is represented with local interface addresses (or similar identifying information, such as an interface "index") over which the parent or child is reachable.

When a multicast data packet arrives at a router, the router uses the group address as an index into the multicast forwarding cache. A copy of the incoming multicast data packet is forwarded over each interface (or to each address) listed in the entry except the incoming interface.

Each router that comprises a CBT multicast, except the core router, is responsible for maintaining its upstream link, provided it has interested downstream receivers, that is, the child interface list is not NULL. A child interface is one over which a member host is directly attached or one over which a downstream on-tree router is attached. This "tree maintenance" is achieved by each downstream router periodically sending a "Keepalive" message (ECHO_REQUEST) to its upstream neighbor, that is, its parent router on the tree. One Keepalive message is sent to represent entries with the same parent, thereby improving scalability on links that are shared by many groups. On multicast-capable links, a keepalive is multicast to the "all-cbt-routers" group (IANA assigned as 224.0.0.15); this has a suppressing effect on any other router for which the link is its parent link. If a parent link does not support multicast transmission, keepalives are unicast.

The receipt of a Keepalive message over a valid child interface immediately prompts a response (ECHO_REPLY), which is either unicast or multicast, as appropriate. The ECHO_REQUEST does not contain any group information; the ECHO_REPLY does, but only periodically. To maintain consistent information between parent and child, the parent periodically reports, in an ECHO_REPLY, all groups for which it has a state, over each of its child interfaces for those groups. This group-carrying echo reply is not prompted explicitly by the receipt of an Echo Request message. A child is notified of the time to expect the next Echo Reply message containing group information in an echo reply prompted by a child's echo request. The frequency of parent group reporting is at the granularity of minutes.

It cannot be assumed all of the routers on a multiaccess link have a uniform view of unicast routing; this is particularly the case when a multiaccess link spans two or more unicast routing domains. This could lead to multiple upstream tree branches being formed (an error condition) unless steps are taken to ensure all routers on the link agree, which is the upstream router for a particular group. CBT routers attached to a multiaccess link participate in an explicit election mechanism that elects a single router, the DR, as the link's upstream router for all groups. Since the DR might not be the link's best next hop for a particular core router, this may result in Join messages being redirected back across a multiaccess link. If this happens, the redirected Join message is unicast across the link by the DR to the best next hop, thereby preventing a looping scenario. This redirection only ever applies to Join messages. While this is suboptimal for Join messages, which are generated infrequently, multicast data never traverses a link more than once (either natively or encapsulated).

In all but the exception case described above, all CBT control messages are multicast over multicast supporting links to the "all-cbt-routers" group, with IP TTL 1. When a CBT control message is sent over a nonmulticast supporting link, it is explicitly addressed to the appropriate next hop.

6.3.1 CBT Control Message Retransmission Strategy

Certain CBT control messages illicit a response of some sort. Lack of response may be due to an upstream router crashing, or the loss of the original message, or its response. To detect these events, CBT retransmits those control messages for which it expects a response, if that response is not forthcoming within the retransmission interval, which varies depending on the type of message involved. There is an upper bound (typically three) on the number of retransmissions of the original message before an exception condition is raised.

For example, the exception procedure for the lack of response to an ECHO_ REQUEST is to send a QUIT_NOTIFICATION upstream and a FLUSH_TREE message downstream for the group. If this router has group members attached, it restarts the joining process to the group's core.

6.3.2 Nonmember Sending

If a nonmember sender's local router is already on tree for the group being sent to, the subnet's upstream router simply forwards the data packet over all outgoing interfaces corresponding to that group's forwarding cache entry. This is in contrast to PIM SM, which must encapsulate data from a nonmember sender, irrespective of whether the local router has joined the tree. This is due to PIM's unidirectional state.

If the sender's subnet is not attached to the group tree, the local DR must encapsulate the data packet and unicast it to the group's core router, where it is deencapsulated and disseminated over all tree interfaces, as specified by the core's forwarding cache entry for the group. The data packet encapsulation method is IP-in-IP. Routers in between a nonmember sender and the group's core need not know anything about the multicast group and indeed may even be multicast unaware. This makes CBT attractive for applications with nonmember senders.

6.4 CORE ROUTER DISCOVERY[3]

This section looks at CBT core router discovery, as described in RFC 2201.

Core router discovery is the most difficult aspect of shared tree multicast architectures, particularly in the context of Interdomain Multicast Routing (IDMR). There have been a number of proposals over the years, including advertising core addresses in a multicast session directory, manual placement, and the Hierarchical Protocol Independent Multicast (HPIM) approach of strictly dividing up the multicast address space into many "hierarchical scopes" and using explicit advertising of core routers between scope levels.

Two options for CBTv2 core discovery are the "bootstrap" mechanism and manual placement. The bootstrap mechanism (as specified with the PIM SM protocol) is applicable only to intradomain core discovery and allows for a "plug-and-play" type operation with minimal configuration. The disadvantage of the bootstrap mechanism is

---

[3]This section is based directly on RFC 2201.

that it is much more difficult to affect the shape, and thus optimality, of the resulting distribution tree. Also, it must be implemented by all CBT routers within a domain. It is unlikely at this stage that the bootstrap mechanism will be appended to a well-known network layer protocol, such as IGMP or ICMP, though this would facilitate its ubiquitous (intradomain) deployment. Therefore, each multicast routing protocol requiring the bootstrap mechanism must implement it as part of the multicast routing protocol itself.

Manual configuration of leaf routers with <core, group> mappings is the other option (*note:* leaf routers only); this imposes a degree of administrative burden: the mapping for a particular group must be coordinated across all leaf routers to ensure consistency. Hence, this method does not scale particularly well. However, it is likely that "better" trees will result from this method, and it is also the only available option for interdomain core discovery currently available. A summary of the operation of the bootstrap mechanism follows (the topic is also revisited in Section 6.5.11). It is assumed that all routers within the domain implement the "bootstrap" protocol, or at least forward bootstrap protocol messages.

A subset of the domain's routers are configured to be CBT candidate core routers. Each candidate core router periodically (default every 60 s) advertises itself to the domain's BSR using Core Advertisement messages. The BSR is itself elected dynamically from all (or participating) routers in the domain. The domain's elected BSR collects Core Advertisement messages from candidate core routers and periodically advertises a Candidate Core set (CC-set) to each other router in the domain using traditional hop-by-hop unicast forwarding. The BSR uses Bootstrap messages to advertise the CC-set. Together, Core Advertisement and Bootstrap messages comprise the bootstrap protocol.

When a router receives an IGMP host membership report from one of its directly attached hosts, the local router uses a hash function on the reported group address, the result of which is used as an index into the CC-set. This is how local routers discover which core to use for a particular group.

Note the hash function is specifically tailored such that a small number of consecutive groups always hash to the same core. Furthermore, Bootstrap messages can carry a "group mask," potentially limiting a CC-set to a particular range of groups. This can help reduce traffic concentration at the core.

If a BSR detects a particular core as being unreachable (it has not announced its availability within some period), it deletes the relevant core from the CC-set sent in its next Bootstrap message. This is how a local router discovers a group's core is unreachable; the router must rehash for each affected group and join the new core after removing the old state. The removal of the "old" state follows the sending of a QUIT_NOTIFICATION upstream and a FLUSH_TREE message downstream.

6.5 PROTOCOL SPECIFICATION DETAILS

In this section, details of the CBT protocol are presented in the context of a single router implementation based on RFC 2189.

6.5.1 CBT HELLO Protocol

The HELLO protocol is used to elect a DR on broadcast-type links. It is also used to elect a designated Border Router (BR) when interconnecting a CBT domain with other domains. Alternatively, the designated BR may be elected as a matter of local policy.

A router represents its status as a link's DR by setting the DR flag on that interface; a DR flag is associated with each of a router's broadcast interfaces. This flag can only assume one of the two values: TRUE or FALSE. By default, this flag is FALSE.

A network manager can preference a router's DR eligibility by optionally configuring a HELLO preference, which is included in the router's HELLO messages. Valid configuration values range from 1 to 254 (decimal), 1 representing the "most eligible" value. In the absence of explicit configuration, a router assumes the default HELLO preference value of 255. The elected DR uses HELLO preference zero (0) in HELLO advertisements, irrespective of any configured preference. The DR continues to use preference zero for as long as it is running.

HELLO messages are multicast periodically to the all-cbt-routers group, 224.0.0.15, using IP TTL 1. The advertisement period is [HELLO_INTERVAL] seconds. HELLO messages have a suppressing effect on those routers that would advertise a "lesser preference" in their HELLO messages; a router resets its [HELLO_INTERVAL] if the received HELLO is "better" than its own. Thus, in steady state, the HELLO protocol incurs very little traffic overhead. The DR election winner is that which advertises the lowest HELLO preference or the lowest addressed in the event of a tie.

The situation where two or more routers attached to the same broadcast link are advertising HELLO preference 0 should never arise. However, should this situation arise, all but the lowest addressed zero advertising router relinquishes its claim as DR immediately by unsetting the DR flag on the corresponding interface. The relinquishing router(s) subsequently advertise their previously used preference value in HELLO advertisements.

6.5.1.1 Sending HELLOs.
When a router starts up, it multicasts two HELLO messages over each of its broadcast interfaces in succession. The DR flag is initially unset (FALSE) on each broadcast interface. This avoids the situation in which each router on a multiaccess subnet believes it is the DR, thus preventing the multiple forwarding of Join requests should they arrive during this startup period. If no "better" HELLO message is received after holdtime seconds, the router assumes the role of DR on the corresponding interface. A router sends a HELLO message whenever its [HELLO_INTERVAL] expires. Whenever a router sends a HELLO message, it resets its hello timer.

6.5.1.2 Receiving HELLOs.
A router does not respond to a HELLO message if the received HELLO is "better" than its own or equally preferred but lower addressed. A router must respond to a HELLO message if that received is lesser preferred (or equally preferred but higher addressed) than would be sent by this router over the same interface. This response is sent on expiry of an interval timer that is

set between zero (0) and [HOLDTIME] seconds when the lesser preferenced HELLO message is received.

6.5.2   JOIN_REQUEST Processing

A JOIN_REQUEST is the CBT control message used to register a member host's interest in joining the distribution tree for the group.

6.5.2.1 Sending JOIN_REQUESTs.

A JOIN_REQUEST can only ever be originated by a leaf router, that is, a router with directly attached member hosts. This Join message is sent hop by hop toward the core router for the group. The originating router caches the <group, NULL, upstream interface> state for each join it originates. This state is known as "transient join state." The absence of a "downstream interface" (NULL) indicates that this router is the Join message originator and is therefore responsible for any retransmissions of this message if a response is not received within [RTX_INTERVAL]. It is an error if no response is received after [JOIN_TIMEOUT] seconds. If this error condition occurs, the joining process may be reinvoked by the receipt of the next IGMP host membership report from a locally attached member host.

Note that if the interface over which a JOIN_REQUEST is to be sent supports multicast, the JOIN_REQUEST is multicast to the all-cbt-routers group using IP TTL 1. If the link does not support multicast, the JOIN_REQUEST is unicast to the next hop on the unicast path to the group's core.

6.5.2.2 Receiving JOIN_REQUESTs.

On broadcast links, JOIN_REQUESTs that are multicast may only be forwarded by the link's DR. Other routers attached to the link may process the join (see below). JOIN_REQUESTs that are multicast over a point-to-point link are only processed by the router on the link that does not have a local interface corresponding to the join's network layer (IP) source address. Unicast JOIN_REQUESTs may only be processed by the router that has a local interface corresponding to the join's network layer (IP) destination address.

With regard to forwarding a received JOIN_REQUEST, if the receiving router is not on tree for the group, is not the group's core router, and has not already forwarded a join for the same group, the join is forwarded to the next hop on the path toward the core. The join is multicast or unicast according to whether the outgoing interface supports multicast. The router caches the following information with respect to the forwarded join: <group, downstream interface, upstream interface>. Subsequent JOIN_REQUESTs received for the same group are cached until this router has received a JOIN_ACK for the previously sent join, at which time any cached joins can also be acknowledged.

If this transient join state is not "confirmed" with a join acknowledgment (JOIN_ACK) message from upstream, the state is timed out after [TRANSIENT_TIMEOUT] seconds.

If the receiving router is the group's core router, the join is "terminated" and acknowledged by means of a JOIN_ACK. Similarly, if the router is on tree and the JOIN_REQUEST arrives over an interface that is not the upstream interface for the group, the join is acknowledged.

If a JOIN_REQUEST for the same group is scheduled to be sent over the corresponding interface (i.e., awaiting a timer expiry), the JOIN_REQUEST is unscheduled.

If this router has a cache-deletion timer [CACHE_DEL_TIMER] running on the arrival interface for the group specified in a multicast join, the timer is cancelled.

6.5.3 JOIN_ACK Processing

A JOIN_ACK is the mechanism by which an interface is added to a router's multicast forwarding cache; thus, the interface becomes part of the group distribution tree.

6.5.3.1 Sending JOIN_ACKs. The JOIN_ACK is sent over the same interface as the corresponding JOIN_REQUEST was received. The sending of the acknowledgement causes the router to add the interface to its child interface list in its forwarding cache for the group, if it is not already. A JOIN_ACK is multicast or unicast according to whether the outgoing interface supports multicast transmission or not.

6.5.3.2 Receiving JOIN_ACKs. The group and arrival interface must be matched to a <group, ..., upstream interface> from the router's cached transient state. If no match is found, the JOIN_ACK is discarded. If a match is found, a CBT forwarding cache entry for the group is created, with "upstream interface" marked as the group's parent interface.

If "downstream interface" in the cached transient state is NULL, the JOIN_ACK has reached the originator of the corresponding JOIN_REQUEST; the JOIN_ACK is not forwarded downstream. If downstream interface is non-NULL, a JOIN_ACK for the group is sent over the downstream interface (multicast or unicast, accordingly). This interface is installed in the child interface list of the group's forwarding cache entry. Once the transient state has been confirmed by transferring it to the forwarding cache, the transient state is deleted.

6.5.4 QUIT_NOTIFICATION Processing

A CBT is "pruned" in the direction downstream to upstream whenever a CBT router's child interface list for a group becomes null.

6.5.4.1 Sending QUIT_NOTIFICATIONs. A QUIT_NOTIFICATION is sent to a router's parent router on the tree whenever the router's child interface list becomes null. If the link over which the quit is to be sent supports multicast transmission, and the sending router is the link's DR, the quit is unicast, otherwise it is multicast.

A QUIT_NOTIFICATION is not acknowledged; once sent, all information pertaining to the group it represents is deleted from the forwarding cache immediately.

To help ensure consistency between a child and parent router given the potential for loss of a QUIT_NOTIFICATION, a total of [MAX_RTX] QUIT_NOTIFICATIONs are sent, each holdtime seconds after the previous one.

The sending of a quit (the first) also invokes the sending of a FLUSH_TREE message over each downstream interface for the corresponding group.

6.5.4.2 Receiving QUIT_NOTIFICATIONs. The group reported in the QUIT_NOTIFICATION must be matched with a forwarding cache entry. If no match is found, the QUIT_NOTIFICATION is ignored and discarded. If a match is found and the arrival interface is a valid child interface in the group entry, how the router proceeds depends on whether the QUIT_NOTIFICATION was multicast or unicast.

If the QUIT_NOTIFICATION was unicast, the corresponding child interface is deleted from the group's forwarding cache entry, and no further processing is required.

If the QUIT_NOTIFICATION was multicast and the arrival interface is a valid child interface for the specified group, the router sets a cache-deletion timer [CACHE_DEL_TIMER].

Because this router might be acting as a parent router for multiple downstream routers attached to the arrival link, [CACHE_DEL_TIMER] interval gives those routers that did not send the QUIT_NOTIFICATION, but received it over their parent interface, the opportunity to ensure that the parent router does not remove the link from its child interface list. Therefore, on receipt of a multicast QUIT_NOTIFICATION over a parent interface, a receiving router schedules a JOIN_REQUEST for the group for sending at a random interval between 0 (zero) and holdtime seconds. If a multicast JOIN_REQUEST is received over the corresponding interface (parent) for the same group before this router sends its own scheduled JOIN_REQUEST, it unschedules the multicasting of its own JOIN_REQUEST.

6.5.5   ECHO_REQUEST Processing

The ECHO_REQUEST message allows a child to monitor reachability to its parent router for a group (or range of groups if the parent router is the parent for multiple groups). Group information is not carried in ECHO_REQUEST messages.

6.5.5.1 Sending ECHO_REQUESTs. Whenever a router creates a forwarding cache entry due to the receipt of a JOIN_ACK, the router begins the periodic sending of ECHO_REQUEST messages over its parent interface. The ECHO_REQUEST is multicast to the "all-cbt-routers" group over multicast-capable interfaces, unless the sending router is the DR on the interface over which the ECHO_REQUEST is being sent, in which case it is unicast (as is the corresponding ECHO_REPLY).

ECHO_REQUEST messages are sent at [ECHO_INTERVAL] second intervals. Whenever an ECHO_REQUEST is sent, [ECHO_INTERVAL] is reset. If no response is forthcoming, any groups present on the parent interface will eventually expire [GROUP_EXPIRE_TIME]. This results in the sending of a QUIT_NOTIFICATION upstream and a FLUSH_TREE message downstream for each group for which the upstream interface was the parent interface.

6.5.5.2 Receiving ECHO_REQUESTs. If an ECHO_REQUEST is received over any valid child interface, the receiving router schedules an ECHO_REPLY message for sending over the same interface; the scheduled interval is between 0 (zero) and holdtime seconds. This message is multicast to the "all-cbt-routers" group over multicast-capable interfaces and unicast otherwise.

If a multicast ECHO_REQUEST message arrives via any valid parent interface, the router resets its [ECHO_INTERVAL] timer for that upstream interface, thereby suppressing the sending of its own ECHO_REQUEST over that upstream interface.

6.5.6 ECHO_REPLY Processing

ECHO_REPLY messages allow a child to monitor the reachability of its parent and help to ensure the group state information is consistent between them.

6.5.6.1 Sending ECHO_REPLY Messages. An ECHO_REPLY message is sent in response to receiving an ECHO_REQUEST message provided the ECHO_REQUEST is received over any one of this router's valid child interfaces. An ECHO_REPLY reports all groups for which the link is its child. ECHO_REPLY messages are unicast or multicast, as appropriate.

6.5.6.2 Receiving ECHO_REPLY Messages. An ECHO_REPLY message must be received via a valid parent interface. For each group reported in an ECHO_REPLY, the downstream router attempts to match the group with one in its forwarding cache for which the arrival interface is the group's parent interface. For each successful match, the entry is "refreshed." If however, after [GROUP_EXPIRE_TIME] seconds a group has not been refreshed, a QUIT_NOTIFICATION is sent upstream, and a FLUSH_TREE message is sent downstream, for the group.

If this router has directly attached members for any of the flushed groups, the receipt of an IGMP host membership report for any of those groups will prompt this router to rejoin the corresponding tree(s).

6.5.7 FLUSH_TREE Processing

The FLUSH_TREE (flush) message is the mechanism by which a router invokes the tearing down of all its downstream branches for a particular group. The flush message is multicast to the "all-cbt-routers" group when sent over multicast-capable interfaces and unicast otherwise.

6.5.7.1 Sending FLUSH_TREE Messages. A FLUSH_TREE message is sent over each downstream (child) interface when a router has lost reachability with its parent router for the group (detected via ECHO_REQUEST and ECHO_REPLY messages). All of the group state is removed from an interface over which a Flush message is sent. A flush can specify a single group or all groups (INADDR_ANY).

6.5.7.2 Receiving FLUSH_TREE Messages. A FLUSH_TREE message must be received over the parent interface for the specified group; otherwise the message is discarded. The Flush message must be forwarded over each child interface for the specified group. Once the Flush message has been forwarded, all of the state for the group is removed from the router's forwarding cache.

6.5.8   Nonmember Sending

Data can be sent to a CBT by a sender not attached to the group tree. The sending host originates native multicast data, which is promiscuously received by a local router, which must be CBT capable. It is assumed the local CBT router knows about the relevant <core, group> mapping and thus can encapsulate (IP-in-IP) the data packet and unicast it to the corresponding core router. On arriving at the core router, the data packet is deencapsulated and disseminated over the group tree in the manner already described.

6.5.9   Timers and Default Values

This section provides a summary of the timers described above together with their recommended default values. Other values may be configured; if so, the values used should be consistent across all CBT routers attached to the same network.

- [HELLO_INTERVAL]: the interval between sending a Hello message. Default: 60 s.
- [HELLO_PREFERENCE]: default: 255 s.
- [HOLDTIME]: generic response interval. Default: 3 s.
- [MAX_RTX]: default maximum number of retransmissions. Default: 3 s.
- [RTX_INTERVAL]: message retransmission time. Default: 5 s.
- [JOIN_TIMEOUT]: raise exception due to tree join failure. Default: $(3.5 \times [\text{RTX\_INTERVAL}])$ s.
- [TRANSIENT_TIMEOUT]: delete (unconfirmed) transient state. Default: $(1.5 \times [\text{RTX\_INTERVAL}])$ s.
- [CACHE_DEL_TIMER]: remove child interface from forwarding cache. Default: $(1.5 \times [\text{HOLDTIME}])$ s.
- [GROUP_EXPIRE_TIME]: time to send a QUIT_NOTIFICATION to our nonresponding parent. Default: $(1.5 \times [\text{ECHO\_INTERVAL}])$ s.
- [ECHO_INTERVAL]: interval between sending ECHO_REQUEST to parent routers. Default: 60 s.
- [EXPECTED_REPLY_TIME]: consider parent unreachable. Default: 70 s.

6.5.10   CBT Packet Formats and Message Types

CBT control packets are encapsulated in IP. CBT has been assigned IP number 7 by IANA.

Figure 6.2. CBT Common Control Packet Header

6.5.10.1 *CBT Common Control Packet Header.* All CBT control messages have a common fixed-length header, as shown in Figure 6.2.

This CBT specification is Version 2.

CBT packet types are:

- Type 0: HELLO
- Type 1: JOIN_REQUEST
- Type 2: JOIN_ACK
- Type 3: QUIT_NOTIFICATION
- Type 4: ECHO_REQUEST
- Type 5: ECHO_REPLY
- Type 6: FLUSH_TREE
- Type 7: Bootstrap message (optional)
- Type 8: Candidate Core Advertisement (optional)
- Address length: address length in bytes of unicast or multicast addresses carried in the control packet.
- Checksum: the 16-bit one's complement of the one's complement sum of the entire CBT control packet.

6.5.10.2 *HELLO Packet Format.* The HELLO packet format is shown in Figure 6.3.

HELLO packet field definitions:

- Preference: sender's HELLO preference.
- Option type: the type of option present in the Option Value field. One option type is currently defined: option type 0 (zero) = BR_HELLO; option value 0 (zero);

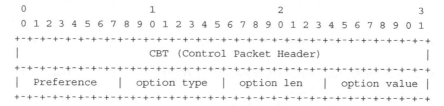

Figure 6.3. HELLO Packet Format

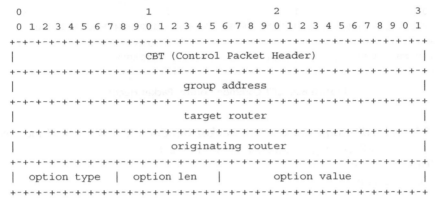

Figure 6.4. JOIN_REQUEST Packet Format

option length 0 (zero). This option type is used with HELLO messages sent by a BR as part of designated BR election.

- Option length: length of the Option Value field in bytes.
- Option value: variable-length field carrying the option value.

6.5.10.3 JOIN_REQUEST Packet Format.   JOIN_REQUEST packet format is shown in Figure 6.4.

JOIN_REQUEST field definitions:

- Group address: multicast group address of the group being joined. For a "wildcard" join this field contains the value of INADDR_ANY.
- Target router: target (core) router for the group.
- Originating router: router that originated this JOIN_REQUEST.
- Option type, option length, and option value: see HELLO packet format.

6.5.10.4 JOIN_ACK Packet Format.   The JOIN_ACK packet format is shown in Figure 6.5.

JOIN_ACK field definitions:

- Group address: multicast group address of the group being joined.
- Target router: router (DR) that originated the corresponding JOIN_REQUEST.
- Option type, option length, and option value: see HELLO packet format.

6.5.10.5 QUIT_NOTIFICATION Packet Format.   The QUIT_NOTIFICATION packet format is shown in Figure 6.6.

QUIT_NOTIFICATION field definitions:

- Group address: multicast group address of the group being joined.

```
 0                   1                   2                   3
 0 1 2 3 4 5 6 7 8 9 0 1 2 3 4 5 6 7 8 9 0 1 2 3 4 5 6 7 8 9 0 1
+-+-+-+-+-+-+-+-+-+-+-+-+-+-+-+-+-+-+-+-+-+-+-+-+-+-+-+-+-+-+-+-+
|                   CBT (Control Packet Header)                 |
+-+-+-+-+-+-+-+-+-+-+-+-+-+-+-+-+-+-+-+-+-+-+-+-+-+-+-+-+-+-+-+-+
|                        group address                         |
+-+-+-+-+-+-+-+-+-+-+-+-+-+-+-+-+-+-+-+-+-+-+-+-+-+-+-+-+-+-+-+-+
|                        target router                         |
+-+-+-+-+-+-+-+-+-+-+-+-+-+-+-+-+-+-+-+-+-+-+-+-+-+-+-+-+-+-+-+-+
|  option type  |  option len   |        option value          |
+-+-+-+-+-+-+-+-+-+-+-+-+-+-+-+-+-+-+-+-+-+-+-+-+-+-+-+-+-+-+-+-+
```

Figure 6.5. JOIN_ACK Packet Format

- Originating child router: address of the router that originates the QUIT_NOTIFICATION.

6.5.10.6 ECHO_REQUEST Packet Format. The ECHO_REQUEST packet format is shown in Figure 6.7.

```
 0                   1                   2                   3
 0 1 2 3 4 5 6 7 8 9 0 1 2 3 4 5 6 7 8 9 0 1 2 3 4 5 6 7 8 9 0 1
+-+-+-+-+-+-+-+-+-+-+-+-+-+-+-+-+-+-+-+-+-+-+-+-+-+-+-+-+-+-+-+-+
|                   CBT (Control Packet Header)                 |
+-+-+-+-+-+-+-+-+-+-+-+-+-+-+-+-+-+-+-+-+-+-+-+-+-+-+-+-+-+-+-+-+
|                        group address                         |
+-+-+-+-+-+-+-+-+-+-+-+-+-+-+-+-+-+-+-+-+-+-+-+-+-+-+-+-+-+-+-+-+
|                   originating child router                   |
+-+-+-+-+-+-+-+-+-+-+-+-+-+-+-+-+-+-+-+-+-+-+-+-+-+-+-+-+-+-+-+-+
```

Figure 6.6. QUIT_NOTIFICATION Packet Format

```
 0                   1                   2                   3
 0 1 2 3 4 5 6 7 8 9 0 1 2 3 4 5 6 7 8 9 0 1 2 3 4 5 6 7 8 9 0 1
+-+-+-+-+-+-+-+-+-+-+-+-+-+-+-+-+-+-+-+-+-+-+-+-+-+-+-+-+-+-+-+-+
|                   CBT (Control Packet Header)                 |
+-+-+-+-+-+-+-+-+-+-+-+-+-+-+-+-+-+-+-+-+-+-+-+-+-+-+-+-+-+-+-+-+
|                   originating child router                   |
+-+-+-+-+-+-+-+-+-+-+-+-+-+-+-+-+-+-+-+-+-+-+-+-+-+-+-+-+-+-+-+-+
```

Figure 6.7. ECHO_REQUEST Packet Format

ECHO_REQUEST field definitions:

- Originating child router: address of the router that originates the ECHO_REQUEST.

6.5.10.7 ECHO_REPLY Packet Format. The ECHO_REPLY packet format is shown in Figure 6.8.
ECHO_REPLY field definitions:

- Originating parent router: address of the router originating this ECHO_REPLY.
- Group address: a list of multicast group addresses for which this router considers itself a parent router with respect to the link over which this message is sent.

6.5.10.8 FLUSH_TREE Packet Format. The FLUSH_TREE packet format is shown in Figure 6.9.
FLUSH_TREE field definitions:

- Group address(es): multicast group address(es) of the group(s) being "flushed."

6.5.11 Core Router Discovery

As discussed earlier in the chapter, there are two available options for CBTv2 core discovery; the bootstrap mechanism (as currently specified with the PIM SM protocol) is applicable only to intradomain core discovery and allows for a "plug and play" type

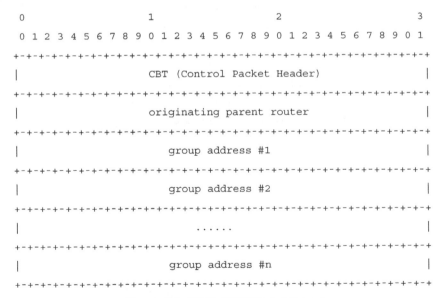

Figure 6.8. ECHO_REPLY Packet Format

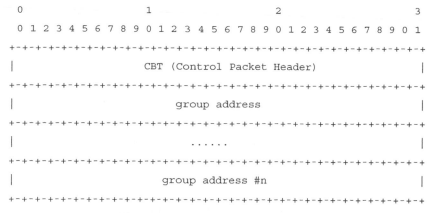

Figure 6.9. FLUSH_TREE Packet Format

operation with minimal configuration. The disadvantage of the bootstrap mechanism is that it is much more difficult to affect the shape, and thus optimality, of the resulting distribution tree. Also, to be applicable, all CBT routers within a domain must implement the bootstrap mechanism.

The other option is to manually configure leaf routers with <core, group> mappings (*note:* leaf routers only); this imposes a degree of administrative burden—the mapping for a particular group must be coordinated across all leaf routers to ensure consistency. Hence, this method does not scale particularly well. However, it is likely that "better" trees will result from this method, and it is also the only available option for interdomain core discovery currently available.

6.5.11.1 Bootstrap Mechanism.

It is unlikely that the bootstrap mechanism will be appended to a well-known network layer protocol, such as IGMP, though this would facilitate its ubiquitous (intradomain) deployment. Therefore, each multicast routing protocol requiring the bootstrap mechanism must implement it as part of the multicast routing protocol itself. A summary of the operation of the bootstrap mechanism follows. It is assumed that all routers within the domain implement the bootstrap protocol, or at least forward bootstrap protocol messages.

A subset of the domain's routers are configured to be CBT candidate core routers. Each candidate core router periodically (default every 60 s) advertises itself to the domain's BSR, using Core Advertisement messages. The BSR is itself elected dynamically from all (or participating) routers in the domain. The domain's elected BSR collects Core Advertisement messages from candidate core routers and periodically advertises a CC-set to each other router in the domain using traditional hop-by-hop unicast forwarding. The BSR uses Bootstrap messages to advertise the CC-set. Together, Core Advertisements and Bootstrap messages comprise the bootstrap protocol.

When a router receives an IGMP host membership report from one of its directly attached hosts, the local router uses a hash function on the reported group address, the

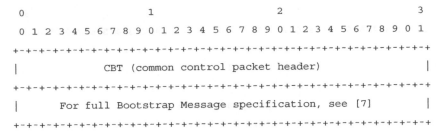

Figure 6.10. Bootstrap Message Format

result of which is used as an index into the CC-set. This is how local routers discover which core to use for a particular group.

Note the hash function is specifically tailored such that a small number of consecutive groups always hash to the same core. Furthermore, Bootstrap messages can carry a "group mask," potentially limiting a CC-set to a particular range of groups. This can help reduce traffic concentration at the core.

If a BSR detects a particular core as being unreachable (it has not announced its availability within some period), it deletes the relevant core from the CC-set sent in its next Bootstrap message. This is how a local router discovers a group's core is unreachable; the router must rehash for each affected group and join the new core after removing the old state. The removal of the "old" state follows the sending of a QUIT_NOTIFICATION upstream and a FLUSH_TREE message downstream.

6.5.11.2 Bootstrap Message Format.   The Bootstrap message format is shown in Figure 6.10.

6.5.11.3 Candidate Core Advertisement Message Format.   The Candidate Core Advertisement message format is shown in Figure 6.11.

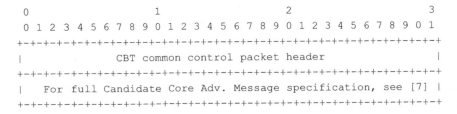

Figure 6.11. Candidate Core Advertisement Message Format

6.6 CBT VERSION 3

The CBT Version 3 specification published as an Internet Draft in 1988 superceded and obsoleted RFC 2189. Changes from RFC 2189 include support for source-specific joining and pruning to provide better CBT transit domain capability, new packet formats, and new robustness features. Unfortunately, most of these changes are not backward compatible with RFC 2189; however, neither at that time nor now has CBT enjoyed widespread implementation or deployment. Specifically, changes from RFC 2189 are [BAL199801]:

- Forwarding cache support for entries of different granularities, that is, (*, G), (*, Core), or (S, G) and support for S and/or G masks for representing S and/or G aggregates
- Included support for joins, quits (prunes), and flushes of different granularities, that is, (*, G), (*, Core), or (S, G), where S and/or G can be aggregated
- Optional one-way join capability
- Improved the LAN HELLO protocol and included a state diagram
- Revised packet format and provided option support for all control packets
- Added downstream state timeout to CBT router
- Revised the CBT "keepalive" mechanism between adjacent on-tree CBT routers
- Overall provided added clarification of protocol events and mechanisms

A brief description of the CBTv3 protocol follows below, based directly on [BAL199801]; it incorporates many of the CBTv2 capabilities described earlier, although, as noted, it is not backward compatible.

6.6.1 The First Step: Joining the Tree

As a first step, a host first expresses its interest in joining a group by multicasting an IGMP host membership report across its attached link. Note that all CBT routers, similar to other multicast protocol routers, are expected to participate in IGMP for the purpose of monitoring directly attached group memberships and acting as IGMP queriers when needed. On receiving an IGMP host membership report, a local CBT router invokes the tree-joining process (unless it has already) by generating a JOIN_REQUEST message, which is sent to the next hop on the path towards the group's core router (how the local router must discover which core to join). This Join message must be explicitly acknowledged (JOIN_ACK) either by the core router itself or by another router that is on the path between the sending router and the core, which itself has already successfully joined the tree.

By default, JOINS/JOIN_ACKS create a bidirectional forwarding state, that is, data can flow in the direction downstream - to upstream or upstream - to downstream. In some circumstances a JOIN/JOIN_ACK may include an option which instantiates a unidirectional forwarding state; an interface over which a unidirectional JOIN_ACK is forwarded (not received) is automatically marked as pruned. Data is permitted to be received via a pruned interface but must not be forwarded over a pruned interface. Prune state can also be instantiated by the QUIT_NOTIFICATION message (see Section 6.6.8).

A JOIN_REQUEST is made unidirectional by the inclusion of the "unidirectional" JOIN option that is copied to the corresponding JOIN_REQUEST options are always copied to the corresponding JOIN_ACK.

CBT now supports source-specific joins/prunes so as to be better equipped when deployed in a transit domain; source-specific control messages are only ever generated by CBT BRs. Source-specific control messages follow G, not S, that is, they are routed toward the core (not S) and no further. Thus, the (S, G) state only exists on the "core tree" in a CBT domain—those routers and links between a BR and a core router.

6.6.2 Transient State

The Join message sets up a transient join state in the router that originates it (a LAN's DR) and the routers it traverses (an exception is described in Section 6.6.9), and this state consists of <group, [source], downstream address, upstream address>; "source" is optional and relevant only to source-specific control messages.

On broadcast networks "downstream address" is the local IP address of the interface over which this router received the join (or IGMP host membership report), and "upstream address" is the local IP address of the interface over which this router forwarded the join (according to this router's routing table). On nonbroadcast networks "downstream address" is the IP address of the join's previous hop, and "upstream address" is the IP address of the next hop (according to this router's routing table). The transient state eventually times out unless the join is explicitly acknowledged. When a join is acknowledged, the transient join state is transferred to the router's multicast forwarding cache, thus becoming "permanent."

If "downstream address" implies a broadcast LAN, the transient state must be able to distinguish between a member host being reachable over that interface and a downstream router being reachable over that interface. This is necessary so that, on receipt of a JOIN_ACK, a router with a transient state knows whether "downstream address" only leads to a group member, in which case the JOIN_ACK need not be forwarded, or whether "downstream address" leads to a downstream router that either originated or forwarded the join prior to this router receiving it, in which case this router must forward a received JOIN_ACK. Precisely how this distinction is made is implementation dependent. A router must also be able to distinguish these two conditions with respect to its forwarding cache.

6.6.3 Getting "On Tree"

A router that terminates a JOIN_REQUEST (see Section 6.6.8) sends a JOIN_ACK in response. A join acknowledgment (JOIN_ACK) traverses the reverse path of the corresponding Join message which is possible due to the presence of the transient join state. Once the acknowledgment reaches the router that originated the Join message, the new receiver can receive traffic sent to the group.

A router is not considered "on tree" until it has received a JOIN_ACK for a previously sent/forwarded JOIN_REQUEST and has instantiated the relevant forwarding state.

Loops cannot be created in a CBT because (a) there is only one active core per group and (b) tree-building/maintenance scenarios that may lead to the creation of tree loops are avoided. For example, if a router's parent router for a group becomes unreachable, the router (child) immediately "flushes" all of its downstream branches, allowing them to individually rejoin if necessary. Transient unicast loops do not pose a threat because a new Join message that loops back on itself will never get acknowledged and thus eventually times out.

6.6.4 Pruning and Prune State

Any of a forwarding cache entry's children can be "pruned" by the immediate downstream router (child); in CBT, pruning is implemented by means of the QUIT_NOTIFICATION message, which is sent hop by hop in the direction downstream to upstream. A pruned child must be distinguishable from a nonpruned child—how is implementation dependent. One possible way would be to associate a "prune bit" with each child in the forwarding cache.

The granularity of a quit (prune) can be (*, G), (*, Core), or (S, G). (*, Core) and (S, G) prunes are only relevant to core tree branches, that is, those routers between a CBT BR and a core (inclusive). (*, G) prunes are applicable anywhere on a CBT.

In previous versions of CBT, a quit was sent by a child router to cause its parent to remove it from the tree. While this capability remains, in this version of CBT a quit can also be sent by a child to make the parent's forwarding state more specific. Refer to Section 6.6.8 for the procedures relating to receiving and forwarding a Quit (Prune) message.

Data is permitted to be received via a pruned interface but must not be forwarded over a pruned interface. Thus, pruning is always unidirectional—it can stop data flowing downstream but does not prevent data from flowing upstream.

CBT BRs are able to take advantage of this unidirectionality; if the BR does not have any directly attached group members and is not serving a neighboring domain with group traffic, it can elect not to receive traffic for the group which is sourced inside, or received via, the CBT domain. At the same time, if the BR is the ingress BR for a particular (*, G), or (S, G), externally sourced traffic for (*, G) or (S, G) need not be encapsulated by the ingress BR and unicast to the relevant core router—the BR can send the traffic using native IP multicast.

6.6.5 The Forwarding Cache

A CBT router must implement a multicast forwarding cache which supports source-specific [i.e., (S, G)] as well as source-independent [i.e., (*, G) and (*, Core)] entries. This forwarding cache is known as the router's Private CBT Forwarding Cache (PFC).

All implementations should also implement a shared (i.e., protocol-independent) multicast forwarding cache—to facilitate interoperability—which is only used by BRs and shared by all protocols operating on the BR (hence "shared"). This forwarding cache is known as the router's Shared Forwarding Cache, or SFC. By having all CBT implementations support an SFC, any CBT router is eligible to become a BR.

(*, Core) entries are only relevant to a CBT PFC. This state is represented in the cache by specifying the core's IP unicast address in place of a group address/group address range.

With respect to representing groups (Gs) in the forwarding cache, G may be an individual Class D 32-bit group address or a prefix representing a contiguous range of group addresses (a group aggregate). Similarly, for source-specific PFC entries, S can be an aggregate. Therefore, the PFC should support the inclusion of masks or mask lengths to be associated with each of S and G.

In CBT, all PFC entries require that an entry's "upstream" interface is distinguishable as such—how is implementation dependent. CBT uses the term "parent" interchangeably with "upstream" and "child/children" interchangeably with "downstream." A core router's parent is always NULL.

Whenever the sending/receiving of a CBT join or prune results in the instantiation of a more specific state in the router [e.g., a (*, Core) state exists, then a (*, G) join arrives], the children of the new entry represent the union of the children from all other less specific forwarding cache entries as well as the child (interface) over which the message was received (if not already included). This is so that at most a single forwarding cache entry needs to be matched with an incoming packet.

Note that in CBT there is no notion of "expected" or "incoming" interface for (S, G) forwarding entries—these are treated just like (*, G) entries.

A forwarding cache entry whose children are all marked as pruned as a result of receiving Quit messages may delete the entry provided there exists no less specific state with at least one nonpruned child.

6.6.6 Packet Forwarding

When a data packet arrives, the forwarding cache is searched for a best matching (according to longest match) entry. If no match is found, the packet is discarded. If the packet arrived natively, it is accepted if it arrives via an on-tree interface, that is, any interface listed in a matching entry; otherwise the packet is discarded. Assuming the packet is accepted, a copy of the packet is forwarded over each other (outgoing) nonpruned interface listed in the matching entry.

If the packet arrived IP-in-IP encapsulated and the packet has reached its final destination, the packet is deencapsulated and treated as described above, except the packet need not have arrived via an on-tree interface according to the matching entry.

6.6.7 The "Keepalive" Protocol

The CBT forwarding state created by JOIN/ACK messages is the soft state. This soft state is maintained by a separate keepalive mechanism rather than by JOIN/ACK refreshes.

The CBT keepalive mechanism operates between adjacent on-tree routers. The keepalive mechanism is implemented by means of group-specific ECHO_REQUEST and ECHO_REPLY messages, with the child routers responsible for periodically (explicitly) querying the parent router. The parent router (implicitly) monitors its children by expecting to periodically receive queries (ECHO_REQUESTs) from each child (per child router on nonbroadcast networks; per child interface on broadcast networks). The repeated absence of either an expected query (ECHO_REQUEST) or expected response (ECHO_REPLY) results in the corresponding interface being marked as pruned in the router's forwarding cache. This constitutes a state timeout due to an exception condition. An interface can also be pruned in an explicit and timely fashion by means of either a QUIT_NOTIFICATION (downstream to upstream) or FLUSH_TREE (upstream to downstream) message.

Note that the network path comprising a CBT branch only changes due to connectivity failure. An implementation could, however, invoke the tearing down and rebuilding of a tree branch whenever an underlying routing change occurs, irrespective of whether that change is due to connectivity failure. This is not CBT's default behavior.

6.6.8 Control Message Precedence and Forwarding Criteria

When a router receives a CBT Join or (Quit) Prune message, if the message contains a state for which the receiving router has no matching (according to longest match) state in its forwarding cache, the receiving router creates a forwarding cache entry for the corresponding state and forwards the control message upstream.

CBT Join and Quit (Prune) messages are forwarded as far upstream as the corresponding core router, or the first router encountered with an equally or less specific state and at least one other nonpruned child for that state. The forwarding state corresponding exactly to the granularity of the join/quit is instantiated in all routers between the join/quit originator and join/quit terminator, inclusive.

A router with a forwarding cache entry whose children are all pruned can remove (delete) the corresponding entry unless there exists a less specific state with at least one nonpruned child. If an entry is eligible for deletion, a quit representing the same granularity as the forwarding cache entry is sent upstream.

CBT Flush messages are forwarded downstream removing all equally and more specific state. A Flush message is terminated by a leaf router or a router with a less specific state; the flush message does not affect the terminating router's less specific state.

6.6.9 Broadcast LANs

It cannot be assumed that all of the routers on a broadcast link have a uniform view of unicast routing; this is particularly the case when a broadcast link spans two or more unicast routing domains. This could lead to multiple upstream tree branches being formed for any one group (an error condition) unless steps are taken to ensure all routers on the link agree on a single LAN upstream forwarding router. CBT routers attached to a broadcast link participate in an explicit election mechanism that elects a single router, the DR; the DR is a "join broker" for all LAN routers insofar as joins are routed according to the DR's view of routing—without a DR there could be conflicts potentially resulting in tree loops. The router that actually forwards a join off-LAN for a group (toward the group's core) is known as the LAN "upstream router" for that group. A group's LAN upstream router may or may not be the LAN DR.

With regards to a JOIN_REQUEST being multicast onto a broadcast LAN, the LAN DR decides over which interface to forward it. Depending on the group's core location, the DR may redirect (unicast) the join back across the same link as it arrived to what it considers is the best next hop toward the core. In this case, the LAN DR does not keep any transient state for the JOIN_REQUEST it passed on. This best next-hop router is then the LAN upstream forwarder for the corresponding group. This redirection only applies to joins, which are relatively infrequent—native multicast data never traverses a link more than once.

For the case where a DR *originates* a join and has to unicast it to a LAN neighbor, the DR must keep a transient state for the join.

On broadcast LANs it is necessary for a router to be able to distinguish between a directly attached (downstream) group member and any (at least one) downstream on-tree router(s). For a router to be able to send a QUIT_NOTIFICATION (prune) upstream, it must be sure it neither has any (downstream) directly attached group members or on-tree routers reachable via a downstream interface. How this is achieved is implementation dependent. One possible way would be for a CBT forwarding cache to maintain two extra bits for each child entry—one bit to indicate the presence of a group member on that interface, the other bit indicating the presence of an on-tree router on that interface. Both these bits must be clear (i.e., unset) before this router can send a QUIT_NOTIFICATION for the corresponding state upstream.

6.6.10   The "all-cbt-routers" Group

The IP destination address of CBT control messages is either the "all-cbt-routers" group address or a unicast address, as appropriate.

All CBT control messages are multicast over broadcast links to the "all-cbt-routers" group (IANA assigned as 224.0.0.15), with IP TTL 1. The exception to this is if a DR decides to forward a control packet back over the interface on which it arrived, in which the DR unicasts the control packet. The IP source address of CBT control messages is the sending router's outgoing interface.

CBT control messages are unicast over nonbroadcast media.

A CBT control message originated or forwarded by a router is never processed by itself.

6.6.11   Nonmember Sending

This process is relevant to nonmember sending where the data is sourced inside the CBT domain. A host always originates native multicast data. All multicast traffic is received promiscuously by CBT routers. All but the LAN's DR discard the packet. The DR looks up the relevant <core, group> mapping, encapsulates (IP-in-IP) the data, and unicasts it to the group's core router. Consequently, no group state is required in the network between the first hop router and the group's core. On arriving at the core router, the data packet is deencapsulated and disseminated over the group tree in the manner already described.

REFERENCES

[BAL199301] T. Ballardie, P. Francist, J. Crowcroft, Core Based Trees (CBT): An Architecture for Scalable Interdomain Multicast Routing, ACM SIGCOMM'93, Ithaca, NY.

[BAL199801] A. Ballardie, B. Cain, Z. Zhang, INTERNET-DRAFT: Core-Based Trees (CBT Version 3) Multicast Routing — Protocol Specification, www3.ietf.org/proceedings/99mar/ I-D/draft-ietf-idmr-cbt-spec-v3-01.txt, August 1998.

[RFC2189] RFC 2189, Core Based Trees (CBT Version 2) Multicast Routing—Protocol Specification, A. Ballardie, September 1997.

[RFC2201] RFC 2201, Core Based Trees (CBT) Multicast Routing Architecture, A. Ballardie, September 1997.

[UCL200701] Department of Computer Science, University College London, Core-Based Trees White Paper, London UK, http://www.cs.ucl.ac.uk/staff/jon/mmbook/book/node78.html.

7

MULTICAST ROUTING—DENSE-MODE PROTOCOLS: PIM DM

This chapter addresses Protocol-Independent Multicast Dense Mode (PIM DM), defined in RFC 3973 (January 2005). PIM DM is a multicast routing protocol that uses the underlying unicast routing information base to flood multicast datagrams to all multicast routers. Prune messages are used to block further messages from propagating to routers without group members. As we have seen in previous chapters, DM is useful when one or more of the following apply: senders and receivers are in geographic/topological proximity, there are few sources and many receivers, the volume of multicast traffic is high, and the stream of multicast traffic is continuous in time. IPTV/DVB-H applications meet these conditions, except for the geographical proximity; however, proximity is effectively achieved by the use of point-to-multipoint satellite distribution.

7.1 OVERVIEW

As we know by now, PIM employs an explicit join model for sparse groups; transmission occurs on a shared tree but it can switch to a per-source tree. PIM DM also uses the

IP Multicast with Applications to IPTV and Mobile DVB-H   by Daniel Minoli
Copyright © 2008 John Wiley & Sons, Inc.

underlying unicast routing information base to flood multicast datagrams to all multicast routers (it does not have a topology discovery mechanism often used by a unicast routing protocol). Prune messages are used to prevent messages from propagating to routers without active group members. PIM DM uses RPF. PIM DM employs the same packet formats PIM SM uses. Note that:

- In PIM DM there are no periodic joins being transmitted, only explicitly triggered prunes and grafts.
- In PIM DM there is no RP. This is advantageous in networks that cannot accept a single point of failure, such as commercial IPTV networks.
- PIM DM does not maintain a keepalive timer associated with each (S,G) route (unlike the case with PIM SM). In PIM DM, route and state information associated with an (S,G) entry is maintained as long as any protocol timer associated with that (S,G) entry is active. Thereafter, all information concerning that (S,G) route is discarded.

When a PIM DM-enabled router receives a packet, it validates the incoming interface with the unicast routing table, and then the packet is sent out to every interface (i.e., it floods) that has not been pruned from the multicast delivery tree. (This is the operation of the RPF algorithm.)

PIM DM does not attempt to develop multicast-specific routes. Instead, it assumes that the routes in the unicast routing table are symmetric. A PIM DM-enabled router initially assumes all downstream interfaces needed to receive multicast traffic. The router floods datagrams to all areas of the network. If some areas do not have receivers for the specific multicast group, PIM DM reactively prunes these branches from the delivery tree. This reactive pruning is done because PIM DM does not obtain downstream receiver information from the unicast routing table. PIM DM requires that the router be able to process a list of prune requests [PAR200601]. See Figure 7.1 for an example of pruning.

Considering the flood-and-prune approach used in PIM DM, one should use it in cases where the large majority of hosts within a domain need to receive the multicast data; here the majority of branches will not be pruned from the delivery tree, and the inefficiencies due to flooding are minimal. IPTV fits this predicament.

7.2 BASIC PIM DM BEHAVIOR

PIM DM makes the assumption that when a source S starts transmitting, all downstream users wish to receive multicast datagrams. Initially, the multicast datagrams are flooded to all areas of the network. PIM DM uses RPF to prevent looping of multicast datagrams while flooding. If some areas of the network do not have group members, PIM DM will prune off the forwarding branch by instantiating a prune state. In IPTV applications, all routers supporting a neighborhood DSL Access Multiplexer (DSLAM) will (typically) require to be receiving all multicast packets (with each content channel using a different multicast address); hence, it is unlikely that pruning will occur, but that may be the case in the middle of the night if nobody is watching TV.

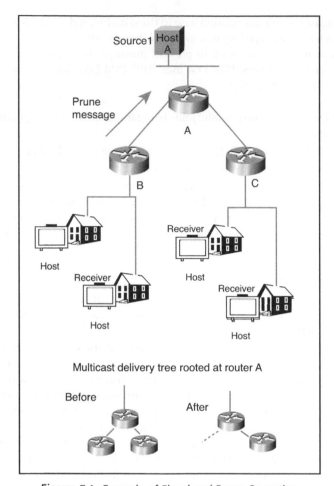

Figure 7.1. Example of Flood-and-Prune Operation

A prune state has a finite lifetime; when that lifetime expires, data will again be forwarded down the previously pruned branch. The broadcast of datagrams followed by the pruning of unwanted branches is referred to as a flood-and-prune cycle. The prune state is associated with an (S,G) pair. When a new member for a group G appears in a pruned area, a router can "graft" toward the source S for the group, thereby activating the pruned branch back into a forwarding branch. To minimize the repeated flooding and pruning associated with a particular (S,G) pair, PIM DM uses a State Refresh message. This message is sent by the router(s) directly connected to the source and is propagated throughout the network; when the message is received by a router on its RPF interface, the State Refresh message causes an existing prune state to be refreshed [RFC3973].

PIM DM has a simplified design compared with multicast routing protocols with built-in topology discovery mechanisms (e.g., DVMRP) and is not dependent on any specific topology discovery protocol. However, this simplification does incur more potential overhead in some applications by causing flooding and pruning activities to take place on some links that could be avoided if sufficient topology information were available. In IPTV applications, increased overhead is opted for in favor of the simplification and flexibility obtained by not relying on a specific topology discovery protocol.

7.3 PROTOCOL SPECIFICATION

The specification of PIM DM consists of several elements:

- Description of the protocol state stored at routers
- Description of the data packet forwarding rules
- Description of the generation and processing of Hello messages
- Description of the join, prune, and graft generation and processing rules
- Description of the state refresh generation and forwarding rules
- Description of the assert generation and processing rules
- PIM DM packet formats
- PIM DM timers and defaults

Only a summary is presented here, with our description based directly on [RFC3973][1]; the interested reader and/or developer should refer to the RFC for complete details.

The RFC uses the notation depicted in Table 7.1. Note that set operations are to be conducted in the order specified. This is due to the fact that $(-)$ is not a true difference operator, because B is not necessarily a subset of A. That is, $A(+)B(-)C = A(-)C(+)B$ is not a true statement unless C is a subset of both A and B.

TABLE 7.1. Set and Other Notation

Notation	Meaning
A (+) B	The union of two sets, A and B
A (−) B	The elements of set A that are not in set B
NULL	The empty set or list
=	Denotes assignment of a variable
==	Denotes a comparison for equality
!=	Denotes a comparison for inequality
Curly braces, namely {and}	Used for grouping

[1]The rest of this chapter is liberally based on RFC 3973.

7.3.1   PIM Protocol State

This section specifies the protocol state that a PIM DM implementation is required to maintain. This state is known as the Tree Information Base (TIB). The TIB holds the state of all the multicast distribution trees at a given router. [RFC3973] defines PIM DM mechanisms in terms of the TIB. However, only a very simple implementation would actually implement packet forwarding operations in terms of this state. Most of the implementations will use this state to build a multicast forwarding table, which would then be updated when the relevant state in the TIB changes. Although the RFC precisely specifies the state to be kept, this does not mean that an implementation of PIM DM has to hold the state in this form; a PIM DM implementation is free to hold whatever internal state it requires and will still be conformant with the specification as long as it results in the same externally visible protocol behavior as an abstract router that holds the following state.

PIM DM does not maintain a keepalive timer associated with each (S,G) route. Instead, route and state information associated with an (S,G) entry must be maintained as long as any timer associated with that (S,G) entry is active. When no timer associated with an (S,G) entry is active, all information concerning that (S,G) route may be discarded.

7.3.1.1   General Purpose State.   A router stores the non-group-specific state shown in Table 7.2.

7.3.1.2   (S,G) State.   For every source/group pair (S,G), a router stores the state shown in Table 7.3.

7.3.1.3   State Summarization Nomenclature.   Table 7.4 defines "macros" used in the descriptions of the state machines and pseudocode in the following sections. The most important macros are those defining the outgoing interface list ("olist") for

TABLE 7.2. Non-Group-Specific State

Router Element	State Information Retained
For each interface	Hello Timer (HT)
	State Refresh Capable
	LAN Delay Enabled
	Propagation Delay (PD)
	Override Interval (OI)
For each neighbor	Information from neighbor's hello
	Neighbor's Gen ID.
	Neighbor's LAN Prune Delay
	Neighbor's Override Interval
	Neighbor's State Refresh Capability
	Neighbor Liveness Timer (NLT)

TABLE 7.3. (S,G) State

Router Element	State Information Retained
For each interface	Local Membership: State: One of {"NoInfo," "Include"} PIM (S,G) Prune State: State: One of {"NoInfo" (NI), "Pruned" (P), "PrunePending" (PP)} Also, Prune Pending Timer (PPT) and Prune Timer (PT) (S,G) Assert Winner State: State: One of {"NoInfo," "I lost Assert" (L), "I won Assert" (W)} Also, Assert-Timer (AT) and assert winner's IP Address and assert winner's Assert Metric

Upstream interface
  specific
	Graft/Prune State:
	State: One of {"NoInfo," "Pruned," "Forwarding" (F),
	  "AckPending" (AP)}
	Also, GraftRetry Timer (GRT) and Override Timer (OT)
	  and Prune Limit Timer (PLT)
	Originator State:
	Source Active Timer (SAT) and State Refresh Timer (SRT)

TABLE 7.4. "Macros" Used in the Descriptions of the State Machines

Macro	Definition
immediate_olist(S,G)	= pim_nbrs (−) prunes(S,G) (+) (pim_include(*,G) (−) pim_exclude(S,G)) (+) pim_include(S,G) (−) lost_assert(S,G) (−) boundary(G)
olist(S,G)	= immediate_olist(S,G) (−) RPF_interface(S)
pim_include(*,G)	= {all interfaces I such that: local_receiver_include(*,G,I)}
pim_include(S,G)	= {all interfaces I such that: local_receiver_include(S,G,I)}
pim_exclude(S,G)	= {all interfaces I such that: local_receiver_exclude(S,G,I)}
RPF_interface(S)	Returns the RPF interface for source S (it returns the · interface used to reach S as indicated by the MRIB)

local_receiver_include(S,G,I)	True if the IGMP module (or other local membership
	  mechanism) has determined that there are local members
	  on interface I that seek to receive traffic sent specifically
	  by S to G

local_receiver_include(*,G,I)	True if the IGMP module or other local membership
	  mechanism has determined that there are local members
	  on interface I that seek to receive all traffic sent to G.
	  Note that this determination is expected to account
	  for membership joins initiated on or by the router.

local_receiver_exclude(S,G,I)	True if local_receiver_include(*,G,I) is true but none of the local members seek to receive traffic from S.
I_Am_Assert_loser(S, G, I)	True if the assert state machine for (S,G) on interface I is in the "I am Assert Loser" state.

TABLE 7.5. Sets Used in the Descriptions of the State Machines

Set	Definition
pim_nbrs	The set of all interfaces on which the router has at least one active PIM neighbor
prunes(S,G)	The set of all interfaces on which the router has received Prune(S,G) messages: prunes(S,G)={all interfaces I such that DownstreamPState(S,G,I) is in pruned state}
lost_assert(S,G)	The set of all interfaces on which the router has lost an (S,G) Assert lost_assert(S,G)={all interfaces I such that lost_assert(S,G,I) == TRUE}
boundary(G)	The set boundary(G)={all interfaces I with an administratively scoped boundary for group G}
RPF'	The RPF neighbor toward a source unless a PIM DM assert has overridden the normal choice of neighbor neighbor RPF'(S,G) {if (I_Am_Assert_loser(S, G, RPF_interface(S))) {return AssertWinner(S, G, RPF_interface(S))} else {return MRIB.next_hop(S)}}
iif	The incoming interface of the packet
S	The source address of the incoming packet
G	The destination address of the packet (group address)

the relevant state. The macros pim_include(*,G) and pim_include(S,G) indicate the interfaces to which traffic might or might not be forwarded because of hosts that are local members on those interfaces.

The sets defined in Table 7.5 are used in the descriptions of the state machines.

7.3.2 Data Packet Forwarding Rules

First, an RPF check is performed to determine whether the packet should be accepted, based on TIB state and the interface on which the packet arrived. The packets that fail the RPF check will not be forwarded, and the router will conduct an assert process for the (S, G) pair specified in the packet. The packets for which a route to the source cannot be found must be discarded. If the RPF check has been passed, an outgoing interface list is constructed for the packet. If this list is not empty, then the packet must be forwarded to all the listed interfaces. If the list is empty, then the router will conduct a prune process for the (S,G) pair specified in the packet.

Upon receipt of a data packet from S addressed to G on interface iif,

$$\text{if (iif} == \text{RPF}_{\text{interface}} (S) \text{ AND UpstreamPState}(S, G) ! = \text{Pruned})$$

$$\{\text{oiflist} = \text{olist}(S, G)\} \text{ else } \{\text{oiflist} = \text{NULL}\}$$

where UpstreamPState(S,G) is the state of the Upstream(S,G) state machine in Upstream Prune, Join, and Graft messages, then the packet is forwarded on all interfaces in the oif list.

7.3.3 Hello Messages

This section describes the generation and processing of Hello messages.

7.3.3.1 Sending Hello Messages. PIM DM uses Hello messages to detect other PIM routers. Hello messages are sent periodically on each PIM-enabled interface. Hello messages are multicast to the ALL-PIM-ROUTERS group. When PIM is enabled on an interface, or when a router first starts, the HT must be set to a random value between 0 and Triggered_Hello_Delay. This prevents synchronization of Hello messages if multiple routers are powered on simultaneously. After the initial Hello message, a Hello message must be sent to every Hello_Period. A single hello timer may be used to trigger sending Hello messages on all active interfaces. The hello timer should not be reset except when it expires.

7.3.3.2 Receiving Hello Messages. When a Hello message is received, the receiving router will record the receiving interface, the sender, and any information contained in recognized options. This information is retained for a number of seconds in the Hold Time field of the Hello message. If a new Hello message is received from a particular neighbor N, the NLT(N,I) must be reset to the newly received hello holdtime. If a Hello message is received from a new neighbor, the receiving router should send its own Hello message after a random delay between 0 and Triggered_Hello_Delay.

7.3.3.3 Hello Message Hold Time. The hold time in the Hello message should be set to a value that can reasonably be expected to keep the hello active until a new Hello message is received. On most links, this will be 3.5 times the value of Hello_Period.

If the hold time is set to 0xFFFF, the receiving router must not time out that Hello message. This feature might be used for on-demand links to avoid keeping the link up with periodic Hello messages. If a hold time of 0 is received, the corresponding neighbor state expires immediately. When a PIM router takes an interface down or changes the IP address, a Hello message with a zero hold time should be sent immediately (with the old IP address if the IP address is changed) to cause any PIM neighbors to remove the old information immediately.

7.3.3.4 Handling Router Failures. If a Hello message is received from an active neighbor with a different Generation ID (GenID), the neighbor has restarted and may not contain the correct (S,G) state. A Hello message should be sent after a random delay between 0 and Triggered_Hello_Delay before any other messages are sent. If the neighbor is downstream, the router may replay the last State Refresh message for any (S,G) pairs for which it is the assert winner indicating prune and assert status to the downstream router. These State Refresh messages should be sent out immediately after the Hello message. If the neighbor is the upstream neighbor for an (S,G) entry, the router may cancel its prune limit timer to permit sending a Prune message and reestablishing a pruned state in the upstream router.

Upon startup, a router may use any State Refresh messages received within Hello_Period of its first Hello message on an interface to establish state information. The state refresh source will be the RPF'(S), and the prune status for all interfaces will be set according to the prune indicator bit in the State Refresh message. If the prune indicator is set, the router should set the PruneLimitTimer to Prune_Holdtime and set the PruneTimer on all downstream interfaces to the state refresh's interval times 2. The router should then propagate the state refresh as described in Section 7.3.5.1.

7.3.3.5 Reducing Prune Propagation Delay on LANs. If all routers on a LAN support the LAN Prune Delay option, then the PIM routers on that LAN will use the values received to adjust their J/P_Override_Interval on that interface and the interface is LAN delay enabled. Briefly, to avoid synchronization of Prune Override (Join) messages when multiple downstream routers share a multiaccess link, sending of these messages is delayed by a small random amount of time. The period of randomization is configurable and has a default value of 3 s.

Each router on the LAN expresses its view on the amount of randomization necessary in the Override Interval field of the LAN Prune Delay option. When all routers on a LAN use the LAN Prune Delay option, all routers on the LAN must set their Override_Interval to the largest override value on the LAN.

The LAN delay inserted by a router in the LAN Prune Delay option expresses the expected message propagation delay on the link and should be configurable by the system administrator. When all routers on a link use the LAN Prune Delay option, all routers on the LAN must set propagation delay to the largest LAN delay.

PIM implementers should enforce a lower bound on the permitted values for this delay to allow for scheduling and processing delays within their router. Such delays may cause received messages to be processed later and triggered messages to be sent later than intended. Setting this LAN prune delay to too low a value may result in temporary forwarding outages, because a downstream router will not be able to override a neighbor's Prune message before the upstream neighbor stops forwarding.

7.3.4 PIM DM Prune, Join, and Graft Messages

This section describes the generation and processing of PIM DM Join, Prune, and Graft messages. Prune messages are sent toward the upstream neighbor for S to indicate that traffic from S addressed to group G is not desired. In the case of downstream routers A and B, where A wishes to continue receiving data and B does not, A will send a join in

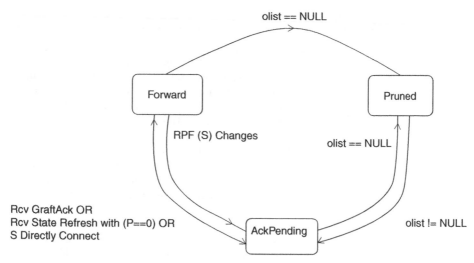

Figure 7.2. Upstream Interface State Machine

response to B's prune to override the prune. This is the only situation in PIM DM in which a Join message is used. Finally, a Graft message is used to rejoin a previously pruned branch to the delivery tree.

7.3.4.1 Upstream Prune, Join, and Graft Messages. The Upstream(S,G) state machine for sending Prune, Graft, and Join messages is shown in Figure 7.2. There are three states, as shown in Table 7.6, and three times, as shown in Table 7.7.

TABLE 7.6. Upstream(S,G) State Machine States

State	Description
Forwarding (F)	This is the starting state of the Upsteam(S,G) state machine. The state machine is in this state if it just started or if oiflist(S,G) != NULL.
Pruned (P)	The set olist(S,G) is empty. The router will not forward data from S addressed to group G.
AckPending (AP)	The router was in the Pruned (P) state, but a transition has occurred in the Downstream (S,G) state machine for one of this (S,G) entry's outgoing interfaces, indicating that traffic from S addressed to G should again be forwarded. A Graft message has been sent to RPF'(S), but a GraftAck message has not yet been received.

TABLE 7.7. State-Machine-Specific Timers

Timer	Description
GraftRetry Timer (GRT(S,G))	This timer is set when a graft is sent upstream. If a corresponding GraftAck is not received before the timer expires, then another graft is sent, and the GraftRetry timer is reset. The timer is stopped when a GraftAck message is received. This timer is normally set to Graft_Retry_Period.
Override Timer (OT(S,G))	This timer is set when a Prune(S,G) is received on the upstream interface where olist(S,G) != NULL. When the timer expires, a Join(S,G) message is sent on the upstream interface. This timer is normally set to t_override.
Prune Limit Timer (PLT(S,G))	This timer is used to rate limit prunes on a LAN. It is only used when the Upstream(S,G) state machine is in the pruned state. A prune cannot be sent if this timer is running. This timer is normally set to t_limit.

In tabular form, the state, machine is defined as follows:

	Previous State		
Event	Forwarding	Pruned	AckPending
Data packet arrives on RPF_Interface(S) AND olist(S,G) == NULL AND PLT (S,G) not running	—>P Send Prune(S,G) Set PLT(S,G)	—>P Send Prune(S,G) Set PLT (S,G)	N/A
State Refresh(S,G) received from RPFÓ(S) AND Prune Indicator == 1	—>F Set OT (S,G)	—>P Reset PLT(S,G)	—>AP Set OT(S,G)
State Refresh (S,G) received from RPFÓ (S) AND Prune Indicator == 0 AND PLT(S,G) not running	—>F	—>P Send Prune (S,G) Set PLT (S,G)	—>F Cancel GRT(S,G)
See Join(S,G) to RPF'(S)	—>F Cancel OT(S,G)	—>P	—>AP Cancel OT(S,G)
See Prune(S,G)	—>F Set OT(S,G)	—>P	—>AP Set OT(S,G)
OT(S,G) Expires	—>F Send Join(S,G)	N/A	—>AP Send Join(S,G)

| Event | Previous State | | |
	Forwarding	Pruned	AckPending
olist(S,G) —>NULL	—>P Send Prune(S,G) Set PLT(S,G)	N/A	—>P Send Prune(S,G) Set PLT (S,G) Cancel GRT (S,G)
olist(S,G) —>non-NULL	N/A	—>AP Send Graft(S,G) Set GRT(S,G)	N/A
RPF' (S) Changes AND olist(S,G) != NULL	—>AP Send Graft(S,G) Set GRT(S,G)	—>AP Send Graft(S,G) Set GRT (S,G)	—>AP Send Graft(S,G) Set GRT(S,G)
RPF' (S) Changes AND olist (S,G) == NULL	—>P	—>P Cancel PLT(S,G)	—>P Cancel GRT(S,G)
S becomes directly connected	—>F	—>P	—>F Cancel GRT(S,G)
GRT(S,G) Expires	N/A	N/A	—>AP Send Graft(S,G) Set GRT(S,G)
Receive GraftAck(S,G) from RPF' (S)	—>F	—>P	—>F Cancel GRT(S,G)

The transition event RcvGraftAck(S,G) implies receiving a GraftAck message targeted to this router's address on the incoming interface for the (S,G) entry. If the destination address is not correct, the state transitions in this state machine must not occur.

TRANSITIONS FROM THE FORWARDING (F) STATE. When the Upstream(S,G) state machine is in the F state, the events shown in Table 7.8 may trigger a transition.

TRANSITIONS FROM THE PRUNED (P) STATE. When the Upstream(S,G) state machine is in the P state, the events shown in Table 7.9 may trigger a transition.

TRANSITIONS FRO THE ACKPENDING(AP) STATE. When the Upstream(S,G) state machine is in the AP state, the events shown in Table 7.10 may trigger a transition.

TABLE 7.8. Events That Trigger a Transition from the F State

Event	Description
Data Packet arrives on RPF_Interface(S) AND olist(S,G) == NULL AND S NOT directly connected	The Upstream(S,G) state machine must transition to the P state, send a Prune(S,G) to RPF'(S), and set PLT(S,G) to t_limit seconds.
State Refresh(S,G) received from RPF'(S)	The Upstream(S,G) state machine remains in an F state. If the received state refresh has the prune indicator bit set to 1, this router must override the upstream router's prune state after a short random interval. If the Override Timer OT(S,G) is not running and the prune indicator bit equals 1, the router must set OT(S,G) to t_override seconds.
See Join(S,G) to RPF'(S)	This event is only relevant if RPF_interface(S) is a shared medium. This router sees another router on RPF_interface(S) send a Join(S,G) to RPF'(S,G). If the OT(S,G) is running, it means that the router had scheduled a join to override a previously received prune. Another router has responded more quickly with a join, so the local router should cancel its OT(S,G), if it is running. The Upstream(S,G) state machine remains in the F state.
See Prune(S,G) AND S NOT directly connected	This event is only relevant if RPF_interface(S) is a shared medium. This router sees another router on RPF_interface(S) send a Prune(S,G). As this router is in the F state, it must override the prune after a short random interval. If OT(S,G) is not running, the router must set OT(S,G) to t_override seconds. The Upstream(S,G) state machine remains in the F state.
OT(S,G) expires AND S NOT directly connected	OT(S,G) expires. The router must send a Join(S,G) to RPF'(S) to override a previously detected prune. The Upstream(S,G) state machine remains in the F state.
olist(S,G) —> NULL AND S NOT directly connected	The Upstream(S,G) state machine must transition to the P state, send a Prune(S,G) to RPF'(S), and set PLT(S,G) to t_limit seconds.
RPF'(S) changes AND olist(S,G) is non-NULL AND S NOT directly connected	Unicast routing or assert state causes RPF'(S) to change, including changes to RPF_Interface(S). The Upstream(S,G) state machine *must* transition to the AP state, unicast a Graft to the new RPF'(S), and set the Graft Retry Timer (GRT(S,G)) to Graft_Retry_Period.
RPF'(S) changes AND olist(S,G) is NULL	Unicast routing or assert state causes RPF'(S) to change, including changes to RPF_Interface(S). The Upstream(S,G) state machine must transition to the P state.

TABLE 7.9. Events That Trigger a Transition from the Upstream(S,G) State

Event	Description
Data arrives on RPF_interface(S) AND PLT(S,G) not running AND S NOT directly connected	Either another router on the LAN desires traffic from S addressed to G or a previous prune was lost. To prevent generating a Prune(S,G) in response to every data packet, the Prune Limit Timer (PLT(S,G)) is used. Once the PLT(S,G) expires, the router needs to send another prune in response to a data packet not received directly from the source. A Prune(S,G) must be sent to RPF'(S), and the PLT(S,G) must be set to t_limit.
State Refresh(S,G) received from RPF'(S)	The Upstream(S,G) state machine remains in a pruned state. If the state refresh has its prune indicator bit set to zero and PLT(S,G) is not running, a Prune(S,G) must be sent to RPF'(S), and the PLT(S,G) must be set to t_limit. If the state refresh has its prune indicator bit set to 1, the router *must* reset PLT(S,G) to t_limit.
See Prune(S,G) to RPF'(S)	A Prune(S,G) is seen on RPF_interface(S) to RPF'(S). The Upstream(S,G) state machine stays in the P state. The router may reset its PLT(S,G) to the value in the Holdtime field of the received message if it is greater than the current value of the PLT(S,G).
olist(S,G)−non-NULL AND S NOT directly connected	The set of interfaces defined by the olist(S,G) macro becomes nonempty, indicating that traffic from S addressed to group G must be forwarded. The Upstream(S,G) state machine must cancel PLT(S,G), transition to the AP state, and unicast a Graft message to RPF'(S). The Graft Retry Timer (GRT(S,G)) must be set to Graft_Retry_Period.
RPF'(S) changes AND olist(S,G) == non-NULL AND S NOT directly connected	Unicast routing or assert state causes RPF'(S) to change, including changes to RPF_Interface(S). The Upstream(S,G) state machine must cancel PLT(S,G), transition to the AP state, send a graft unicast to the new RPF'(S), and set GRT(S,G) to Graft_Retry_Period.
RPF'(S) changes AND olist(S,G) == NULL AND S NOT directly connected	Unicast routing or assert state causes RPF'(S) to change, including changes to RPF_Interface(S). The Upstream(S,G) state machine stays in the P state and *must* cancel the PLT(S,G) timer.
S becomes directly connected	Unicast routing changed so that S is directly connected. The Upstream(S,G) state machine remains in the P state.

TABLE 7.10. Events That Trigger a Transition from the AP State

Event	Description
State Refresh(S,G) received from RPF'(S) with prune indicator == 1	The Upstream(S,G) state machine remains in an AP state. The router must override the upstream router's prune state after a short random interval. If the Override Timer OT (S,G) is not running and the prune indicator bit equals 1, the router must set OT(S,G) to t_override seconds.
State Refresh(S,G) received from RPF'(S) with prune indicator == 0	The router must cancel its Graft Retry Timer (GRT(S,G)) and transition to the F state.
See Join(S,G) to RPF'(S,G)	This event is only relevant if RPF_interface(S) is a shared medium. This router sees another router on RPF_interface(S) send a Join(S,G) to RPF'(S,G). If the OT(S,G) is running, it means that the router had scheduled a join to override a previously received prune. Another router has responded more quickly with a join, so the local router SHOULD cancel its OT(S,G), if it is running. The Upstream(S,G) state machine remains in the AP state.
See Prune(S,G)	This event is only relevant if RPF_interface(S) is a shared medium. This router sees another router on RPF_interface(S) send a Prune(S,G). As this router is in AP state, it must override the prune after a short random interval. If OT(S,G) is not running, the router *must* set OT(S,G) to t_override seconds. The Upstream(S,G) state machine remains in AP state.
OT(S,G) Expires	The OT(S,G) expires. The router must send a Join(S,G) to RPF'(S). The Upstream(S,G) state machine remains in the AP state.
olist(S,G) −> NULL	The set of interfaces defined by the olist(S,G) macro becomes null, indicating that traffic from S addressed to group G should no longer be forwarded. The Upstream(S,G) state machine must transition to the P state. A Prune(S,G) must be multicast to the RPF_interface(S), with RPF'(S) named in the upstream neighbor field. The GRT(S,G) *must* be cancelled, and PLT(S,G) must be set to t_limit seconds.
RPF'(S) changes AND olist(S,G) does not become NULL AND S NOT directly connected	Unicast routing or assert state causes RPF'(S) to change, including changes to RPF_Interface(S). The Upstream(S,G) state machine stays in the AP state. A graft *must* be unicast to the new RPF'(S) and the GRT(S,G) reset to Graft_Retry_Period
RPF'(S) changes AND olist(S,G) == NULL	Unicast routing or assert state causes RPF'(S) to change, including changes to RPF_Interface(S). The Upstream(S,G)

TABLE 7.10 (*Continued*)

Event	Description
AND S NOT directly connected	state machine *must* transition to the P state. The GRT(S,G) must be cancelled.
S becomes directly connected	Unicast routing has changed so that S is directly connected. The graft retry timer *must* be cancelled, and the Upstream(S,G) state machine *must* transition to the F state.
GRT(S,G) expires	The GRT(S,G) expires for this (S,G) entry. The Upstream(S,G) state machine stays in the AP state. Another Graft message for (S,G) should be unicast to RPF'(S) and the GRT(S,G) reset to Graft_Retry_Period. It is recommended that the router retry a configured number of times before ceasing retries.
See GraftAck(S,G) from RPF'(S)	A GraftAck is received from RPF'(S). The graft retry timer must be cancelled, and the Upstream(S,G) state machine *must* transition to the F state.

7.3.4.2 Downstream Prune, Join, and Graft Messages. The Prune(S,G) downstream state machine for receiving Prune, Join, and Graft messages on interface I is shown in Figure 7.3. This state machine must always be in the NoInfo state on the upstream interface. It contains three states, as shown in Table 7.11. Table 7.12 lists times.

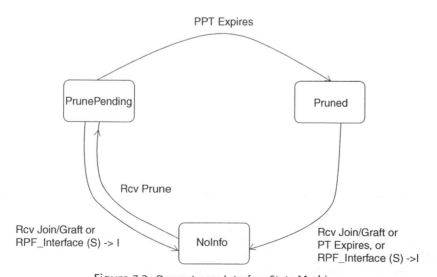

Figure 7.3. Downstream Interface State Machine

TABLE 7.11. Prune(S,G) Downstream State Machine States

State	Description
NoInfo(NI)	The interface has no (S,G) prune state, and neither the Prune Timer (PT(S,G,I)) nor the Prune Pending Timer ((PPT(S,G,I)) is running
PrunePending(PP)	The router has received a Prune(S,G) on this interface from a downstream neighbor and is waiting to see whether the prune will be overridden by another downstream router. For forwarding purposes, the prune pending state functions exactly like the NoInfo state.
Pruned(P)	The router has received a Prune(S,G) on this interface from a downstream neighbor, and the prune was not overridden. Data from S addressed to group G is no longer being forwarded on this interface

In tabular form, the state machine is as follows:

		Previous State	
Event	NoInfo	PrunePend	Pruned
Receive Prune(S,G)	->PP Set PPT(S,G,I)	->PP	->P Reset T(S,G,I)
Receive Join(S,G)	->NI ->NI Send GraftAck	->NI Cancel PPT(S,G,I)	->NI Cancel T(S,G,I)
Receive Graft(S,G)		->NI send GraftAck cancel PPT(S,G,I)	->NI Send GraftAck cancel PT(S,G,I)
PPT(S,G) expires	N/A	->P Set PT (S,G,I)	N/A
PT(S,G) expires	N/A	N/A	->NI
RPF_Interface(S) becomes I	->NI	->NI cancel PPT(S,G,I)	->NI cancel PT(S,G,I)
Send State Refresh(S,G) out I	->NI	->PP	->P reset PT(S,G,I)

The transition events "Receive Graft(S,G)," "Receive Prune(S,G)," and "Receive Join(S,G)" denote receiving a Graft, Prune, or Join message in which this router's address on I is contained in the message's Upstream Neighbor field. If the Upstream Neighbor

TABLE 7.12. Prune(S,G) Downstream State Machine Timers

Timer	Description
Prune Pending Timer (PPT(S,G,I))	This timer is set when a valid Prune(S,G) is received. Expiry of the PPT(S,G,I) causes the interface to transition to the pruned state.
Prune Timer (PT(S,G,I))	This timer is set when the PPT(S,G,I) expires. Expiry of the PT(S,G,I) causes the interface to transition to the NoInfo (NI) state, thereby allowing data from S addressed to group G to be forwarded on the interface.

field does not match this router's address on I, then these state transitions in this state machine must not occur.

TRANSITIONS FROM THE NOINFO STATE. When the Prune(S,G) downstream state machine is in the NI state, the events identified in Table 7.13 may trigger a transition.

TRANSITIONS FROM THE PRUNEPENDING (PP) STATE. When the Prune(S,G) downstream state machine is in the PP state, the events identified in Table 7.14 may trigger a transition.

TABLE 7.13. Events That Trigger a Transition from the NI State

Event	Description
Receive Prune(S,G)	A Prune(S,G) is received on interface I with the upstream neighbor field set to the router's address on I. The Prune(S,G) downstream state machine on interface I must transition to the PP state. The Prune Pending Timer (PPT(S,G,I)) must be set to J/P_Override_Interval if the router has more than one neighbor on I. If the router has only one neighbor on interface I, then it should set the PPT(S,G,I) to zero, effectively transitioning immediately to the P state.
Receive Graft(S,G)	A Graft(S,G) is received on the interface I with the upstream neighbor field set to the router's address on I. The Prune(S,G) downstream state machine on interface I stays in the NI state. A GraftAck(S,G) MUST be unicast to the originator of the Graft(S,G) message.

TABLE 7.14. Events That Trigger a Transition from the PP State

Event	Description
Receive Join(S,G)	A Join(S,G) is received on interface I with the upstream neighbor field set to the router's address on I. The Prune(S,G) downstream state machine on interface I must transition to the NI state. The Prune Pending Timer (PPT(S,G,I)) must be cancelled.
Receive Graft(S,G)	A Graft(S,G) is received on interface I with the upstream neighbor field set to the router's address on I. The Prune(S,G) downstream state machine on interface I must transition to the NI state and must unicast a GraftAck message to the graft originator. The PPT(S,G,I) must be cancelled.
PPT(S,G,I) expires	The PPT(S,G,I) expires, indicating that no neighbors have overridden the previous Prune(S,G) message. The Prune(S,G) downstream state machine on interface I must transition to the P state. The Prune Timer (PT(S,G,I)) is started and *must* be initialized to the received Prune_Hold_Time minus J/P_Override_Interval. A PruneEcho(S,G) must be sent on I if I has more than one PIM neighbor. A PruneEcho(S,G) is simply a Prune(S,G) message multicast by the upstream router to a LAN, with itself as the upstream neighbor. Its purpose is to add additional reliability so that if a join that should have overridden the prune is lost locally on the LAN, the PruneEcho(S,G) may be received and trigger a new Join message. A PruneEcho(S,G) is optional on an interface with only one PIM neighbor. In addition, the router must evaluate any possible transitions in the Upstream(S,G) state machine. RPF_Interface(S) becomes interface I. The upstream interface for S has changed. The Prune(S,G) downstream state machine on interface I must transition to the NI state. The PPT(S,G,I) must be cancelled.

TRANSITIONS FROM THE PRUNE (P) STATE. When the Prune(S,G) downstream state machine is in the P state, the events identified in Table 7.15 may trigger a transition.

7.3.5 State Refresh

This section describes the major portions of the state refresh mechanism.

TABLE 7.15. Events That Trigger a Transition from the P State

Event	Description
Receive Prune(S,G)	A Prune(S,G) is received on the interface I with the Upstream Neighbor field set to the router's address on I. The Prune(S,G) downstream state machine on interface I remains in the P state. The Prune Timer (PT(S,G,I)) should be reset to the holdtime contained in the Prune(S,G) message if it is greater than the current value.
Receive Join(S,G)	A Join(S,G) is received on the interface I with the Upstream Neighbor field set to the router's address on I. The Prune(S,G) downstream state machine on interface I must transition to the NI state. The PT(S,G,I) must be cancelled. The router must evaluate any possible transitions in the Upstream(S,G) state machine.
Receive Graft(S,G)	A Graft(S,G) is received on interface I with the Upstream Neighbor field set to the router's address on I. The Prune(S,G) downstream state machine on interface I must transition to the NI state and send a GraftAck back to the graft's source. The PT(S,G,I) must be cancelled. The router must evaluate any possible transitions in the Upstream(S,G) state machine.
PT(S,G,I) expires	The PT(S,G,I) expires, indicating that time again is to flood data from S addressed to group G onto interface I. The Prune(S,G) downstream state machine on interface I must transition to the NI state. The router must evaluate any possible transitions in the Upstream(S,G) state machine.
RPF_Interface(S) becomes interface I	The upstream interface for S has changed. The Prune(S,G) downstream state machine on interface I must transition to the NI state. The PT(S,G,I) must be cancelled.
Send State Refresh(S,G) out to interface I	The router has refreshed the Prune(S,G) state on interface I. The router *must* reset the PT(S,G,I) to the holdtime from an active prune received on interface I. The holdtime used should be the largest active one but may be the most recently received active prune holdtime.

7.3.5.1   Forwarding of State Refresh Messages. When a State Refresh message, is received, it is forwarded according to the following pseudocode:

```
if (iif != RPF_interface(S)) return;
if (RPF'(S) != srcaddr(SRM)) return;
if (StateRefreshRateLimit(S,G) == TRUE) return;

for each interface I in pim_nbrs {
  if (TTL(SRM) == 0 OR (TTL(SRM)-1) < Threshold(I))
    continue;/* Out of TTL, skip this interface */
  if (boundary(I,G))
    continue;/* This interface is scope boundary, skip it */
  if (I == iif)
    continue;/* This is the incoming interface, skip it */
  if (lost_assert(S,G,I) == TRUE)
    continue;/* Let the Assert Winner do State Refresh */

Copy SRM to SRM' /* Make a copy of SRM to forward */

  if (I contained in prunes(S,G)) {
    set Prune Indicator bit of SRM' to 1;
    if StateRefreshCapable(I) == TRUE
      set PT(S,G) to largest active holdtime read from a Prune
      message accepted on I;
  } else {
    set Prune Indicator bit of SRM' to 0;
  }

  set srcaddr(SRM') to my_addr(I);
  set TTL of SRM' to TTL(SRM)-1;
  set metric of SRM' to metric of unicast route used to reach S;
  set pref of SRM' to preference of unicast route used to reach S;
  set mask of SRM' to mask of route used to reach S;

if (AssertState == NoInfo) {
  set Assert Override of SRM' to 1;
  } else {
  set Assert Override of SRM' to 0;
  }
  transmit SRM' on I;
  }
```

The pseudocode above employs the macro definitions listed in Table 7.16.

TABLE 7.16. Macro Definitions Used for Forwarding of State Refresh Messages

Macro	Definition
Boundary(I,G)	TRUE if an administratively scoped boundary for group G is configured on interface I
StateRefreshCapable(I)	TRUE if all neighbors on an interface use the state refresh option
StateRefreshRateLimit(S,G)	TRUE if the time elapsed since the last received State Refresh(S,G) is less than the configured RefreshLimitInterval
TTL(SRM)	Returns the TTL contained in the State Refresh Message, SRM. This is different from the TTL contained in the IP header.
Threshold(I)	Returns the minimum TTL that a packet must have before it can be transmitted on interface I
srcaddr(SRM)	Returns the source address contained in the network protocol (e.g., IPv4) header of the SRM
my_addr(I)	Returns this node's network (e.g., IPv4) address on interface I

7.3.5.2 *State Refresh Message Origination.* This section describes the origination of State Refresh messages. These messages are generated periodically by the PIM DM router directly connected to a source. One Origination(S,G) state machine exists per (S,G) entry in a PIM DM router. The Origination(S,G) state machine shown in Figure 7.4 has the states defined in Table 7.17. Timers used in this state machine are defined in Table 7.18.

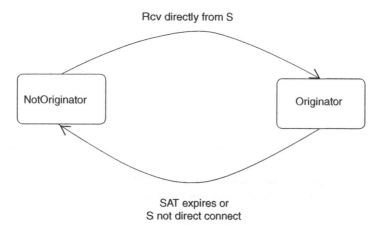

Figure 7.4. State Refresh State Machine

TABLE 7.17. States for Origination(S,G) State Machine

State	Description
NotOriginator (NO)	This is the starting state of the Origination(S,G) state machine. While in this state, a router will not originate State Refresh messages for the (S,G) pair.
Originator (O)	When in this state the router will periodically originate State Refresh messages. Only routers directly connected to S may transition to this state.

TABLE 7.18. Timers Used State Machine

Timer	Description
State Refresh Timer (SRT(S,G))	This timer controls when State Refresh messages are generated. The timer is initially set when that Origination(S,G) state machine transitions to the O state. It is cancelled when the Origination(S,G) state machine transitions to the NO state. This timer is normally set to StateRefreshInterval.
Source Active Timer (SAT(S,G))	This timer is first set when the Origination(S,G) state machine transitions to the O state and is reset on the receipt of every data packet from S addressed to group G. When it expires, the Origination(S,G) state machine transitions to the NO state. This timer is normally set to SourceLifetime.

In tabular form, the state machine is defined as follows:

	Previous State	
Event	NotOriginator	Originator
Receive data from S and S directly connected	->O Set SRT(S,G) Set SAT(S,G)	->O Reset SAT(S,G)
SRT(S,G) expires	N/A	->O Send StateRefresh(S,G) reset SRT(S,G)
SAT(S,G) expires	N/A	->NO Cancel SRT(S,G)
S no longer directly connected	->NO	->NO Cancel SRT(S,G) Cancel SAT(S,G)

TRANSITIONS FROM THE NOTORIGINATOR (NO) STATE. When the Originating(S,G) state machine is in the NO state, the event shown in Table 7.19 may trigger a transition.

TRANSITIONS FROM THE ORIGINATOR (O) STATE. When the Origination(S,G) state machine is in the O state, the events shown in Table 7.20 may trigger a transition.

TABLE 7.19. Events That Trigger a Transition from the NO State

Event	Description
Data packet received from directly connected Source S addressed to group G	The router must transition to an O state, set SAT(S,G) to SourceLifetime, and set SRT(S,G) to StateRefreshInterval. The router should record the TTL of the packet for use in State Refresh messages

7.3.6 PIM Assert Messages

7.3.6.1 *Assert Metrics.* Assert metrics are defined as follows:

```
struct assert_metric{
  metric_preference;
  route_metric;
  ip_address;
};
```

TABLE 7.20. Events That Trigger a Transition from the O State

Event	Description
Receive data packet from S addressed to G	The router remains in the O state and must reset SAT(S,G) to SourceLifetime. The router should increase its recorded TTL to match the TTL of the packet if the packet's TTL is larger than the previously recorded TTL. A router may record the TTL based on an implementation-specific sampling policy to avoid examining the TTL of every multicast packet it handles.
SRT(S,G) expires	The router remains in the O state and must reset SRT(S,G) to StateRefreshInterval. The router must also generate State Refresh messages for transmission, as described in the state refresh forwarding rules (Section 7.3.5.1), except for the TTL. If the TTL of data packets from S to G are being recorded, then the TTL of each State Refresh message is set to the highest recorded TTL. Otherwise, the TTL is set to the configured state refresh TTL. Let I denote the interface over which a State Refresh message is being sent. If the Prune(S,G) downstream state machine is in the P state, then the prune indicator bit must be set to 1 in the State Refresh message being sent over I. Otherwise, the prune indicator bit must be set to 0
SAT(S,G) expires	The router must cancel the SRT(S,G) timer and transition to the NO state
S is no longer directly connected	The router must transition to the NO state and cancel both the SAT(S,G) and SRT(S,G)

When assert_metrics are compared, the metric_preference and route_metric field are compared in order, where the first lower value wins. If all fields are equal, the IP address of the router that sourced the Assert message is used as a tiebreaker, with the highest IP address winning.

An assert metric for (S,G) to include in (or compare against) an Assert message sent on interface I should be computed using the following pseudocode:

```
assert_metric
my_assert_metric(S,G,I) {
  if (CouldAssert(S,G,I) == TRUE) {
  return spt_assert_metric(S,G,I)
  } else {
  return infinite_assert_metric()
  }
}
```

spt_assert_metric(S,I) gives the assert metric that we use if one is sending an assert based on the following active (S,G) forwarding state:

```
assert_metric
spt_assert_metric(S,I) {
  return { 0,MRIB.pref(S),MRIB.metric(S),my_addr(I)}
}
```

MRIB.pref(X) and MRIB.metric(X) are the routing preference and routing metrics associated with the route to a particular (unicast) destination X, as determined by the MRIB.; my_addr(I) is simply the router's network (e.g., IP) address associated with the local interface I.

infinite_assert_metric() gives the assert metric that one needs to send an assert but does not match the (S,G) forwarding state:

```
assert_metric
infinite_assert_metric() {
  return { 1,infinity,infinity,0}
}
```

7.3.6.2 *AssertCancel Messages.* An AssertCancel(S,G) message is simply an Assert message for (S,G) with infinite metric. The assert winner sends this message when it changes its upstream interface to this interface. Other routers will see this metric, causing those with forwarding state to send their own asserts and reestablish an assert winner.

AssertCancel messages are simply an optimization. The original assert timeout mechanism will eventually allow a subnet to become consistent; the Assert-Cancel mechanism simply causes faster convergence. No special processing is required for an AssertCancel message, as it is simply an Assert message from the current winner.

7.3.6.3 Assert State Macros. The macro lost_assert(S,G,I) is used in the olist computations of state summarization nomenclature and is defined as follows:

```
bool lost_assert(S,G,I) {
  if ( RPF_interface(S) == I ) {
    return FALSE
  } else {
    return (AssertWinner(S,G,I) != me AND
      (AssertWinnerMetric(S,G,I) is better than
      spt_assert_metric(S,G,I)))
  }
}
```

AssertWinner(S,G,I) defaults to NULL, and AssertWinnerMetric(S,G,I) defaults to infinity when in the NI state.

7.3.6.4 (S,G) Assert Message State Machine. The (S,G) assert state machine for interface I is shown in Figure 7.5. There are three states as depicted in Table 7.21.

In addition, an Assert Timer (AT(S,G,I)) is used to time out the assert state.

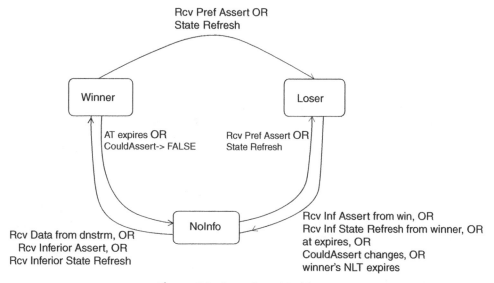

Figure 7.5. Assert State Machine

TABLE 7.21. States for (S,G) Assert State Machine

State	Description
NoInfo (NI)	This router has no (S,G) assert state on interface I.
I am Assert Winner (W)	This router has won an (S,G) assert on interface I. It is now responsible for forwarding traffic from S destined for G via interface I.
I am Assert Loser (L)	This router has lost an (S,G) assert on interface I. It must not forward packets from S destined for G onto interface I.

In tabular form, the state machine is defined as follows:

	Previous State		
Event	NoInfo	Winner	Loser
An (S,G) data packet received on downstream interface	->W Send Assert(S,G) set AT(S,G,I)	->W Send Assert(S,G) set AT(S,G,I)	->L
Receive Inferior (Assert or State Refresh) from Assert Winner	N/A	N/A	->NI Cancel AT(S,G,I)
Receive Inferior (Assert or State Refresh) from nonAssert winner and CouldAssert==TRUE	->W Send Assert(S,G) set AT(S,G,I)	->W Send Assert(S,G) set AT(S,G,I)	->L
Receive Preferred Assert or State Refresh	>L Send Prune(S,G) set AT(S,G,I)	->L Send Prune(S,G) set AT(S,G,I)	->L Set AT(S,G,I)
Send State Refresh	->NI	->W reset AT(S,G,I)	N/A
AT(S,G) Expires	N/A	->NI	->NI
CouldAssert -> FALSE	->NI	->NI Cancel AT(S,G,I)	->NI Cancel AT(S,G,I)
CouldAssert -> TRUE	->NI	N/A	->NI Cancel AT(S,G,I)
Winner's NLT(N,I) Expires	N/A	N/A	->NI Cancel AT(S,G,I)
Receive Prune(S,G), Join(S,G) or Graft(S,G)	->NI	->W Assert(S,G)	->L Send

TABLE 7.22. Events That Trigger a Transition from the NI State

Event	Description
An (S,G) data packet arrives on downstream interface I	An (S,G) data packet arrived on a downstream interface. It is optimistically assumed that this router will be the assert winner for this (S,G). The assert state machine must transition to the "I am Assert Winner" state, send an Assert(S,G) to interface I, store its own address and metric as the assert winner, and set the Assert_Timer (AT(S,G,I) to Assert_Time, thereby initiating the assert negotiation for (S,G).
Receive Inferior (Assert or State Refresh) and CouldAssert(S,G,I) ==TRUE	An assert or state refresh is received for (S,G) that is inferior to our own assert metric on interface I. The assert state machine *must* transition to the "I am Assert Winner" state, send an Assert(S,G) to interface I, store its own address and metric as the assert winner, and set AT(S,G,I) to Assert_Time.
Receive Preferred Assert or State Refresh	The received assert or state refresh has a better metric than this router's, and, therefore, the assert state machine *must* transition to the "I am Assert Loser" state and store the assert winner's address and metric. If the metric was received in an assert, the router must set AT(S,G,I) to Assert_Time. If the metric was received in a state refresh, the router must set AT(S,G,I) to three times the received state refresh interval. If CouldAssert(S,G,I) == TRUE, the router must also multicast a Prune(S,G) to the assert winner with a prune holdtime equal to the assert timer and evaluate any changes in its Upstream(S,G) state machine.

Terminology: A "preferred assert" is one with a better metric than the current winner. An "inferior assert" is one with a worse metric than my_assert_metric(S,G,I).

The state machine uses the following macro:

```
CouldAssert(S,G,I) = (RPF_interface(S) != I)
```

TRANSITIONS FROM NI STATE. In the NI state, the events shown in Table 7.22 may trigger transitions.

TRANSITIONS FROM WINNER STATE. When in "I am Assert Winner" state, the events shown in Table 7.23 trigger transitions.

TRANSITIONS FROM LOSER STATE. When in "I am Assert Loser" state, the transitions shown in Table 7.24 can occur.

7.3.6.5 Rationale for Assert Rules.
The following is a summary of the rules for generating and processing Assert messages. It is not intended to be definitive (the

TABLE 7.23. Events That Trigger a Transition from the "I am Assert Winner" State

Event	Description
An (S,G) data packet arrives on downstream interface I	An (S,G) data packet arrived on a downstream interface. The assert state machine remains in the "I am Assert Winner" state. The router must send an Assert(S,G) to interface I and set the Assert Timer (AT(S,G,I)) to Assert_Time.
Receive Inferior Assert or State Refresh	An (S,G) assert is received containing a metric for S that is worse than this router's metric for S. Whoever sent the assert is in error. The router must send an Assert(S,G) to interface I and reset AT(S,G,I) to Assert_Time.
Receive Preferred Assert or State Refresh	An (S,G) assert or state refresh is received that has a better metric than this router's metric for S on interface I. The assert state machine must transition to "I am Assert Loser" state and store the new assert winner's address and metric. If the metric was received in an assert, the router must set AT(S,G,I) to Assert_Time. If the metric was received in a state refresh, the router must set AT(S,G,I) to three times the state refresh interval. The router must also multicast a Prune(S,G) to the assert winner, with a prune holdtime equal to the assert timer, and evaluate any changes in its Upstream(S,G) state machine.
Send State Refresh	The router is sending a State Refresh(S,G) message on interface I. The router must set AT(S,G,I) to three times the state refresh interval contained in the State Refresh(S,G) message.
AT(S,G,I) Expires	The (S,G) AT(S,G,I) expires. The assert state machine must transition to the NI state.
CouldAssert(S,G,I) -> FALSE	This router's RPF interface changed, making CouldAssert(S,G,I) false. This router can no longer perform the actions of the Assert winner, so the assert state machine must transition to NI state, send an AssertCancel(S,G) to interface I, cancel the AT(S,G,I), and remove itself as the assert winner.

state machines and pseudocode provide the definitive behavior). Instead, it provides some rationale for the behavior.

1. The assert winner for (S,G) must act as the local forwarder for (S,G) on behalf of all downstream members.
2. PIM messages are directed to the RPF' neighbor and not to the regular RPF neighbor.

TABLE 7.24. Events That Trigger a Transition from the "I am Assert Loser" State

Event	Description
Receive Inferior Assert or State Refresh from Current Winner	An assert or state refresh is received from the current Assert winner that is worse than this router's metric for S (typically, the winner's metric became worse). The assert state machine *must* transition to NI state and cancel the Assert Timer (AT(S,G,I)). The router *must* delete the previous assert winner's address and metric and evaluate any possible transitions to its Upstream(S,G) state machine. Usually this router will eventually reassert and win when data packets from S have started flowing again.
Receive Preferred Assert or State Refresh	An assert or state refresh is received that has a metric better than or equal to that of the current assert winner. The assert state machine remains in the Loser (L) state. If the metric was received in an assert, the router must set the AT(S,G,I) to Assert_Time. If the metric was received in a state refresh, the router *must* set the AT(S,G,I) to three times the received state refresh interval. If the metric is better than the current assert winner, the router must store the address and metric of the new assert winner, and if CouldAssert(S,G,I) (b) V. Mirsa and D. E. Draper, Biopolymers **48**, 113(1998). See also ref. 71 and 72.== TRUE, the router must multicast a Prune(S,G) to the new assert winner.
AT(S,G,I) expires	The (S,G) AT(S,G,I) expires. The assert state machine *must* transition to NI state. The router must delete the assert winner's address and metric. If CouldAssert == TRUE, the router must evaluate any possible transitions to its Upstream(S,G) state machine.
CouldAssert –> FALSE	CouldAssert has become FALSE because interface I has become the RPF interface for S. The assert state machine *must* transition to NI state, cancel AT(S,G,I), and delete information concerning the assert winner on I.
CouldAssert –> TRUE	CouldAssert has become TRUE because interface I used to be the RPF interface for S, and now it is not. The assert state machine *must* transition to NI state, cancel AT(S,G,I), and delete information concerning the assert winner on I.
Current Assert Winner's NeighborLiveness Timer Expires	The current assert winner's NeighborLiveness Timer (NLT(N,I)) has expired. The Assert state machine must transition to the NI state, delete the assert winner's address and metric, and evaluate any possible transitions to its Upstream(S,G) state machine
Receive Prune(S,G), Join(S,G), or Graft(S,G)	A Prune(S,G), Join(S,G), or Graft(S,G) message was received on interface I with its upstream neighbor address set to the router's address on I. The router must send an Assert(S,G) on the receiving interface I to initiate an assert negotiation. The assert state machine remains in the assert L state. If a Graft(S,G) was received, the router must respond with a GraftAck(S,G).

3. An assert loser that receives a Prune(S,G), Join(S,G), or Graft(S,G) directed to it initiates a new assert negotiation so that the downstream router can correct its RPF'(S).

4. An assert winner for (S,G) sends a cancelling assert when it is about to stop forwarding on an (S,G) entry. Example: If a router is being taken down, then a cancelling assert is sent.

7.3.7 PIM Packet Formats

All PIM DM packets use the same format as PIM SM packets discussed in Chapter 5. All PIM control messages have IP number 103. All PIM DM messages must be sent with a TTL of 1. All PIM DM messages except Graft and GraftAck messages must be sent to the ALL-PIM-ROUTERS group. Graft messages should be unicast to the RPF'(S). GraftAck messages *must* be unicast to the sender of the graft.

The IPv4 ALL-PIM-ROUTERS group is 224.0.0.13. The IPv6 ALL-PIM-ROUTERS group is FF02::D.

7.3.7.1 PIM Header. As discussed in Chapter 5, all PIM Control messages have the header shown in Figure 7.6.

7.3.7.2 Hello Message Format. Refer to Chapter 5.

7.3.7.3 Join/Prune Message Format. Refer to Chapter 5.

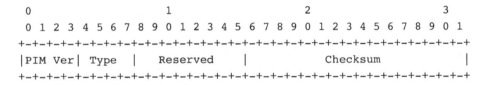

```
 0                   1                   2                   3
 0 1 2 3 4 5 6 7 8 9 0 1 2 3 4 5 6 7 8 9 0 1 2 3 4 5 6 7 8 9 0 1
+-+-+-+-+-+-+-+-+-+-+-+-+-+-+-+-+-+-+-+-+-+-+-+-+-+-+-+-+-+-+-+-+
|PIM Ver| Type  |    Reserved   |            Checksum           |
+-+-+-+-+-+-+-+-+-+-+-+-+-+-+-+-+-+-+-+-+-+-+-+-+-+-+-+-+-+-+-+-+
```

PIM Ver PIM version number is 2.

Type: Types for specific PIM messages:
0 = Hello
1 = Register (PIM SM only)
2 = Register Stop (PIM SM only)
3 = Join/Prune
4 = Bootstrap (PIM SM only)
5 = Assert
6 = Graft
7 = GrafTack
8 = Candidate RP Advertisement (PIM SM only)
9 = State Refresh

Figure 7.6. PIM Control Message

7.3.7.4 Assert Message Format. Refer to Chapter 5.

7.3.7.5 Graft Message Format. PIM Graft messages use the same format as Join/Prune messages, except that the Type field is set to 6. The source address must be in the Join section of the message. The Holdtime field should be zero and should be ignored when a graft is received.

7.3.7.6 GraftAck Message Format. PIM GraftAck messages are identical in format to the received Graft message, except that the Type field is set to 7. The Upstream Neighbor Address field should be set to the sender of the Graft message and should be ignored upon receipt.

7.3.7.7 State Refresh Message Format. PIM State Refresh messages have the format shown in Figure 7.7.

PIM Ver, Type, Reserved, Checksum: Described in PIM SM (see Chapter 5).

Multicast Group Address: The multicast group address in the encoded multicast address format given in PIM SM (see Chapter 5).

Source Address: The address of the data source in the encoded unicast address format given in PIM SM (see Chapter 5).

Originator Address: The address of the first hop router in the encoded unicast address format given in PIM SM (see Chapter 5).

R: The RP-tree bit. Set to 0 for PIM DM. Ignored upon receipt.

Metric Preference: The preference value assigned to the unicast routing protocol that provided the route to the source.

Metric: The cost metric of the unicast route to the source. The metric is in units applicable to the unicast routing protocol used.

```
 0                   1                   2                   3
 0 1 2 3 4 5 6 7 8 9 0 1 2 3 4 5 6 7 8 9 0 1 2 3 4 5 6 7 8 9 0 1
+-+-+-+-+-+-+-+-+-+-+-+-+-+-+-+-+-+-+-+-+-+-+-+-+-+-+-+-+-+-+-+-+
|PIM Ver| Type  |   Reserved    |            Checksum           |
+-+-+-+-+-+-+-+-+-+-+-+-+-+-+-+-+-+-+-+-+-+-+-+-+-+-+-+-+-+-+-+-+
|          Multicast Group Address (Encoded Group Format)       |
+-+-+-+-+-+-+-+-+-+-+-+-+-+-+-+-+-+-+-+-+-+-+-+-+-+-+-+-+-+-+-+-+
|             Source Address (Encoded Unicast Format)           |
+-+-+-+-+-+-+-+-+-+-+-+-+-+-+-+-+-+-+-+-+-+-+-+-+-+-+-+-+-+-+-+-+
|           Originator Address (Encoded Unicast Format)         |
+-+-+-+-+-+-+-+-+-+-+-+-+-+-+-+-+-+-+-+-+-+-+-+-+-+-+-+-+-+-+-+-+
|R|                    Metric Preference                        |
+-+-+-+-+-+-+-+-+-+-+-+-+-+-+-+-+-+-+-+-+-+-+-+-+-+-+-+-+-+-+-+-+
|                            Metric                             |
+-+-+-+-+-+-+-+-+-+-+-+-+-+-+-+-+-+-+-+-+-+-+-+-+-+-+-+-+-+-+-+-+
|    Masklen     |     TTL       |P|N|O|Reserved |   Interval    |
+-+-+-+-+-+-+-+-+-+-+-+-+-+-+-+-+-+-+-+-+-+-+-+-+-+-+-+-+-+-+-+-+
```

Figure 7.7. Refresh Message

Masklen: The length of the address mask of the unicast route to the source.

TTL: Time to Live of the State Refresh message. Decremented each time the message is forwarded. Note that this is different from the IP header TTL, which is always set to 1.

P: Prune indicator flag. This must be set to 1 if the state refresh is to be sent on a pruned interface. Otherwise, it must be set to 0.

N: Prune Now flag. This should be set to 1 by the state refresh originator on every third State Refresh message and should be ignored upon receipt. This is for compatibility with earlier versions of state refresh.

O: Assert Override flag. This should be set to 1 by upstream routers on a LAN if the Assert Timer (AT(S,G)) is not running and should be ignored upon receipt. This is for compatibility with earlier versions of state refresh.

Reserved: Set to zero and ignored upon receipt.

Interval: Set by the originating router to the interval (in seconds) between consecutive State Refresh messages for this (S,G) pair.

REFERENCES

[PAR200601] L. Parziale,W. Liu, et al., TCP/IP Tutorial and Technical Overview, IBM Press, Redbook Abstract, 2006, IBM Form Number GG24-3376-07, 2006.

[RFC3973] RFC 3973, Protocol Independent Multicast—Dense-Mode (PIM—DM): Protocol Specification (Revised), J. Nicholas, W. Siadak, January 2005.

8

OTHER DENSE-MODE MULTICAST ROUTING PROTOCOLS: DVMRP AND MOSPF

This chapter provides a short overview of other DM MRPs not covered so far, specifically Distance Vector Multicast Routing Protocol (DVMRP) and Multicast Open Shortest Path First (MOSPF). These protocols are generally not used in current IPTV/DVB-H applications, but MOSPF may have applicability at some future point in time. Portions of this discussion are based on the pertinent RFCs.

8.1 DISTANCE VECTOR MULTICAST ALGORITHM

8.1.1 Overview

In previous chapters we discussed the processes typically used for the creation of source-based multicast trees. As noted, these distribution trees can be built by

- a distance-vector algorithm that may be implemented separately from the unicast routing algorithm (as is the case with DVMRP discussed below) or using the information present in the underlying unicast routing table (as is the case with PIM DM) or

- a link-state algorithm (as is the case with MOSPF, also discussed below).

The distance vector multicast algorithm builds a multicast delivery tree using a variant of the RPF technique. In broad terms, the technique is as follows: when a multicast router receives a multicast data packet, if the packet arrives on the interface used to reach the source of the packet, the packet is forwarded over all outgoing interfaces, except leaf subnets with no members attached; a "leaf" subnet is a subnet that no router would use to reach the source of a multicast packet. If the data packet does not arrive over the link that would be used to reach the source, then the packet is discarded. This constitutes a "broadcast-and-prune" approach to multicast tree construction: when a data packet reaches a leaf router, if that router has no membership registered on any of its directly attached subnetworks, the router sends a Prune message one hop back toward the source. The receiving router then checks its leaf subnets for group membership and checks whether it has received a prune from all of its downstream routers (downstream with respect to the source). If so, the router itself can send a Prune message upstream over the interface leading to the source. The sender and receiver of a Prune message must cache the $<S, G>$ pair being reported for a "lifetime," typically of minutes. Unless a router's prune information is refreshed by the receipt of a new prune for $<$source, group$>$ before its "lifetime" expires, that information is removed, allowing data to flow over the branch again. The state that expires in this way is referred to as of "soft state" [RFC2201].

Note that routers that do not lead to group members still have to deal with overhead generated by Prune messages. For wide-area multicasting this technique does not scale (as discussed in Chapter 6).

8.1.2 Basic DVMRP Operation

DVMRP[1] is defined in RFC 1075 (1988) and uses RPF. It is an interior gateway protocol [operate within an Autonomous System (AS)] used to build per-source, per-group multicast delivery trees. As described above and in Chapter 3, when a router receives a packet, it floods the packet out of all paths except the one that leads back to the packet's source. If a downstream router does not wish to receive a particular multicast group because there are no active members, the router can send a Prune message back up the distribution tree to inhibit subsequent packets from reaching it. DVMRP periodically refloods the network in an effort to make sure that any new users that wish to receive a particular group G are reachable over the distribution tree. There is a direct correlation between the frequency of the reflooding and the time required for a new receiver to join the group and receive the data stream. In turn, the necessity for frequent reflooding limits the scalability of DVMRP, as we noted in previous chapters.

---

[1] DVMRP has been used to support MBONE, a multicast service over the Internet, by establishing tunnels between DVMRP-capable machines; MBONE was used widely in the research community.

Note that:

- DVMRP builds per-source trees based on routing information collected via protocol exchanges.
- DVMRP prunes the per-source broadcast tree to generate a multicast delivery tree; DVMRP utilizes the RPF algorithm to establish the set of downstream interfaces used to forward multicast traffic.

DVMRP uses its own routing process; this routing is based on hop counts and is similar to the Routing Information Protocol (RIP). DVMRP does not route unicast datagrams, hence a router that needs to process both multicast and unicast datagrams must be configured with two separate routing processes. Note, as a consequence, that the path that the multicast traffic uses to reach a destination may not be the same as the path that the unicast traffic uses to reach the same destination. While in principle this is not necessarily a problem of its own, the implications are that a dual state must be maintained at a router.

A key operation of DVMRP is the neighbor discovery operation. A DVMRP router dynamically discovers its neighbors by periodically transmitting Neighbor Probe messages over each of its local interfaces. The transmitted message contains a list of neighbor routers from which Neighbor Probe messages have been received. Upon receiving a Probe message that contains its own address in the neighbor list, the pair of routers establishes a two-way neighbor adjacency relationship. Messages are transmitted to the multicast address 224.0.0.4 *"all-DVMRP-routers"* (See Chapter 2).

Another key operation is the routing table creation operation. The DVMRP algorithm is based on hop counts and the algorithm computes the set of reverse paths identified in the RPF algorithm. As part of the process, the routing table is exchanged between each neighbor router. The algorithm makes use of a metric configured on every router interface. Each router advertises the network number, mask, and metric of each interface; it also advertises routes received from neighbor routers. As is the case for other distance vector protocols, when a route is received, the interface metric is added to the advertised metric; this adjusted metric is then used to determine the best upstream path to the source [PAR200601].

The creation of a list of dependent downstream routers is also important. The DVMRP algorithm utilizes the exchange of a routing information mechanism to notify upstream routers that a specific downstream router requires these upstream routers to forward multicast traffic to this downstream router. DVMRP accomplishes this as described next. If a downstream router selects an upstream router as the next hop to a particular source, then the routing updates from the downstream router have a metric set to a very large number ("infinity") for the source network. When the upstream DVMRP router receives the advertisement, it adds the downstream router to the list of *dependent downstream routers* for this source. This technique provides the information needed to prune the multicast delivery tree [PAR200601]. DVMRP prevents the forwarding of duplicate packets by enforcing the concept of a *designated forwarder* for each source. This is accomplished as follows: when routers exchange their routing table, each router makes note of the peer's metric to reach the source network. By convention, it will be the router with the lowest metric that is responsible for forwarding data to the shared network (if multiple routers have the same metric, then the router with the lowest IP address becomes the designated forwarder for the network).

Building and maintaining multicast delivery trees is obviously a key operation of the protocol. The RPF algorithm is used in a DVMRP environment to forward multicast datagrams. As described in Chapter 3, with RPF, if a datagram is received via the interface that represents the best path to the source, then the router forwards the datagram along the set of downstream interfaces. This set contains each downstream interface included in the multicast delivery tree.

If a multicast router has no dependent downstream neighbors through a specific interface, the network as seen from that interface is called a *leaf network*. If a network is a leaf for a given source, and if there are no members of a particular group on the network, then there are no recipients for datagrams from the source to the group on that network. That network's parent router can forgo sending those datagrams on that network; this is also called "truncating" the shortest path tree. The algorithm that tracks and uses this information is the Truncated Reverse Path Broadcasting (TRPB) algorithm [RFC1075]. If a new router connects to a leaf network, packets are forwarded on that network only if there are hosts/receivers that are members of the specific multicast group as determined through the IGMP and the local group database that is generated from IGMP transactions. If the group address is currently listed and the router is the designated forwarder for the source, then, and only then, the interface is included in the multicast delivery tree.

Pruning of the multicast tree is important in order to optimize network resources. At first, all networks that are nonleaf networks are included in the multicast delivery tree. However, routers connected to leaf networks abrogate an interface when there are no longer any active receivers/members participating in the specific multicast group; thereafter, multicast packets are no longer forwarded through the interface. If and when a router is able to remove all of its downstream interfaces for a specific group, it notifies its upstream neighbor (by sending a Prune message to the upstream neighbor) that it no longer is in need of traffic from that particular source and group pair. In turn, if the upstream neighbor receives Prune messages from each of the dependent downstream routers on a given interface, the upstream router can remove this interface from the multicast delivery tree. In turn, again, if this upstream router is able to prune all of its interfaces from the tree, it sends a Prune message to its upstream router. This process continues until all unused branches have been pruned from the delivery tree. In order to eliminate the possibility of using outdated prune information, each Prune message contains a prune lifetime timer that indicates the length of time that the prune is to remain in effect.

DVMRP routers use graft messages to reattach portions of the network to the multicast delivery tree. This is needed because IP multicast is required to accommodate dynamic group membership. A Graft message is sent upon receiving an IGMP MR for a group that has previously been pruned. Distinct Graft messages are transmitted to the appropriate upstream neighbor for each source network that has been Pruned. Receipt of a Graft message is acknowledged with a Graft ACK message; if an acknowledgment is not received within the graft timeout period, the request is retransmitted. ACKs enable the sender to distinguish between a misrouted graft packet and an inactive device.

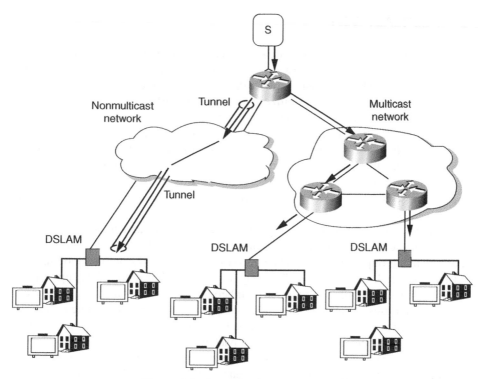

Figure 8.1. Example of a DVMRP Tunnel

In addition to its native functionality, DVMRP can tunnel IP multicast datagrams through networks containing nonmulticast routers. Here the datagrams are encapsulated in unicast IP packets and forwarded through the network. When the packet is received at the remote end of the tunnel, it is deencapsulated and forwarded through the remaining subnetwork using DVMRP multicast methods (as discussed in the previous paragraphs). See Figure 8.1 for a pictorial example of tunneling.

The frequent reflooding procedure limits the scalability of DVMRP to large user populations. In an IPTV application, one would have a (super)source but several hundred groups G. As it can be seen in Table 8.1 (expanded from Table 6.1), between 10,000 and 50,000 table entries per router are required. This is generally at the mid-high-end of what a router typically is able to support.

TABLE 8.1. Amount of State Required by CBT and DVMRP

Number of groups	200	400
Group size (no. of members)	10,000	50,000
No. of services per group	0.5%	0.25%
No. of DVMRP router entries	10K	50K

8.2   MULTICAST OSPF

MOSPF is a multicast extension to OSPF Version 2 that is described in RFC 1584. MOSPF provides the ability to forward multicast datagrams from one IP network to another (i.e., through Internet routers). MOSPF is a link-state multicast algorithm that is employed in networks that already utilize OSPF for unicast IP routing (it is not a separate multicast routing protocol per se). The multicast extensions make use of the existing OSPF topology database to create a source-rooted shortest path delivery tree. While OSPF relies only on the destination address, MOSPF forwards a multicast datagram on the basis of both the datagram's source and destination (this is also called source/destination routing).

As discussed in RFC 2201, routers implementing a link-state algorithm periodically collect reachability information related to their directly attached neighbors, then flood this throughout the routing domain using the so-called link-state update packets. Stephen Deering extended the link-state algorithm for multicasting by having a router additionally detect group membership changes on its incident links before flooding this information in link-state packets. This way, each router has a complete, up-to-date image of a domain's topology and group membership. Upon receiving a multicast data packet, a router uses its membership and topology information to calculate a shortest path tree rooted at the sender subnetwork; on the assumption that the router is on the computed tree, the router forwards the data packet over the interfaces defined by its calculation. Hence, multicast data packets only traverse routers leading to members either directly attached or further downstream. That is, the delivery tree is a true multicast tree right from the start. However, the flooding of group membership information is the predominant factor preventing the link-state multicast algorithm being applicable over a wide-area network. The other limiting factor is the processing cost of the Dijkstra calculation to compute the shortest path tree for each active source [RFC2201].

The OSPF link-state database provides a complete description of the topology of an AS. OSPF allows an AS to be segmented into multiple areas; areas are generally utilized for traffic management purposes. However, when this is done, complete knowledge of the AS's topology is lost. By adding a new type of link-state advertisement, the group membership Link-State Advertisements (LSAs), the location of all multicast group members is defined in the database. The path of a multicast datagram can then be calculated by building a shortest path tree rooted at the datagram's source. All branches not containing multicast members are pruned from the tree. These pruned shortest path trees are initially built when the first datagram is received (i.e., on demand). The results of the shortest path calculation are then cached for use by subsequent datagrams having the same source and destination.

When forwarding multicasts between areas, only incomplete shortest path trees can be built; this may lead to some inefficiency in routing. An analogous situation exists when the source of the multicast datagram lies in another AS. In both cases (i.e., the source of the datagram belongs to a different OSPF area or to a different AS) the neighborhood immediately surrounding the source is unknown. In these cases the source's neighborhood is approximated by OSPF summary link advertisements or by OSPF AS external link advertisements, respectively. Routers running MOSPF can be intermixed with nonmulticast OSPF routers. Both types of routers can interoperate when forwarding regular (unicast) IP data traffic. The forwarding extent of IP multicasts is limited by the number of MOSPF routers present in the AS (and their interconnection, if any). An ability to "tunnel" multicast datagrams through nonmulticast routers is *not* provided. In MOSPF, just as in the OSPF protocol, datagrams (multicast or unicast) are routed "as is" — they are not further encapsulated or deencapsulated as they transit the AS [RFC1584].

MOSPF forwards a multicast datagram to a group G by building a shortest path delivery tree rooted at the datagram's source S using information contained in the link-state database. Branches in the shortest path delivery tree that do not have a corresponding group membership LSA are pruned, because these branches do not contain any multicast members for the group G. Note that all routers generate an identical shortest path delivery tree for a specific multicast datagram and there is a single path between the datagram source and any specific destination. The tree is recomputed when a link-state change occurs or when the forwarding information ages (times out).

As a multicast datagram is forwarded along its shortest path tree, the datagram is delivered to each member of the destination multicast group. As is the case for PIM, on each network segment, one MOSPF router is selected to be the DR. The DR is responsible for generating periodic IGMP host membership queries. The DR is also responsible for accumulating IGMP MRs. Routers ignore any MRs received on a network where they are not the DR, thus ensuring that each network segment appears in the local group database of at most one router and also preventing datagrams from being duplicated as they are transmitted to local group members. Every router transmits in a flooding mode a group membership LSA for each multicast group that has at least one entry in the router's local group database. The forwarding of the multicast datagram has the following properties [RFC1584]:

- The path taken by a multicast datagram depends on both the datagram's source and its multicast destination; this is called source/destination routing—this is in contrast to most unicast datagram forwarding algorithms (as is the case for OSPF) that route based solely on destination.
- The path taken between the datagram's source and any particular destination group member is the least cost path available. Cost is expressed in terms of the OSPF link-state metric. For example, if the OSPF metric represents delay, a minimum-delay path is chosen. OSPF metrics are configurable. A metric is assigned to each outbound router interface, representing the cost of sending a packet on that interface. The cost of a path is the sum of its constituent (outbound) router interfaces.
- MOSPF takes advantage of any commonality of least cost paths to destination group members. However, when members of the multicast group are spread out

over multiple networks, the multicast datagram must at times be replicated. This replication is performed as few times as possible (at the tree branches), taking maximum advantage of common path segments.

- For a given multicast datagram, all routers calculate an identical shortest path tree. There is a single path between the datagram's source and any particular destination group member. This means that, unlike OSPF's treatment of regular (unicast) IP data traffic, there is no provision for equal-cost multipath.
- On each packet hop, MOSPF normally forwards IP multicast datagrams as data link multicasts. There are two exceptions. First, on nonbroadcast networks, since there are no data link multicast/broadcast services, the datagram must be forwarded to specific MOSPF neighbors. Second, a MOSPF router can be configured to forward IP multicasts on specific networks as data link unicasts, in order to avoid datagram replication in certain anomalous situations.

As noted, the location of every group member is communicated to the rest of the network. This ensures that multicast datagrams can be forwarded to each member. OSPF uses group membership LSAs to track the location of each group member. These LSAs are stored in the OSPF link-state database that effectively describes the topology of the AS [PAR200601].

While MOSPF optimizes the path to any given group member, it does not necessarily optimize the use of the internetwork as a whole. To do so, instead of calculating source-based shortest path trees, something similar to a minimal spanning tree (containing only the group members) would need to be calculated. This type of minimal spanning tree is called a Steiner tree in the literature.

In a multiple-area environment, provisions need to be made to maintain global topology information because a router is only aware of the network topology within the local area. Within an OSPF area, the Area Border Router (ABR[2]) forwards routing information and data traffic between areas; in an MOSPF environment this function is performed by an *interarea multicast forwarder*. The interarea multicast forwarder forwards group membership information and multicast datagrams between areas. Because group membership LSAs are only flooded within an area, a process in the interarea multicast forwarder is needed to convey membership information between areas. To do this, each interarea multicast forwarder summarizes the attached areas' group membership information and forwards this information to OSPF backbone. This announcement consists of a group membership LSA listing each group containing members in the nonbackbone area. The advertisement supports the same function as the summary LSAs generated in a standard OSPF area. Membership information for the nonbackbone area is summarized into the backbone; however, this information is not readvertised into other nonbackbone areas. To forward multicast data traffic between areas, a *wildcard multicast receiver* is utilized. This is a router to which all multicast traffic, regardless of destination, is forwarded. In nonbackbone areas, all interarea multicast forwarders are wildcard multicast receivers. This ensures that all multicast traffic that

---

[2] Aka Autonomous System Border Router (ASBR).

originates in a nonbackbone area is forwarded to an interarea multicast forwarder. This router sends the multicast datagrams to the backbone area; because the backbone has complete knowledge of all group membership information, the datagrams are then forwarded to the appropriate group members in other areas [PAR200601].

REFERENCES

[PAR200601] L. Parziale, W. Liu, et al., TCP/IP Tutorial and Technical Overview, IBM Press, Redbook Abstract, IBM Form Number GG24-3376-07, 2006.

[RFC1075] RFC 1075, Distance Vector Multicast Routing Protocol, D. Waitzman, C. Partridge, S. Deering, November 1988

[RFC1584] RFC 1584, Multicast Extensions to OSPF, J. Moy, March 1994.

[RFC2201] RFC 2201, Core Based Trees (CBT) Multicast Routing Architecture, A. Ballardie, September 1997.

9

IP MULTICASTING IN IPv6 ENVIRONMENTS

This chapter discusses IPv6 and multicast applications. The first part is a short tutorial on IPv6; the second part looks at multicast-specific issues. IPv6 is now seeing major deployment in Europe and Asia; eventually, it will also see deployment in North America.

9.1 OPPORTUNITIES OFFERED BY IPv6

The IPv6 is now gaining momentum as an improved network layer protocol. There is a lot of commercial interest and activity in Europe and Asia, and as of press time, there was also some traction in the United States. For example, the U.S. Department of Defense (DoD) announced that from October 1, 2003, all new developments and procurements needed to be IPv6 capable; the DoD's goal was to complete the transition to IPv6 for all intra- and internetworking across the agency by 2008. In 2005, the U.S. Government Accountability Office (GAO) recommended that all agencies become proactive in planning a coherent transition to IPv6. The expectation is that in the next few years, a transition to this new protocol will occur worldwide [MIN200801].

IP Multicast with Applications to IPTV and Mobile DVB-H   by Daniel Minoli
Copyright © 2008 John Wiley & Sons, Inc.

IPv6 is considered to be the next generation IP ([MIN200801], [HAG200201], [MUR200501], [SOL200401], [ITO200401], [MIL200001], [GRA200001], [DAV200201], [LOS200301], [GON199801], [DEM200301], [GOS200301], [MIN200601], [WEG199901]). The current version of IP, IPv4, has been in use for almost 30 years and exhibits some challenges in supporting emerging demands for address space cardinality, high-density mobility, multimedia, and strong security. This is particularly true in developing domestic and defense department applications utilizing peer-to-peer networking. IPv6 is an improved version of IP that is designed to coexist with IPv4 and eventually provide better internetworking capabilities than IPv4 [IPV200401].

IPv6 offers the potential of achieving the scalability, reacheability, end-to-end interworking, QoS, and commercial-grade robustness for data as well as for Voice Over IP (VoIP), IPTV distribution, and triple-play networks; these capabilities are mandatory mileposts of the technology if it is to replace the Time Division Multiplexing (TDM) infrastructure around the world.

IPv6 was initially developed in the early 1990s because of the anticipated need for more end-system addresses based on anticipated Internet growth, encompassing mobile phone deployment, smart home appliances, and billions of new users in developing countries (e.g., in China and India). New technologies and applications such as VoIP, "always-on access" (e.g., DSL and cable), Ethernet-to-the-home, converged networks, and evolving ubiquitous computing applications will be driving this need even more in the next few years [IPV200501]. A converged network utilizing IPv6 supports both local- and wide-area components as well as private and carrier-provided communications domains; the IPv6/IPv4 network can support video delivery, VoIP, Internet, intranet, and wireless services.

Basic Network Address Translation (NAT) is a method by which IP addresses (specifically IPv4 addresses) are transparently mapped from one group to another. Specifically, private "nonregistered" addresses are mapped to a small set (as small as 1) of public registered addresses; this impacts the general addressability, accessibility, and "individuality" of the device. Network Address Port Translation (NAPT) is a method by which many network addresses and their TCP/UDP ports are translated into a single network address and its TCP/UDP ports. Together, these two methods, referred to as traditional NAT, provide a mechanism to connect a realm with private addresses to an external realm with globally unique registered addresses [RFC3022].

NAT is a short-term solution for the anticipated Internet growth phenomenon and a better solution is needed for address exhaustion. There is a recognition that NAT techniques make the internetworking, the applications, and even the devices more complex and this means a cost overhead [IPV200501]. The expectation is that IPv6 can make IP devices less expensive, more powerful, and even consume less power; the power issue not only is important for environmental reasons but also improves operability (e.g., longer battery life in portable devices, such as mobile phones).

Corporations and government agencies will be able to achieve a number of improvements with IPv6. IPv6 can improve a firm's intranet, with benefits such as follows:

- Expanded addressing capabilities
- Serverless autoconfiguration ("plug-and-play") and reconfiguration
- More efficient and robust mobility mechanisms
- End-to-end security, with built-in, strong IP layer encryption, and authentication
- Streamlined header format and flow identification
- Enhanced support for multicast and QoS
- Extensibility—improved support for feature options/extensions

While the basic function of IP is to move information across networks, IPv6 has more capabilities built into its foundation than IPv4. A key capability is the significant increase in address space. For example, all devices could have a public IP address, so that they can be uniquely tracked. Today, inventory management of dispersed Information Technology (IT) assets cannot be achieved with IP mechanisms; during the inventory cycle, someone has to manually verify the location of each desktop computer. With IPv6, one can use the network to verify that such equipment is there; even non-IT equipment in the field can also be tracked, by having an IP address permanently assigned to it. IPv6 also has extensive automatic configuration (autoconfiguration) mechanisms and reduces the IT burden, thereby making configuration essentially plug-and-play.

9.2   INTRODUCTORY OVERVIEW OF IPv6

IP was designed in the 1970s for the purpose of connecting computers that were in separate geographic locations. Computers on a campus were connected by means of local networks, but these local networks were separated into essentially stand-alone islands. Internet, as a name to designate the protocol and more recently the worldwide information network, simply means "internetwork," that is, a connection between networks. In the beginning, the protocol had only military use, but computers from universities and enterprises were quickly added. The Internet as a worldwide information network is the result of the practical application of IP, that is, the result of the interconnection of a large set of information networks [IPV200501]. Starting in the early 1990s, developers realized that the communication needs of the 21st century needed a protocol with some new features and capabilities while at the same time retaining the useful features of the existing protocol.

While link-level communication does not generally require a node identifier (address) since the device is intrinsically identified with the link-level address, communication over a group of links (a network) does require unique node identifiers (addresses). The IP address is an identifier that is applied to each device connected to an IP network. In this setup, different elements taking part in the network (servers, routers, user computers, etc.) communicate among each other using their IP address as an entity identifier. In IPv4, addresses consist of four octets. For ease of human conversation, IP addresses are represented as separated by periods, for example, 166.74.110.83, where the decimal numbers are a shorthand (and corresponds to) the binary code described by the byte in question (an 8-bit number takes a value in the 0–255 range). Since the IPv4 address has 32 bits there are nominally 2^{32} different IP addresses (approximately four billions nodes if all combinations are used).

IPv6 is the Internet's next-generation protocol, which was at first called IPng ("Internet Next Generation"). The IETF developed the basic specifications during the 1990s to support a migration to a new environment. IPv6 is defined in RFC 2460, which obsoletes RFC 1883. [The "version 5" reference was employed for another use (an experimental real-time streaming protocol), and to avoid any confusion, it was decided not to use this nomenclature.]

9.2.1 IPv6 Benefits

IPv4 has proven, by means of its long life, to be a flexible and powerful networking mechanism. However, IPv4 is starting to exhibit limitations, not only with respect to the need for an increase of the IP address space, driven, for example, by new populations of users in countries such as China and India and by new technologies with "always connected devices" (DSL, cable, networked PDAs, 2.5G/3G mobile telephones, etc.), but also in reference to a potential global rollout of VoIP. IPv6 creates a new IP address format, so that the number of IP addresses will not exhaust for several decades or longer even though an entire new crop of devices are expected to connect to Internet.

IPv6 also adds improvements in areas such as routing and network autoconfiguration. Specifically, new devices that connect to the Internet will be "plug-and-play" devices. With IPv6 one is not required to configure dynamic nonpublished local IP addresses, the gateway address, the subnetwork mask, or any other parameters. When plugged into the network, the equipment automatically obtains all requisite configuration data [IPV200501].

The advantages of IPv6 can be summarized as follows:

- Scalability: IPv6 has 128-bit addresses versus 32-bit IPv4 addresses. With IPv4, the theoretical number of available IP addresses are $2^{32} - 10^{10}$. IPv6 offers a 2^{128} space. Hence, the number of available unique node addresses is $2^{128} - 10^{39}$.
- Security: IPv6 includes security in its specifications such as payload encryption and authentication of the source of the communication.
- Real-time applications: To provide better support for real-time traffic (e.g., VoIP), IPv6 includes "labeled flows" in its specifications. By means of this mechanism routers can recognize the end-to-end flow to which transmitted packets belong. This is similar to the service offered by MPLS, but it is intrinsic with the IP mechanism rather than an add-on. Also, it preceded this MPLS feature by a number of years.

- Plug-and-play: IPv6 includes a plug-and-play mechanism that facilitates the connection of equipment to the network. The requisite configuration is automatic.
- Mobility: IPv6 includes more efficient and enhanced mobility mechanisms, particularly important for mobile networks.
- Optimized protocol: IPv6 embodies IPv4 best practices but removes unused or obsolete IPv4 characteristics. This results in a better optimized IP.
- Addressing and routing: IPv6 improves the addressing and routing hierarchy.
- Extensibility: IPv6 has been designed to be extensible and offers support for new options and extensions.

9.2.2 Traditional Addressing Classes for IPv4

With IPv4, the 32-bit address can be represented as AdrClass|netID|host. The network portion can contain either a network ID or a network ID and a subnet. Every network and every host or device has a unique address, by definition. The traditional IPv4 address classes were as follows:

- Traditional Class A address: Class A uses the first bit of the 32-bit space (bit 0) to identify it as a Class A address; this bit is set to 0. Bits $1-7$ represent the network ID and bits $8-31$ identify the PC, terminal device, or host/server on the network. This address space supports $2^7 - 2 = 126$ networks and approximately 16 million devices (2^{24}) on each network. By convention, the use of an "all 1s" or "all 0s" address for both the network ID and the host ID is prohibited (which is the reason for subtracting the 2 above).
- Traditional Class B address: Class B uses the first 2 bits (bit 0 and bit 1) of the 32-bit space to identify it as a Class B address; these bits are set to 10. Bits $2-15$ represent the network ID and bits $16-31$ identify the PC, terminal device, or host/server on the network. This address space supports $2^{14} - 2 = 16,382$ networks and $2^{16} - 2 = 65,134$ devices on each network.
- Traditional Class C address: Class C uses the first 3 bits (bit 0, bit 1, and bit 2) of the 32-bit space to identify it as a Class C address; these bits are set to 110. Bits $3-23$ represent the network ID and bits $24-31$ identify the PC, terminal device, or host/server on the network. This address space supports about 2 million networks ($2^{21} - 2$) and $2^8 - 2 = 254$ devices on each network.
- Traditional Class D address: This class is used for broadcasting and/or multicasting: wherein all devices on the network receive the same packet. Class D uses the first 4 bits (bit 0, bit 1, bit 2, and bit 3) of the 32-bit space to identify it as a Class D address; these bits are set to 1110.

Classless Interdomain Routing (CIDR), described in RFC 1518, RFC 1519, and RFC 2050, is yet another mechanism that was developed to help alleviate the problem of exhaustion of IP addresses and growth of routing tables. The concept behind CIDR is that blocks of multiple addresses (for example, blocks of Class C address) can be combined, or aggregated, to create a larger classless set of IP addresses, with more hosts allowed. Blocks of Class C network numbers are allocated to each network service provider; organizations using the network service provider for Internet connectivity are allocated subsets of the service provider's address space as required. These multiple Class C addresses can then be summarized in routing tables, resulting in fewer route advertisements. The CIDR mechanism can also be applied to blocks of Class A and B addresses [TEA200401]. All of this assumes, however, that the institution in question already has an assigned set of public, registered IP addresses; it does not address the issue of how to get additional public, registered, globally unique IP addresses.

9.2.3 Network Address Translation Issues in IPv4

IPv4 addresses can be from an officially assigned public range or from an internal intranet private (but not globally unique) block. Internal intranet addresses may be in the ranges of 10.0.0.0/8, 172.16.0.0/12, and 192.168.0.0/16. In the internal intranet private address case, a NAT function is employed to map the internal addresses to an external public address when the private-to-public network boundary is crossed. This, however, imposes a number of limitations, particularly since the number of registered public addresses available to a company is almost invariably much smaller (as small as 1) than the number of internal devices requiring an address.

As noted, IPv4 theoretically allows up to 2^{32} addresses, based on a four-octet address space. Public, globally unique addresses are assigned by the IANA. IP addresses are addresses of network nodes at layer 3; each device on a network (whether the Internet or an intranet) must have a unique address. In IPv4, it is a 32-bit (4-byte) binary address used to identify a host's network ID. It is represented by the nomenclature *a.b.c.d* (each of *a*, *b*, *c*, and *d* being from 1 to 255 (0 has a special meaning). Examples are 167.168.169.170, 232.233.229.209, and 200.100.200.100.

The problem is that during the 1980s many public registered addresses were allocated to firms and organizations without any consistent control. As a result, some organizations have more addresses than they actually need, giving rise to the present dearth of available "registerable" layer 3 addresses. Furthermore, not all IP addresses can be used due to the fragmentation described above.

One approach to the issue would be a renumbering and a reallocation of the IPv4 addressing space. However, this is not as simple as it appears since it requires worldwide coordination efforts. Moreover, it would still be limited for the human population and the quantity of devices that will be connected to the Internet in the medium-term future [IPV200501]. At this juncture, and as a temporary and pragmatic approach to alleviate the dearth of addresses, NAT mechanisms are employed by organizations and even home users. This mechanism consists of using only a small set of public IPv4 addresses for an entire network to access the Internet. The myriad of internal devices are assigned IP addresses from a specifically designated range of Class A or Class C addresses that are locally unique but are duplicatively used and reused within various organizations. In some cases (e.g., residential Internet access use via DSL or cable), the legal IP address is only provided to a user on a time-lease basis, rather than permanently.

A number of protocols cannot travel through a NAT device and hence the use of NAT implies that many applications (e.g., VoIP) cannot be used effectively in all instances. As a consequence, these applications can only be used in intranets. Examples include [IPV200501] the following:

- Multimedia applications such as videoconferencing, VoIP, or video-on-demand/ IPTV do not work smoothly through NAT devices. Multimedia applications make use of RTP and Real-Time Control Protocol (RTCP). These in turn use UDP with dynamic allocation of ports and NAT does not directly support this environment.

- Kerberos authentication needs the source address and the source address in the IP header is often modified by NAT devices.

- IPSec is used extensively for data authentication, integrity, and confidentiality. However, when NAT is used, IPSec operation is impacted, since NAT changes the address in the IP header.

- Multicast, although possible in theory, requires complex configuration in a NAT environment and hence, in practice, is not utilized as often as could be the case.

The need for obligatory use of NAT disappears with IPv6.

9.2.4 IPv6 Address Space

The format of IPv6 addressing is described in RFC 2373. As noted, an IPv6 address consists of 128 bits, rather than 32 bits as with IPv4 addresses. The number of bits correlates to the address space as follows:

IP Version	Size of Address Space
IPv6	128 bits, which allows for 2^{128} or $340,282,366,920,938,463,463,374,607,431,768,211,456$ (3.4×10^{38}) possible addresses
IPv4	32 bits, which allows for 2^{32} or $4,294,967,296$ possible addresses

The relatively large size of the IPv6 address is designed to be subdivided into hierarchical routing domains that reflect the topology of the modern-day Internet. The use of 128 bits provides multiple levels of hierarchy and flexibility in designing hierarchical addressing and routing. The IPv4-based Internet currently lacks this flexibility [MSD200401].

The IPv6 address is represented as eight groups of 16 bits each separated by the ":" character. Each 16-bit group is represented by four hexadecimal digits, that is, each digit has a value between 0 and F (0,1, 2, ... A, B, C, D, E, F with $A = 10$, $B = 11$, etc., to $F = 15$). What follows is an IPv6 address example:

3223:0BA0:01E0:D001:0000:0000:D0F0:0010

An abbreviated format exists to designate IPv6 addresses when all endings are 0. For example,

3223:0BA0::

is the abbreviated form of the following address:

3223:0BA0:0000:0000:0000:0000:0000:0000

Similarly, only one 0 is written, removing 0s in the left side and four 0s in the middle of the address. For example, the address

3223:BA0:0:0:0:0::1234

is the abbreviated form of the following address:

3223:0BA0:0000:0000:0000:0000:0000:1234

There is also a method to designate groups of IP addresses or subnetworks that is based on specifying the number of bits that designate the subnetwork, beginning from left to right, using remaining bits to designate single devices inside the network. For example, the notation

3223:0BA0:01a0::/48

indicates that the part of the IP address used to represent the subnetwork has 48 bits. Since each hexadecimal digit has 4 bits, this points out that the part used to represent the subnetwork is formed by 12 digits, that is: "3223:0BA0:01A0." The remaining digits of the IP address would be used to represent nodes inside the network.

There are a number of special IPv6 addresses, as follows:

- Auto-return or loopback virtual address: This address is specified in IPv4 as the 127.0.0.1 address. In IPv6 this address is represented as ::1.
- Not specified address (::): This address is not allocated to any node since it is used to indicate absence of address.
- IPv6 over IPv4 dynamic/automatic tunnel addresses: These addresses are designated as IPv4-compatible IPv6 addresses and allow the sending of IPv6 traffic over IPv4 networks in a transparent manner. They are represented as, for example, ::156.55.23.5.
- IPv4 over IPv6 addresses automatic representation: These addresses allow for IPv4-only nodes to still work in IPv6 networks. They are designated as "mapped from IPv4 to IPv6 addresses" and are represented as ::FFFF:, for example, ::FFFF.156.55.43.3.

9.2.5   Basic Protocol Constructs

Table 9.1 lists basic IPv6 terminology while Table 9.2 shows the core protocols that comprise IPv6.

A scope is a subset of the network; multiple scopes are defined within IPv6, as illustrated in Figure 9.1. Table 9.3 shows the address and associated reachability scopes. The reachability of *node-local addresses* is "the same node"; the reachability of

TABLE 9.1. Basic IPv6 Terminology

Address	An IP layer identifier for an interface or a set of interfaces.
Host	Any node that is not a router.
Interface	A node's attachment to a link.
Link	A communication facility or medium over which nodes can communicate at the link layer, that is, the layer immediately below IP. Examples are Ethernet (simple or bridged); PPP links, X.25, frame relay, or ATM networks; and Internet (or higher) layer "tunnels," such as tunnels over IPv4 or IPv6 itself.
Link-layer identifier	A link-layer identifier for an interface. Examples include IEEE 802 addresses for Ethernet network interfaces and E.164 addresses for ISDN links.
Link-local address	An IPv6 address having a link-only scope, indicated by having the prefix (FE80::/10), that can be used to reach neighboring nodes attached to the same link. Every interface has a link-local address.
Multicast address	An identifier for a set of interfaces typically belonging to different nodes. A packet sent to a multicast address is delivered to all interfaces identified by that address.
Neighbor	A node attached to the same link.
Node	A device that implements IP.
Packet	An IP header plus payload.
Prefix	The initial bits of an address, or a set of IP addresses that share the same initial bits.
Prefix length	The number of bits in a prefix.
Router	A node that forwards IP packets not explicitly addressed to itself.
Unicast address	An identifier for a single interface. A packet sent to a unicast address is delivered to the interface identified by that address.

link-local addresses is "the local link"; the reachability of *site-local addresses*[1] is "the private intranet"; and the reachability of *global addresses* is "the IPv6-enabled Internet." IPv6 interfaces can have multiple addresses that have different reachability scopes. For example, a node may have a link-local address, a site-local address, and a global address. *Note*: IPv6 actually has possible 15 scopes, as hex 0 to hex *F*; some of these scopes are unused.

Like IPv4, IPv6 is a connectionless, unreliable datagram protocol used primarily for addressing and routing packets between hosts. Connectionless means that a session is not established before exchanging data. Unreliable means that delivery is not guaranteed. IPv6 always makes a best effort attempt to deliver a packet. An IPv6 packet might be lost, delivered out of sequence, duplicated, or delayed. IPv6 per se does not attempt to recover from these types of errors. The acknowledgment of packets delivered and the recovery of lost packets is done by a higher layer protocol, such as TCP [MSD200401]. From a packet forwarding perspective IPv6 operates just like IPv4. An IPv6 packet, also known as an IPv6 datagram, consists of an IPv6 header and an IPv6 payload.

---

[1] Site-local unicast addresses were deprecated by the IETF in 2003; their description herewith is for historical reference.

TABLE 9.2. Key IPv6 Protocols

Protocol	Description
Internet Protocol version 6 (IPv6): RFC 2460	IPv6 is a connectionless datagram protocol used for routing packets between hosts.
Internet Control Message Protocol for IPv6 (ICMPv6): RFC 2463	ICMPv6 is a mechanism that enables hosts and routers that use IPv6 communication to report errors and send simple status messages.
Multicast Listener Discovery (MLD): RFC 2710, RFC 3590, RFC 3810	MLD is a mechanism that enables one to manage subnet multicast membership for IPv6. MLD uses a series of three ICMPv6 messages. MLD replaces IGMPv3 that is employed for IPv4.
Neighbor Discovery (ND): RFC 2461	ND is a mechanism that is used to manage node-to-node communication on a link. ND uses a series of five ICMPv6 messages. ND replaces ARP, ICMPv4 Router Discovery, and the ICMPv4 Redirect message; it also provides additional functions.

The IPv6 header consists of two parts, the IPv6 base header and optional extension headers. Functionally, the optional extension headers and upper layer protocols, for example, TCP, are considered part of the IPv6 payload. Table 9.4 shows the fields in the IPv6 base header. IPv4 headers and IPv6 headers are not directly interoperable: hosts and/or routers must use an implementation of both IPv4 and IPv6 in order to recognize and process both header formats. This gives rise to a number of complexities in the migration process between the IPv4 and the IPv6 environments. However, techniques have been developed to handle these migrations.

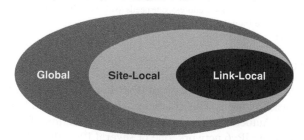

Figure 9.1. Scope in IPv6

TABLE 9.3. Address and Associated Reachability Scopes

Address scope/ Reachability	Description
Node-local addresses to reach same node	Used to send PDUs to the same node: • Loopback address (PDUs addressed to the loopback address are never sent on a link or forwarded by an IPv6 router—this is equivalent to the IPv4 loopback address) • Node-local multicast address
Link-local addresses to reach local link[a]	Used to communicate between hosts devices (e.g., servers, VoIP devices, etc.) on the link; these addresses are always configured automatically: • Unspecified address. It indicates the absence of an address and is typically used as a source address for PDUs that are attempting to verify the uniqueness of a tentative address (it is equivalent to the IPv4 unspecified address). The unspecified address is never assigned to an interface or used as a destination address. • Link-local unicast address • Link-local multicast address
Site-local addresses to reach the private intranet (internetwork)[a, b]	Used between nodes that communicate with other nodes in the same site; site-local addresses are configured by router advertisement: • Site-local unicast address—these addresses are not reachable from other sites, and routers must not forward site-local traffic outside of the site. Site-local addresses can be used in addition to aggregatable global unicast addresses. • Site-local multicast address
Global addresses to reach the Internet (IPv6 enabled); also known as aggregatable global unicast addresses	Globally routable and reachable addresses on the IPv6 portion of the Internet (they are equivalent to public IPv4 addresses); global addresses are configured by router advertisement: • Global unicast address • Other scope multicast address Global addresses are designed to be aggregated or summarized to produce an efficient, hierarchical addressing and routing structure.

[a]When one specifies a link-local or site-local address, one needs to also specify a scope ID, which further defines the reachability scope for these (nonglobal) addresses.
[b]See note 1 in this chapter.

9.2.6   IPv6 Autoconfiguration

"Autoconfiguration" is a new characteristic of IPv6 that facilitates network management and system setup tasks by users. This characteristic is often called "plug-and-play" or "connect-and-work." Autoconfiguration facilitates initialization of user devices: after connecting a device to an IPv6 network, one or several IPv6 globally unique addresses are automatically allocated.

TABLE 9.4. IPv6 Base Header

IPv6 Header Field	Length, bits	Function
Version	4	Identifies the version of the protocol. For IPv6, the version is 6.
Class	8	Intended for originating nodes and forwarding routers to identify and distinguish between different classes or priorities of IPv6 packets.
Flow Label	20	(Sometimes referred to as flow ID) Defines how traffic is handled and identified. A flow is a sequence of packets sent either to a unicast or a multicast destination. This field identifies packets that require special handling by the IPv6 node. The following list shows the ways the field is handled if a host or router does not support Flow Label field functions: If the packet is being sent, the field is set to zero. If the packet is being received, the field is ignored.
Payload Length	16	Identifies the length, in octets, of the payload. This field is a 16-bit unsigned integer. The payload includes the optional extension headers, as well as the upper layer protocols, for example, TCP.
Next Header	8	Identifies the header immediately following the IPv6 header. The following shows examples of the next header: 00 = Hop-by-hop options 01 = ICMPv4 04 = IP in IP (encapsulation) 06 = TCP 17 = UDP 43 = Routing 44 = Fragment 50 = Encapsulating security payload 51 = Authentication 58 = ICMPv6
Hop Limit	8	Identifies the number of network segments, also known as links or subnets, on which the packet is allowed to travel before being discarded by a router. The hop limit is set by the sending host and is used to prevent packets from endlessly circulating on an IPv6 internetwork. When forwarding an IPv6 packet, IPv6 routers must decrease the hop limit by 1 and must discard the IPv6 packet when the hop limit is 0.
Source Address	128	Identifies the IPv6 address of the original source of the IPv6 packet.
Destination Address	128	Identifies the IPv6 address of the intermediate or final destination of the IPv6 packet.

The "autoconfiguration" process is flexible but it is also somewhat complex. The complexity arises from the fact that various policies are defined and implemented by the network administrator. Specifically, the administrator determines the parameters that will be assigned automatically. At a minimum (and/or when there is no network administrator), the allocation of a link-local address is often included. The link-local address allows communication with other nodes placed in the same physical network. Note that "link" has somewhat of a special meaning in IPv6, as follows: a communication facility or medium over which nodes can communicate at the link layer, that is, the layer immediately below IPv6. Examples are Ethernets (simple or bridged); PPP links; an X.25 packet-switched network, a frame relay network or a cell relay/ATM network, and internet(working) layer (or higher layer) "tunnels," such as tunnels over IPv4 or IPv6 itself [RFC2460].

Two autoconfiguration basic mechanisms exist: (i) "stateful" and (ii) "stateless." Both mechanisms can be used in a complementary manner and/or simultaneously to define parameter configurations [IPV200501].

Stateless autoconfiguration is also described as "serverless." Here, the presence of configuration servers to supply profile information is not required. In this environment, manual configuration is required only at the host level and a minimal configuration at the router level is occasionally needed. The host generates its own address using a combination of the information that it possesses (in its interface or network card) and the information that is periodically supplied by the routers. Routers determine the prefix that identifies networks associated to the link under discussion. The "interface identifier" identifies an interface within a subnetwork and is often, and by default, generated from the MAC address of the network card. The IPv6 address is built combining the 64 bits of the interface identifier with the prefixes that routers determine as belonging to the subnetwork. If there is no router, the interface identifier is self-sufficient to allow the PC to generate a link-local address. The link-local address is sufficient to allow the communication between several nodes connected to the same link (the same local network).

Stateful configuration requires a server to send the information and parameters of network connection to nodes and hosts. Servers maintain a database with all addresses allocated and a mapping of the hosts to which these addresses have been allocated, along with any information related with all requisite parameters. In general, this mechanism is based on the use of DHCPv6.

Stateful autoconfiguration is often employed when there is a need for rigorous control in reference to the address allocated to hosts (in stateless autoconfiguration the only concern is that the address be unique). Depending on the network administrator policies, it may be required that some addresses be allocated to specific hosts and devices in a permanent manner; here, the stateful mechanism is employed on this subset of hosts, but the control of the remaining parameters and/or nodes could be less rigorous. In some environments there are no policy requirements on the importance of the allocated addresses. In this situation the stateless mechanism can be used.

IPv6 addresses are "leased" to an interface for a fixed established time (including an infinite time). When this "lifetime" expires, the link between the interface and the address is invalidated and the address can be reallocated to other interfaces. For the suitable management of address expiration time, an address goes through two states (stages) while it is affiliated to an interface [IPV200501]:

(a) At first, an address is in a "preferred" state, so its use in any communication is not restricted.
(b) After that, an address becomes "deprecated," indicating that its affiliation with the current interface will (soon) be invalidated.

While it is in deprecated state, the use of the address is discouraged, although it is not forbidden. However, when possible, any new communication (for example, the opening of a new TCP connection) must use a preferred address. A deprecated address should only be used by applications that already used it before and in cases where it is difficult to change this address to another address without causing a service interruption.

To insure that allocated addresses (granted either by manual mechanisms or by autoconfiguration) are unique in a specific link, the *link duplicated address detection algorithm* is used. The address to which the duplicated address detection algorithm is being applied to is designated (until the end of this algorithmic session) as an "attempt address." In this case, it does not matter that such address has been allocated to an interface and received packets are discarded.

Next, we describe how an IPv6 address is formed. The lowest 64 bits of the address identify a specific interface and these bits are designated as "interface identifier." The highest 64 bits of the address identify the "path" or the "prefix" of the network or router in one of the links to which such interface is connected. The IPv6 address is formed by combining the prefix with the interface identifier.

It is possible for a host or device to have IPv6 and IPv4 addresses simultaneously. Most of the systems that currently support IPv6 allow the simultaneous use of both protocols. In this way, it is possible to support communication with IPv4-only networks as well as IPv6-only networks and the use of the applications developed for both protocols [IPV200501].

Is it possible to transmit IPv6 traffic over IPv4 networks via tunneling methods. This approach consists of "wrapping" the IPv6 traffic as IPv4 payload data: IPv6 traffic is sent "encapsulated" into IPv4 traffic, and at the receiving end this traffic is parsed as IPv6 traffic. Transition mechanisms are methods used for the coexistence of IPv4 and/or IPv6 devices and networks. For example, an "IPv6-in-IPv4 tunnel" is a transition mechanism that allows IPv6 devices to communicate through an IPv4 network. The mechanism consists of creating the IPv6 packets in a normal way and eccapsulating them in an IPv4 packet. The reverse process is undertaken in the destination machine, which deencapsulates the IPv6 packet.

There is a significant difference between the procedures to allocate IPv4 addresses, which focus on the parsimonious use of addresses (since addresses are a scarce resource and should be managed with caution), and the procedures to allocate IPv6 addresses, which focus on flexibility. ISPs deploying IPv6 systems follow the Regional Internet Registries (RIRs) policies relating to how to assign IPv6 addressing space among their clients. RIRs are recommending ISPs and operators allocate to each IPv6 client a /48 subnetwork; this allows clients to manage their own subnetworks without using NAT. (The implication is that the need for NAT disappears in IPv6.)

In order to allow its maximum scalability, IPv6 uses an approach based on a basic header, with minimum information. This differentiates it from IPv4 where different options are included in addition to the basic header. IPv6 uses a header "concatenation" mechanism to support supplementary capabilities. The advantages of this approach include the following:

- The size of the basic header is always the same and is well known. The basic header has been simplified compared with IPv4, since only 8 fields are used instead of 12. The basic IPv6 header has a fixed size, hence, its processing by nodes and routers is more straightforward. Also, the header's structure aligns to 64 bits, so that new and future processors (64 bits minimum) can process it in a more efficient way.

- Routers placed between a source point and a destination point (that is, the route that a specific packet has to pass through) do not need to process or understand any "following headers." In other words, in general, interior (core) points of the network (routers) only have to process the basic header, while in IPv4 all headers must be processed. This flow mechanism is similar to the operation in MPLS yet precedes it by several years.

- There is no limit to the number of options that the headers can support (the IPv6 basic header is 40 octets in length, while the IPv4 one varies from 20 to 60 octets, depending on the options used).

In IPv6, interior/core routers do not perform packet fragmentation, but the fragmentation is performed end to end. That is, source and destination nodes perform, by means of the IPv6 stack, the fragmentation of a packet and the reassembly, respectively. The fragmentation process consists of dividing the source packet into smaller packets or fragments [IPV200501].

A "jumbogram" is an option that allows an IPv6 packet to have a payload greater than 65,535 bytes. Jumbograms are identified with a 0 value in the payload length in the IPv6 header field and include a jumbo payload option in the hop-by-hop option header. It is anticipated that such packets will be used, in particular, for multimedia traffic.

This preliminary overview of IPv6 highlights the advantages of the new protocol and its applicability to a whole range of applications, including VoIP.

9.3   MIGRATION AND COEXISTENCE

Migration is expected to be fairly complex. Initially, internetworking between the two environments will be critical. Existing IPv4 endpoints and/or nodes will need to run dual-stack nodes or convert to IPv6 systems. Fortunately, the new protocol supports IPv4-compatible IPv6 addresses, which is an IPv6 address format that employs embedded IPv4 addresses. Tunneling, which we already described in passing, will play a major role in the beginning:

There are a number of requirements that are typically applicable to an organization wishing to introduce an IPv6 service [6NE200501]:

- The existing IPv4 service should not be adversely disrupted (e.g., as it might be by router loading of encapsulating IPv6 in IPv4 for tunnels).
- The IPv6 service should perform as well as the IPv4 service (e.g., at the IPv4 line rate and with similar network characteristics).
- The service must be manageable and be able to be monitored (thus tools should be available for IPv6 as they are for IPv4).
- The security of the network should not be compromised due to the additional protocol itself or weakness of any transition mechanism used.
- An IPv6 address allocation plan must be drawn up.

Well-known interworking mechanisms include the following [RFC2893]:[2]

- Dual IP layer (also known as dual stack): A technique for providing complete support for both IPs—IPv4 and IPv6—in hosts and routers.
- Configured tunneling of IPv6 over IPv4: Point-to-point tunnels made by encapsulating IPv6 packets within IPv4 headers to carry them over IPv4 routing infrastructures.
- Automatic tunneling of IPv6 over IPv4: A mechanism for using IPv4-compatible addresses to automatically tunnel IPv6 packets over IPv4 networks.

Tunneling techniques include the following [RFC2893]:

- IPv6-over-IPv4 tunneling: The technique of encapsulating IPv6 packets within IPv4 so that they can be carried across IPv4 routing infrastructures.
- Configured tunneling:
  - IPv6-over-IPv4 tunneling where the IPv4 tunnel endpoint address is determined by configuration information on the encapsulating node. The tunnels can be either unidirectional or bidirectional. Bidirectional configured tunnels behave as virtual point-to-point links.
  - Automatic tunneling: IPv6-over-IPv4 tunneling where the IPv4 tunnel endpoint address is determined from the IPv4 address embedded in the IPv4-compatible destination address of the IPv6 packet being tunneled.

— IPv4 multicast tunneling: IPv6-over-IPv4 tunneling where the IPv4 tunnel endpoint address is determined using ND. Unlike configured tunneling this does not require any address configuration, and unlike automatic tunneling it does not require the use of IPv4-compatible addresses. However, the mechanism assumes that the IPv4 infrastructure supports IPv4 multicast.

Applications (and the lower layer protocol stack) need to be properly equipped. There are four cases [RFC4038]:

Case 1: IPv4-only applications in a dual-stack node. IPv6 is introduced in a node, but applications are not yet ported to support IPv6. The protocol stack is as follows:

```
+-------------------------+
|      appv4              | (appv4 — IPv4-only applications)
+-------------------------+
| TCP / UDP / others| (transport protocols — TCP, UDP, SCTP, DCCP, etc.)
+-------------------------+
|   IPv4 | IPv6           | (IP protocols supported/enabled in the OS)
+-------------------------+
```

Case 2: IPv4-only applications and IPv6-only applications in a dual-stack node. Applications are ported for IPv6-only. Therefore, there are two similar applications, one for each protocol version (e.g., ping and ping6). The protocol stack is as follows:

```
+-------------------------+ (appv4— IPv4-only applications)
| appv4 | appv6   | (appv6— IPv6-only applications)
+-------------------------+
|TCP / UDP / others| (transport protocols —TCP, UDP, SCTP, DCCP, etc.)
+-------------------------+
|   IPv4 | IPv6           | (IP protocols supported/enabled in the OS)
+-------------------------+
```

Case 3: Applications supporting both IPv4 and IPv6 in a dual-stack node. Applications are ported for both IPv4 and IPv6 support. Therefore, the existing IPv4 applications can be removed. The protocol stack is as follows:

```
+---------------------------+
|    appv4/v6           | (appv4/v6— applications supporting both IPv4 and IPv6)
+---------------------------+
|TCP / UDP / others| (transport protocols —TCP, UDP, SCTP, DCCP, etc.)
+---------------------------+
|   IPv4 | IPv6           | (IP protocols supported/enabled in the OS)
+---------------------------+
```

Case 4: Applications supporting both IPv4 and IPv6 in an IPv4-only node. Applications are ported for both IPv4 and IPv6 support, but the same applications may also have to work when IPv6 is not being used [e.g., disabled from the Operating System (OS)]. The protocol stack is as follows:

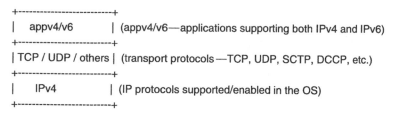

The first two cases are not interesting in the longer term; only a few applications are inherently IPv4 or IPv6 specific and should work with both protocols without having to care about which one is being used.

9.4 MULTICAST WITH IPv6

Next, we focus on multicast issues, including layer 3 addressing. Note at this juncture that IPv6 multicast does not support DM.

9.4.1 IPv6 Multicast Addresses

Figure 9.2 depicts the IPv6 multicast address. In IPv6, multicast addresses begin with the format prefix 1111 1111 (FF in hex). The format prefix is followed by two fields, each 4 bits long: flags and scope. The flag field T initially indicated whether the address was permanent or transient. RFC 3306 added a P (prefix) flag; this flag allows part of the group address to include the source networks unicast prefix, which creates a globally unique group address. The R flag is used to indicate that the RP address is embedded in the group address; with embedded RP, the flags R, P, and T are set to 1. The scope is a subset of the network, as discussed earlier. The remaining 112 bits of the IPv6 address are the group ID.

9.4.2 MAC Layer Addresses

MAC layer addresses consist of 24 bits for the Organizational Unit Identifier (OUI) and 24 bits for the serial number of the Ethernet NIC. For a multicast environment the MAC address format uses a special OUI. As we saw in Chapter 2, the OUI for IPv4 multicast is 00:00:5E with the least significant bit most significant octet set and with only half of this address space allocated to IP multicast. The implication of the fact that only 23 bits are available for the group address means a potential address overlap at layer 2. A different OUI format is used for IPv6 multicast. The leading two octets are set to hex 33-33, and the remaining four octets are available for address mapping from the last 32 bits of the 128-bit IPv6 multicast address. See Figure 9.3 for an example.

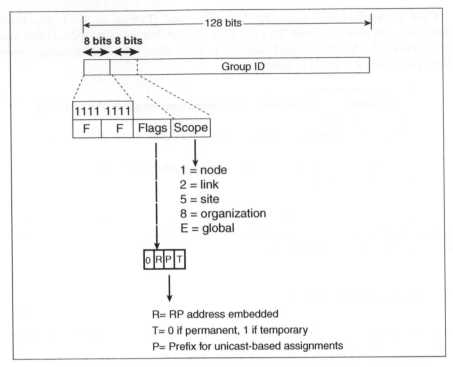

Figure 9.2. IPv6 Multicast Addressing

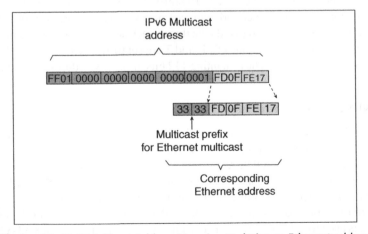

Figure 9.3. IPv6 Multicast Address Mapping to derive an Ethernet address

9.4.3 Signaling

Just as is the case in IPv4, IPv6 hosts (receivers) must signal a router with its desire to receive data from a specific group. IPv6 multicast does not use IGMP but rather uses MLD. MLDv1 is similar to IGMPv2, and MLDv2 is similar to IGMPv3. This topic is revisited in Chapter 10.

9.4.4 RP Approaches

Recall that in SM PIM sources must send their traffic to an RP; this traffic is in turn forwarded to receivers on a shared distribution tree. In IPv6, auto-RP is not currently available; however, there is a BSR for IPv6; also there is static configuration of an RP (embedded RP). Static use is acceptable in the intradomain, but not within the interdomain. Embedded RP is a viable solution for those applications that cannot leverage SSM and that require a PIM SM model to interoperate across multiple domains [CIS200701]. *Embedded RP uses the R flag discussed above: when the flags R, P, and T are set to 1, this indicates that the RP address is embedded in the group address.

REFERENCES

[6NE200501] 6NET, D2.2.4: Final IPv4 to IPv6 Transition Cookbook for Organisational/ISP (NREN) and Backbone Networks, Version:1.0, Project Number: IST-2001-32603, CEC Deliverable Number 32603/UOS/DS/2.2.4/A1, February 4, 2005.

[CIS200701] Cisco Systems, Internet Protocol (IP) Multicast Technology Overview and White Papers, Cisco Systems, San Jose, CA.

[DAV200201] J. Davies, *Understanding IPv6*, Microsoft Press, 2002.

[DEM200301] Desmeules, Cisco Self-Study: Implementing IPv6 Networks (IPV6), Pearson Education, May 2003.

[GON199801] M. Goncalves, K. Niles, *IPv6 Networks*, McGraw-Hill Osborne, 1998.

[GOS200301] S.Goswami, *Internet Protocols: Advances, Technologies, and Applications*, Kluwer Academic Publishers, May 2003.

[GRA200001] B. Graham, *TCP/IP Addressing: Designing and Optimizing Your IP Addressing Scheme*, 2nd ed., Morgan Kaufmann, 2000.

[HAG200201] S. Hagen, *IPv6 Essentials*, O'Reilly, 2002.

[HUI199701] C. Huitema, *IPv6 the New Internet Protocol*, 2nd ed., Prentice-Hall, 1997.

[IPV200401] IPv6Forum, IPv6 Vendors Test Voice, Wireless and Firewalls on Moonv6, http://www.ipv6forum.com/modules.php?op=modload&name=News&file=article&sid=15&mode=thread&order=0&thold=0, November 15, 2004.

[IPV200501] IPv6 Portal, http://www.ipv6tf.org/meet/faqs.php.

[ITO200401] J. Itojun Hagino, *IPv6 Network Programming*, Butterworth-Heinemann, 2004.

[LEE200501] H. K. Lee, *Understanding IPv6*, Springer-Verlag, New York, 2005.

[LOS200301] P. Loshin, *IPv6: Theory, Protocol, and Practice*, 2nd ed., Elsevier Science & Technology Books, 2003.

[MIL199701] M.A. Miller, *Implementing IPv6: Migrating to the Next Generation Internet Protocol*, Wiley, 1997.

[MIL200001] M. Miller, P. E. Miller, *Implementing IP V6: Supporting the Next Generation Internet Protocols*, 2nd ed., Hungry Minds, 2000.

[MIN200601] D. Minoli, *VoIP over IPv6*, Elsevier, 2006.

[MIN200801] J. J. Amoss, D. Minoli, *Handbook of IPv4 to IPv6 Transition Methodologies for Institutional and Corporate Networks*, TF-ARBCH, New York, 2008.

[MSD200401] Microsoft Corporation, MSDN Library, Internet Protocol, http://msdn.microsoft. com, 2004.

[MUR200501] N. R. Murphy, D. Malone, *IPv6 Network Administration*, O'Reilly & Associates, 2005.

[RFC2460] RFC 2460, Internet Protocol, Version 6 (IPv6) Specification, S. Deering, R. Hinden, December 1998.

[RFC2893] RFC 2893, Transition Mechanisms for IPv6 Hosts and Routers, R. Gilligan, E. Nordmark, August 2000.

[RFC3022] RFC 3022, Traditional IP Network Address Translator (Traditional NAT), P. Srisuresh, K. Egevang, January 2001.

[RFC3306] RFC 3306, Unicast-Prefix-Based IPv6 Multicast.

[RFC4038] RFC 4038, Application Aspects of IPv6 Transition, M-K. Shin, Ed., Y-G. Hong, J. Hagino, P. Savola, E.M. Castro, March 2005.

[SOL200401] H. S. Soliman, *Mobile IPv6*, Pearson Education, 2004.

[TEA200401] D. Teare, C. Paquet, *CCNP Self-Study: Advanced IP Addressing*, Cisco Press, June 11, 2004.

[WEG199901] J. D. Wegner, *IP Addressing and Subnetting, Including IPv6*, Elsevier Science & Technology Books, 1999.

10

MULTICAST LISTENER DISCOVERY

Just as is the case in IPv4, IPv6 hosts (receivers) signal a router with their desire to receive data from a specific group. IPv6 multicast does not use the IGMP but rather the Multicast Listener Discovery (MLD) protocol. MLD is used by an IPv6 router to discover the presence of multicast listeners on directly attached links and to discover which multicast addresses are of interest to those neighboring nodes. MLDv1 is similar to IGMPv2, and MLDv2 is similar to IGMPv3. MLDv2 adds the ability for a node to report interest in listening to packets with a particular multicast address only from specific source addresses, or from all sources except for specific source addresses, this being similar to SSM. Recall that SSM is a form of multicast where a receiver must specify both the network layer address of the source and the multicast destination address to receive the multicast datagrams of interest.

This chapter provides an overview of MLD based on RFC 2710,[1] Multicast Listener Discovery (MLD) for IPv6, and RFC 3810, Multicast Listener Discovery Version 2 (MLDv2) for IPv6. The focus is on MLDv1. Due to the commonality of

IP Multicast with Applications to IPTV and Mobile DVB-H   by Daniel Minoli
Copyright © 2008 John Wiley & Sons, Inc.

function, the term Group Management Protocol (GMP) is sometimes used to refer to both IGMP and MLD.

10.1   OVERVIEW OF MLDv1[2]

MLD [RFC 2710, RFC 3550, RFC 3810] specifies the protocol used by an IPv6 router to discover the presence of multicast listeners (i.e., nodes wishing to receive multicast packets) on its directly attached links and to discover which multicast addresses are of interest to those neighboring nodes. MLD enables IPv6 routers to discover the presence of multicast listeners. This information is then provided to the multicast routing protocol being used by the router to ensure that multicast packets are delivered to all links where there are interested receivers. MLD is derived from Version 2 of IPv4's IGMPv2. One important difference is that MLD uses ICMPv6 message types (IP 58) rather than IGMP message types (IP 2).

MLD is an asymmetric protocol, specifying different behaviors for multicast listeners and for routers. For those multicast addresses to which a router itself is listening, the router performs both parts of the protocol, the "multicast router part" and the "multicast address listener part," including responding to its own messages. If a router has more than one interface to the same link, it needs to perform the router part of the MLD over only one of those interfaces. Listeners, on the contrary, must perform the listener part of MLD on all interfaces from which an application or upper layer protocol has requested reception of multicast packets.

Note that a multicast router may itself be a listener of one or more multicast addresses; in this case it performs both the multicast router part and the multicast address listener part of the protocol to collect the multicast listener information needed by its multicast routing protocol on the one hand and to inform itself and other neighboring multicast routers of its listening state on the other hand.

10.2   MESSAGE FORMAT

MLD is a subprotocol of ICMPv6, namely, MLD message types are a subset of the set of ICMPv6 messages, and MLD messages are identified in IPv6 packets by a preceding next header value of 58. All MLD messages are sent with a link-local IPv6 source address, an IPv6 hop limit of 1, and an IPv6 Router Alert option in a Hop-by-Hop Options header. (The Router Alert option is necessary to cause routers to examine MLD messages sent to multicast addresses in which the routers themselves have no interest.)

MLD messages have the format depicted in Figure 10.1.

---

[2] The discussion of Sections 10.1–10.5 is based on and summarized from RFC 2710.

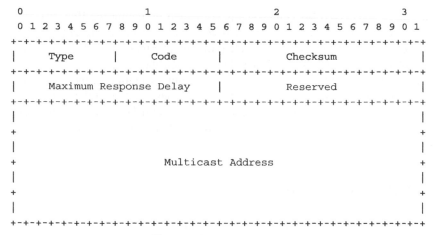

```
 0                   1                   2                   3
 0 1 2 3 4 5 6 7 8 9 0 1 2 3 4 5 6 7 8 9 0 1 2 3 4 5 6 7 8 9 0 1
+-+-+-+-+-+-+-+-+-+-+-+-+-+-+-+-+-+-+-+-+-+-+-+-+-+-+-+-+-+-+-+-+
|      Type     |      Code     |            Checksum           |
+-+-+-+-+-+-+-+-+-+-+-+-+-+-+-+-+-+-+-+-+-+-+-+-+-+-+-+-+-+-+-+-+
|     Maximum Response Delay     |            Reserved           |
+-+-+-+-+-+-+-+-+-+-+-+-+-+-+-+-+-+-+-+-+-+-+-+-+-+-+-+-+-+-+-+-+
|                                                               |
+                                                               +
|                                                               |
+                       Multicast Address                       +
|                                                               |
+                                                               +
|                                                               |
+-+-+-+-+-+-+-+-+-+-+-+-+-+-+-+-+-+-+-+-+-+-+-+-+-+-+-+-+-+-+-+-+
```

Figure 10.1. MLD Messages Format

There are three types of MLD messages:

1. Multicast Listener Query (type = decimal 130), also known as "Query." There are two subtypes of Multicast Listener Query messages (differentiated by the contents of the Multicast Address field):
   - General Query, used to learn which multicast addresses have listeners on an attached link.
   - Multicast-Address-Specific Query, used to learn if a particular multicast address has any listeners on an attached link.
2. Multicast Listener Report (type = decimal 131), also known as "Report."
3. Multicast Listener Done (type = decimal 132), also known as "Done."

The *Code* field is initialized to zero by the sender; ignored by receivers.

The *Checksum* field is the standard ICMPv6 checksum, covering the entire MLD message plus a "pseudoheader" of IPv6 header fields.

The *Maximum Response Delay* field is meaningful only in Query messages and specifies the maximum allowed delay before sending a responding report, in units of milliseconds. In all other messages, it is set to zero by the sender and ignored by receivers.

Varying this value allows the routers to tune the "leave latency" (the time between the moment the last node on a link ceases listening to a particular multicast address and the moment the routing protocol is notified that there are no longer any listeners for that address. It also allows tuning of the burstiness of MLD traffic on a link.

The *Reserved* field is initialized to zero by the sender; ignored by receivers.

In a Query message, the *Multicast Address* field is set to zero when sending a general query and set to a specific IPv6 multicast address when sending a multicast-address-specific query. In a Report or Done message, the Multicast Address field holds a specific IPv6 multicast address to which the message sender is listening or is ceasing to listen, respectively.

The length of a received MLD message is computed by taking the IPv6 payload length value and subtracting the length of any IPv6 extension headers present between the IPv6 header and the MLD message. If that length is greater than 24 octets, it indicates that there are other fields present beyond the fields described above, perhaps belonging to a future backwards-compatible version of MLD. An implementation of the version of MLD specified in this document must not send an MLD message longer than 24 octets, and must ignore anything past the first 24 octets, of a received MLD message. In all cases, the MLD checksum must be computed over the entire MLD message, and not just the first 24 octets.

10.3 PROTOCOL DESCRIPTION

Routers use MLD to learn that multicast addresses have listeners on each of their attached links. Each router keeps a list, for each attached link, of which multicast addresses have listeners on that link and a timer associated with each of those addresses. Note that the router needs to learn only that listeners for a given multicast address are present on a link; it does not need to learn the identity (e.g., unicast address) of those listeners or even how many listeners are present.

For each attached link, a router selects one of its link-local unicast addresses on that link to be used as the IPv6 source address in all MLD packets it transmits on that link.

For each interface over which the router is operating the MLD protocol, the router must configure that interface to listen to all link-layer multicast addresses that can be generated by IPv6 multicasts. For example, an Ethernet-attached router must set its Ethernet address reception filter to accept all Ethernet multicast addresses that start with the hexadecimal value 3333 (as covered in Chapter 9); in the case of an Ethernet interface that does not support the filtering of such a range of multicast addresses, it must be configured to accept all Ethernet multicast addresses to meet the requirements of MLD.

With respect to each of its attached links, a router may assume one of the two roles: querier or nonquerier. There is normally only one querier per link. All routers start up as a querier on each of their attached links. If a router hears a Query message whose IPv6 source address is numerically less than its own selected address for that link, it must become a nonquerier on that link. If the timer [Other Querier Present Interval] passes without receiving, from a particular attached link, any queries from a router with an address less than its own, a router resumes the role of querier on that link.

A querier for a link periodically sends (with timer [Query Interval]) a general query on that link to solicit reports of all multicast addresses of interest on that link. On startup, a router should send as many general queries as specified by [Startup Query Count] spaced closely together (based on the [Startup Query Interval] timer) on all attached links to quickly and reliably discover the presence of multicast listeners on those links.

General queries are sent to the link-scope all-nodes multicast address (FF02::1) with a Multicast Address field of 0 and a maximum response delay defined by the timer [Query Response Interval].

When a node receives a general query, it sets a delay timer for each multicast address to which it is listening on the interface from which it received the query, excluding the link-scope all-nodes address and any multicast addresses of scope 0 (reserved) or 1 (node-local). Each timer is set to a different random value, using the highest clock granularity available on the node, selected from the range [0,Maximum Response Delay] with the maximum response delay as specified in the query packet. If a timer for any address is already running, it is reset to the new random value only if the requested maximum response delay is less than the remaining value of the running timer. If the query packet specifies a maximum response delay of zero, each timer is effectively set to zero, and the action specified below for timer expiration is performed immediately.

When a node receives a multicast-address-specific query, if it is listening to the queried multicast address on the interface from which the query was received, it sets a delay timer for that address to a random value selected from the range [0,Maximum Response Delay], as above. If a timer for the address is already running, it is reset to the new random value only if the requested maximum response delay is less than the remaining value of the running timer. If the query packet specifies a maximum response delay of zero, the timer is effectively set to zero, and the action specified below for timer expiration is performed immediately.

If a node's timer for a particular multicast address on a particular interface expires, the node transmits a report to that address via that interface; the address being reported is carried in both the IPv6 Destination Address field and the MLD Multicast Address field of the report packet. The IPv6 hop limit of 1 (as well as the presence of a link-local IPv6 source address) prevents the packet from traveling beyond the link to which the reporting interface is attached.

If a node receives another node's report from an interface for a multicast address while it has a timer running for that same address on that interface, it stops its timer and does not send a report for that address, thus suppressing duplicate reports on the link.

When a router receives a report from a link, if the reported address is not already present in the router's list of multicast addresses having listeners on that link, the reported address is added to the list, its timer is set to [Multicast Listener Interval], and its appearance is made known to the router's multicast routing component. If a report is received for a multicast address that is already present in the router's list, the timer for that address is reset to [Multicast Listener Interval]. If an address's timer expires, it is assumed that there are no longer any listeners for that address present on the link; so it is deleted from the list and its disappearance is made known to the multicast routing component.

When a node starts listening to a multicast address on an interface, it should immediately transmit an unsolicited report for that address on that interface in case it is the first listener on the link. To cover the possibility of the initial report being lost or damaged, it is recommended that it be repeated once or twice after short delays [Unsolicited Report Interval] (a simple way to accomplish this is to send the initial report and then act as if a multicast-address-specific query was received for that address and set a timer appropriately).

When a node ceases to listen to a multicast address on an interface, it should send a single Done message to the link-scope all-routers multicast address (FF02::2), carrying in its Multicast Address field the address to which it is ceasing to listen. If the node's most recent Report message was suppressed by hearing another Report message, it may send nothing, as it is highly likely that there is another listener for that address still present on the same link. If this optimization is implemented, it must be able to be turned off but should also default to on.

When a router in the querier state receives a Done message from a link, if the multicast address identified in the message is present in the querier's list of addresses having listeners on that link, the querier sends [Last Listener Query Count] multicast-address-specific queries, one every [Last Listener Query Interval] to that multicast address. These multicast-address-specific queries have their maximum response delay set to [Last Listener Query Interval]. If no reports for the address are received from the link after the response delay of the last query has passed, the routers on the link assume that the address no longer has any listeners there; the address is therefore deleted from the list and its disappearance is made known to the multicast routing component. This process is continued to its resolution (i.e., until a report is received or the last multicast-address-specific query is sent with no response) despite any transition from querier to nonquerier on this link.

Routers in the Nonquerier state must ignore Done messages.

When a router in the Nonquerier state receives a multicast-address-specific query, if its timer value for the identified multicast address is greater than [Last Listener Query Count] times the maximum response delay specified in the message, it sets the address's timer to that latter value.

10.4 NODE STATE TRANSITION DIAGRAM

Node behavior is more formally specified by the state transition diagram below. A node may be in one of the three possible states with respect to any single IPv6 multicast address on any single interface:

- "Nonlistener" state, when the node is not listening to the address on the interface (i.e., no upperlayer protocol or application has requested reception of packets to that multicast address). This is the initial state for all multicast addresses on all interfaces; it requires no storage in the node.
- "Delaying listener" state, when the node is listening to the address on the interface and has a report delay timer running for that address.
- "Idle listener" state, when the node is listening to the address on the interface and does not have a report delay timer running for that address.

There are five significant events that can cause MLD state transitions:

- "Start listening" occurs when the node starts listening to the address on the interface. It may occur only in the nonlistener state.

- "Stop listening" occurs when the node stops listening to the address on the interface. It may occur only in the delaying listener and idle listener states.
- "Query received" occurs when the node receives either a valid General Query message or a valid Multicast-Address-Specific Query message. To be valid, the Query message must come from a link-local IPv6 source address, be at least 24 octets long, and have a correct MLD checksum. The Multicast Address field in the MLD message must contain either zero (a general query) or a valid multicast address (a multicast-address-specific query). A general query applies to all multicast addresses on the interface from which the query is received. A multicast-address-specific query applies to a single multicast address on the interface from which the query is received. Queries are ignored for addresses in the nonlistener state.
- "Report received" occurs when the node receives a valid MLD Report message. To be valid, the Report message must come from a link-local IPv6 source address, be at least 24 octets long, and have a correct MLD checksum. A report applies only to the address identified in the Multicast Address field of the Report, on the interface from which the report is received. It is ignored in the nonlistener or idle listener state.
- "Timer expired" occurs when the report delay timer for the address on the interface expires. It may occur only in the delaying listener state.

All other events, such as receiving invalid MLD messages or MLD message types other than Query or Report, are ignored in all states.

There are seven possible actions that may be taken in response to the above events:

- "Send report" for the address on the interface. The Report message is sent to the address being reported.
- "Send done" for the address on the interface. If the flag saying we were the last node to report is cleared, this action may be skipped. The Done message is sent to the link-scope all-routers address (FF02::2).
- "Set flag" that we were the last node to send a report for this address.
- "Clear flag" since we were not the last node to send a report for this address.
- "Start timer" for the address on the interface using a delay value chosen uniformly from the interval [0,Maximum Response Delay], where the maximum response delay is specified in the query. If this is an unsolicited report, the timer is set to a delay value chosen uniformly from the interval [0,Unsolicited Report Interval].
- "Reset timer" for the address on the interface to a new value using a delay value chosen uniformly from the interval [0, Maximum Response Delay], as described in "start timer."
- "Stop timer" for the address on the interface.

See Figure 10.2 for the protocol state machine. In all of the following state transition diagrams, each state transition arc is labeled with the event that causes the transition

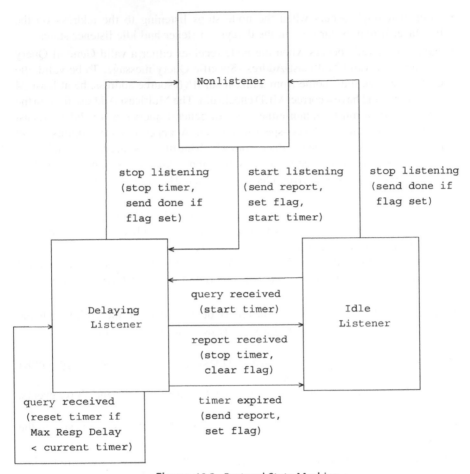

Figure 10.2. Protocol State Machine

and, in parentheses, any actions taken during the transition. Note that the transition is always triggered by the event; even if the action is conditional, the transition still occurs.

The link-scope all-nodes address (FF02::1) is handled as a special case. The node starts in the idle listener state for that address on every interface, never transitions to another state, and never sends a Report or Done message for that address.

MLD messages are never sent for multicast addresses whose scope is 0 (reserved) or 1 (node-local).

MLD messages are sent for multicast addresses whose scope is 2 (link-local), including solicited-node multicast addresses, except for the link-scope all-nodes address (FF02::1).

10.5   ROUTER STATE TRANSITION DIAGRAM

Router behavior is more formally specified by the state transition diagrams of Figures 10.3–10.5.

A router may be in one of the two possible states with respect to any single attached link:

- "Querier," when this router is designated to transmit MLD queries on this link.
- "Nonquerier," when there is another router designated to transmit MLD queries on this link.

The following three events can cause the router to change states:

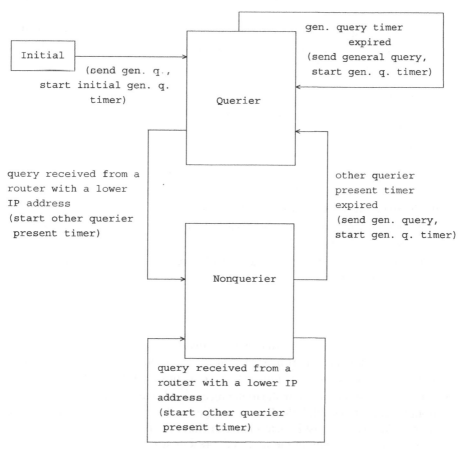

Figure 10.3. Router State Diagram

- "Query timer expired" occurs when the timer set for query transmission expires. This event is significant only when in the querier state.
- "Query received from a router with a lower IP address" occurs when a valid MLD query is received from a router on the same link with a lower IPv6 source address. To be valid, the Query message must come from a link-local IPv6 source address, be at least 24 octets long, and have a correct MLD checksum.
- "Other querier present timer expired" occurs when the timer set to note the presence of another querier with a lower IP address on the link expires. This event is significant only when in the nonquerier state.

There are three actions that may be taken in response to the above events:

- "Start general query timer" for the attached link to [Query Interval].
- "Start other querier present timer" for the attached link to [Other Querier Present Interval].
- "Send general query" on the attached link. The general query is sent to the link-scope all-nodes address (FF02::1) and has a maximum response delay of [Query Response Interval].

A router starts in the Initial state on all attached links and immediately transitions to the querier state. In addition, to keep track of which multicast addresses have listeners, a router may be in one of the three possible states with respect to any single IPv6 multicast address on any single attached link:

- "No listeners present" state, when there are no nodes on the link that have sent a report for this multicast address. This is the initial state for all multicast addresses on the router; it requires no storage in the router.
- "Listeners present" state, when there is a node on the link that has sent a report for this multicast address.
- "Checking listeners" state, when the router has received a Done message but has not yet heard a report for the identified address.

There are five significant events that can cause router state transitions:

- "Report received" occurs when the router receives a report for the address from the link. To be valid, the Report message must come from a link-local IPv6 source address, be at least 24 octets long, and have a correct MLD checksum.
- "Done received" occurs when the router receives a Done message for the address from the link. To be valid, the Done message must come from a link-local IPv6 source address, be at least 24 octets long, and have a correct MLD checksum. This event is significant only in the listerners present state and when the router is a querier.

- "Multicast-address-specific query received" occurs when a router receives a multicast-address-specific query for the address from the link. To be valid, the Query message must come from a link-local IPv6 source address, be at least 24 octets long, and have a correct MLD checksum. This event is significant only in the listeners present state and when the router is a nonquerier.
- "Timer expired" occurs when the timer set for a multicast address expires. This event is significant only in the listeners present or checking listeners state.
- "Retransmit timer expired" occurs when the timer set to retransmit a multicast-address-specific query expires. This event is significant only in the checking listeners state.

There are seven possible actions that may be taken in response to the above events:

- "Start timer" for the address on the link — also resets the timer to its initial value [Multicast Listener Interval] if the timer is currently running.
- "Start timer*" for the address on the link — this alternate action sets the timer to the minimum of its current value and either [Last Listener Query Interval] × [Last Listener Query Count] if this router is a querier or the maximum response delay in the query message × [Last Listener Query Count] if this router is a nonquerier.
- "Start retransmit timer" for the address on the link [Last Listener Query Interval].
- "Clear retransmit timer" for the address on the link.
- "Send multicast-address-specific query" for the address on the link. The multi-cast-address-specific query is sent to the address being queried and has a maximum response delay of [Last Listener Query Interval].
- "Notify routing +" internally notify the multicast routing protocol that there are listeners to this address on this link.
- "Notify routing −" internally notify the multicast routing protocol that there are no longer any listeners to this address on this link.

The state diagrams that follow apply per group per link (one for routers in the querier state and one for routers in the nonquerier state). The transition between querier and nonquerier states on a link is handled specially. All groups on that link in the no listeners present or listeners present state switch state transition diagrams when the querier/nonquerier state transition occurs. However, any groups in checking listeners state continue with the same state transition diagram until the checking listeners state is exited. For example, a router that starts as a querier, receives a Done message for a group, and then receives a query from a router with a lower address (causing a transition to the nonquerier state) continues to send multicast-address-specific queries for the group in question until it either receives a report or its timer expires, at which time it starts performing the actions of a nonquerier for this group.

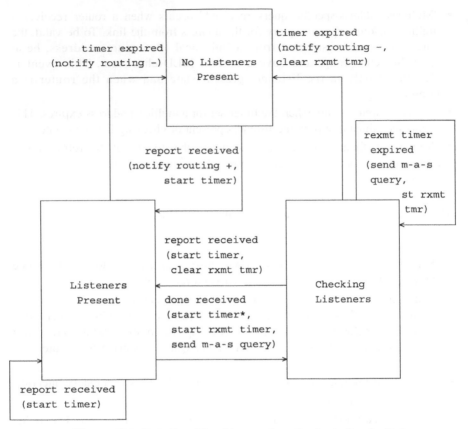

Figure 10.4. State Transition Diagram for a Router in Querier State

The state transition diagram for a router in the querier state is shown in Figure 10.4. The state transition diagram for a router in the nonquerier state is similar, but nonqueriers do not send any messages and are only driven by message reception. See Figure 10.5.

10.6   OVERVIEW OF MLDv2

The MLDv2 protocol, when compared to MLDv1, adds support for "source filtering," that is, the ability for a node to report interest in listening to packets only from specific source addresses, as required to support source-specific multicast defined in RFC 3569, or from all but specific source addresses sent to a particular multicast address. MLDv2 is designed to be interoperable with MLDv1. RFC 3810 (June 2004) updates RFC 2710. Below is a summary of MLDv2 based directly on the RFC. Developers and interested parties should consult the RFC outright.

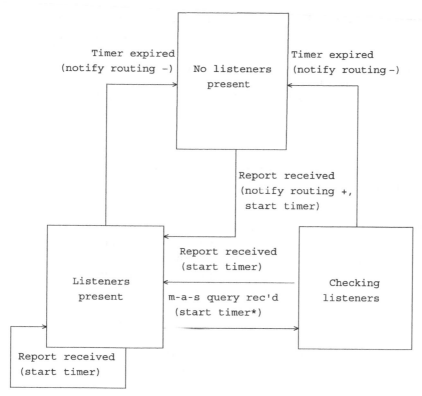

Figure 10.5. The State Transition Diagram for a Router in Nonquerier State

10.6.1 Protocol Overview

As noted already, MLD is an asymmetric protocol; it specifies separate behaviors for multicast address listeners (i.e., hosts or routers that listen to multicast packets) and multicast routers. The purpose of MLD is to enable each multicast router to learn, for each of its directly attached links, which multicast addresses and sources have interested listeners on that link. The information gathered by MLD is provided to whichever multicast routing protocol is used by the router to ensure that multicast packets are delivered to all links where there are listeners interested in such packets.

Multicast routers only need to know that at least one node on an attached link is listening to packets for a particular multicast address from a particular source; a multicast router is not required to individually keep track of the interests of each neighboring node.

A multicast router performs the *router part* of the MLDv2 protocol on each of its directly attached links. If a multicast router has more than one interface connected to the same link, it only needs to operate the protocol on one of those interfaces. The router behavior depends on whether there are several multicast routers on the same subnet or not. If that is the case, a querier election mechanism is used to elect a single multicast router to be in the querier state. This router is called the querier. All multicast routers on the subnet listen to the messages sent by multicast address listeners and maintain the same multicast listening information state so that they can take over the querier role should the present querier fail. Nevertheless, only the querier sends periodic or triggered query messages on the subnet.

A multicast address listener performs the *listener part* of the MLDv2 protocol on all interfaces on which multicast reception is supported, even if more than one of those interfaces are connected to the same link.

10.6.2 Building Multicast Listening State on Multicast Address Listeners

Upper layer protocols and applications that run on a multicast address listener node use specific service interface calls to ask the IP layer to enable or disable reception of packets sent to specific multicast addresses. The node keeps the multicast address listening state for each socket on which the service interface calls have been invoked. In addition to this per-socket multicast listening state, a node must also maintain or compute a multicast listening state for each of its interfaces. Conceptually, that state consists of a set of records, with each record containing an IPv6 multicast address, a filter mode, and a source list. The filter mode may be either INCLUDE or EXCLUDE. In the INCLUDE mode, reception of packets sent to the specified multicast address is enabled only from the source addresses listed in the source list. In the EXCLUDE mode, reception of packets sent to the given multicast address is enabled from all the source addresses *except* those listed in the source list.

At most one record per multicast address exists for a given interface. This per-interface state is derived from the per-socket state but may differ from it when different sockets have differing filter modes and/or source lists for the same multicast address and interface. After a multicast packet has been accepted from an interface by the IP layer, its subsequent delivery to the application connected to a particular socket depends on the multicast listening state of that socket (and possibly also on other conditions, such as what transport layer port the socket is bound to). Note that MLDv2 messages are not subject to source filtering and must always be processed by hosts and routers.

10.6.3 Exchanging Messages between the Querier and the Listening Nodes

There are three types of MLDv2 query messages: general queries, multicast address-specific queries, and multicast address- and source-specific queries. The querier periodically sends general queries to learn multicast address listener information from an attached link. These queries are used to build and refresh the multicast address listener state inside all multicast routers on the link.

Nodes respond to these queries by reporting their per-interface multicast address listening state through Current State Report messages sent to a specific multicast address of all MLDv2 routers on the link listen to. On the contrary, if the listening state of a node changes, the node immediately reports these changes through a State Change Report message. The state change report contains either filter mode change records, source list change records, or records of both types.

Both router and listener state changes are mainly triggered by the expiration of a specific timer or the reception of an MLD message (listener state change can also be triggered by the invocation of a service interface call). Therefore, to enhance protocol robustness, in spite of the possible unreliability of message exchanges, messages are retransmitted several times. Furthermore, timers are set so as to take into account the possible message losses and to wait for retransmissions.

Periodic general queries and current state reports do not apply this rule in order to not to overload the link; it is assumed that, in general, these messages do not generate state changes, their main purpose being to refresh the existing state. Thus, even if one such message is lost, the corresponding state will be refreshed during the next reporting period.

As opposed to current state reports, state change reports are retransmitted several times in order to avoid them being missed by one or more multicast routers. The number of retransmissions depends on the so-called robustness variable. This variable allows tuning the protocol according to the expected packet loss on a link. If a link is expected to be lossy (e.g., a wireless connection), the value of the robustness variable may be increased. MLD is robust to [Robustness Variable] − 1 packet losses. The RFC recommends a default value of 2 for the robustness variable.

If more changes to the same per-interface state entry occur before all the retransmissions of the state change report for the first change have been completed, each additional change triggers the immediate transmission of a new state change report. Retransmissions of the new state change report will be scheduled as well, in order to ensure that each instance of state change is transmitted at least [Robustness Variable] times.

If a node on a link expresses, through a state change report, its desire to no longer listen to a particular multicast address (or source), the querier must query for other listeners of the multicast address (or source) before deleting the multicast address (or source) from its multicast address listener state and stopping the corresponding traffic. Thus, the querier sends a multicast address-specific query to verify whether there are nodes still listening to a specified multicast address or not. Similarly, the querier sends a multicast address- and source-specific query to verify whether, for a specified multicast address, there are nodes still listening to a specific set of sources or not.

Both multicast address-specific queries and multicast address- and source-specific queries are only sent in response to state change reports and never in response to current state reports. This distinction between the two types of reports is needed to avoid the router treating all multicast listener reports as potential changes in state. By doing so, the fast leave mechanism of MLDv2 might not be effective if a state change report is lost, and only the following current state report is received by the router. Nevertheless, it avoids an increased processing at the router, and it reduces the MLD traffic on the link.

Nodes respond to the above queries through current state reports, which contain their per-interface multicast address listening state, only for the multicast addresses (or sources) being queried.

As stated earlier, in order to ensure protocol robustness, all the queries, except the periodic general queries, are retransmitted several times within a given time interval. The number of retransmissions depends on the robustness variable. If, while scheduling new queries, there are pending queries to be retransmitted for the same multicast address, the new queries and the pending queries have to be merged. In addition, host reports received for a multicast address with pending queries may affect the contents of those queries.

Protocol robustness is also enhanced through the use of the S flag (suppress router-side processing). As described above, when a multicast address-specific or a multicast Address- and source-specific query is sent by the querier, a number of retransmissions of the query are scheduled. In the original (first) query the S flag is clear. When the querier sends this query, it lowers the timers for the concerned multicast address (or source) to a given value; similarly, any nonquerier multicast router that receives the query lowers its timers in the same way. Nevertheless, while waiting for the next scheduled queries to be sent, the querier may receive a report that updates the timers. The scheduled queries still have to be sent, in order to ensure that a nonquerier router keeps its state synchronized with the current querier (the nonquerier router might have missed the first query). Nevertheless, the timers should not be lowered again, as a valid answer was already received. Therefore, in subsequent queries the querier sets the S flag.

10.6.4 Building Multicast Address Listener State on Multicast Routers

Multicast routers that implement MLDv2 (whether they are in the querier state or not) keep state per multicast address per attached link. This multicast address listener state consists of a filter mode, a filter timer, and a source list, with a timer associated to each source from the list. The filter mode is used to summarize the total listening state of a multicast address to a minimum set such that all nodes' listening states are respected. The filter mode may change in response to the reception of particular types of Report messages or when certain timer conditions occur.

A router is in the INCLUDE mode for a specific multicast address on a given interface if all the listeners on the link interested in that address are in the INCLUDE mode. The router state is represented through the notation INCLUDE (A), where A is a list of sources, called the "include list." The include list is the set of sources that one or more listeners on the link have requested to receive. All the sources from the include list will be forwarded by the router. Any other source that is not in the include list will be blocked by the router.

A source can be added to the current include list if a listener in the INCLUDE mode sends a current state or a state change report that includes that source. Each source from the include list is associated with a source timer that is updated whenever a listener in the INCLUDE mode sends a report that confirms its interest in that specific source. If the timer of a source from the include list expires, the source is deleted from the include list.

Besides this "soft leave" mechanism, there is also a "fast leave" scheme in MLDv2; it is also based on the use of source timers. When a node in the INCLUDE mode expresses its desire to stop listening to a specific source, all the multicast routers on the link lower their timers for that source to a given value. The querier then sends a multicast address and source-specific query to verify whether there are other listeners for that source on the link or not. If a report that includes this source is received before the timer expiration, all the multicast routers on the link update the source timer. If not, the source is deleted from the include list.

A router is in the EXCLUDE mode for a specific multicast address on a given interface if there is at least one listener in the EXCLUDE mode for that address on the link. When the first report is received from such a listener, the router sets the filter timer that corresponds to that address. This timer is reset each time an EXCLUDE mode listener confirms its listening state through a current state report. The timer is also updated when a listener, formerly in the INCLUDE mode, announces its filter mode change through a State Change Report message. If the filter timer expires, it means that there are no more listeners in the EXCLUDE mode on the link. In this case, the router switches back to the INCLUDE mode for that multicast address.

When the router is in the EXCLUDE mode, the router state is represented by the notation EXCLUDE (X,Y), where X is called the "requested list" and Y is called the "exclude list." All sources, except those from the exclude list, will be forwarded by the router. The requested list has no effect on forwarding. Nevertheless, the router has to maintain the requested list for the following two reasons:

1. To keep track of sources that listeners in the INCLUDE mode listen to. This is necessary to assure a seamless transition of the router to the INCLUDE mode when there is no listener in the EXCLUDE mode left. This transition should not interrupt the flow of traffic to listeners in the INCLUDE mode for that multicast address. Therefore, at the time of the transition, the requested list should contain the set of sources that nodes in the INCLUDE mode have explicitly requested.

    When the router switches to the INCLUDE mode, the sources in the requested list are moved to the include list, and the exclude list is deleted. Before switching, the requested list can contain an inexact guess of the sources that listeners in the INCLUDE mode listen to—might be too large or too small. These inexactitudes are due to the fact that the requested list is also used for fast blocking purposes, as described below. If such a fast blocking is required, some sources may be deleted from the requested list to reduce the router state. Nevertheless, in each such case the filter timer is updated as well. Therefore, listeners in the INCLUDE mode will have enough time, before an eventual switching, to reconfirm their interest in the eliminated source(s) and rebuild the requested list accordingly. The protocol ensures that when a switch to the INCLUDE mode occurs, the requested list is accurate.

2. To allow the fast blocking of previously unblocked sources. If the router receives a report that contains such a request, the concerned sources are added to the requested list. Their timers are set to a given small value, and a multicast address and source-specific query is sent by the querier to check whether there are nodes on the link still interested in those sources or not. If no node announces its interest

in receiving those specific source, the timers of those sources expire. Then, the sources are moved from the requested list to the exclude list. From then onwards, the sources will be blocked by the router.

10.7 SOURCE FILTERING

What follows is a brief discussion of source filtering based on RFC 4604. The term "Source Filtering GMP (SFGMP)" is used to refer jointly to the IGMPv3 and MLDv2 group management protocols. The use of source-specific multicast is facilitated by small changes to the SFGMP protocols on both hosts and routers. SSM defines general requirements that must be followed by systems that implement the SSM service model; this document defines the concrete application of those requirements to systems that implement IGMPv3 and MLDv2. In doing so, RFC 4604 defines modifications to the host and router portions of IGMPv3 and MLDv2 for use with SSM and presents a number of clarifications to their behavior when used with SSM addresses. RFC 4604 updates the IGMPv3 and MLDv2 specifications.

One should note that SSM can be used by any host that supports source filtering APIs and whose operating system supports the appropriate SFGMP. The SFGMP modifications, as described in RFC 4604, make SSM work better on an SSM-aware host (but they are not strict prerequisites for the use of SSM).

The 232/8 IPv4 address range is currently allocated for SSM by the IANA. In IPv6, the FF3x::/32 range (where x is a valid IPv6 multicast scope value) is reserved for SSM semantics, although today SSM allocations are restricted to FF3x::/96.

A host that knows the SSM address range and is capable of applying SSM semantics to it is described as an "SSM-aware" host. A host or router may be configured to apply SSM semantics to addresses other than those in the IANA-allocated range. The GMP module on a host or router *should* have a configuration option to set the SSM address range(s). If this configuration option exists, it *must* default to the IANA-allocated SSM range. The mechanism for setting this configuration option must at least allow for manual configuration. Protocol mechanisms to set this option may be defined in the future.

If the host IP module of an SSM-aware host receives a non-source-specific request to receive multicast traffic sent to an SSM destination address, it *should* return an error to the application. On a non-SSM-aware host, an application that uses the wrong API [e.g., "join(G)," "IPMulticastListen(G,EXCLUDE(S1))" for IGMPv3 or "IPv6MulticastListen(G,EXCLUDE(S2))" for MLDv2] to request delivery of packets sent to an SSM address will not receive the requested service because an SSM-aware router (following the rules of this document) will refuse to process the request, and the application will receive no indication other than a failure to receive the requested traffic.

RFC 4604 documents the behavior of an SSM-aware host with respect to sending and receiving the following GMP message types:

- IGMPv1/v2 and MLDv1 Reports (2.2.1)
- IGMPv3 and MLDv2 Reports (2.2.2)

- IGMPv1 Queries, IGMPv2 and MLDv1 General Queries (2.2.3)
- IGMPv2 Leave and MLDv1 Done (2.2.4)
- IGMPv2 and MLDv1 Group Specific Query (2.2.5)
- IGMPv3 and MLDv2 Group Specific Query (2.2.6)
- IGMPv3 and MLDv2 Group-and-Source Specific Query (2.2.7)

Refer to the RFC for details.

REFERENCES

[RFC2710] RFC 2710, Multicast Listener Discovery (MLD) for IPv6, S. Deering, W. Fenner, B. Haberman, October 1999, updated by RFC 3590, RFC 3810.

[RFC3810] RFC 3810, Multicast Listener Discovery Version 2 (MLDv2) for IPv6, R. Vida, Ed., L. Costa, Ed., June 2004.

[RFC4604] RFC 4604, Using Internet Group Management Protocol Version 3 (IGMPv3) and Multicast Listener Discovery Protocol Version 2 (MLDv2)for Source-Specific Multicast, H. Holbrook, B. Cain, B. Haberman, August 2006.

11

IPTV APPLICATIONS

Entertainment is "big business" all over the world. Major markets include North America, Europe, Asia, and South America. The annual residential cable TV revenue was estimated to be $75 billion in 2007 in the United States alone, providing services to about 66 million subscribers. IPTV services are initially targeted by traditional telephone companies as a way to enter the just-named market; eventually cable TV companies may adopt the same technology. traditional telephone companies ("telcos") have seen erosions in their revenues and they seek ways to increase their ARPU (Average Revenue Per User) using video services and "triple/quadruple play."[1] This chapter provides a terse overview to the topic; the discussion is not intended to be comprehensive or to be completely systematic: to do justice to the topic an entire lengthy textbook is needed.

11.1 OVERVIEW AND MOTIVATION

As noted in Chapter 1, IPTV deals with approaches, technologies, and protocols to deliver commercial-grade SD and HD entertainment-quality real-time linear and

---

[1] Triple play is the delivery of voice, Internet, and video services to a customer. Quadruple play adds wireless services.

IP Multicast with Applications to IPTV and Mobile DVB-H by Daniel Minoli
Copyright © 2008 John Wiley & Sons, Inc.

on-demand video content over IP-based networks, while meeting all prerequisite quality of service, quality of experience, conditional access (security), blackout management (for sporting events), emergency alert system, closed captions, parental controls, Nielsen rating collection, secondary audio channel, picture-in-picture, and guide data requirements of the content providers and/or regulatory entities. Typically, IPTV makes use of MPEG-4 encoding to deliver 200–300 SD channels and 20–40 HD channels; viewers need to be able to switch channels within 2 s or less; also, the need exists to support multi-STB/multiprogramming (say two to four) within a single domicile.

IPTV (also known in some quarters as telco TV) is not to be confused with simple delivery of video over an IP network, including video streaming, which has been possible for over two decades; IPTV supports all business, billing, provisioning, and content protection requirements that are associated with commercial video distribution. IP-based service needs to be comparable to that received over cable TV or DBS. In addition to TV sets, the content may also be delivered to a personal computer. MPEG-4, which operates at 2.5 Mbps for SD video and 8–11 Mbps for HD video, is critical to telco-based video delivery over a copper-based plant because of the bandwidth limitations of that plant, particularly when multiple simultaneous streams need to be delivered to a domicile; MPEG-2 would typically require a higher bit rate for the same perceived video quality [MIN199501, MIN200301].

Hence, in summary, an IPTV system must provide, as a minimum, the same service and content as extant cable networks, including broadcast television, local channels, premium channels, Pay Per View (PPV), music, and Personal Digital Recorder (PDR[2]) services. SD and HD channels must be supported. Very high availability (no less than 99.999%) must also be supported.

With the significant erosion in revenues from traditional voice services on wireline-originated calls (both in terms of depressed pricing and a shift to VoIP over broadband Internet services delivered over cable TV infrastructure), and with the transition of many customers from wireline to wireless services, the traditional telephone carriers find themselves in need of generating new revenues by seeking to deliver video services to their customers. Traditional phone carriers find themselves challenged in the voice arena (by VoIP and other providers); their Internet services are also challenged in the broadband Internet access arena (by cable TV companies); and, their video services are nascent and challenged by a lack of deployed technology. Multimedia (and new media) services are a way to improve telco revenues.

Table 11.1 depicts the gains in ARPU that can be achieved by adding linear programming and nonlinear programming (e.g., VoD and PDR services). Line rentals and voice calls contribute an ARPU of $38; adding broadband brings the figure to $68. Adding video services increases this figure by $52, to a total of $120.

IPTV is in the early stage of technical and market development worldwide. The U.S. telco IPTV market opportunity is projected by market research firms to reach

---

[2] These are also called Digital Video Recorders (DVRs) or Personal Video Recorders (PVRs).

TABLE 11.1. Monthly ARPU for U.S. Telcos

Service	Monthly ARPU	Incremental Gross Margin	Incremental Gross Profit per User per Month
Line rental	$16	94%	$15
Voice calls	$22	82%	$18
Broadband	$30	97%	$29
Basic video	$20	50%	$10
VoD	$12	75%	$9
DVR	$10	80%	$8
HDTV	$10	80%	$8
Total	$120	81%	$97

Source: Light Reading, Nov. 28, 2005.

10 million subscribers by 2012 and about 65 million subscribers worldwide. That could represent an IPTV services market of $6–$8 billion in the United States and $39–$52 billion worldwide by 2012; the Compound Annual Growth Rate (CAGR) is 35–40% for the next 5 years according to some. Table 11.2 depicts some press time stats and Table 11.3 depicts a forecast for the next few years.

According to press time data from Infonetics Research, worldwide IPTV equipment revenue reached about $425 million in the first quarter of 2007. According to the same market research, worldwide IPTV equipment manufacturer revenue increased over 150% in 2006, passing the $1 billion mark. While the IPTV equipment market is expected to grow at a more moderate pace in coming years, most equipment categories are forecast to at least double or triple between 2006 and 2010 [INF200701]. It has been estimated that to deploy the systems needed to deliver IPTV, carriers will spend in the range of $20 billion between 2007 and 2012 in the United States alone. There appears to be a favorable regulatory support in the United States for the entrance of the telcos into the video field. However, telcos may face franchising rights challenges. It is worth noting that historically the cable TV/pay TV market has been insensitive to economic cycles.

Table 11.4 provides a basic glossary of IPTV service concepts from Nortel [NOR200601]; refer to the glossary at the back of the book for a more exhaustive listing.

11.2 BASIC ARCHITECTURE

Figures 11.1–11.3 depict typical architectures for linear IPTV.

Figure 11.1 shows a content aggregator preparing the content at a single source S for terrestrial distribution of the content to multiple remote telcos. This example depicts the telcos acquiring the service from an aggregator/distributor, rather than performing that fairly complex function on their own, which can be fairly expensive to architect, develop, set up, and maintain. The operator must sign an agreement with each content *provider*; hundreds of agreements are, therefore, required to cover the available channels and VoD content. Aggregators provide the content to the operator, typically over satellite delivery, and do a lot of the signal normalization and CA work. However, an additional per-channel agreement with one or more content *aggregators* is also needed.

TABLE 11.2. Cable TV Statistics (2006/2007)

U.S. Cable TV	U.S. Television Households (December 2006)[a]	111,600,000
Industry Statistics	Basic Cable Subscribers (December 2006)[a]	65,600,000
	Cable Penetration of TV Households (December 2006)[a]	58.8%
	Occupied Homes Passed by Cable (December 2006)[a]	112,600,000
	Cable Headends (March 2007)[b]	8,360
	Premium Cable Units (December 2006)[a]	50,600,000
	Cable Systems (2006)[c]	7,090
	Annual Cable Revenue (residential) (2007 estimate)[a]	$74.7 billion
	Total Advertising Revenue (2007 estimate)[a]	$26.9 billion
	Annual Franchise Fees Paid by Cable Industry (2006)[d]	$2.8 billion
Cable's Private Investment	Cable Industry Construction/Upgrade Expenditures (2006)[a]	$12.4 billion
	Schools Served by *Cable in the Classroom* (August 2006)[e]	81,665
	Students Served by *Cable in the Classroom* (August 2006)[e]	44,157,959
Broadband Deployment	Digital Cable Customers (March 2007)[a]	34,012,000
	Residential Cable High-Speed Data Subscribers (December 2006)[a]	28,900,000
	Total Cable High-Speed Data Subscribers (March 2007)[a] (includes commercial customers)	32,712,000
	Housing Units Passed by Cable High-Speed Data Service (2006)[f]	119,100,000
	Residential Cable Telephony Customers (March 2007)[d]	10,800,000
	Homes Passed by Cable HDTV Service (June 2006)[d]	97,000,000
Value and Prices	National Video Programming Services/Networks (June 2005)[g]	531
	Major Television Awards Won by Cable in 2006[h]	61
	Average Monthly Price for Expanded Basic Programming Packages (2007 estimate)[a]	$42.76
Competition	Subscribers to Non-Cable Multichannel Video Program Distributors (e.g., DBS, etc.) (December 2006)[d]	32,100,000

Courtesy: National Cable & Telecommunications Association
[a]Kagan Research, LLC
[b]A.C. Nielsen Media Research
[c]Warren Communications News, Inc.
[d]National Cable & Telecommunications Association
[e]Cable in the Classroom
[f]U.S. Census Bureau and Kagan Research, LLC estimates. Housing units include occupied, seasonal, and vacant households
[g]Federal Communications Commission, Twelfth Annual Video Competition Report (March 2006)
[h]Academy of Television Arts & Sciences and Grady College of Journalism, University of Georgia

TABLE 11.3. U.S. Television Subscription Households by Type of Service 2005–2011

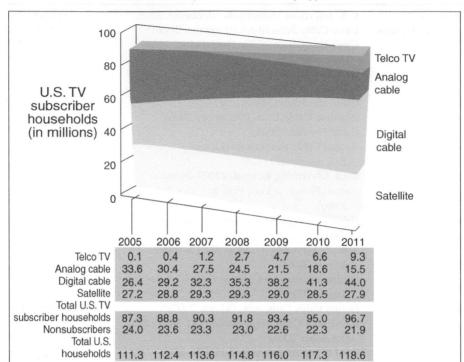

	2005	2006	2007	2008	2009	2010	2011
Telco TV	0.1	0.4	1.2	2.7	4.7	6.6	9.3
Analog cable	33.6	30.4	27.5	24.5	21.5	18.6	15.5
Digital cable	26.4	29.2	32.3	35.3	38.2	41.3	44.0
Satellite	27.2	28.8	29.3	29.3	29.0	28.5	27.9
Total U.S. TV subscriber households	87.3	88.8	90.3	91.8	93.4	95.0	96.7
Nonsubscribers	24.0	23.6	23.3	23.0	22.6	22.3	21.9
Total U.S. households	111.3	112.4	113.6	114.8	116.0	117.3	118.6

Source: Forrester Research Inc.

Note: This figure shows DSL delivery, likely ADSL2+/VDSL, but a FTTH can also be used.

Note: This figure does not show the middleware server either distributed at the telco headend or centralized at the content aggregator.

Note: This figure does not show the content acquisition; the uniform transcoding (e.g., using MPEG-4) is only hinted by the device at the far left.

Note: This figure does not show the specifics of how the Entitlement Control Message (ECM) and Entitlement Management Message (EMM) to support the conditional access function are distributed resiliently. This is typically done in-band for the ECMs and out-of-band [e.g., using a Virtual Private Network (VPN) over the Internet] for the EMMs.

Note: This figure does not show the video-on-demand overlay is deployed over the same infrastructure to deliver this and other advanced services.

Note: This figure does not show a blackout management system, which is needed to support substitution of programming for local sport events.

Note: This figure does not show how the tribune programming data is injected into the IPTV system, which is needed for scheduling/programming support.

Figure 11.2 is an architecture that is basically similar to that of Figure 11.1, but the distribution to the remote telcos is done via a satellite broadcast technology. Satellite delivery is typical of how cable TV operators today receive their signals

TABLE 11.4. Basic Glossary of IPTV Service Concepts

A la carte VoD	VoD where one pays for each item viewed (similar to PPV). Typically the subscriber has one day to view the content.
DVRs	Devices (perhaps built into the STB) that provide the ability to "time-shift" television viewing. DVRs use a hard disk to record the content. As such, they can record hundreds of hours of content, and subscribers can directly access any recording without "fast forwarding" through other programs. DVRs are integrated into the IPTV system. From the operator's Electronic Program Guide (EPG), the subscriber simply scrolls to the content to be recorded and hits a "record" button.
Free on-Demand VoD	VoD where access and content is free, as stimulus to buy the overall service.
Linear programming	Real-time TV content, including national channels, local channels, sports channels, and premium channels.
Near Video on Demand (nVoD)	Service similar to PPV. While PPV service starts the movie every two hours, nVoD service shows the same movie on several channels, each starting as little as 15 min apart. Hence the subscriber has a short wait time until the movie begins.
PPV programming	Services that are ordered on-the-fly (or prereserved at some point prior to a broadcast), which requires that the subscriber pay an additional fee to view specific content. Like standard television service, PPV content is broadcast at a set time.
Premium VoD	VoD where one pays an additional monthly fee for premium content such as recent movies.
Pull VoD	VoD system that stores content within the operator network. Upon request, the content is streamed to the subscriber. The advantage is that the user can select from a large, centrally stored content library. The disadvantage is that bandwidth must be allocated to each subscriber viewing VoD content.
Push VoD	VoD system that automatically downloads the VoD content to the subscriber's DVR. This download is done during offpeak times or at low priority, eliminating the need for additional bandwidth. The downside is that this makes some of the DVR disk unavailable to the subscriber. As such, this approach is practical only for the latest content, which will be viewed by a relatively large number of subscribers.
Subscription VoD	VoD where one pays a monthly fee for access to all content in the standard library.
Time-shifted viewing	As enhancements to television service that allows content to be viewed at a time which is more convenient to the subscriber.
VoD	Service that allows the subscriber to view content whenever he or she wants from a library of stored content. VoD supports a complete set of VCR-like functions, including rewind, pause, and fast forward.

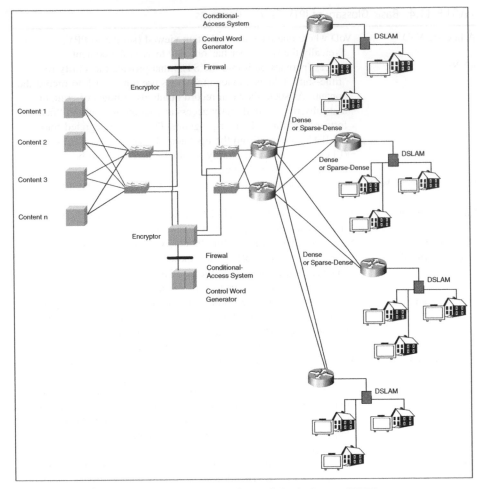

Figure 11.1. Typical Terrestrial-Based Single-Source IPTV System

from various media content producers (e.g., ABC/Disney, CNN, UPN, Discovery, A&E). In the case of the cable TV/Multiple Systems Operators (MSOs), the operator would typically have (multiple) satellite antenna(s) accessing multiple transponders on a satellite or on multiple satellites and then combine these signals for distribution. See Figure 11.3 for a pictorial example. In contrast, in the architecture of Figure 11.4, the operator will need only one receive antenna because the signal aggregation (conditional access, middleware administration, etc.) is done at the central point of content aggregation.

Zooming in a bit, the technology elements (subsystems) involved in linear IPTV include the following:

- Content aggregation
- Uniform transcoding

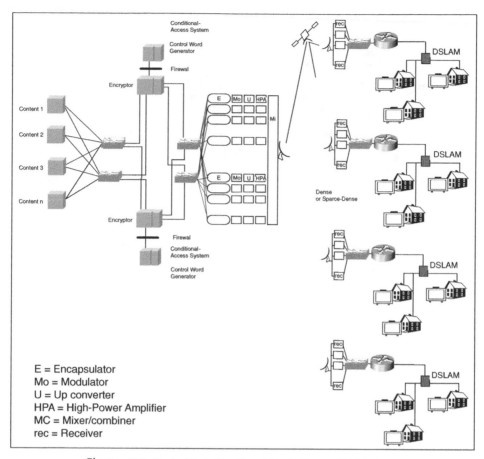

Figure 11.2. Typical Satellite-Based Single-Source IPTV System

- Conditional-access management
- Encapusulation
- Long-haul distribution
- Local distribution
- Middleware
- STBs
- Catcher (for VoD services)

Each of these technologies/subcomponents has its own specific design requirements, architectures, and considerations. Furthermore, these systems have to interoperate for an end-to-end complete solution that has a high QoE for the user, and it is easy to manage and reliable.

In turn, each of these subsystems can be viewed as a vendor-provided platform. Different vendors have different product solutions to support these subsystems; generally

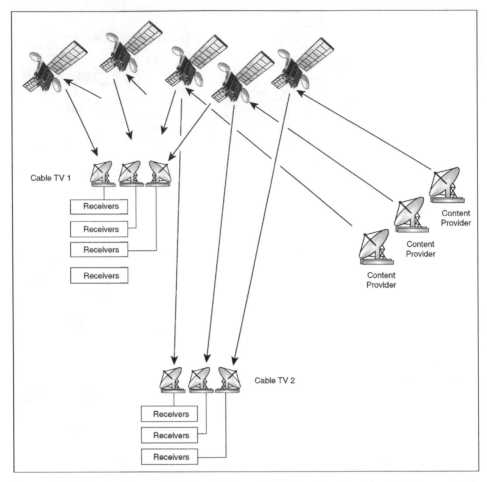

Figure 11.3. Disadvantages of Distributed Source IPTV: Requires Need for Dish Farms at Each Telco and for All Ancillary Subsystems

no one vendor has a true end-to-end solution. Hence, each of the following can be seen as a subsystem platform in its own right:

- Content aggregation
- Uniform transcoding
- Conditional-access management
- Encapusulation
- Long-haul distribution
- Local distribution
- Middleware
- STBs
- Catcher (for VoD services)

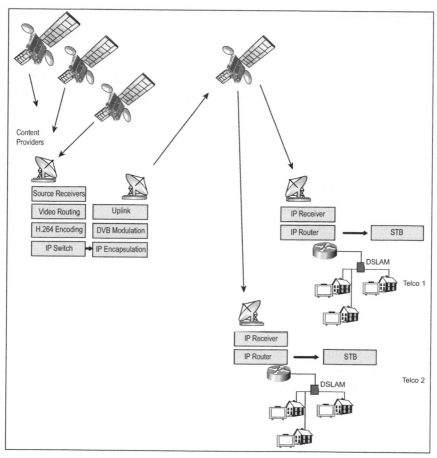

Figure 11.4. Advantages of Single Source IPTV: Obviates Need for Dish Farms at Each Telco

Operators can be classified as follows:

- High-end telcos (tier 1)
- Midtier telcos (tier 2)
- Small telcos (tier 3)
- High-end cable TV (tier 1) (future)
- Midtier cable TV (tier 2) (future)
- Smallcable TV (tier 3) (future)

One can anticipate several phases in the deployment of IPTV as follows:

- Phase 1—IPTV introduced by the telcos for commercial delivery of entertainment-grade video over their IP/MPLS networks (2007–2010).
- Phase 2—IPTV introduced by the cable TV companies for commercial delivery of entertainment-grade video over their cable infrastructure (speculative, 2010+).

- Phase 3—IPTV to morph to Internet TV for commercial delivery of any video content but of entertainment-grade quality over the Internet/broadband Internet access connections (2011+).

Applications such as video are very sensitive to end-to-end delay, jitter, and (uncorrectable) packet loss; QoS considerations are critical. These networks tend to have fewer hops, and pruning may be somewhat trivially implemented by making use of a simplified network topology.

11.2.1 Content Aggregation Subsystem

Content aggregation can be done in a distributed fashion or preferably (and more cost effectively) at a central site. Central site aggregation has the advantage that a uniform video/audio/conditional-access discipline can be applied to all video of interest.

Content can be downloaded from existing satellites (assuming that the proper authorization from the content owner is secured) or even delivered to the central site with a terrestrial facility (e.g., a point-to-point DS3 facility, a single-hop GbE connection), or even via the Internet, although the latter may introduce degradation right up front. At this juncture, the content from the satellites is received in encrypted form and needs to be decrypted.

When using existing content already distributed by a group of satellites (say in MPEG-2, MPEG-4, or other format), the content aggregation site can use a farm of satellite dishes pointing to the various satellites (as shown in Figure 11.4) or a single simulsat antenna, which is a large antenna that can look at 24–36 satellites simultaneously.

Generally C-band links are used (4 GHz in the downlink, 6 GHz in the uplink, 500 MHz bandwidth over 24 transponders using vertical and horizontal polarization, resulting in a usable transponder capacity of 45–75 Mbps—depending on modulation/FEC scheme). C-band has been used for several decades and has good transmission characteristics, particularly in the presence of rain, which typically affects high-frequency transmission. See Table 11.5 for some details. The individual C-band dishes are typically 3.8–4.5 m in diameter, and the simulsat antenna is usually 7 or 11 m in (toroidal) size.

The various signals are received by Integrated Receiver-Decoders (IRDs) that are tuned to the specific transponder (and subchannel) of interest. The IRDs have to be authorized by the ultimate content provider in order to be decrypted and decoded. The output of the IRDs is typically in Serial Digital Interface (SDI) format. See Appendix 11.A for some information on SDI.

The signals are typically routed (via a video router) to a bank of MPEG-4 encoders that generate both an SD (or an HD if that was the original format) version and a more compact SD (or HD) Picture-in-Picture (PIP) version (including PIP audio). MPEG-4 operates at 2.5 Mbps for SD video and 8–11 Mbps for HD video. The encoders typically output IP packets, each containing seven Transport Stream (TS) datagrams for that video program. See Figures 11.5 and 11.6. The approach is taken that an MPEG-2 infrastructure exists, and so an overlay of IP onto MPEG-2 TS is done [just as was the case a few years

TABLE 11.5. Satellite Band Details

Band	Characteristics	Considerations
C-band (5 GHz uplink and 4 GHz downlink)	• Relatively immune to atmospheric effects • Popular band, but on occasion it is congested on the ground (see note at right) • Bandwidth (~500 MHz/36-MHz transponders) allows video and high data rates • Provides good performance for video transmission • Proven technology with long heritage and good track record • Common in heavy-rain zones	• Requires large antennas (3.8–4.5 m or larger, especially on the transmit side) • Large footprints • Best performing band in the context of rain attenuation • Potential interference due to terrestrial microwave systems
Ku-band (14–14.5 GHz uplink and 11.7–12.2 GHz downlink)	• Moderate- to low-cost hardware • Highly suited to VSAT networks • Spot beam footprint permits use of smaller earth terminals, 1–3 m wide in moderate rain zones	• Attenuated by rain and other atmospheric moisture • Spot beams generally focused on land masses • Not ideal in heavy-rain zones
DBS-band (12.2–12.7 GHz downlink)	• Simplex • Multiple feeds for access to satellite neighborhoods • Small RO antennas	• Attenuated by rain and other atmospheric moisture
Ka-band (18.3–18.8 GHz and 19.7–20.2 GHz downlink)	• Microspot footprint • Very small terminals, much less than 1 m • High data rates are possible, 500–1000 Mbps	• Rain attenuation • Obstruction interference due to heavy rainfall

back with overlaying IP over an Asynchronus Transfer Mode (ATM) infrastructure]. Really, all that means is that chipsets had previously developed for MPEG-2 devices (e.g., receivers) and a desire existed in manufacturers to make use of that existing hardware technology. The IP Encapsulator (IPE), as this technology is known, receives IP packets from an Ethernet/IP connection and encapsulates selected packets into an MPEG-2 transport stream per DVB or Advanced Television Systems Committee (ATSC) specifications.

11.2.2 Uniform Transcoding Subsystem

At this stage all signals are uniformly encoded with MPEG-4 encoders, with the goal of achieving a consistent aggregate signal in terms of video and audio quality. Figure 11.7

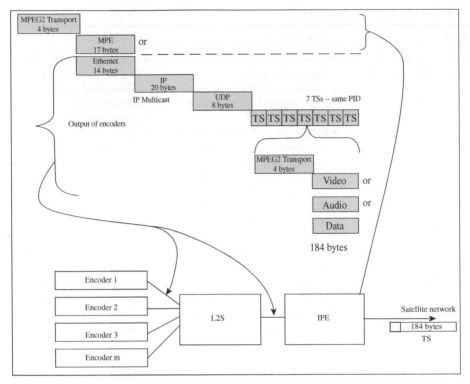

Figure 11.5. Encapsulation Function over Existing MPEG-2 Infrastructure

depicts the basic MPEG-2/4 framework. Each Elementary Stream (ES) output by an MPEG audio, video, and (some) data encoders contain a single type of (usually compressed) signal. There are a number of types of ES, including:

- Digital control data
- Digital audio
- Digital video
- Digital data

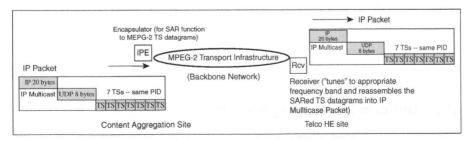

Figure 11.6. Segmentation and Reassembly over 'Existing' MPEG-2 Infrastructure

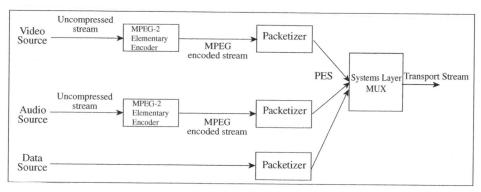

Figure 11.7. MPEG-2 Framework

For video and audio, the information is organized into *access units*, each representing a fundamental unit of encoding. For example, in video, an access unit will usually be a complete encoded video frame. Each ES is an input to an MPEG-2 processor (e.g., a video compressor) which accumulates the data into a stream of Packetized Elementary Stream (PES) packets. The compression is achieved using the Discrete Cosine Transform (DCT). A PES packet may be a fixed- or variable-sized block, with up to 65,536 octets per block, and includes a 6-byte protocol header. A PES is usually organized to contain an integral number of ES access units. In MPEG-2 networks, an IP address must be associated with a PID[3] and a specific transmission multiplex.

Video compression is the basic enabler for IPTV and DVB-H. Compression—decompression (codec) algorithms make it possible to capture, store, and transmit digital video signals. Codec technology has continuously improved in the last decade. One has

- industry standards, such as MPEG-2, MPEG-4 AVC (aka, MPEG-4 Part 10), H.264/AVC [ITU Joint Video Team (JVT) with the International Organization for Standardization (ISO)], and AVS (Chinese national video coding standard) and
- proprietary algorithms, such as On2, Real Video, Nancy, and Windows Media Video (WMV). WMV was originally a Microsoft proprietary algorithm that is now also standardized by SMPTE as VC-1.

The most recent codecs, H.264/AVC and VC-1, represent the third generation of video compression technology. Both codecs achieve very high compression ratios utilizing the available processing power in low-cost Integrated Circuits (ICs). Compression ratios of 100:1–400:1, but with good quality, are desirable and are achievable. Codecs now being developed by the ITU and MPEG include ITU/MPEG Joint Scalable

---

[3] Some also call this the Program ID.

TABLE 11.6. Data Rates of Video, Which Mandates the Use of Compression Algorithms

Picture	Pixels	Lines	Uncompressed Bit Rate (Mbps)			
			10 fps B&W	10 fps Color	10 fps B&W	30 fps Color
SQCIF	128	96	0.98	1.47	2.95	4.42
QCIF	176	144	2.03	3.04	6.08	9.12
CIF	352	288	8.11	12.17	24.33	36.50
4CIF	704	576	32.44	48.66	97.32	145.98
16CIF	1408	1152	129.76	194.4	380.28	583.93

Video Coding, an amendment to H.264/AVC, and PEG multiview video coding. Table 11.6 depicts the data rates encountered in digital video, which mandates the use of compression algorithms [SIP200701]. Figure 11.8 illustrates the history of video codec standardization.

The encoder will typically generate IP packets. See Figure 11.9. These have a source IP address and a multicast IP address. Video content can also be identified by the PID, as was shown in Figure 2.7. As noted in Chapter 2, the PID is a 13-bit field that is used to uniquely identify the stream to which the packet belongs (e.g., PES packets corresponding to an ES) generated by the MPEG-4 encoder/multiplexer. The PID allows the receiver to differentiate the stream to which each received packet belongs; effectively, it allows the receiver to accept or reject PES packets at a high level without burdening the receiver with extensive processing. A packet with an unknown PID or one with a PID which is not required by the receiver is discarded. Some PID values are predefined and are used to indicate various streams of control information. For a user to receive a particular transport stream, the user must first determine the PID being used and then filter packets which have a matching PID value. To enable the user to identify which PID corresponds to which program, a special set of streams, known as *signaling tables*, are transmitted with a description of each program carried within the MPEG-2 transport stream [FAI200101]. Signaling tables are sent separately to PES and are not

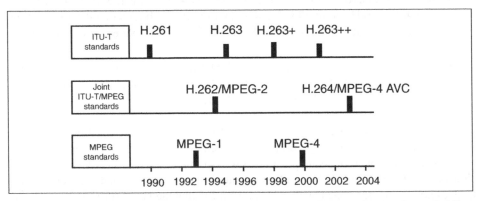

Figure 11.8. Compression Standards That Have Evolved over the Years (Approximate Publication Date)

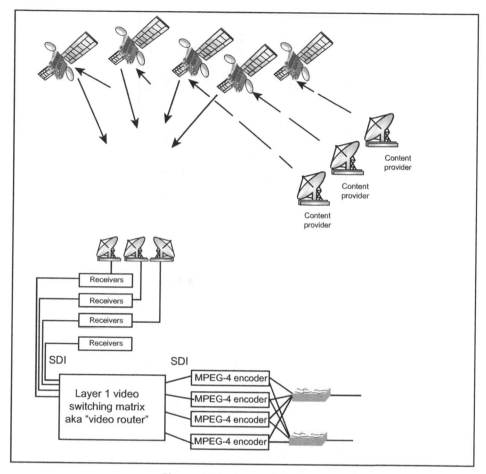

Figure 11.9. Transcoding Stage

synchronized with the elementary streams (i.e., they are an independent control channel).

Considerations for the encoder include:

- Bandwidth requirements for SD channels
- Ability to cap the variable bit rate, particularly for DSL delivery systems
- Bandwidth requirements for PIP for SD channels
- Types of audio/secondary audio channels to be supported
- Bandwidth requirements for audio
- Bandwidth requirements for HD channels
- Ability to cap the variable bit rate, particularly for DSL delivery systems
- Bandwidth requirements for PIP for HD channels
- Types of audio/secondary audio channels to be supported

TABLE 11.7. Compression Applications/Characteristics

| | Design Concern | | | | | | | | |
Application	Low Bitrate	Multiformal Decoders	Right Management	High Quality	Random Access	Low Cost	Error Robustness	Current Technology	Target Technology
Internet streaming	●	●	●					WMV9, Real Video, MPEG-4, Quicktime	H.264, WMV9
DVD				●	●	●		MPEG-2MP	
Digital terrestrial TV				●			●	MPEG-2	MPEG-2, H.264, AVS 1.0
Satellite TV	●			●			●	MPEG-2	H.264 HP
IPTV	●		●	●			●	MPEG-2, MPEG-4	MPEG-4
Digital video to handset	●		●	●		●		WMV9, H.264, MPEG-4	MPEG-4
Personal video recorders				●	●		●	MPEG-2	H.264, WMV9

TABLE 11.8. MPEG-4 Profiles

Profile	Estimated Improved Efficiency over MPEG-2	Decoder Complexity over MPEG-2	Application
Baseline	1.5 times better	2.5 times more complex	Low delay, video phone
Extended	1.75 times better	3.5 times more complex	DVB-H
Main	2.0 times better	4 times more complex	IPTV, broadcast video applications, packaged media

- Bandwidth requirements for HD audio
- Alarms and auto switchover upon device failure
- Power consumption and physical size

Tables 11.7 and 11.8 provide some basic information on encoder applications and features.

More details on MPEG-2/4 are provided in Appendix 11.3B.

11.2.3 Conditional-Access Management Subsystem

Satellite and cable delivery-based video streams are made available only to authorized users by the use of one or more of a variety of CASs. CA is basically a user authorization system that provides the STB with credentials to decode the encrypted video signal. CA is implemented using a CAS typically residing in a physically secure (separate) room at the content aggregation site. As can be seen in Figures 11.1 and 11.2, the individual IP multicast streams are encrypted for secure delivery to entitled users. In IPTV (and cable TV for that matter), symmetric encryption is typically the norm (although some systems do use public-key encryption).

Content streams are individually encrypted using triple DES (Data Encryption Standard) or AES. Keys are rotated, typically every 15 s. Also, portions of the key may be sent via different means (e.g., a portion over the satellite and a portion over another network, e.g., a VPN tunnel). CASs are very complex and not well documented in general.

A CAS relies on two types of messages:

- *Entitlement Control Message.* Message sent at periodic intervals (e.g., 15 s) that contains the encrypted code word, that is, the encrypted decryption key to be used by the STB to descramble the packets. They represent a method to send secret keys. ECMs have their PIDs at the TS level and their multicast address at the IP level.

- *Entitlement Management Message.* Message that controls the remote decryption client in the STB. EMMs entitle the subscriber to watch events by sending an authorization to the STB. They are usually sent every 12 h. EMMs have their PIDs at the TS level and their multicast address at the IP level.

ECM keys are extracted from the multicast stream. ECMs control the decryption of the events. To watch an event the subscriber must be entitled to watch the event (receive the EMM) and be able to decrypt the scrambled event (have the latest ECM). EMMs might be sent (but not always) via a separate path. Different CAS systems make use of the ECMs/EMMs in somewhat different ways.

11.2.3.1   Overview.   In a DVB context, CA is a security mechanism used to control the access to broadcast content (including video and audio, interactive services, etc.) through the transmission of encrypted signals and the programmable regulation of their decryption by a system such as smart cards [CON200701]. There are some standards available for CA, but vendors have generally developed vendor-proprietary systems.

A CAS uses encryption to prevent unauthorized reception. There also has to be a process to protect the secret keys that are transmitted with the signal to enable the descrambler to operate. The algorithm that is used for the encryption itself is generally a public algorithm (e.g., Triple DES and AES) or it is an open (but not publicly known) algorithm, such as the DVB-CSA. However, the key distribution mechanism is typically proprietary to each CA vendor. To handle key distribution the CAS adds two types of data to the multicast stream; these are known as CA messages. CA messages consist of already named ECMs and EMMs. Together these control the ability of individual users (or groups of users) to watch scrambled content. The scrambler key, called the *control word*, must be transmitted to the receiver in encrypted form as an ECM (sometimes called the *multisession key*). The CA subsystem in the receiver decrypts the control word only when authorized to do so; that authority is sent to the receiver in the form of an EMM. This layered approach is fundamental to all proprietary CAS in use today. The control word is typically changed at intervals of 10–15 s; this interval is called the crypto period. The ECM changes at the same frequency. The EMM is typically changed every 12–24 h. Encrypting of signal is typically done using dedicated hardware. See Figure 11.10 [DIG200701].

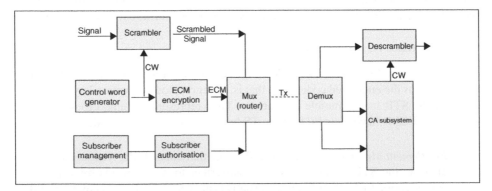

Figure 11.10. Basic CAS

The CAS supports the following two types of IPTV traffic [NOR200601]:

- *Broadcast/Linear TV* Broadcast television traffic must be encrypted "on the fly" to protect against piracy and service theft.
- *Video on Demand* Content providers require that VoD content be encrypted before it is stored on the VoD server. Stored content must be periodically reencrypted as a further preventive measure.

One simplified example is shown in Figures 11.11 and 11.12. Here a code word generator sends a newly generated key (generated every 15 s) for symmetric encryption to the stream encryptor. The code word is also sent to an Entitlement Management Messages Generator (EMMG) and Entitlement Control Messages Generator (ECMG). The SMS (Service Management System) portion of the system manages subscriber information, subscribers' device information, and ordered program information. The smart card is used for the management and control of subscriber and program delivery. The ECMG/EMMG manages encryption and packaging of entitlements and controls words for scrambled service. The EMMG has a database of preregistered smart cards, which tells it if the card that is associated with a specific STB is entitled to the overall program/service (where program is a collection of individual video channels). The ECM contains a scrambled version of the code word. In this system, the STB is equipped with a smart card. The client on the STB uses the arriving EMMs to update entitlement information on the smart card and keys in the arriving ECMs to decrypt the IP streams comprising the program/service. These messages enable or disable a client's access to privileged data content coming through the CAS.

In this example ECMs contain the code word; the data required by the smart card or SoftClient to decrypt the content are sent in ECMs. Control words change on a regular basis and so an ECM always contains two ECMs (now and next) to ensure continuous

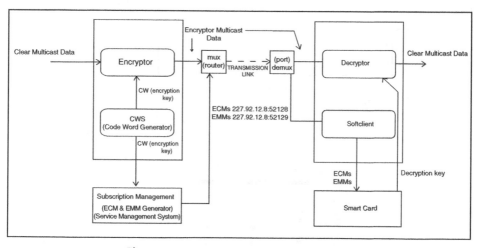

Figure 11.11. Example of CAS—Logical View

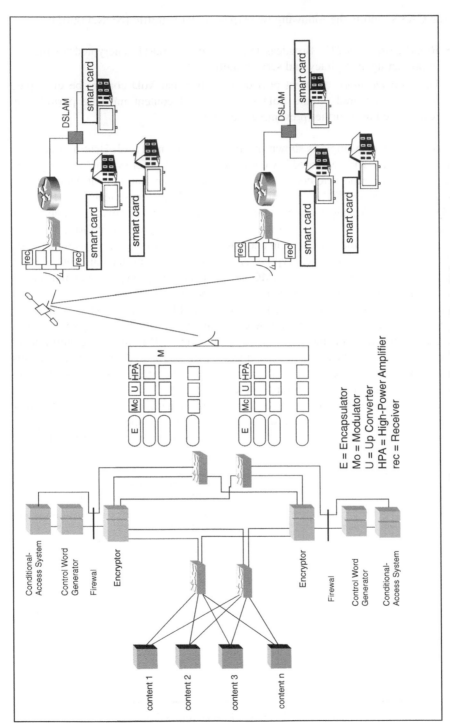

Figure 11.12. Example of CAS—Physical View

E = Encapsulator
Mo = Modulator
U = Up Converter
HPA = High-Power Amplifier
rec = Receiver

viewing. ECMs are specific to the scrambled content and are the same for all subscribers. EMMs are used to deliver the entitlements to, and manage, the entitlements on the Smart Card or SoftClient. EMMs are subscriber-specific, and can be divided into three categories:

- Messages for managing a subscriber's entitlements
- Messages for performing security-related functions
- Messages relating to the management of applications on the STB

The code words are generated randomly and are changed frequently. ECM and EMM messages are encrypted with the multilevel keys.

11.2.3.2 Standards. As noted, vendors have developed vendor-specific solutions. Conditional access is not fully specified in DVB, but a collection of tools are available, specifically (i) DVB Common Scrambling Algorithm and (ii) the DVB Simulcrypt Mechanism (DVB-SIM), which allows different CAS to coexist on one service. In DVB, there are two CA interoperability scenarios envisaged [DVB200701]:

SimulCrypt is a mechanism whereby a single transport stream can contain several CAS. This enables different CA decoder populations (potentially with different CAS installed) to receive and correctly decode the same video and audio streams.

MultiCrypt revolves around the specification of a Common Interface (CI) which, when installed in the set-top box or television, permits the user to switch manually between CAS. Thus, a viewer presented with a CAS that is not installed in his or her box simply switches cards.

The DVB standards are:

- DVB-CSA, Standard Ref: ETR 289, Edition: 1.0, Support for Use of Scrambling and Conditional Access within Digital Broadcasting Systems
- Standard Ref: TR 102 035, Edition: 1.1.1, Implementation Guidelines of the DVB Simulcrypt Standard
- Standard Ref: ETSI TS 101 197, Edition: 1.2.1, DVB SimulCrypt: Headend Architecture and Synchronization
- Standard Ref: ETSI TS 103 197, Edition: 1.4.1, Headend Implementation of SimulCrypt

Common Interface. In the mid 1990s the DVB came to the realization that a single standard could not be agreed upon and thus settled for defining a common framework within which different systems could exist and compete. They defined an interface structure, the common interface, to allow the STB to receive signals from several service providers operating different CAS (the common interface connector also allows plug-in cards for other functions besides CA; e.g., it is proposed to provide audio description for the visually impaired using a common interface card). Since then the European Commission has required the use of a common interface mechanism for all integrated TV sets (excluding STBs, which may employ embedded CAS) [DIG200701].

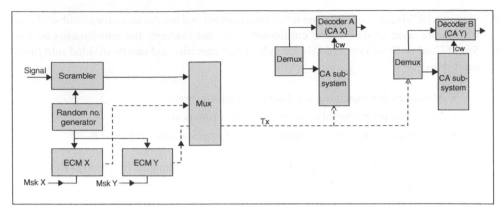

Figure 11.13. SimulCrypt

SimulCrypt. This allows two CAS to work side by side, transmitting separate entitlement messages to two separate types of STBs, with different CAS. It also gives the multiplex provider the opportunity to increase the viewer base by cooperating with other multiplex operators. See Figure 11.13. If a viewer wishes to receive services from different providers who do not simulcrypt each other's ECMs, the only option is to acquire separate decryption for each CAS. The common interface enables a *MultiCrypt* environment, allowing an additional CA system to be added as a module. In practice, the possibility of MultiCrypt encourages the parties to conclude a SimulCrypt agreement [DIG200701].

11.2.3.3 Additional Details.[4]

In a DVB system, scrambling can operate at either the level of the entire transport stream or the level of individual elementary streams. There is no provision for scrambling a service in its own right, but the same effect is achieved by scrambling all of the elementary streams in a service. In the case of scrambled elementary streams, not all of the data are actually scrambled; the packet headers are left unscrambled so that the decoder can work out their contents and handle them correctly. In the case of transport stream scrambling, only the headers of the transport packets are left unencrypted; everything else is scrambled. The scrambling (and descrambling) process relies on three pieces of information:

- The code word (aka control word)
- The service key
- The user key

The code word is encrypted using the service key, providing the first level of protection. This service key may be common to a group of users, and typically each

---

[4] This section is based on reference [BRO200701].

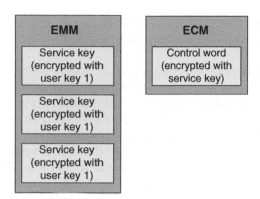

Figure 11.14. Embedding Code Words and Service Keys in ECMs and EMMs

encrypted service will have one service key. This encrypted code word is broadcast in an ECM every few seconds and is what the decoder in the STB needs to descramble a service.

Next, one has to make sure that authorized users (i.e., those who have paid) can decrypt the code word, but that only authorized users can decrypt it. To do this, the service key is itself encrypted using the user key. Each user key is unique to a single user, and so the service key must be encrypted with the user key for each user that is authorized to view the content. Once the system has encrypted the service key, it is broadcast as part of an EMM. Since there is a lot more information to be broadcast (the encrypted service key must be broadcast for each user), these are broadcast less frequently; each EMM is broadcast every 12–24 h, although some CASs broadcast them every half hour. See Figure 11.14.

Often (but not always) the encryption algorithm is symmetric, where the same key is used for encryption and decryption in the case of the service and user keys. When the receiver gets a CA message, it is passed to the CAS. In the case of an EMM, the receiver will check whether the EMM is intended for that receiver (usually by checking the CA serial number or smart card number); and if it is, it will use its copy of the user key to decrypt the service key. The service key is then used to decrypt any ECMs that are received for that service and recover the control word. Once the receiver has the correct control word, it can use this to initialize the descrambling hardware and actually descramble the content.

While not all CAS use the same algorithms (and it is impossible to know, because technical details of the CA algorithms are not made public), they all work in basically the same way. There may be some differences, and the EMMs may sometimes be used for other CA-related tasks besides decrypting service keys, such as controlling the pairing of a smart card and an STB so that the smart card will work correctly in that receiver.

In order to generate the EMMs correctly, the CAS needs to have some information about which subscribers are entitled to watch which shows. The SMS is used to set which channels (or shows) an individual subscriber can watch. This is typically a large database of all the subscribers that is connected to the billing system and to the CA system and is used to control the CAS and decide which entitlements should be generated for which users. The SMS and CAS are usually part of the same package from the CA vendor.

The ECMs and EMMs are broadcast as part of the service. The PIDs for the CA data are listed in the Conditional Access Table (CAT), and different PIDs can be used for the ECMs and EMMs. This makes it easier for remultiplexing, where some of the CA data (the ECMs) may be kept, while other data (the EMMs) may be replaced.

A DVB receiver may contain several descrambling modules, each of which takes a transport stream as input. Each module is logically the same, as we have described above, but different modules may be capable of handling different CASs. The DVB-CI allows a receiver to swap CA modules by defining a standard interface for the CAS. The DVB-CI uses a PCMCIA interface for the CA module—any module that complies with the DVB-CI specification will work in any receiver equipped with a DVB-CI slot. DVB-CI is not the only standard interface for scrambling systems; the OpenCable POD interface is also in use and in some cases is more popular that DVB-CI.

While NDS and Nagravision are the two most common CASs on the market at press time, other CASs are provided by Conax, Irdeto Access, Verimatrix, Widevine, Philips (the CryptoWorks system), and France Telecom (the Viaccess system). There are other systems from companies, such as Motorola, who make CASs, but these are not often used in DVB systems. DVB systems can offer pluggable encryption modules using the DVB-CI, which uses a PCMCIA card to contain the encryption hardware and software. This means that the user can switch encryption systems (for instance, if they change their cable company) without having to replace the entire STB. This is a big advantage for open standards and really enables the move from a vertical market to a horizontal one.

Some companies (NDS, for instance) are reportedly not convinced of the security of the DVB-CI system, and so not all CASs are available as CI modules. The Advanced Television Systems Committee (ATSC) uses a similar, though slightly more secure, mechanism called the POD (Point of Deployment) module, known as CableCARD in OpenCable systems. These are more widely deployed in U.S. markets, and all OCAP receivers will include a CableCARD slot.

11.2.4 Encapsulation Subsystem

The MPEG standard (ISO138181) [ISO200001] defines mechanisms of multiplexing more than one stream (video, audio, and data) to produce one program. The standard provides basic framework for integrated video, audio and, data services. As noted, the service provided by a MPEG-2 transport multiplex offers a number of parallel channels, which correspond to logical links (forming the MPEG TS) [ISO200001, CLA200301]. The MPEG-2 TS has been widely accepted not only for providing digital TV services but also as a subnetwork technology for building IP networks. Each MPEG-2 TS channel is uniquely identified by the PID value carried in the header of fixed-length MPEG-2 TS packets. The PID value is a 13-bit field and, thus, the number of channels is limited to 8192, some of which are reserved. Nonreserved TS logical channels may be used to carry audio [ISO200003], video [ISO200002], IP datagrams [ISO200004, ETS200301], ATS200001], or other private data.

```
+--------+---------------------------+-----------------+
| Header |            PDU            | Integrity Check |
+--------+---------------------------+-----------------+
<-------------------- SNDU ------------------------->
```

Figure 11.15. Encapsulation of a Subnetwork IPv4 or IPv6 PDU to Form an MPEG-2 Payload Unit

MPE is a scheme used in DVB that encapsulates PDUs; each Section is sent in a series of TS packets using a single TS logical channel [ETS200301]. The MPEG-2 TS has been widely accepted not only for providing digital TV services but also as a subnetwork technology for building IP networks. Examples of systems using MPEG-2 include the DVB and ATSC standards for digital television. To make use of an MPEG-2 TS environment, a network device, known as an encapsulator,[5] receives PDUs (e.g., IP packets or Ethernet frames) and formats these into Subnetwork Data Units (SNDUs). An encapsulation (or convergence) protocol transports each SNDU over the MPEG-2 TS service and provides the appropriate mechanisms to deliver the encapsulated PDU to the receiver IP interface. In forming an SNDU, the encapsulation protocol typically adds header fields that carry protocol control information, such as the length of SNDU, receiver address, multiplexing information, payload type, and sequence numbers. The SNDU payload is typically followed by a trailer which carries an integrity check [e.g., Cyclic Redundancy Check (CRC)]. When required, an SNDU may be fragmented across a number of TS packets. See Figures 11.15 and 11.16 [RFC4259]. Examples of existing encapsulation/convergence protocols include AAL5 an ITU standard) and MPEG-2 MPE (an ETSI/DVB standard). In summary, the standard DVB way of carrying IP datagrams in an MPEG-2 TS is to use MPE; with MPE each IP datagram is encapsulated into one MPE section. A stream of MPE sections is then put into an ES, that is, a stream of MPEG-2 TS packets with a particular PID. Each MPE section has a 12-B header, a 4-B CRC (CRC-32) tail, and a payload length, which is identical to the length of the IP datagram, which is carried by the MPE section [FAR200601].

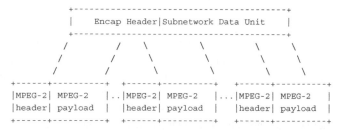

Figure 11.16. Encapsulation of a PDU (e.g., IP Packet) into a Series of MPEG-2 TS Packets. Each TS Packet Carries a Header with a Common ID Value Denoting the MPEG-2 TS Logical Channel

---

[5] This is also known as an IP Encapsulator (IPE)

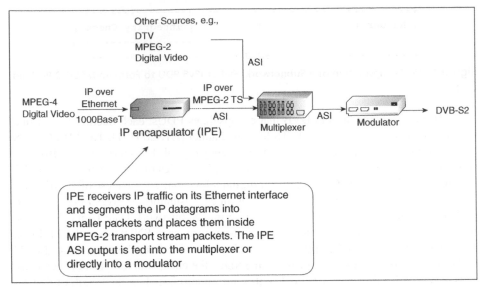

Figure 11.17. Encapsulator Function

Data for transmission over the MPEG-2 transport multiplex is passed to an encapsulator that typically receives PDUs (Ethernet frames, IP datagrams, or other network layer packets). It formats each PDU into a series of TS packets (usually after adding an encapsulation header), which is sent over a TS logical channel. In a simple example, one or more TS logical channels are processed by a MPEG-2 multiplexor resulting in a TS multiplex. In more complex examples, the same TS logical channel may be fed to multiple MPEG-2 multiplexors and these may, in turn, feed other MPEG-2 multiplexors (remultiplexing). In all cases, the final result is a TS multiplex, which is transmitted over the physical bearer towards the receiver [CLA200301]. The output of an encapsulator is typically ASI (Asynchronous Serial Interface). See Figure 11.17 for a pictorial view. Appendix 11.C provides additional information on the encapsulation process.

Note: DVB-ASI is a serial data transmission protocol that transports MPEG-2 (*compressed*) TS packets over copper-based cables or optical links, typically within a center. DVB-ASI is used as a serial link between equipment in broadcast facilities. The maximum line rate is 270 Mbps and multiple transport streams can be multiplexed on the 270 Mbps. The encoder/statistical multiplexer places stuffing data when there is no MPEG data to send; for example, 11 Mbps of MPEG is sent such that only 11 Mbps is used in the network and not the full 270 Mbps. ASI is defined in TR 101 891 Version 1.1.1 "Digital Video Broadcasting (DVB); Professional Interfaces: Guidelines for the Implementation and Usage of the DVB Asynchronous Serial Interface (ASI)," and in EN 50083–9 CENELEC/December 2002 "Cable Networks for Television Signals, Sound Signals and Interactive Services. Part 9: Interfaces for CATV/SMATV Headends." See Figure 11.18.

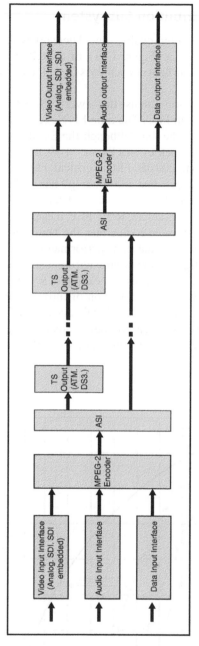

Figure 11.18. ASI Application

11.2.5 Long-Haul Distribution Subsystem

The long-haul network can be a high-quality routed network with very tightly controlled latency, jitter, and packet loss (e.g., Figure 11.1), or a satellite-based one-hop network (e.g., Figure 11.2). The backbone network supports IP multicast, very typically PIM DM or PIM sparse-dense.

For satellite delivery, the norm is to use the newer DVB-S2 modulation scheme. It is an 8-PSK-based technology with FEC. The ratio Eb/No (energy per bit over noise) is a reasonable guide for quality of the link (although the Es/No—energy per symbol over noise—would be an even better metric). See Figure 11.19. Because satellite transmission can attenuate the signal by up to 200 dB, FEC is critical. FEC is a family of well-known simplex error correction techniques that add "coding" bits to the information bits at the transmit end (encoder) which enables the decoder to determine which bits are in error and correct them (up to a limit). For example, R 5/4 FEC means one coding bit is added for every four information bits. The more coding bits, the "stronger" the code (requires less transmit power or link quality to get the same performance), but more coding bits mean more bandwidth required. High coding is an environment where one uses R 1/2; low coding is an environment where one uses, for example, R 7/8. Typical satellite FEC is either convolutional/Viterbi with Reed–Solomon or turbo coding. Typical turbo codes provide about a 2-dB advantage over conventional codes. Viterbi soft-decision decoding has been the norm (~4.4 dB gain). Turbo coding advanced recently (~6.3 dB gain). Low-Density Parity Check (LDPC) is the newest (~7.8 dB gain).

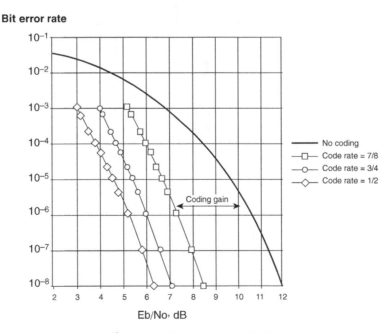

Figure 11.19. Advantage of FEC

TABLE 11.9. Link Performance Requirements for Satellite Links Operating with Various Modulation Technologies

Coding/Modulation		Required Eb/No (dB)
DVB/QPSK	R 1/2	4.5
	R 2/3	5.0
	R 3/4	5.5
	R 7/8	6.4
DVB/8PSK	R 2/3	6.9
	R 5/6	8.9
Turbo QPSK	R 1/2	2.7
	R 5/8	3.3
	R 3/4	3.9
	R 5/6	4.5
	R 7/8	4.7
Turbo 8PSK	R 2/3	5.4
	R 3/4	6.4
	R 5/6	7.7

Table 11.9 shows the DVB specs for Eb/No required for various modulation and coding rates (includes RS); Turbo values are from vendor specs; the new DVB-S2 standard specifies LDPC coding in lieu of Turbo codes, which are slightly better than the values shown in the table for turbo. An Eb/No of 6–9 dB (and a C/N—carrier-to-noise ratio—of 12 dB) is desirable. In this satellite-based design, jitter is nonexistent.

A set of international standards for digital TV has been developed by the DVB Project, an industry consortium with about 300 members, and published by a Joint Technical Committee (JTC) of ETSI, CENELEC, and European Broadcasting Union (EBU). These are collectively known as Digital Video Broadcast. IPTV makes use of a number of these standards, particularly when making use of satellite links. Standards have emerged in the past 10 years for defining the physical layer and data-link layer of a distribution system, as follows:

- Satellite video distribution (DVB-S and DVB-S2)
- Cable video distribution (DVB-C)
- Terrestrial television video distribution (DVB-T)
- Terrestrial television for handheld mobile devices (DVB-H)

Distribution systems differ mainly in the modulation schemes used (because of specific technical constraints):

- DVB-S (SHF) employs QPSK.
- DVB-S2 employs QPSK, 8PSK, 16APSK or 32APSK; 8PSK is the most common at this time (it supports 30 megasymbols pre satellite transponder and provides a

usable rate in the 75-Mbps range, or about 25 SD-equivalent MPEG-4 video channels).

- DVB-C (VHF/UHF) employs Quadrature Amplitude Modulation (QAM): 64-QAM or 256-QAM.
- DVB-T (VHF/UHF) employs 16-QAM or 64-QAM (or QPSK) along with Coded Orthogonal Frequency Division Multiplexing (COFDM).

Devices interact with the physical layer via a Synchronous Parallel Interface (SPI), Synchronous Serial Interface (SSI), or ASI. All information in DVB is transmitted in MPEG-2 transport streams with some additional constraints (DVB-MPEG).

11.2.6 Local Distribution Subsystem

The local distribution network is typically a high-quality routed network with very tightly controlled latency, jitter, and packet loss. The local distribution network is typically comprised of a metropolitan core tier and a consumer distribution tier. See Figure 11.20.

In the metropolitan core tier, IPTV is generally transmitted using the telco's private "carrier-grade" IP network. The network engine can be pure IP based, MPLS based (layer "2.5"), metro Ethernet based (Layer 2), optical SONET/Optical Transport Network (OTN) based (layer 1), or a combination thereof. A (private) wireless network, such as WiMax, can also be used. The backbone network supports IP multicast, very typically PIM DM or PIM sparse–dense.

The consumer distribution tier, the final leg, is generally (but not always) DSL based at this time (e.g., VDSL or ADSL2+); other technologies, such as PON (Passive Optical Network) may also be used (see Table 11.10). A bandwidth in the range 20–50 Mbps is generally desirable for delivery of IPTV services. For example, the simultaneous viewing of an HD channel along with two SD channels would require about 17 Mbps; Internet access would require additional bandwidth. Therefore, the 20 Mbps is seen as a lower bound on the bandwidth. As an example, in the United States Verizon is implementing Fiber to the Premises (FTTP) technologies, delivering fiber to the subscriber's domicile; this supports high bandwidth, but it requires significant investments. AT&T is implementing Fiber To The Curb (FTTC) in some markets, using existing copper for only the last 1/10 of a mile, and Fiber to the Node (FTTN) in other markets, terminating the fiber run within a few thousand feet of the subscriber. These approaches lower the upfront cost but limit the total bandwidth.

The receivers (STBs) use IGMP to gain real-time access to programming.

It is important to keep the telco-level network (the metropolitan core tier) streamlined with as few routed hops as possible and with plenty of bandwidth between links and with high-power nodal routers in order to meet the QoS requirements of IPTV. Otherwise, pixilation, tiling, waterfall effects, and even blank screens will be an issue. It is important to properly size all layer 2 and layer 3

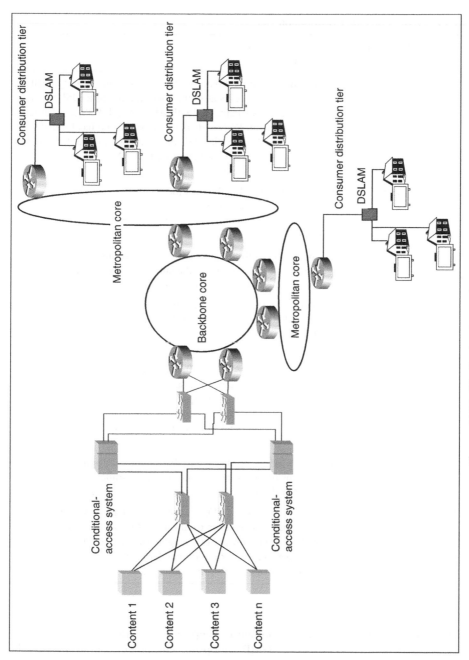

Figure 11.20. Distribution Networks

TABLE 11.10. Consumer Distribution Tier

Approach for the Consumer Distribution Tier	Description
"Classical"	• DSL delivers digital data over a copper connection, typically using the existing local loop. There are multiple DSL variants (as covered in Chapter 1) with ADSL2 and ADSL2+ being the most prevalent. DSL is distance sensitive and has limited bandwidth. As a result, DSL oftencannot be used alone; fiber must be deployed to connect to a DSLAM located in an outside plant cabinet.
Under deployment	• Fiber to the Neighborhood: Fiber is extended to each neighborhood where IPTV service is to be supported. A small-size DSLAM in each neighborhood supports a few dozen subscribers.
	• Fiber to the Curb: Fiber is extended to within (typically) less than 1/10th of a mile from the subscriber site. Each fiber typically supports one to three subscribers.
	• Fiber to the Premises/Home/Subscriber/Business (FTTP, FTTH, FTTS, FTTB): Fiber reaches the subscriber site
New/future	• PON technology can be used to deliver service using end-to-end fiber. A single fiber emanates from the central office, and a passive splitter in the outside plant splits the signal to support multiple subscribers. Broadband PON (BPON) supports up to 32 subscribers per port, whereas Gigabit PON (GPON) supports up to 128 subscribers per port.
	• Fixed wireless WiMax. Note that WiMax-supports only 17 Mbps of shared bandwidth over a 2.5-mile radius (and less at higher distances) and is therefore rather limited.
Cable operators	• Hybrid Fiber Coax (HFC) is the traditional technology used by cable operators. Fiber is used for the first section, from the headend to the subscriber's neighborhood. The link is then converted to coax for the remainder of the connection, terminating at the subscriber premises.

devices in the network. It is also important to keep multicast traffic from "splashing back" and flood unrelated ports. IGMP snooping and other techniques may be appropriate.

Keep in mind that the end-off point at the headend, the demark between the IPTV content provider and the telco, will need administrative and management connectivity back to the CAS (for the EMMs) and also for the middleware function when that is done in a centralized fashion.

11.2.7 Middleware Subsystem

Middleware is the software system used for delivering an IPTV service to the consumer. IPTV middleware is the software that manages the interaction of network elements from the headend through to the STB. There may be a server portion to the middleware in the headend, or at a central network point, and a client portion that resides in the STB. The middleware allows a customer to select from a list of available video programs. Press time providers included Microsoft, Widevine, Myrio/Siemens, Minerva, and Orca, among others. Companies using Microsoft's IPTV platform include AT&T U-Verse TV, BT, Swisscom, Bell Canada, Telecom Italia, among others. Functions include subscriber control, service definition, content control, and systems control. IPTV middleware supports the basic operation of the IPTV system with functions such as subscriber authentication, channel selection, an electronic program guide, and VoD services.

The middleware is typically a client/server architecture where the client resides on the STB. The middleware controls the user experience and, because of this, it defines how the consumer interacts with the service. For example, the user interface and services available to a consumer [such as electronic program guide (EPG), VoD, or pay-per-view service] are all made available and controlled through the middleware. The ease of managing multiple services is a function of the two-way IP network. This IP architecture provides a standard for applications and services to be integrated into the network, and IPTV becomes just one of these applications. The differentiating factor in an IP service model is convergence. Because of the common structure for applications and services, convergence can be realized for network elements, applications, and Operations/ Business Support Systems (OSS/BSS). Therefore, managing multiple services becomes a matter of managing the same services through the network and distributing them to multiple end-user environments [BRD200701].

Typical capabilities include [FOU200701]:

User Management The middleware provides the dynamic User Interface (UI) to the STB. It also keeps track of the STB security ID, as well as maintaining the STB usage log for billing and security purposes. It provides the Web-based STB remote control capability. The STBs can also be remotely upgraded. The UI of the STB may be customized and assigned to individual users or multiple user groups.

Content Management The software provides flexible control over that content. For example, one can apply different costs to different content types, decide on the usage pattern, or create different packages for different content groups.

Infrastructure Management The middleware allows the administrator to configure server roles and functions and control input and output parameters. The middleware provides manual and automated tools for load balancing. It can monitor the availability of all servers and can activate a failover mechanism in the event of finding a component failure.

11.2.8 Set-Top Boxes

The STB is the subscriber's device that provides access to the IPTV services and network. On the network side it has an Ethernet interface (e.g., 100Base-T) and on the user side a

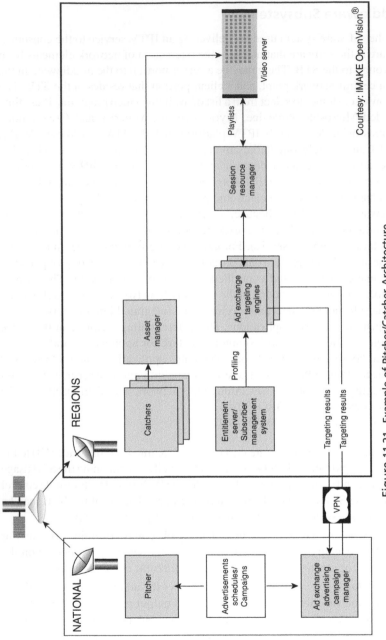

Figure 11.21. Example of Pitcher/Catcher Architecture

variety of TV interfaces. The STB must decrypt the incoming signal; therefore, it must have access to the CAS both at provisioning time as well as in real time to process the ECMs and EMMs. It needs a chipset to run the decryption. Also, it must be able to take IP packets that contain the encapsulated MPEG-4 TS and convert that into a displayable video signal by supporting the deencapsulation and the decoding function. Importantly, the STB must support the middleware function. The middleware supports the user interface and the ability to navigate the EPG, order new channels, VoD, DVR, etc. Also, it must support SAP, closed captions, EAS (Emergency Alert System), parental controls, picture-in-picture display, and multistream viewing (e.g., support three separate TV sets in three separate rooms—this is sometimes done by packaging three units into one chassis and using short-distance RF signaling to support the two secondary room remote Controls). Typical STB manufactures include, but are not limited to, Cisco Scientific Atlanta, Amino, LG Electronics, Motorola, Philips, Samsung, and Thomson Multimedia.

11.2.9 Catcher (for VoD Services)

There are three primary components to a VoD system [NOR200601]:

- *VoD Server* This device stores the content. Some VoD servers are proprietary hardware; others are software that works with commercial server and storage equipment.
- *VoD Catcher* This equipment receives new content from the content provider (such as a movie studio) via satellite. The brand/model of a VoD catcher is specified by the content provider to work with the "VoD pitcher" used by the content provider since there are no industry standards. An operator may need several VoD catchers to receive content from multiple sources.
- *VoD Cache* The VoD cache is a distributed VoD server. Frequently accessed content may be pushed to caching equipment located closer to the user.

The broad pitcher/catcher architecture has been defined by CableLabs®. Figure11.21 shows an example of a commercial implementation. Video server providers include, but are not limited to, Kasenna and Bitband.

APPENDIX 11.A: SERIAL DIGITAL INTERFACE BASICS

SDI is a standard for transporting *uncompressed* standard-definition digital video serially over coax cable. It is defined by ANSI/SMPTE 259 M, ITU-R BT.656, and other related standards and practices. SDI is the most common interface used by the media industry for production (e.g., editing machines, storage, cameras, and monitors). It is used both for PAL/Europe and NTSC/North America/Asia. The SDI signal is typically used locally in the production facilities (e.g., TV station) or between closely located sites using point-to-point fiber solutions. SDI carries uncompressed video of different formats as well as SDTI (Serial Digital Transport Interface)

SMPTE 259M:

Video type	Standard	Bit rate
NTSC composite digital video	SMPTE 244M	143 Mbps
PAL composite digital video	IEC 61179	177 Mbps
NTSC & PAL 4:2:2 *component* digital video (13.5 MHz sample rate)	SMPTE 125M ITU-R BT.601	270 Mbps
16x9 wide-screen NTSC & PAL 4:2:2 *component* digital video (18 MHz sample rate)	SMPTE 267M ITU-R BT.601	360 Mbps

SMPTE 344M: 540 Mbps SDI bit rate

High-Definition SDI (HD-SDI):

Transports *uncompressed* high-definition video serially over video coax cable or fiber

Two bit rates:

–1.485 Gbps
–1.485/1.001 Gbps-primarily used in North America

Figure 11.A1. SDI Rates

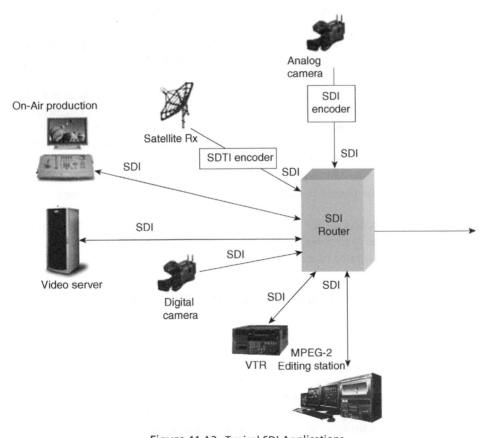

Figure 11.A2. Typical SDI Applications

transport streams. SDI's basic data rate is uncompressed-270 Mbps streams; it supports distances on 100 m on coax and 2 km on fiber. Figure 11.A1 depicts other supported rates. An *uncompressed* HD version has also been defined. Figure 11.A2 depicts a typical application.

APPENDIX 11.B: MPEG BASICS

11.B.1   MPEG-2 Transport/Multiplexing Mechanisms

In its true form, the MPEG standards define multiplexing methodologies for transporting video (or other signals); specifically, the MPEG-2 systems layer provides a standardized method of providing integrated video, audio, and data services. In a more colloquial fashion, they define video compression technologies[6] that transcode digital TV signals from uncompressed (SD) signals at around 170 Mbps to 2.5–4 Mbps and from uncompressed (HD) signals at around 500 Mbps to 8–12 Mbps. Typically "programs" consist of primarily one video channel and one or more audio channels; the data streams also handled by MPEG are used to broadcast program-related data and close captioning (other applications may be supported at a future time, e.g., data download or Internet-based information). Figure 11.B1 is a simplified protocol stack that will assist understanding of the protocol hierarchy.

```
+-+-+-+-+--------------------+----+---+
|T|V|A|O|                    |        |
|e|i|u|t|                    |   S    |
|l|d|d|h|         IP         |   I    |
|e|e|i|e|                    |        |
|t|o|o|r|                    |   T    |
|e| | | |                    |   a    |
|x| | | |         +---+----+-+   b    |
|t| | | |         |   | MPE |     1    |
| | | | | +--+--+  +------+    e    |
| | | | | | AAL5 |ULE|  Priv.|        |
+-+-+-+-+------+   | Sect. +-+--+--+
|  PES  | ATM  |   |      | Section |
+-------------+---+----+------+-------+
|            MPEG-2 TS              |
+----------------------------------+
```

Figure 11.B1. Simplified Protocol Hierarchy

---

[6] ISO/IEC MPEG-4 Part-2 video specification does not specify the design of an encoder. It defines only the syntax and semantics of a coded bit stream. Therefore, an encoder has proprietary design.

The most basic component in MPEG is the *elementary stream*. A program (e.g., a television video program) typically contains a combination of ESs (say, one for video, one or more for audio, one for control data). Each ES generated at the output of an MPEG audio encoder and an MPEG video encoder contains a single type of (usually compressed) signal. For video and audio, the information is organized into *access units*, each representing a fundamental unit of encoding; for example, in video, an access unit usually is a complete encoded video frame [FAI200101]. A packetization function (typically within the encoder stage) accumulates the data into a stream of *packetized elementary stream* packets. See Figure 11.B2.

A PES datagram is a fixed (or variable) sized block, with up to 65,536 bytes per block. A PES is usually organized to contain an integral number of ES access units. Figure 11.B3 depicts the PES format.

The MPEG-2 standard defines two ways for multiplexing different elementary stream types: (i) program stream, and (ii) transport stream. See Figure 11.B4.

An MPEG-2 *program stream* (MPEG-2 PS) is principally intended for storage and retrieval from storage media. It supports grouping of video, audio, and data elementary streams that have a common time base. Each PS consists of only one content (TV) program. The PS is used in error-free environments; for example, DVDs use the MPEG-2 PS. A PS is a group of tightly coupled PES packets referenced to the same time base.

An MPEG-2 *transport stream* (MPEG-2 TS) combines multiple PESs (which may or may not have a common time base) into a single stream and multiplexes these PESs into one stream, along with information for synchronizing between them. At the same time, the TS segments the PES into the smaller fixed-size TS packets. An entire video frame may be mapped in one PES packet. PES headers distinguish PES packets of various streams and also contain time stamp information. PESs are generated by the packetization process; the payload consists of the data bytes taken sequentially from the original ES. There are some constraints for forming TS packets: (i) The first byte of the PES packet must be the first byte of the transport packet payload and (ii) each transport packet must contain data from only one PES packet.

A TS may correspond to a single TV program; this type of TS is normally called a *Single-Program Transport Stream* (SPTS). In most cases one or more SPTSs are combined to form a *Multiple-Program Transport Stream* (MPTS). This larger aggregate also contains the control information [*Program-Specific Information* (PSI)] required to coordinate the DVB system and any other data that is to be sent [FAI200101].

As noted, the TS consists of a stream of short fixed-length TS packets. A TS is intended for non-error-free environments (i.e., environments that entail a transmission link). The MPEG-2 TS packet length is 188 bytes long[7] (4-byte header + adaptation field, or payload, or both); hence, each packet comprises 184 bytes of payload and a 4-byte header. A TS packet starts with a TS header of 4 bytes, followed by 184-byte Adaptation field (a header extension) and payload (information section).

---

[7] The MPEG TS packet size equates to eight ATM cells, assuming 8 B overhead from the ATM Adaptation Layer (AAL).

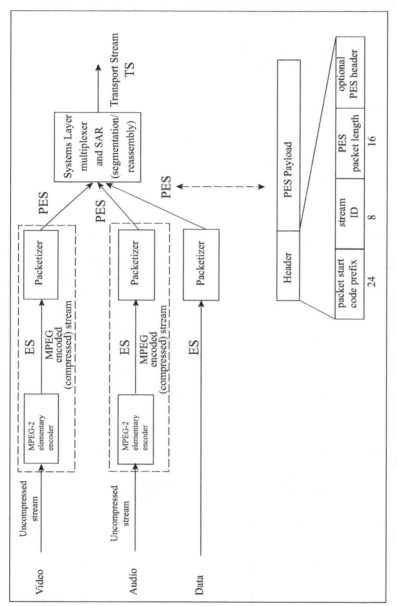

Figure 11.B2 Combining of PESs into a TS

273

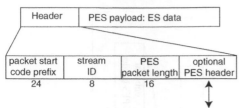

- PES Indicators (provide additional information about the stream to assist the decoder at the receiver):
  - PES_Scrambling_Control—defines whether scrambling is used and the chosen scrambling method
  - PES_Priority—indicates priority of the current PES packet
  - data_alignment_indicator—indicates if the payload starts with a video or audio start code
  - copyright information—indicates if the payload is copyright protected
  - original_or_copy—Indicates if this is the original ES
- Flags field (1 byte) (defines the following optional fields, which, if present, are inserted before the start of the PES payload):
  - *Presentation Time Stamp* (PTS) and possibly a *Decode Time Stamp* (DTS)—For audio/video streams these are time stamps, which may be used to synchronise a set of elementary streams and control the rate at which they are replayed by the receiver
  - *Elementary Stream Clock Reference* (ESCR)
  - *Elementary Stream rate*—Rate at which the ES was encoded
  - *Trick Mode*—indicates the video/audio is not the normal ES
  - *Copyright Information*—set to 1 to indicate a copyright ES
  - CRC—this may be used to monitor errors in the previous PES packet
  - *PES Extension Information*—may be used to support MPEG-1 streams

Figure 11.B3. PES Packet Format

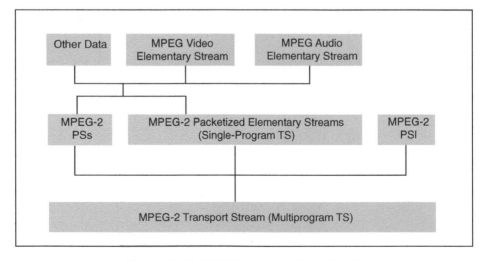

Figure 11.B4. ES/PES Carriage in PSs and/or TSs

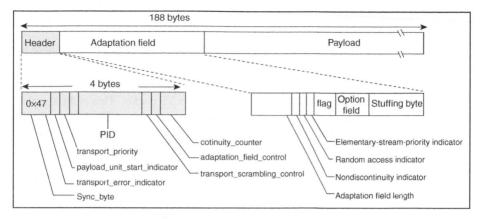

Figure 11.B5. MPEG-2 TS Format

A key field in the TS header, which plays the important role in the downstream use of the TS, is the 13-bit PID. The PID[8] determines to which program a TS packet belongs to, and the PID is also unique for each program. In MPEG-2 systems, TS logical channels are identified by their PIDs and provide multiplexing, addressing, and error reporting. The PID value is a 13-bit field; thus, the number of available channels ranges from 0 to 8191 decimal ($0 \times 1FFF$ in hexadecimal), some of which are reserved for transmission of PSI (also called SI) tables. Nonreserved TS logical channels may be used to carry audio, video, IP packets, or other data. The value 8191 decimal ($0 \times 1FFF$) indicates a null packet that is used to maintain the physical bearer bit rate when there are no other MPEG-2 TS packets to be sent [RFC4259]. The Adaptation field supports various options and it may or may not be present. The presence of an Adaptation field is indicated by the Adaptation field control bits in a TS packet. If present, the Adaptation field directly follows the 4-byte packet header, before any user payload data; it contains a variety of information used for timing and control, including the *Program Clock Reference* (*PCR*) field. Byte stuffing is used to ascertain that the TS packet is always 188 bytes long; any remainder portion of the TS packet payload is stuffed with bytes with value $0 \times FF$ (in some instances the Adaptation field is present only to provide the stuffing function). See Figure 11.B5. The MPEG-TS is not a time division multiplex function because packets with any PID may be inserted into the TS at any time by the TS multiplexor. If no packets are available at the multiplexor, it inserts null packets (denoted by a PID value of $0 \times 1FFF$) to retain the specified TS bit rate [FAI200101]. By comparison with PS, with TS it is easy to detect start and end of frames; it is also easy to recover from packet loss/ corruption. However, it is more difficult to produce and demultiplex than the PS. Mapping functions are required to relate TS logical channels to IP addresses, to map

---

[8] There are similarities between the way PIDs are used and the operation of virtual channels in ATM. However, unlike ATM, a PID defines a unidirectional broadcast channel and not a point-to-point link. Contrary to ATM, there is, as yet, no specified standard interface for MPEG-2 connection setup or for signaling.

TS logical channels to IP-level QoS, and to associate IP flows with specific subnetwork capabilities.

Figure 11.B6 puts the PES and TS concepts together. Two options are available for inserting a PES packet into the TS packet payload [FAI200101]:

1. Carry only one PES (or part of a single PES) in a TS packet. This is the simplest environment from both the encoder and receiver viewpoints. This allows the TS packet header to indicate the start of the PES, but since a PES packet may have an arbitrary length, it also requires the remainder of the TS packet to be padded, ensuring correct alignment of the next PES to the start of a TS packet.

2. In general, a given PES packet spans several TS packets, so that the majority of TS packets contain continuation data in their payloads. When a PES packet begins, the payload_unit_start_indicator bit is set to 1, which means the first byte of the TS payload contains the first byte of the PES packet header. Only one PES packet can start in any single TS packet. The TS header also contains the PID so that the receiver can accept or reject PES packets at a high level without burdening the receiver with excessive processing. This approach, however, has an efficiency impact on short PES packets.

The TS stream also includes PSI information. PSI consists of transport packets used by the decoder to acquire information about the TS. The tables consist of a description of the ESs that need to be combined to build programs and a description of the programs. Each PSI table is carried in a sequence of PSI sections; the length of a section allows a decoder to identify the next section in a packet. Tables are sent periodically by including them in the transmitted transport multiplex [FAI200101]. PSI tables include:

- Program Association Table (PAT)—contains list of all programs in the TS along with the PID for the program map table for each program. The PAT is sent with the well-known PID value of 0×000.
- Program Map Table (PMT)—contains the PID for each of the channels associated with a particular program.
- Network Information Table (NIT)—(Optional; content is private—not part of MPEG standard) used to provide information about the physical network, for example, channel frequencies, service originator, and service name.
- Conditional-Access Table (CAT)—defines type of scrambling used and PID values of TSs which contain the conditional-access management and entitlement information (EMMs)). The CAT is sent with the well-known PID value of 0×001.

To identify the required PID to demultiplex a particular PES, the remote device searches for a description in the PAT. The PAT lists all programs in the multiplex; each content program is associated with a set of PIDs (one for each PES) that correspond to a PMT carried as a separate PSI section. There is one PMT per program. DVB also adds a number of additional tables. See Figure 11.B7 for a pictorial example.

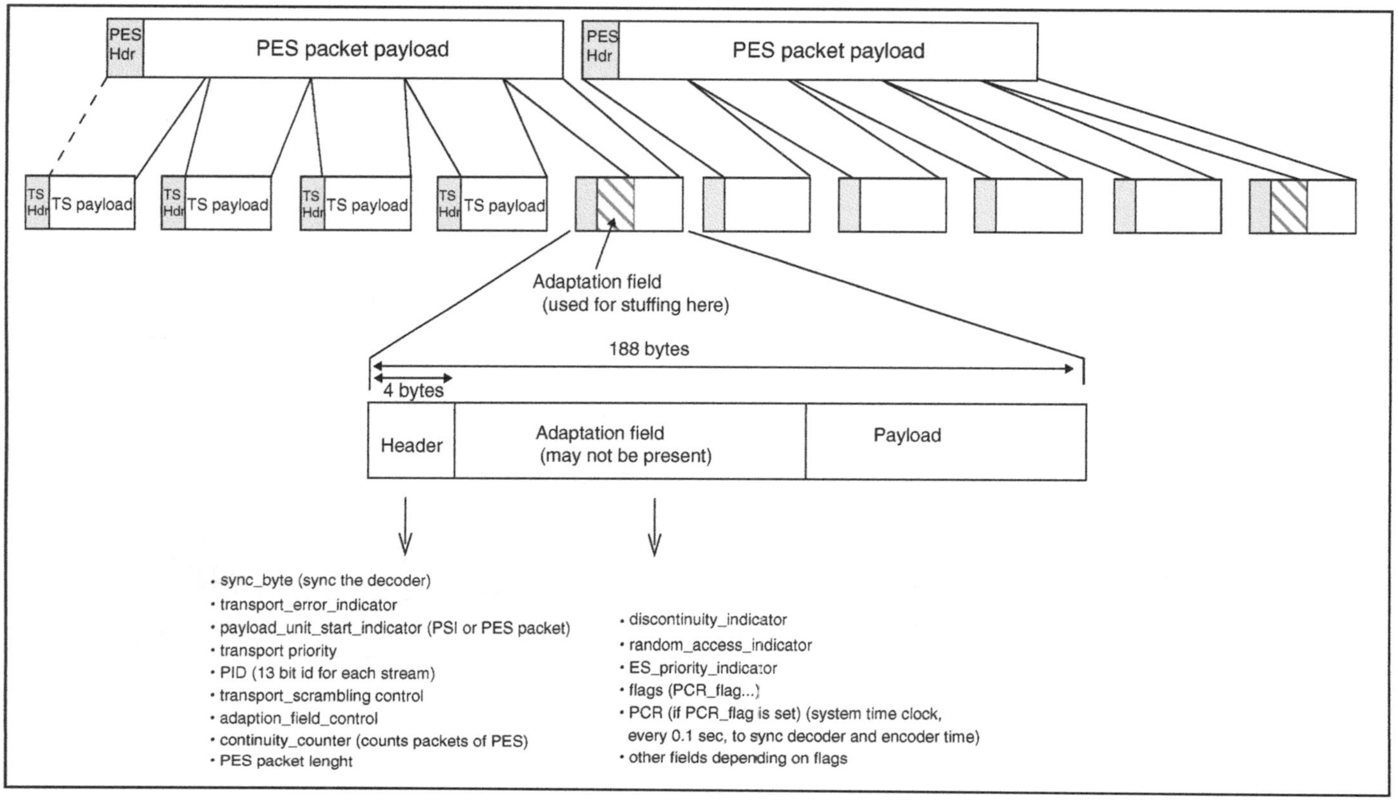
PES Hdr
PES packet payload
PES Hdr
PES packet payload
TS Hdr
TS payload
TS Hdr
TS payload
TS Hdr
TS payload
TS Hdr
TS payload
Adaptation field
(used for stuffing here)
188 bytes
4 bytes
Header
Adaptation field
(may not be present)
Payload
• sync_byte (sync the decoder)
• transport_error_indicator
• payload_unit_start_indicator (PSI or PES packet)
• transport priority
• PID (13 bit id for each stream)
• transport_scrambling control
• adaption_field_control
• continuity_counter (counts packets of PES)
• PES packet lenght
• discontinuity_indicator
• random_access_indicator
• ES_priority_indicator
• flags (PCR_flag...)
• PCR (if PCR_flag is set) (system time clock,
every 0.1 sec, to sync decoder and encoder time)
• other fields depending on flags

Figure 11.B6. A Sequence of PESs Leads to a Sequence of Uniform TS Packets

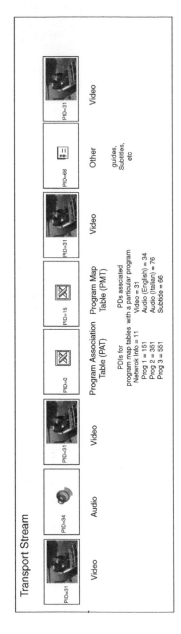

Figure 11.B7. Single-Program Transport Stream (Video, Audio, and PSI PES)

As implied pictorially in Figure 11.B7, TSs consist of a number of related ESs (e.g., the video and audio of a TV program), where the decoding of the ESs requires synchronization to ensure that the audio playback is aligned with the corresponding video frames. Time stamps are typically sent in the transport stream. Threre are two types of time stamps:

- Reference Time Stamp—time stamps that provide an indication of *the current time*. *Reference* time stamps are found in the transport packet adaptation PCR field.
- DTS or PTS—These time stamps are inserted in the proximity of the material to which they refer (normally in the PES packet header). They indicate the exact moment where a video frame or an audio frame has to be decoded or presented to the user, respectively. These rely on reference time stamps for operation.

11.B.2   IPTV/IP Transmission over TS Logical Channels

The mechanisms discussed above are used in typical IPTV applications. RFC 4259 captures this process very well. The description that follows below is based directly on RFC 4259.

An MPEG-2 transport multiplex offers a number of parallel channels, which are known as TS logical channels. Each TS logical channel is uniquely identified by the PID value that is carried in the header of each MPEG-2 TS packet. TS logical channels are independently numbered on each MPEG-2 TS multiplex (MUX). In most cases, the data sent over the TS logical channels will differ for different multiplexes. Figure 11.B8 shows a set of TS logical channels sent using two MPEG-2 TS multiplexes (A and B). There are cases where the same data may be distributed over two or more multiplexes (e.g., some PSI tables; multicast content that needs to be received by receivers tuned to either MPEG-2 TS; unicast data where the receiver may be in either/both of two potentially overlapping MPEG-2 transmission cells). In Figure 11.B8, each multiplex carries three MPEG-2 TS logical channels. These TS logical channels may differ (TS-LC-A-1, TS-LC-A-2, TS-LC-B-2, TS-LC-B-1) or may be common to both MPEG-2 TS multiplexes (i.e., TS-LC-A-3 and TS-LC-B-3 carry identical content).

In a simple example, one or more TS logical channels are processed by an MPEG-2 multiplexor, resulting in a TS multiplex. The TS multiplex is forwarded over a physical bearer toward one or more receivers (see Figure 11.B9). In a more complex example, the same TS may be fed to multiple MPEG-2 multiplexors and these may, in turn, feed other MPEG-2 multiplexors (remultiplexing). Remultiplexing may occur in several places. One example is a satellite that provides on-board processing of the TS packets, multiplexing the TS logical channels received from one or more uplink physical bearers (TS multiplex) to one (or more in the case of broadcast/multicast) downlink physical bearer (TS multiplex). As part of the remultiplexing process, a remultiplexor may renumber the PID values associated with one or more TS logical channels to prevent clashes between input TS logical channels with the same PID carried on different input multiplexes. It may also modify and/or insert new SI data into the control plane.

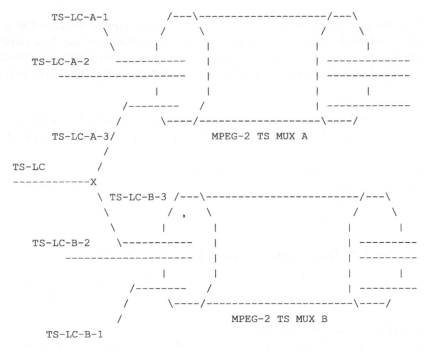

Figure 11.B8. Example Showing MPEG-2 TS Logical Channels Carried over Two MPEG-2 TS Multiplexes

In all cases, the final result is a TS multiplex that is transmitted over the physical bearer toward the receiver.

Packet data for transmission over an MPEG-2 transport multiplex is passed to an encapsulator, sometimes known as a gateway. This receives PDUs such as Ethernet frames or IP packets and formats each into an SNDU by adding an encapsulation header and trailer. The SNDUs are subsequently fragmented into a series of TS packets. To receive IP packets over an MPEG-2 TS multiplex, a receiver needs to identify the specific TS multiplex (physical link) and also the TS logical channel (the PID value of a logical link). It is common for a number of MPEG-2 TS logical channels to carry SNDUs; therefore, a receiver must filter (accept) IP packets sent with a number of PID values and must independently reassemble each SNDU.

A receiver that simultaneously receives from several TS logical channels must filter the other unwanted TS logical channels by employing, for example, specific hardware support. Packets for one IP flow (i.e., a specific combination of IP source and destination addresses) must be sent using the same PID. It should not be assumed that all IP packets are carried on a single PID, as in some cable modem implementations, and multiple PIDs must be allowed in the architecture. Many current hardware filters limit the maximum number of active PIDs (e.g., 32), although if needed, future systems may reasonably be expected to support more.

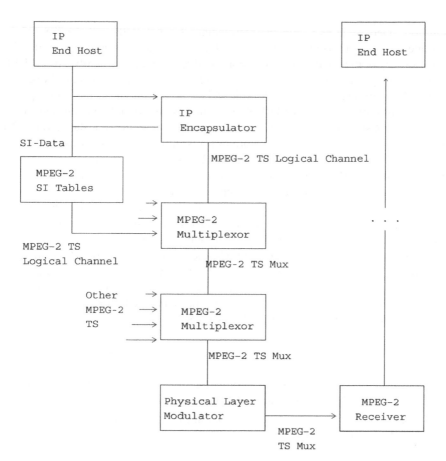

Figure 11.B9. An Example Configuration for a Unidirectional Service for IP Transport over MPEG-2

In some cases, receivers may need to select TS logical channels from a number of simultaneously active TS multiplexes. To do this, they need a multiple physical receive interfaces [e.g., radio frequency (RF) front ends and demodulators]. Some applications also envisage the concurrent reception of IP packets over other media that may not necessarily use MPEG-2 transmission.

11.B.3   Compression Technology

This section provides a brief overview of compression technology.

The goal of IPTV is to deliver digital video using an IP network infrastructure; however, this must be done using video compression methods. Standard-definition (NTSC) video is typically digitized at 720×480 using 4:2:2 YCrCb at 30 frames per second, which results in an uncompressed data rate of over 165 Mbps. Even lower resolution video, such as Common Intermediate Format (CIF[9]) (352×288 4:2:0 at 30 frames/second), utilized in video streaming applications, requires over 36 Mbps. Direct delivery of these video streams is not possible except on a true fiber-based FTTH system—since this data rate is many times more than what can be achieved over DSL systems. Furthermore, storing one 90-min NTSC video movie in the uncompressed 4:2:2 YCrCb form requires over 110 Gbytes—this is not possible on consumer media such as DVD-R since this data is 25 times the storage capability of a standard DVD-R. Obviously, compression is needed to store or transmit digital video. A compression of ratio of 100 : 1 (for IPTV) and 400 : 1 (for DVB-H) is sought; one wishes to encode digital video by using as few bits as possible while maintaining visual quality. Typical factors to consider when selecting the codec for an application include the visual quality requirements for the application, the environment (speed, latency, and error characteristics) of the transmission channel or storage media, the desired resolution, the target bit rate, the color depth, the number of frames per second, whether the content and/or display are progressive or interlaced, and the cost of real-time implementation of the encoding and decoding. Typically newer algorithms, such as H.264/AVC, achieve higher compression but require increased processing, which can impact the cost for encoding and decoding devices, system power dissipation, and system memory [GOL200601]. For IPTV, the industry is settling on MPEG-4 at 2.5–3 Mbps for SD, 8–11 Mbps for HD, and 384 kbps for DVB-H.

Two key standards organizations that have defined video codecs over the years are:

- The ITU, which is focused on telecommunication applications and has developed the H.261, H.262, H.263, and H.264 standards for low-bit-rate video telephony.
- The ISO, which is focused on consumer applications and has defined MPEG-1, MPEG-2, and MPEG-4.

On occasions, the groups have worked together, such as in the Joint Video Team (JVT), to define the MPEG-4 Part 10. ITU and MPEG continue to define new standards for improved efficiency; for example, standards being developed at press time included ITU/MPEG Joint Scalable Video Coding (an amendment to H.264/AVC) and MPEG Multiview Video Coding. H.264 also recently defined a new mode, Fidelity Range Extension, to address professional digital editing, HD-DVD, and lossless coding applications. In addition to industry standards, a number of vendor-developed solutions have emerged in recent years, especially for Internet-based streaming media applications. These proprietary systems include Real Networks Real Video (RV10), Microsoft Windows Media Video 9 (WMV9) series, ON2 VP6, and Nancy. In 2003, Microsoft proposed to the Society for Motion Picture and Television Engineers (SMPTE) that the WMV9 bitstream and syntax be standardized, which is now the SMPTE VC-1 standard. These codecs, however, are not generally used in IPTV applications.

---

[9] Common Intermediate Format is a set of standard video formats used principally in videoconferencing applications. The original CIF [also known as Full CIF (FCIF)] has a resolution of 352×288; QCIF— Quarter CIF has a resolution 176×144; SQCIF—Subquarter CIF (resolution 128×96); 4CIF—$4 \times$ CIF has a resolution 704×576; 16CIF—$16 \times$ CIF has a resolution 1408×1152.

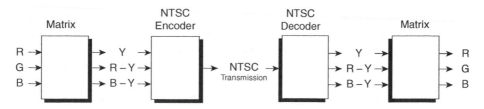

Figure 11.B10. Traditional Mapping of Color Space

In the next few paragraphs we provide a basic overview of video digitization; eventually a digitized signal is delivered to an encoder.

Color spaces are mathematical representations of color. Three common color spaces are RGB, YUV, and YCbCr.

The Video signal originating from a TV studio camera is considered a baseband component where the three-color components (red, green, and blue) are distinct signals. Original NTSC systems sought to maintain compatibility with black-and-white TV sets, and to do so, the R, G, B color space in video signals was converted to the Y, U, V color space where

- Y is luminous information (lightness)
- $U = B - Y$
- $V = R - Y$

(see Figure 11.B10). Hence, in a composite signal, which is the signal used for traditional analog TV distribution:

- RGB components from the camera are generally translated to a set of color difference components (such as Y, R − Y, B − Y) before being encoded to NTSC or PAL for transmission (in modern equipment all these operations may take place in the camera).
- The composite signal must be decoded in the receiver to a color difference format and then translated to RGB for display.

If RGB-to-YUV color space conversion is done maintaining full-bandwidth chroma (hue plus saturation), the conversion is called a 4 : 4 : 4 sampling. If conversion is carried out on chroma samples every other pixel, it is termed a 4 : 2 : 2 sampling scheme. Specifically:

- A 4:2:2 sampling halves chroma resolution horizontally, resulting in a 33% saving in bandwidth compared to a 4 : 4 : 4 sampling.
- A 4:2:0 sampling reduces chroma bandwidth even more, halving overall bandwidth.

In noninterlaced video scan, lines are displayed sequentially down the display unit (that is, display line 1, 2, 3, 4, ..., n). This is also called progressive scanning. In interlaced video, alternate scan lines are displayed sequentially down the display, with even fields being shown in one frame (lines 2, 4, 6, 8, ..., n) and odd fields being shown in the next frame (1, 3, 5, 7, ..., $n-1$).

Similar concepts apply to digital TV. YCbCr is the component color space defined by ITU-R BT.601 to support digital TV: $Cr = R - Y$ and $Cb = B - Y$. The ranges of the digital numbers are

- Y nominal range: 16–235
- Cb and Cr nominal range: 16–240 with zero corresponding to 128
- Y and CbCr components have different bandwidth and dynamic ranges

YCbCr components are not independent; it is possible to generate "invalid" RGB values if YCbCr values are improperly modified.

As in the YUV case, various sampling rates are possible: sampling ratio of Y : Cb : Cr are 4:4:4; 4:2:2; 4:1:1; 4:2:0.

- YCbCr Color Space—4:4:4 YCbCr
  - See Figure 11.B11
  - Each sample has Y, Cb, and Cr data
  - 13.5 or 18 MHz sample rate
  - 720 or 960 active samples per line
- YCbCr Color Space—4:2:2 YCbCr
  - See Figure 11.B12
  - Consumer and PC applications

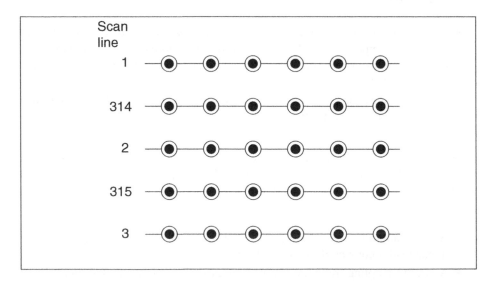

Figure 11.B11. YCbCr Color Space—4:4:4 YCbCr Sampling (625-Line System)

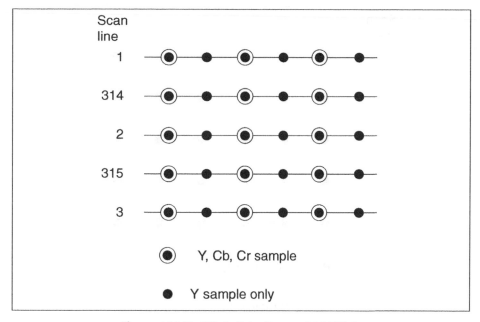

Figure 11.B12. YCbCr Color Space—4:2:2 YCbCr

- Each sample has Y data
  o 13.5 or 18 MHz sample rate
  o 720 or 960 active samples per line
- Every other sample (horizontally) has Cb and Cr data
  o 6.75 or 9 MHz sample rate
  o 360 or 480 active samples per line
- YCbCr Color Space—4:1:1 YCbCr
  - See Figure 11.B13
  - Consumer applications (DVC and TV)
  - Each sample has Y data
    o 13.5 or 18 MHz sample rate
    o 720 or 960 active samples per line
  - Every fourth sample (horizontally) has Cb and Cr data
    o 3.375 or 4.5 MHz sample rate
    o 180 or 240 active samples per line
- YCbCr Color Space—4:2:0 YCbCr
  - Two types of 4:2:0 notation
    o Version used for internal processing by MPEG 1, H.261, and H.263: Noninterlaced video only
    o Version used for internal processing by MPEG 2: Noninterlaced or interlaced Video
  - YCbCr Color Space—4:2:0 Sampling for MPEG 1/2/4, H.261, and H.263: see Figure 11.B14
  - YCbCr Color Space—4:2:0 Sampling for MPEG 2 (noninterlaced): see Figure 11.B15.

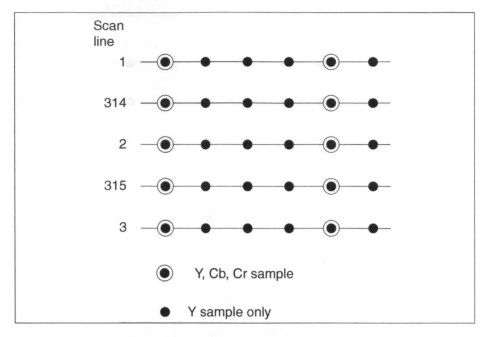

Figure 11.B13. YCbCr Color Space—4:1:1 YCbCr

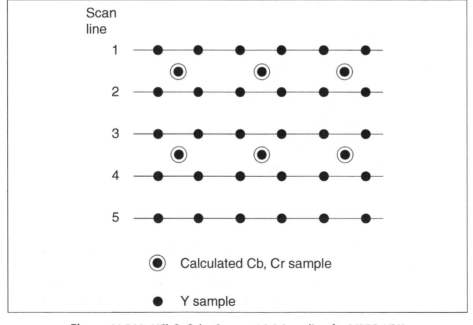

Figure 11.B14. YCbCr Color Space—4:2:0 Sampling for MPEG 1/2/4

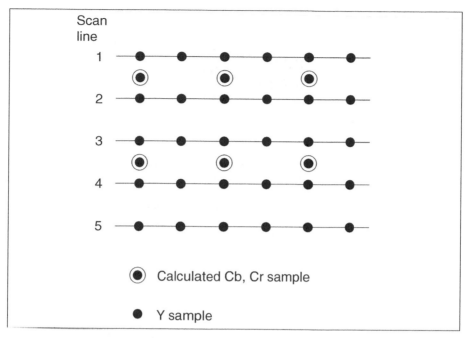

Figure 11.B15 YCbCr Color Space—4:2:0 Sampling for MPEG 2 (Noninterlaced)

A typical IPTV codec has interlaced 4:2:2 input and outputs ESs or PESs. See Figure 11.B16.

Next we discuss some basic constructs that are part of the MPEG coding schemes.

A *video sequence* is a sequence of frames that begins with a sequence header (may contain additional sequence headers), includes one or more groups of pictures, and ends with an end-of-sequence code. A *Group of Pictures* (GOP) is comprised of a header and a series of one or more pictures intended to allow random access into the video sequence. A *picture* is the primary coding unit of a video sequence. A picture consists of three rectangular matrices representing luminance (Y) and two chrominance (Cb and Cr) values. The Y matrix has an even number of rows and columns. The Cb and Cr matrices are (usually) half the size of the Y matrix in each direction (horizontal and vertical) (details on this below). A *slice* is one or more "contiguous" macroblocks (the order of the macroblocks within a slice is from left to right and top to bottom). Slices are important in the handling of errors—if the bit stream contains an error, the decoder can skip to the start of the next slice. A *Macroblock* (MB) is a16-pixel by 16-line section of luminance components and the corresponding 8-pixel by 8-line section of the two chrominance components. Figure 11.B15 shows the spatial location of luminance and chrominance components. A macroblock contains four Y blocks, one Cb block, and one Cr block. Numbers correspond to the ordering of the blocks in the data stream, with block 1 first. Each macroblock relates to 16 pixels by 16 lines of Y and the spatially corresponding 8 pixels by 8 lines of Cb and Cr. That is, a macroblock consists of four luminance blocks

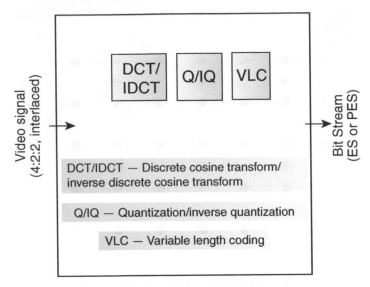

Figure 11.B16. High-Level View of Encoder

and two spatially corresponding color difference blocks: (i) Each luminance block thus relates to 8 pixels by 8 lines of Y (16×16 Y pixels). (ii) Each chrominance block thus relates to 8 pixels by 8 lines of Cb or Cr, but these last are in 4:2:2 mode, resulting in 4 points for them in each 8×8 Y block (4:2:2 -> "8:4:4", namely: $8 \times 8 : 4 \times 4 : 4 \times 4$) ($8 \times 8$ Cr and 8×8 Cb). Figure 11.B.17 illustrates some of these concepts.

A *Cb and Cr* diagram shows the relative x-y locations of the luminance and chrominance components. Note that for every four luminance values, there are two associated chrominance values: one Cb value and one Cr value. See Figure 11.B18; note that the location of the Cb and Cr values is the same, so only one circle is shown in the figure.

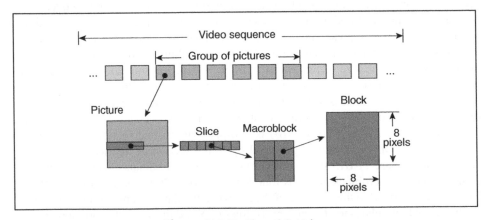

Figure 11.B17. Cb and Cr Values

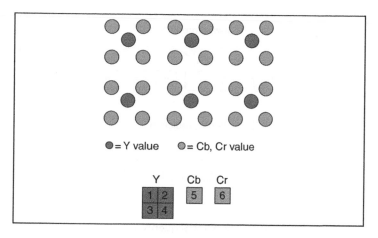

Figure 11.B18. Cb and Cr Values

Intra pictures (I-pictures) are coded using only information present in the picture itself:

- I-pictures provide potential random access points into the compressed video data.
- I-pictures use only transform coding and provide moderate compression.
- I-pictures typically use about 2 bits per coded pixel.

Predicted pictures (P-pictures) are coded with respect to the nearest previous I- or P-picture (technique is called forward prediction; see Figure 11.B19):

- P-pictures serve as a prediction reference for B-pictures (bidirectionally interpolated pictures) and future P-pictures. P-pictures use motion compensation to provide more compression than is possible with I-pictures. Unlike I-pictures, P-pictures can propagate coding errors because P-pictures are predicted from previous reference (I- or P-) pictures.

Bidirectional pictures (B-pictures) are pictures that use both a past and future picture as a reference (technique is called bidirectional prediction; see Figure 11.B19):

- B-pictures provide the most compression and do not propagate errors because they are never used as a reference.
- Bidirectional prediction also decreases the effect of noise by averaging two pictures.

The MPEG algorithms allow the encoder to choose the frequency and location of I-pictures; the choice is based on an application's need for random accessibility and location of scene cuts in a video sequence (in applications where random access is important, I-pictures are typically used two times a second). The encoder also chooses

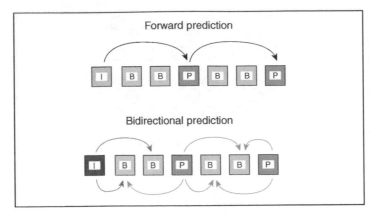

Figure 11.B19. Basic Sequence of Frames

the number of B-pictures between any pair of reference (I- or P-) pictures. The choice is based on factors such as the amount of memory in the encoder and the characteristics of the material being coded. A typical arrangement of I-, P-, and B-pictures, in the order in which they are displayed, is shown in Figure 11.B20.

11.B.3.1   Video Coding Principles

The next few paragraphs provide a quick overview of the topic based on an excellent paper by Golston and A. Rao [GOL200601].

Figure 11.B21 shows a typical video codec. Video coding is based on the principles of quantization, Motion-Compensated (MC) prediction, discrete transforms, and entropy coding. Modern video coders utilize block-based processing; each macroblock typically contains four 8×8 luminance blocks and two 8×8 chrominance blocks (for chroma format 4:2:0). In MC, compression is achieved by predicting each macroblock of pixels in a frame of video from a similar region of a recently coded ("reference") video frame. For example, background areas often stay the same from one frame to the next and do not need to be retransmitted in each frame.

Motion Estimation (ME) is the process of determining for each MB in the current frame, the 16×16 region of the reference frame that is most similar to it. ME is usually the

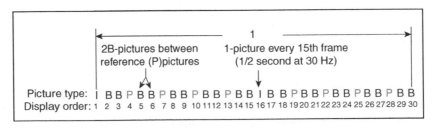

Figure 11.B20. Basic Sequence of Frames

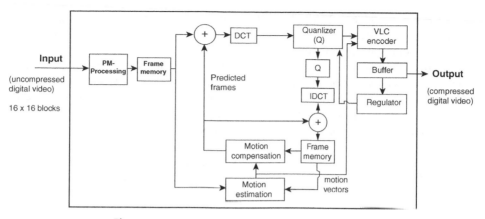

Figure 11.B21. Motion-Compensated Video Coder

most performance-intensive function in video compression. Information on the relative location of the most similar region for each block in the current frame ("motion vector") is transmitted to the decoder. The residual after MC is divided into 8×8 blocks, each encoded using a combination of transform coding, quantization, and variable-length coding. Transform coding, such as Discrete Cosine Transform (DCT), exploits spatial redundancy in the residual signal. Quantization removes perceptual redundancy and reduces the amount of data required to encode the residual. Variable-length coding exploits the statistical nature of the residual coefficients. The process of redundancy removal via MC is reversed in the decoder, and the predicted data from the reference frame is combined with the encoded residual data to generate back a representation of the original video frame.

In a video codec, an individual frame may be encoded using one of the three modes: I, P, or B, as discussed above. A few frames referred to as Intra (I) frames are encoded independently without reference to any other frame (no motion compensation). Some frames may be coded using MC with a previous frame as reference (forward prediction). These frames are referred to as Predicted (P) frames. B frames, or Bidirectional predicted frames, are predicted from both past frames as well as frames slated to appear after the current frame. A benefit of B frames is the ability to match a background area that was occluded in the previous frame but can be found in a subsequent frame using backward prediction. Bidirectional prediction can allow for decreased noise by averaging both forward and backward prediction. Leveraging this feature in encoders requires additional processing since ME has to be performed for both forward and backward prediction, which can effectively double the motion estimation computational requirements. Additional memory is also needed at both encoder and decoder to store two reference frames. B frame tools require a more complex data flow since frames are decoded out of order with respect to how they are captured and need to be displayed. This feature results in increased latency and, thus, is not suitable for some real-time sensitive applications. Until the introduction of H.264, B frames were not used for prediction allowing tradeoffs to be made for some applications. For example, they can be skipped in low-frame-rate applications without impacting the decoding of future I and P frames.

11.B.3.1.1 MPEG-2/H.262. MPEG-2 was developed targeting digital television and soon became the most successful video compression standard thus far. MPEG-2 addressed both standard progressive video (where a video sequence consists of a succession of frames each captured at regularly spaced time instants) as well as interlaced video, which is popular in the television world. In interlaced video, two sets of alternate rows of pixels (each called a field) in the image are captured and displayed alternately. Until recently, this approach was particularly suited to the physics of most TV displays on the market. MPEG-2 supports standard television resolutions, including interlaced 720×480 at 60 fields per second for NTSC used in the United States and Japan and interlaced 720×576 at 50 fields per second for PAL used in Europe and other countries.

MPEG-2 builds on MPEG-1 with extensions to support interlaced video and also much wider motion compensation ranges. MPEG-2 encoders, taking full advantage of the wider search range and the higher resolution, require significantly more processing than H.261 and MPEG-1. Interlaced coding tools in MPEG-2 include the ability to optimize the motion compensation supporting both field- and frame-based predictions and support for both field- and frame-based DCT/Inverse Discrete Cosine Transform (IDCT). MPEG-2 performs well at compression ratios around 30:1. The quality achieved with MPEG-2 at 4–8 Mbps was acceptable for consumer video applications, and it soon became deployed in applications including digital satellite, digital cable, DVDs, and lately high-definition TV.

In addition, MPEG-2 adds scalable video coding tools to support multiple layer video coding, namely, temporal scalability, spatial scalability, SNR (Signal-to-Noise Ratio) scalability, and data partitioning. Although related profiles were defined in MPEG-2 for scalable video applications, the main profile that supports single-layer coding is the sole MPEG-2 profile that is widely deployed in the mass market today. The MPEG-2 main profile is often referred to as simply MPEG-2. The processing requirements for MPEG-2 decoding were initially very high for general purpose processors and even DSPs. Optimized fixed-function MPEG-2 decoders were developed and became inexpensive over time due to the high volumes. MPEG-2 proved that the availability of cost-effective silicon solutions is a key ingredient for the success and deployment of video codec standards.

11.B.3.1.2 MPEG-4. MPEG-4 was initiated by the ISO as a follow-on to the success of MPEG-2. Some of the early objectives were increased error robustness to support wireless networks, better support for low-bit-rate applications, and a variety of new tools to support merging graphic objects with video. Most of the graphics features have not yet gained significant traction in products, and implementations have focused primarily on the improved low-bit-rate compression and error resiliency.

MPEG-4 Simple Profile (SP) starts from H.263 baseline and adds new tools for improved compression, including:

- Unrestricted Motion Vectors—supports prediction for objects when they partially move outside of the boundaries of the frame.
- Variable Block Size Motion Compensation—allows motion compensation at either 16×16 or 8×8 block granularity.

- Context Adaptive Intra DCT DC/AC Prediction—allows the DC/AC DCT coefficients to be predicted from neighboring blocks either to the left or above the current block.
- Extended dynamic range of quantized AC coefficients from $[-127:127]$ in H.263 to $[-2047, 2047]$ to support high-fidelity video.

Error resiliency features added to support recovery in packet loss conditions include:

- Slice Resynchronization—establishes slices within images that allow quicker resynchronization after an error has occurred. Unlike MPEG-2 packet sizes, MPEG-4 packet sizes are delinked from the number of bits used to represent an MB. As a result, resynchronization is possible at equal intervals in the bit stream irrespective of the amount of information per MB.
- Data Partitioning—a mode that allows partitioning the data within a video packet into a motion part and DCT data part by separating these with a unique motion boundary marker. This allows more stringent checks on the validity of motion vector data. If an error occurs, you can have better visibility into the point where the error occurs, thus avoiding the discarding of all the motion data when an error is found.
- Reversible Variable-Length Coding (VLC–VLC)—code tables designed to allow decoding backward as well as forward. When an error is encountered, it is possible to sync at the next slice or start code and work back to the point where the error occurred.
- New Prediction (NEWPRED)—mainly designed for fast error recovery in real-time applications, where the decoder uses a reverse channel to request additional information from the encoder in the event of packet losses.

The MPEG-4 Advanced Simple Profile (ASP) starts from the simple profile and adds B frames and interlaced tools (for level 4 and up) similar to MPEG-2. It also adds quarter-pixel motion compensation and an option for global motion compensation. MPEG-4 advanced simple profile requires significantly more processing performance than the simple profile and has higher complexity and coding efficiency than MPEG-2.

MPEG-4 was used initially in Internet streaming and became adopted, for example, by Apple's QuickTime player. MPEG-4 simple profile is now finding usage in mobile streaming applications.

11.B.3.1.3   H.264/MPEG-4 AVC. One of the most important developments in video coding in the last few years has been the definition of the H.264/MPEG-4 AVC standard by the JVT of the ITU and the ISO/IEC. The ITU approved the new H.264 standard in May 2003. The ISO approved the standard in October 2003 as MPEG-4 Part 10, Advanced Video Coding. H.264/AVC delivers a significant breakthrough in compression efficiency generally achieving around 2x compression versus MPEG-2 and MPEG-4 simple profile. In formal tests conducted by the JVT, H.264 delivered a coding efficiency improvement of 1.5x or greater in 78% of the 85 test cases, with 77% of those showing improvements of 2x or greater and as high as 4x for some cases. The improvement offered by H.264 creates new market opportunity, such as the following possibilities:

- VHS-quality video at about 600 kbps. This can enable video delivery on demand over ADSL lines.
- An HD movie can fit on one ordinary DVD instead of requiring new laser optics.

When H.264 was standardized, it supported three profiles—baseline, main, and extended. Later, an amendment called Fidelity Range Extension (FRExt) introduced four additional profiles referred to as the high profiles. Earlier, the baseline profile and main profile generated interest the most. The baseline profile requires less computation and system memory and is optimized for low latency. It does not include B frames due to its inherent latency or CABAC due to the computational complexity. The baseline profile is a good match for video telephony applications as well as other applications that require cost-effective real-time encoding.

The main profile provides the highest compression but requires significantly more processing than the baseline profile, making it difficult to use in low-cost real-time encoding and low-latency applications. Broadcast and content storage applications are primarily interested in the main profile to leverage the highest possible video quality at the lowest bit rate.

While H.264 uses the same general coding techniques as previous standards, it has many new features that distinguish it from previous standards, which combined improve coding efficiency. The main differences are:

- Intraprediction and Coding—H.264 uses spatial domain of intraprediction to predict the pixels in an intra-MB from the neighboring pixels in adjacent blocks. The prediction residual along with the prediction modes is coded, rather than the actual pixels in the block. This results in a significant improvement in intracoding efficiency.
- Interprediction and Coding—Interframe coding in H.264 leverages most of the key features in earlier standards and adds both flexibility and functionality, including multiple options for block sizes for motion compensation, quarter-pel motion compensation, multiple reference frames, generalized bidirectional prediction, and adaptive loop deblocking.
- Variable Vector Block Sizes—Motion compensation can be performed using a number of different block sizes. Individual motion vectors can be transmitted for blocks as small as 4×4, so, up to 32 motion vectors may be transmitted for a single MB in the case of bidirectional prediction. Block sizes of $16 \times 8, 8 \times 16, 8 \times 8, 8 \times 4$, and 4×8 are also supported. Smaller block sizes improve the ability to handle fine motion detail and results in better subjective quality, including the absence of large blocking artifacts.
- Multiple Reference Frame Prediction—Up to 16 different reference frames can be used for interpicture coding, resulting in better subjective video quality and more efficient coding. Providing multiple reference frames can also help make the H.264 bit stream more error resilient. Note that this feature leads to increased

memory requirement for both the encoder and the decoder since multiple reference frames must be maintained in memory.

- Adaptive Loop Deblocking Filter—H.264 uses an adaptive deblocking filter that operates on the horizontal and vertical block edges within the prediction loop to remove artifacts caused by the block prediction errors. The filtering is generally based on 4×4 block boundaries, in which up to three pixels on either side of the boundary may be updated using a four-tap filter.

- Integer Transform—Previous standards that use DCT had to define rounding-error tolerances for fixed-point implementations of the inverse transform. Drifts caused by mismatches in the IDCT precision between the encoder and decoder were a source of quality loss. H.264 gets around the problem by using an integer 4×4 spatial transform, which is an approximation of the DCT. The small 4×4 shape also helps reduce blocking and ringing artifacts.

- Quantization and Transform Coefficient Scanning—Transform coefficients are quantized using scalar quantization with no widened dead zone. Different quantization step sizes can be chosen for each MB, similar to prior standards, but the step sizes are increased at a compounding rate of approximately 12.5%, rather than by a constant increment. Also, finer quantization step sizes are used for the chrominance component, especially when the luminance coefficients are coarsely quantized.

- Entropy Coding—Unlike previous standards that offered a number of static VLC tables depending on the type of data under consideration, H.264 uses a context-adaptive VLC for the transform coefficients and a single universal VLC approach for all the other symbols. The main profile also supports a new Context-Adaptive Binary Arithmetic Coder (CABAC). The CAVLC is superior to previous VLC implementations but without the full cost of CABAC.

- CABAC—It uses a probability model to encode and decode the syntax elements, such as transform coefficients and motion vectors. To increase the coding efficiency of arithmetic coding, the underlying probability model is adapted to the changing statistics within a video frame through a process called context modeling. Context modeling provides estimates of conditional probabilities of the coding symbols. Utilizing suitable context models, the given intersymbol redundancy can be exploited by switching between different probability models, according to already coded symbols in the neighborhood of the current symbol. Each syntax element maintains a different model (e.g., motion vectors and transform coefficients have different models). CABAC can provide up to about 10% bitrate improvement over CAVLC.

- Weighted Prediction—It forms the prediction for bidirectionally interpolated macroblocks by using the weighted sum of forward and backward predictions, which leads to higher coding efficiency when scene changes fade.

11.B.3.1.4 Fidelity Range Extension. In 2004, a new amendment called Fidelity Range Extension was added to the H.264 standard. This extension introduced an additional set of tools into H.264 and also allowed the use of additional color spaces, video formats, and bit depths. Additional support for lossless interframe coding and stereo-view video was introduced. The FRExt amendment introduced four new profiles to H.264:

- High Profile (HP) for standard 4:2:0 chroma sampling with 8-bit color per component.
- New tools were introduced for this profile; described in more detail below.
- High 10 Profile (Hi10P) for 10-bit color with standard 4:2:0 chroma sampling for higher fidelity video displays.
- High 4:2:2 10-bit color profile (H422P) useful for source editing functions such as alpha blending.
- High 4:4:4 12-bit color profile (H444P) for the highest quality source editing and color fidelity supporting lossless coding for regions of the video and a new integer color space transform (from RGB to YUV and back).

Among the new profiles, H.264 HP, which maintains 8-bit components and 4:2:0 chroma sampling, appears especially promising to the broadcast and DVD community. Some experiments show as much as 3x gain for H.264 HP over MPEG-2. Below are the key additional tools introduced in H.264 HP:

- Adaptive Residual Block Size and Integer 8×8 Transform—The residual blocks can be switched between 8×8 and 4×4 blocks for transform coding. A new 16-bit integer transform for 8×8 blocks. The older 4×4 transform can continue to be used for smaller block sizes.
- 8×8 Luma Intraprediction—Additional eight modes were added to allow luma intra-macroblocks to perform intraprediction on 8×8 blocks in addition to previously 16×16 and 4×4 blocks.
- Quantization Weighting—New quantization weighting matrices for quantization of 8×8 transform coefficients.
- Monochrome—Supports coding of black-and-white video.

11.B.3.2   Windows Media Video 9/VC-1

Windows Media is a leading format for music and video subscription services and streaming video on the Internet. In 2002, Microsoft introduced the Windows Media Video 9 (WMV9) series codec providing a major improvement in video compression efficiency. WMV9 is also standardized in SMPTE as VC-1. Similar to H.264, the WMV9 series codec includes many advanced coding tools, although there are differences in the specifics. WMV9's ME allows quarter-pel bicubic (using four-tap approximate bicubic filters) interpolation in addition to support for $^1/_2$ pixel bilinear interpolation. It also includes an in-loop deblocking filter similar to H.264, but with different details on the filters and decisions. Some other important features are:

- Multiple VLC Tables—WMV9 main profile contains multiple sets of VLC tables that are optimized for different types of content. Tables can be switched at a frame level to adjust to the characteristics of the input video.

- DCT/IDCT Transform Switch—WMV9 supports multiple DCT block sizes, including 8×8, 8×4, 4×8, and 4×4, and uses a special 16-bit integer transform and inverse transform.
- Quantization—Both regular step-size-based quantization and dead-zone quantization are used. Use of dead-zone quantization allows substantial savings at lower bit rates.

Another interesting feature is the ability to use an explicit fading compensating for scenes involving fading. This improves the quality of motion compensation in these scenarios. WMV9/VC-1 achieves significant performance improvements over MPEG-2 and MPEG-4 simple profile and has fared well in some perceptual quality rating comparisons with H.264. WMV9 is also standardized as a compression option for the upcoming HD-DVD and Blu-ray formats.

11.B.3.3 AVS

In 2002, the Audio-Video Standard Working Group established by the Ministry of Information Industry of China announced an effort to create a national standard for mobile multimedia, broadcast, DVD, etc. The video standard, referred to as AVS, consists of two related parts, a AVS-M for mobile video applications and AVS1.0 for broadcast and DVD. The AVS standards are similar to H.264. AVS1.0 supports both interlaced and progressive modes. AVS allows the use of two previous reference frames for P frames while allowing one future and one previous frame for B frames. In the interlaced mode, up to four fields are allowed for reference. Frame/field coding in the interlaced mode can be performed at a frame-level only, unlike H.264, where MB-level adaptation of this option is allowed. AVS has a loop filter similar to H.264, which can be disabled at a frame level. Also, no loop filter is required in B-pictures. The intraprediction is done on 8×8 blocks. MC allows up to $\frac{1}{4}$ pel for luma blocks. The block sizes for ME can be 16×16, 16×8, 8×16, or 8×8. The transform is a 16-bit based 8×8 integer transform, similar to WMV9. VLC is based on context-adaptive 2-D run/level coding. Four different Exp-Golomb codes are used. The code used for each quantized coefficient is adaptive to the previous symbols within the same 8×8 block. Since Exp-Golomb tables are parametric, table sizes are small. The visual quality of AVS 1.0 for progressive video sequences is marginally inferior to H.264 main profile at the same bit rate. AVS-M is targeted especially at mobile video applications and overlaps with H.264 baseline profile. It only supports progressive video, I and P frames, and no B frames. The main AVS-M coding tools include 4×4 block-based intraprediction, quarter-pel motion compensation, integer transform and quantization, context-adaptive VLC, and a highly simplified loop-filter. Similar to H.264 baseline profile, in AVS-M the motion vector block size can be down to 4×4, and consequently an MB can have up to 16 motion vectors. Multiple frame prediction is used, but it only requires up to two reference frames. A subset of H.264 HRD/SEI messages is also defined in AVS-M. On average and with similar settings, the coding efficiency of AVS-M is about 0.3 dB, worse than the H.264 baseline profile, whereas decoder complexity is about 20% lower.

The material in this section is based directly on a paper by Golston and Rao [GOL200601].

APPENDIX 11.C: ENCAPSULATION FOR TRANSMISSION OF IP DATAGRAMS OVER MPEG-2/DVB NETWORKS

To make use of an MPEG-2 TS environment, a network device, known as an encapsulator, receives PDUs (e.g., IP packets or Ethernet frames) and formats these into SNDUs. The MPE method provides a mechanism for transporting data network protocols, such as IP on top of the MPEG-2 TSs DVB networks. The DVB family of standards currently defines a mechanism for transporting an IP packet or Ethernet frame using the MPE; an equivalent scheme is also supported in ATSC. MPE allows transmission of IP packets or [by using Logical Link Control (LLC)] Ethernet frames by encapsulation within a table section (with the format used by the control plane associated with the MPEG-2 transmission). The MPE specification includes a set of optional header components and requires decoding of the control headers. This processing is suboptimal for Internet traffic, since it incurs significant receiver processing overhead and some extra link overhead [RFC4259].

MPE is a data link-layer protocol defined by DVB (included in ETSI TS 301 192 and also ATSC A/90) MPE uses MPEG-2 private table sections to carry the user datagrams. The section header is used to convey

- the frame's destination MAC address,
- optional ISO/IEC 8802-2 LLC and ISO/IEC 8802-1 Subnetwork Attachment Point (SNAP) information,
- a payload scrambling indication, and
- a MAC address scrambling indication.

Figure 11.C1 depicts the positioning of MPE [RFC4259].

MPE supports unicast (datagrams targeted to a single receiver), multicast (datagrams targeted to a group of receivers), and broadcast (datagrams targeted to all receivers). The 48-bit MAC addresses are used for addressing receivers; however, DVB does not specify how the MAC addresses are allocated to the receivers. IP packets are processed at the edge of a MPEG-2 transmission network by an encapsulator gateway that fragments and forwards the packets using MPEG-2 TS. As the data leave the MPEG-2 networks, a receiver restores the original IP packets and forwards these to the end host or IP network. Using MPE, each IP packet arriving at an MPEG encapsulator gateway has an MPE header attached to form a PDU. The amount of overhead is a function of the size and timing of the IP packets being sent. The entire PDU is then fragmented to form a series of MPEG-2 TS packets. MPE usually adds a lot of overhead for encapsulation, for example, 17 bytes of header/trailer for IPv4 and 25 bytes for IPv6 (use of LLC/SNAP). The current MPE, defined by DVB, is based on the MPEG-2 control plane [using Digital Storage Media Command and Control (DSM-CC)]. This scheme has

```
+-+-+-+-+------+-------------+---+--+--+---------+
|T|V|A|O|  O   |             | O |S |O |         |
|e|i|u|t|  t   |             | t |I |t |         |
|1|d|d|h|  h   |     IP      | h |  |h | Other   |
|e|e|i|e|  e   |             | e |T |e |protocols|
|t|o|o|r|  r   |             | r |a |r | native  |
|e| | | |      |             |   |b |  | over    |
|x| | | |      | +---+----+-+ |1 |  |MPEG-2 TS|
|t| | | |      | |   | MPE | |e |  |         |
| | | | | +--+---+  +------+ |  |  |         |
| | | | | | AAL5 |ULE|Priv. | |  |  |         |
+-+-+-+-+---+------+  |      +-+--+--+         |
|  PES  |   ATM    |  |Sect. |Section|         |
+-------+----------+---+------+-------+---------+
|                MPEG-2 TS                      |
+---------+-------+----------------+-----------+
|Satellite| Cable | Terrestrial TV | Other PHY |
+---------+-------+----------------+-----------+
```

Figure 11.C1. MPE Positioning

seen widespread use in a variety of MPEG-2 transmission networks, including DVB-S. DSM-CC is a format for transmission of data and control information defined by the ISO MPEG-2 standard that is carried in an MPEG-2 private section. Figure 11.C2 illustrates the packet format of the MPE method [HON200501].

The existing standards carry heritage from legacy implementations. These have reflected the limitations of technology at the time of their deployment (e.g., design decisions driven by audio/video considerations, rather than IP networking requirements). IPv6, MPLS, and other network layer protocols are not natively supported. Together, these justify the development of a new encapsulation that will be truly IP centric. Carrying IP packets over a TS logical channel involves several convergence protocol functions. New encapsulation mechanisms are now being sought. Since a majority of MPEG-2 transmission networks are bandwidth limited, encapsulation protocols must, therefore, add minimal overhead to ensure good link efficiency while providing adequate network services. They also need to be simple to minimize processing, robust to errors and security threats, and extensible to a wide range of services [RFC4259].

Work was underway at press time in the IETF [IP over DVB (ipdvb) Group] to develop new protocols and architectures to enable better deployment of IP over MPEG-2 transport and provide easier interworking with IP networks. Appropriate standards are needed to support transmission of IPv4 and IPv6 datagrams between IP networks connected using MPEG-2 transport subnetworks. This includes options for encapsulation, dynamic unicast address resolution for IPv4/IPv6, and the mechanisms needed to map routed IP multicast traffic to the MPEG-2 transport subnetwork. Standards will be

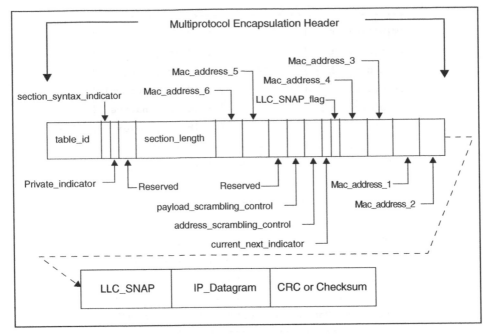

Figure 11.C2. MPE Header

appropriate to both MPE and any alternative encapsulation method developed (MPE will continue to be deployed in the future to develop new markets; any alternative encapsulation would need to coexist with MPE). The developed protocols may also be applicable to other multicast-enabled subnetwork technologies supporting large numbers of directly connected systems.

An encapsulation method that has emerged recently is the Unidirectional Lightweight Encapsulation (ULE) defined in RFC 4326. An ULE is layered direct on TS. This approach is known as data piping and it is a new encapsulation method or mechanism for the transport of IPv4 and IPv6 datagrams directly over ISO MPEG-2 TS as TS private data. ULE also supports DVB architecture, the ATSC system, and other similar MPEG-2-based transmission systems. ULE encapsulation does not add a lot of overhead for encapsulation. The ULE header is much smaller and less complex than the MPE header [HON200501].

REFERENCES

[ATS200001] A/90, ATSC Data Broadcast Standard, Advanced Television Systems Committee (ATSC), Doc. A/090, 2000.

[BRD200701] Broadband Services Forum, IPTV Explained—Part 1 in a BSF Series, Fremont, CA, www.broadbandserivcesforum.org.

[BRO200701] Broadcast Engineering Basics, http://www.interactivetvweb.org/tutorial/dtv-intro/dtv-transmission.shtml.

[CLA200301] H. D. Clausen Bernhard, Collini-Nocker, et al., Simple Encapsulation for Transmission of IP Datagrams over MPEG-2/DVB Networks, Internet Engineering Task Force, draft-unisal-ipdvb-enc-00.txt, May 2003.

[DIG200701] Digital TV Group, Conditional Access (CA) Tutorial, http://www.dtg.org.uk/reference/tutorial_ca.html.

[DVB200701] DVB Organization, Standards, http://www.dvb.org/technology/standards_specifications/conditional_access/index.xml.

[ETS200301] EN 301 192, Specifications for Data Broadcasting, v1.3.1, European Telecommunications Standards Institute (ETSI), http://www.etsi/org, May 2003.

[FAI200101] G. Fairhurst, MPEG-2 Digital Video, Background to Digital Video, University of Aberdeen, King's College, Dept. of Engineering, Aberdeen, UK, http://www.erg.abdn.ac.uk/research/future-net/digital-video/mpeg2-trans.html, January 2001.

[FAI200501] G. Fairhurst, M-J. Montpetit, Address Resolution for IP Datagrams over MPEG-2 Networks, Internet Draft, draft-ietf-ipdvb-ar-00.txt, IETF ipdvb, June 2005.

[FAR200601] G. Faria, J. A. Henriksson, E. Stare, P. Talmola, DVB-H: Digital Broadcast Services to Handheld Devices, *Proceedings of the IEEE*, vol. 94, no. 1, January 2006, page 194.

[FOU200701] FOURCAST MEDIA Ltd., IPTV Middleware, Sheffield, South Yorkshire.

[GOL200601] J. Golston, A. Rao, Video Codecs Tutorial: Trade-Offs with H.264, VC-1, and Other Advanced Codecs, *EE Times*, March 30, 2006.

[HON200501] T. C. Hong, W. T. Chee, R. Budiarto, Simulation and Design of IP over DVB Using Multi-Protocol Encapsulation and Ultra Lightweight Encapsulation, National Computer Science Postgraduate Colloquium 2005 (NaCSPC'05), Penang, Malaysia June 27–28, 2005.

[INF200701] Infonetics Reports on IPTV, Light Reading, June 28, 2007.

[ISO200001] ISO/IEC IS 13818-1, 'Information Technology—Generic Coding of Moving Pictures and Associated Audio Information—Part 1: Systems,' International Organization for Standardization (ISO), 2000.

[ISO200002] ISO/IEC DIS 13818-2, Information Technology—Generic Coding of Moving Pictures and Associated Audio Information: Video, International Organization for Standardization (ISO).

[ISO200003] ISO/IEC 13818-3: Information Technology—Generic Coding of Moving Pictures and Associated Audio Information—Part 3: Audio, International Organization for Standardization (ISO), 1995.

[ISO200004] ISO/IEC IS 13818–6, Information Technology—Generic Coding of Moving Pictures and Associated Audio Information—Part 6: Extensions for DSM-CC Is a Full Software Implementation, International Organization for Standardization (ISO).

[JAC200601] M. Jacklin, Going DVB: Getting Started, http://broadcastengineering. com/mag/broadcasting_going_dvb_getting, March 1, 2006.

[MIN199501] D. Minoli, *Video Dialtone Technology: Digital Video over ADSL, HFC, FTTC, and ATM*, McGraw-Hill, New York, 1995.

[MIN200001] D. Minoli, Digital Video Technologies, video section in K. Terplan and Morreale, Editors, *The Telecommunications Handbook,* IEEE Press, 2000.

[MIN200301] D. Minoli, *Telecommunications Technology Handbook*, 2nd ed., Artech House, Norwood, MA, 2003.

[NOR200601] Nortel, Position Paper: Introduction to IPTV, Nortel, Research Triangle Park, NC, 2006.

[RFC4259] RFC 4259, A Framework for Transmission of IP Datagrams over MPEG-2 Networks, M-J. Montpetit, G. Fairhurst, et al., November 2005.

[SIP200701] Spirent Communications, High Quality Mobile TV: The Challenge for Operators to Deliver High-Quality TV to Mobiles, White Paper, Spirent, Eatontown, NJ, February 2007.

12

DVB-H: HIGH-QUALITY TV TO CELL PHONES

This chapter discusses standards-based technologies used to deliver high-quality real-time TV to cell phones. This global standard behind these open technologies is DVB-H developed by the ETSI.[1] DVB-H focuses on physical layer technology; encapsulation is used at the data link layer and IP multicast technology is used at the network layer. This environment is also known as Mobile Digital TV (mDTV). There appears to be strong market interest for mobile TV services to be delivered on cell phones and/or PDAs. mDTV services are expected to grow very rapidly: some analysts are predicting yearly sales of over 250 million DVB-H terminals by 2010. This chapter provides a terse overview to the topic; the discussion is not intended to be comprehensive or completely systematic: to do justice to the topic an entire lengthy textbook is needed.

[1]At press time an initiative by the newly formed Open Mobile Video Coalition (OMVC) sought to develop a different technology intended to be used by the U.S. TV over-the-air broadcasters to deliver video to handheld (cell phones) without using cellular technology. However DVB-H has been around for several years and it is already a standard. The OMVC work targeted a standard by February 17, 2009, when analog TV broadcasting ceases in the United States.

IP Multicast with Applications to IPTV and Mobile DVB-H   by Daniel Minoli
Copyright © 2008 John Wiley & Sons, Inc.

12.1 BACKGROUND AND MOTIVATION

The cell phone/PDA screen is considered a "third" content delivery interface point by many (the first is the TV screen, and the second is the PC screen). There is keen industry interest in delivering video to cell phones as a way to support an unmet need and also increase Average Rate per User[2] (ARPU). Figure 12.1 depicts one industry forecast for mDTV services in the United States.

   mDTV is of interest to the entire wireless market—operators, handset OEMs, infrastructure, and semiconductor providers, but for the DTV market in the United States to take off, open standards must see implementation [TEX200701]. Initial mDTV services use streaming video over the cellular network; the downside of this approach is that it uses voice bandwidth and in so doing lowers the overall capacity of the network for all users. The commercial breakthrough will arise from live broadcast TV. By design, mDTV will offer high-quality live broadcast TV (20–30 frames per second; QCIF-QVGA format) accompanied by full audio. Additional services will be available as a menu/guide system and pay-per-view channels to enhance the viewing experience [PIE200501]. Open standards offer advantages over proprietary technologies and networks controlled by a single company; consumers benefit from the innovation and less expensive devices. Portable handsets with relatively large, high-resolution Liquid Crystal Display (LCD) screens, powerful CPUs, and long battery life provide users viewing enjoyment along with freedom of movement. Compression/decompression standards with reduced bandwidth requirements and acceptable quality video signals have emerged in the past 15 years as discussed in the previous chapter. Also, fueling expansion is the development of cellular networks from second generation (2G) through third generation (3G) and soon to fourth generation (4G) [SIP200701].

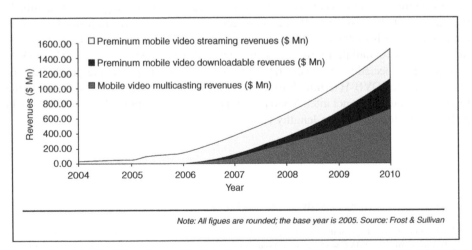

Figure 12.1. Mobile Video Server Market: Revenues from Different Types of Mobile Video Servers (U.S.) 2004–2010

---

[2] Some also favor the expansion average rate per unit.

Video-to-cell phone services (real-time TV or looped stored content) have by and large used vendor-proprietary approaches up to now. In order to make the service more broadly available, standards are needed, just like off-the-air TV is possible through the use of open standards. There are several standards for mDTV used in various geographies [TEX200701]:

- DMB (Digital Media Broadcast) has deployed today in Korea with several handsets already in the market to support the standard and is expanding to Europe and other parts of Asia.
- ISDB-T (Integrated Services Digital Broadcast-Terrestrial) is the standard in Japan.
- DVB-H is quickly gaining ground with trials in Europe, the United States, and parts of Asia.
- 3G networks: While the economics and bandwidth requirements of streaming live broadcasts over the cellular network are still being assessed at this time, the use of 3G networks to download clips or full television shows to PDA/cell-phone memory is practical.[3]
- OMVC — see Appendix 12.A.

As implied above, there are other "nonopen" technologies that have been developed for mDTV, including MediaFLO™. Table 12.1 provides a comparison [TEX200701]. This chapter focuses on DVB-H. While there are number of frequency plans to support DVB-H, especially internationally, in the United States, the 700–800-MHz area is now being considered; this relieves (at least initially) the 3G bandwidth-limitation issues just noted for video delivery to handhelds. DVB-H is an extension of the DVB-T standard. Additional features have been added to support handheld and mobile reception. Lower power consumption for mobile terminals and secured reception in the mobility environments are key features of the standard. It is meant for IP-based services. DVB-H can share the DVB-T MUX with MPEG-2/MPEG-4 services, so it can be part of the IPTV infrastructure described in the previous chapter, except that lower bit rates are used for transmission (typically in the 384-kbps range). The content aggregation point is similar to that described in Chapter 11, including the use of CASs. Since the middle of this decade, a number of network operators, equipment providers, and content providers have conducted or are conducting several DVB-H trials around the world.

DVB-H was published as ETSI standard EN 302 304 in November 2004. This standard is an umbrella standard defining how to combine the existing (now updated) ETSI standards to form the DVB-H system. The basic standards in DVB-H are as follows:

- *ETSI EN 302 304:* "Digital Video Broadcasting (DVB); Transmission System for Handheld Terminals (DVB-H)"

---

[3]One of the issues with 3G is bandwidth. One could recall from the recent discussions regarding Apple's release of the iPhone that the handheld (iPhone) got much better reviews than the (specific) carrier that one had to subscribe to in order to use that device: the carrier did not have its 3G (high-speed) data network deployed throughout the United States, which means that some of the key features (such as Web browsing) do not run as fast as consumers may have hoped.

TABLE 12.1. Mobile DTV Technologies

	DVB-H	MediaFLO™	ISDB-T	DMB	3G	OMVC
Standard	Open	Proprietary	Open	Open	Open	Open (future)
Regions	U.S., Europe, parts of Asia	U.S.	Japan	Korea, expanding to other countries	Worldwide	U.S.
Air interface	Orthogonal Frequency Division Multiplexing (OFDM)	OFDM	OFDM (subbanded)	OFDM	—	AVSB
Service availability	Mid 2005, open U.S. spectrum nationwide today	2006 (locally through analog TV channels)	Early 2006	Today	Today expanding rollout	None
Handset availability	Today from several OEMs	2006	2006	Today from several OEMs	Today from several vendors	2009

- *Draft ETSI TR 102 377 V1.1.1 (2005-01):* "Digital Video Broadcasting (DVB); DVB-H Implementation Guidelines"
- *Draft ETSI TR 159 r12:* "Digital Video Broadcasting (DVB); DVB-H Implementation Guidelines"

Mobile DTV has the potential to positively impact the bottom line, ARPU, of distributors, multimedia content suppliers, and telcos. Specifically, there are a number of business opportunities for mobile DTV, including the following [PIE200501]:

Carriers (telcos)

- DVB-H allows them to increase ARPU with a new service to existing customers
- Reduce churn rate
- Attract new customers with competitive services and channel offerings through mobile DTV
- Gain additional revenue from interactive services and advertising
- Make deals with content providers or aggregators on their own to deliver content to their subscribers.

Content providers/broadcasters

- Deliver the programming for the mobile phone
- Gain additional viewers for their content with no or low investment
- Gain additional revenue from ads and content

- Play in multiple areas of the value chain as desired, including possibility of purchasing spectrum and deploying their own broadcast network if desired

Infrastructure companies: Provide the towers and transmitting equipment.
Handset OEMs: Develop handset for consumers. DVB-H allows them to:

- Gain revenue with phone upgrades as mobile DTV services increases in popularity
- Develop new mobile phone designs that are small but deliver the performance and screen resolution for crisp, clear images
  Some, however, including this author, have a concern that in an attempt to add a screen to a cell phone handset, the speaker portion of the handset is being severely compromised in size. In some cell phone models, where the ear would naturally line up when the cell phone is in use, there is instead a $2'' \times 2''$ screen with a trivial speaker element placed literally on the rim (rather than center) of the upper shell portion of the phone. This arrangement runs quite contrary to the physiognomy of the ear, which would prefer the speaker closer to the center of the upper portion of the phone. This design has the effect of making the voice quality really marginal, especially for use in noisy environments (e.g., in a car) or for older users. Manufacturers need to ascertain that the voice quality remains at an acceptable level as they contemplate the video use of the cell phone. The potential use of a Bluetooth earpiece does not invalidate this design concern, because the earpiece is not always in use or is pragmatically inappropriate

Silicon vendors: Develop chip sets and software for mobile phones.
Software third parties: Deliver additional software and applications for mobile phones.

Figures 12.2–12.4 provide basic graphical views of DVB-H/mobile DTV environments. Notice the CAS. The backbones make use of IP multicast. A DVB-H network is typically a combination of [PIE200501]:

- Terrestrial fixed lines (e.g., SONET/SDH/OTN) between the TV production center and the satellite teleport.
- A satellite primary distribution network from the Earth station to the individual terrestrial microwave towers present in several markets distributed over the country or market regions. Satellite, in general, is the most efficient and lowest cost solution for primary distribution and broadcast applications over a wide geographic coverage.
- Terrestrial DVB-H SFN per market cell or region. The SFN allows the reuse of the frequency spectrum over adjacent DVB-H cells. In the United States, bandwidth in the range 700–800 MHz is being targeted for use, but other bands may also be used.

Delivery (transmission) mechanisms for cell phone reception fall into two categories [SIP200701]:

- Unicast transmission where each subscriber receives a dedicated video channel. The various 3G protocols—e.g., evolutions of either Universal Mobile

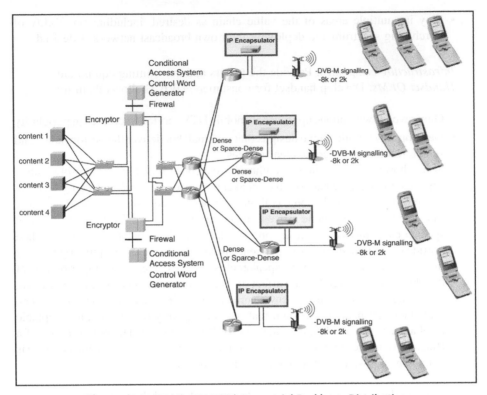

Figure 12.2. Mobile DTV With Terrestrial Backbone Distribution

Telecommunications System (UMTS) [Wideband Code Division Multiple Access (WCDMA)] or CDMA2000—are unicast protocols with fixed limits using their total upper bandwidth. WCDMA is a symmetric protocol, whereas all other protocols are asymmetric with most of their bandwidth devoted to the downlink, as shown in Table 12.2.

- Multicast or broadcast transmissions, through which all subscribers in range receive the same signal containing multiple channels. Subscribers select the channel they wish to display. Traditional TV is a broadcast mechanism; IPTV is a multicast mechanism, as are DVB-H, DMB, and MediaFLO™.

DVB-H, DMB, and MediaFLO™ need to deal with bandwidth constraints because while each video channel may be watched by many subscribers simultaneously, the bandwidth available per channel is limited. These bandwidth constraints are mitigated through the use of state-of-the-art compression standards that provide good-enough quality for a handheld at 384 kbps. Because of the constrained data rates suggested for individual DVB-H services and the small displays of typical handheld terminals, the classical audio and video coding schemes used in digital broadcasting do not suit DVB-H well; therefore, the DVB-H standard replaces MPEG-2 video with H.264/AVC or other high-efficiency video coding standards [FAR200601]. As noted in the previous

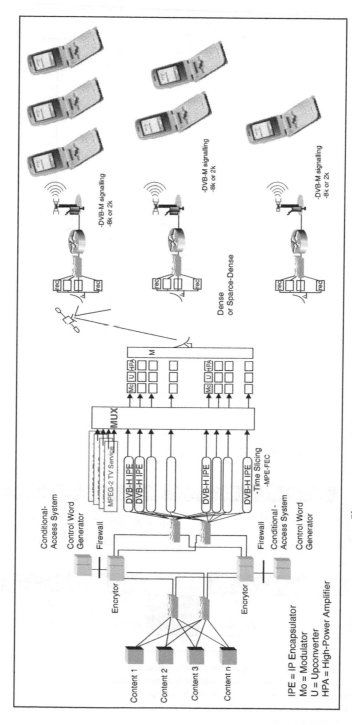

Figure 12.3. Mobile DTV With Satellite Backbone Distribution

IPE = IP Encapsulator
Mo = Modulator
U = Upconverter
HPA = High-Power Amplifier

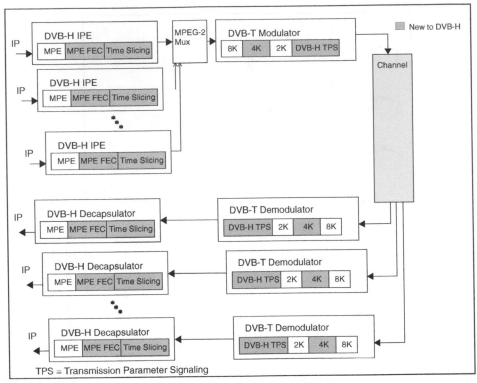

Figure 12.4. DVB-H Framework

TABLE 12.2. Unicast Protocols: 3G Approaches

	2003	2004	2005	2006	2007		2009	2010
CDMA2000	1XEVDO				EVDO Rev. A	EVDO Rev. B	EVDO Rev. C	
UMTS	WCDMA Rel. 99			HSDPA Rel. 5		HSUPA Rel. 6	HSPA+ Rel. 7	HSPA+ Rel. 8

CDMA2000 (Mbit/s)	1xEVDO	Rev. A	Rev. B	Rev. C
Down link Data rate	2.4	3.1	3.1-73	70-200
Up link Data rate	0.153	1.8	1.8-27	30-45

CDMA2000 (Mbit/s)	WCDMA	HSDPA	HSUPA	HSPA+
Down link Data rate	0.384	1.8-72	7.2	40
Up link Data rate	0.384	0.384	5.8	10

Note: Total cell (sector) bandwidth is comparatively small, typically 2–3 Mbps at the low end and 20 Mbps at the higher end. This puts an upper limit on the total number of simultaneous subscribers who can watch video (perhaps an absolute maximum of 100 or so). WiMAX is better for total system throughput (approximately 40–80 Mbps) but may reach a bottleneck when subscribers reach a few hundred.

Courtesy: Spirent Communications.

TABLE 12.3. Vendor-Proprietary Mobile DTV Systems (Partial List)

	MediaFLO	Modeo
Spectrum	6 MHz at 700 MHz	5 MHz at 1.6 GHz
Transmission Standard	Proprietary non-IP based	DVB-H
Strength	Carrier commitment	DVB-H open standard
Weakness	Proprietary system	Limited spectrum
		Low-power spectrum license
		Need carrier commitment

chapter, H.264/AVC/MPEG-4 Part 10 embodies significant advances in compression capability and recently was adopted for PlayStation Portable, iPod, Nero Digital product suite, CoreAVC video decoder, Mac OS X v10.4, and HD-DVD/Blu-ray. Several prototype DVB-H phones have been developed by major handset manufacturers (e.g., but not limited to LG). It is expected that there will be a number of trials in the United States launching in 2007, with full-scale deployments starting in 2008 into 2009.

Qualcomm (MediaFLO) and Crown Castle (Modeo) both publicly announced mobile video services. A quick snapshot of these technologies is provided in Table 12.3. These are not currently DVB-H-based.

12.2 BASIC DVB-H TECHNOLOGY

DVB-H is seen as a "proven technology" because it is based on the DVB standard used in Europe for terrestrial and satellite DTV transmission but has a low-power mode for battery-powered devices. A DVB-H system is a combination of elements of the physical and link layers, as well as service information. At the physical layer, it uses an OFDM air interface technology and includes a technique for power reduction in the tuner. OFDM is a good choice for mobile TV air interface because it offers good spectral efficiency, immunity to multipath interference, and good mobile performance and works well in single-frequency networks such as those planned for mobile TV. DVB-H uses time slicing so that the tuner can be switched off most of the time and is only on during short transmission bursts. This allows the tuner to operate over a reduced input bandwidth and also conserves power. In the United States, DVB-H will be deployed using clear and "ready-for-use" spectrum available today, without interfering with the existing analog TV stations or other TV or wireless services [TEX200701].

The Digital Video Broadcast (DVB) Project started research work related to mobile reception of DVB—Terrestrial (DVB-T) signals in 1998, accompanying the introduction of commercial terrestrial digital TV services in Europe. In 2000, the EU-sponsored Motivate (Mobile Television and Innovative Receivers) Project concluded that mobile reception of DVB-T is possible, but it implies dedicated broadcast networks. It was recognized that mobile services are more demanding in robustness (i.e., constellation and coding rate) than broadcast networks planned for fixed DVB-T reception. Later in 2002, the EU-sponsored Multimedia Car Platform (MCP) Project explored the behavior of antenna diversity reception that by introducing spatial diversity in addition to the frequency and time diversities provided by the DVB-T transmission layer improved sufficiently reception performance to allow a mobile receiver to access DVB-T signals broadcast for fixed receivers. While DVB-T shows sufficient flexibility to permit mobile broadcast services, it is not ideally suited for these applications. As a consequence, in early 2002, the DVB community was asked to provide technical specifications to allow delivery of rich multimedia contents to handheld terminals, a property that has been missing in the original DVB-T. This would make it possible to receive TV-type services in a small, handheld device like a mobile phone [FAR200601].

Handheld terminals (defined as a lightweight, battery-powered apparatus) require specific features from the transmission system serving them, as defined in ETSI TR 102 377 V1.2.1 (2005-11):

- The transmission system must offer the possibility to repeatedly turn the power off to some parts of the reception chain. This reduces the average power consumption of the receiver.
- The transmission system must ensure that it is easy for receivers to move from one transmission cell to another while maintaining the DVB-H service.
- For a number of reception scenarios (indoor, outdoor, pedestrian, and inside a moving vehicle), the transmission system must offer sufficient flexibility and scalability to allow the reception of DVB-H services at various speeds while optimizing transmitter coverage.
- Since services are expected to be delivered in environments that suffer high levels of human-made electromagnetic noise, the transmission system needs to offer the means to mitigate their effects on the performance of the receiving terminal.
- Since DVB-H aims to provide a generic way to serve handheld terminals in various parts of the world, the transmission system must offer the flexibility to be used in various transmission bands and channel bandwidths.

As noted, the DVB-H system is defined based on the existing DVB-T standard for fixed and in-car reception of digital TV; the main additional elements in the link layer (i.e., the layer above the physical layer) are time slicing and additional FEC coding. Figure12.5 depicts the DVB-H protocol stack.

DVB-H makes use of the following technological elements for the link and physical layers:

- Link layer:
  - Time slicing is used in order to reduce the average power consumption of the receiving terminal and enable smooth and seamless frequency handover when the user leaves one service area in order to enter a new cell. Time slicing reduces the average power in the receiver front end up to about 90–95%. Time slicing is mandatory for DVB-H. With DVB-H, a device has a need to receive audio/video

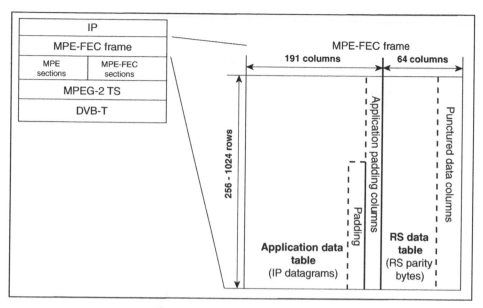

Figure 12.5. DVB-H Protocol Stack

services transmitted over IP on ESs at a relatively low bit rate, typically at 384 kbps. The MPEG-2 TS may, however, have a much higher bit rate, for example, 10 Mbps. The particular ES of interest thus occupies only a fraction (in this example, 3.8%) of the total MPEG-2 TS bit rate. In order to reduce power consumption, one would ideally like the receiver to demodulate and decode only the 3.8% portion of interest, and not the full MPEG-2 TS. With time slicing this is possible, since the MPE sections of a particular ES are sent in high-bit-rate bursts instead of with a constant low bit rate. During the time between the bursts—the off-time—no sections of the particular ES are transmitted. This allows the receiver to power off completely during the off-time. The receiver, however, needs to know when to power on again to receive the next burst. Refer to [FAR200601] for a tutorial description of this process or to the standard itself.

– Forward error correction for multiprotocol encapsulated data (MPE-FEC) is not mandatory for DVB-H. MPE-FEC is used to improve signal robustness. The objective of MPE-FEC is to improve the C/N and Doppler performance in mobile channels and to improve the tolerance to impulse interference. This is accomplished through the introduction of an additional level of error correction where the parity data is sent in separate MPE-FEC sections. With MPE-FEC, a flexible amount of the transmission capacity is allocated to parity overhead. The MPE-FEC overhead can be fully compensated by choosing a slightly weaker transmission code rate while still providing far better performance than DVB-T (without MPE-FEC) for the same

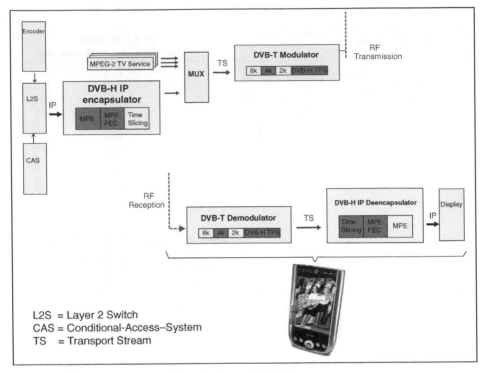

Figure 12.6. A DVB-H System

throughput. This MPE-FEC scheme allows high-speed single-antenna DVB-T reception using 8K/16-QAM or even 8K/64-QAM signals. In addition, MPE-FEC provides good immunity to impulse noise interference. The payload of DVB-H is IP datagrams or other network layer datagrams are encapsulated into MPE sections. Figure 12.6 expands the view shown in Figure 12.4.

These functions are typically implemented in the IP Encapsulator (IPE) at the transmission end and in the DVB-H device at the receiving end.

- Physical layer: DVB-H makes use of DVB-T but with the following technical elements specifically targeting DVB-H use:
  - DVB-H signaling in the Transmission Parameter Signaling (TPS) bits to enhance and speed up service discovery. A cell identifier is also carried in the TPS-bits to support quicker signal scan and frequency handover on mobile receivers. DVB-H signaling is mandatory for DVB-H.
  - 4K mode for trading off mobility and SFN cell size, allowing single-antenna reception in medium SFNs at very high speed, adding flexibility for the network design. 4K mode is not mandatory for DVB-H.

– In-depth symbol interleaver for the 2K and 4K modes to further improve the robustness in mobile environments and impulse noise conditions. In-depth symbol interleavers for 2K and 4K are not mandatory for DVB-H.

Hence, the physical layer has four extensions to the existing DVB-T physical layer [FAR200601]:

1. The bits in TPS have been upgraded to include two additional bits to indicate presence of DVB-H services and possible use of MPE-FEC to enhance and speed up the service discovery.

2. A new 4K OFDM mode is adopted for trading off mobility and SFN cell size, allowing single-antenna reception in medium SFNs at very high speeds. 4K mode is an option for DVB-H complementing the 2K and 8K modes that are available as well. The objective of the 4K mode is to improve network planning flexibility by trading off mobility and SFN size.

3. A new way of using the symbol interleaver of DVB-T has been defined. For 2K and 4K modes, the operator may select (instead of native interleaver that interleaves the bits over one OFDM symbol) the option of an in-depth interleaver that interleaves the bits over four or two OFDM symbols, respectively. This approach brings the basic tolerance to impulse noise of these modes up to the level attainable with the 8K mode and also improves the robustness in mobile environment. To further improve robustness of the DVB-H 2K and 4K modes in a mobile environment and impulse noise reception conditions, an in-depth symbol interleaver has also been added to the standard.

4. The 5 MHz channel bandwidth to be used in nonbroadcast bands. This is of interest, for example, in the United States, where a network of about 1.7 GHz is running using DVB-H with a 5-MHz channel.

DVB-T only has 2K (1705 carriers) and 8K (6817 carriers) modes. DVB-H adds a 4K (3409 carriers) mode; it allows the designer to trade off mobility and SFN cell size. See Figure 12.7. Enhanced in-depth interleavers (distributes burst errors over a larger timescale so that FEC is able to correct the errors) in 2K and 4K modes. DVB-H is backward compatible to DVB-T.

12.2.1 DVB-H Mobile Devices

A DVB-H terminal device includes the following functionality (see Figure 12.8) [FAR200601]:

• DVB-H receiver (a DVB-T demodulator, a time-slicing module, and an optional MPE-FEC module). The DVB-T demodulator recovers the MPEG-2 TS packets from the received DVB-T RF signal. It offers three transmission modes: 8K, 4K, and 2K with the corresponding signaling. The time-slicing module controls the

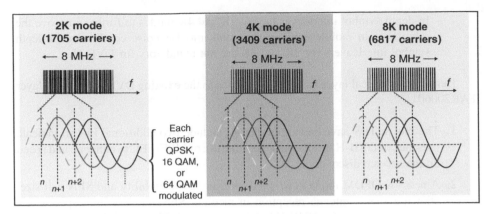

Figure 12.7. Modulation In DVB-H

receiver to decode the wanted service and shut off during the other service bits. It aims to reduce receiver power consumption while also enabling a smooth and seamless frequency handover. The MPE-FEC module provided by DVB-H offers, in addition to the error correction in the physical layer transmission, a complementary FEC function that allows the receiver to cope with particularly difficult reception situations.

- The DVB-H terminal itself. The handheld terminal decodes/uses IP services only. Note that the 4K mode and the in-depth interleavers are not available, for compatibility reasons, in cases where the multiplex is shared between services intended for fixed DVB-T receivers and services for DVB-H devices.

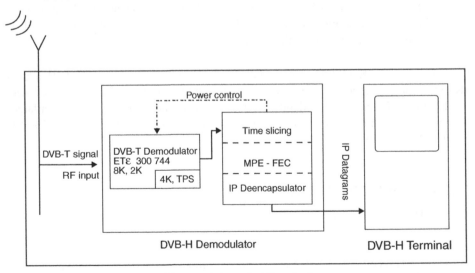

Figure 12.8. DVB-H Terminal

APPENDIX 12.A: OPEN MOBILE VIDEO COALITION EFFORTS

At press time, a coalition of almost 800 local stations in the United States were working to bring live over-the-air broadcast TV to mobile television devices by 2008. The broadcasting groups were working with the Digital TV (DTV) standard body ATSC to create a new standard to allow broadcasters to transmit live video and non-real-time data services to mobile phones and other handheld devices via their existing digital TV spectrum without interfering with their current HD or SD programming. The Open Mobile Video Coalition (OMVC) has established the goal to have the technology standard in place by February 17, 2009, when analog TV broadcasts will cease in the United States [DIC200701]. The OMVC, which has enlisted financial support form the National Association of Broadcasters and technical help from the Association for Maximum Service Television (MSTV), represents 422 commercial stations in 142 markets covering 103 million U.S. TV households as well as 361 public TV stations. Members include station groups ION, Belo, Fox, Gannett, Gray, NBC/Telemundo, Sinclair, Tribune, Cox, Dispatch, Freedom, LIN, Meredith, Media General, Post-Newsweek, Raycom, Schurz, and the Association of Public Television Stations.

   The technical challenge is not trivial. It requires the transmission of robust signals to small, portable devices within the existing 6-MHz DTV channel, without interfering with the core programming services stations are already providing with their 19.4 Mbps of digital throughput. The request for proposals that the ATSC circulated in mid-2007 asked for a system that could not only deliver live, advertiser-supported TV to cellphones but also support subscription services, non-real-time download services for on-demand playback, datacasting applications, interactive TV, and real-time navigation data for automobiles. Preliminary proposals were submitted in 2007 by 10 companies and/or groups of companies, including Coding Technologies, Coherent Logix, DTS, LG Electronics and Harris Corp., Mobile DTV Alliance, Micronas Semiconductor, Nokia, Samsung Electronics Co., and Rohde & Schwarz, Thomson, and Qualcomm. Some proposals related to full mobile DTV systems, such as MPH (Mobile Pedestrian Handheld) from LG/Harris and A-VSB (Advanced-Vestigial Side Band) from Samsung/Rohde & Schwarz, both of which were demonstrated at the NAB show in Las Vegas in April 2007. There were two proposals being considered at press time. (1) The MPH system, which LG and Harris formally documented in an 80-page submission to the ATSC late in 2007, has been undergoing continual development since it was first unveiled at the NAB show. LG has created an MPH receiver chip that will allow it to soon demonstrate much smaller from-factor mobile devices than the "big box" it used to demonstrate MPH in Las Vegas; such devices would have a single antenna less than 3 inches long. (2) As an alternative proposal, Samsung was refining its A-VSB system since first demonstrating it in a shuttle bus at the Consumer Electronics Show in early 2007. The goal of OMVC was to reach a compromise, inclusive solution and then proceed to implementation, in competition with DVB-H-based solutions [DIC200701].

REFERENCES

[DIC200701] G. Dickson, Mobile TV Takes Flight, *Broadcasting & Cable*, November 12, 2007.

[FAR200601] G. Faria, J. A. Henriksson, E. Stare, P. Talmola, DVB-H: Digital Broadcast Services to Handheld Devices, *Proceedings of the IEEE*, vol. 94, no. 1, January 2006, page 194.

[PIE200501] R. Pieck, DVB-H Broadcast to Mobile Devices, White Paper, Newtec America, Inc., Stamford, CT, www.newtecamerica.com, September 14, 2005.

[SIP200701] Spirent Communications, High Quality Mobile TV The Challenge for Operators to Deliver High-Quality TV to Mobiles, White Paper, Spirent, Eatontown, NJ, February 2007.

[TEX200701] Texas Instruments, DVB-H Mobile Digital TV for the U.S., White Paper, Texas Instruments, Dallas, TX.

GLOSSARY

This Glossary contains basic multicast/IPTV terminology compiled from numerous industry sources, as noted.

(*,*,RP) Route Entry   In PIM SM, (*,*,RP) refers to any source and any multicast group that maps to the RP included in the entry. The routers along the shortest path branches between a domain's RP(s) and its PMBRs keep (*,*,RP) state and use it to determine how to deliver packets toward the PMBRs if data packets arrive for which there is not a longer match. The wildcard group in the (*,*,RP) route entry is represented by a group address of 224.0.0.0 and a mask length of 4 bits [RFC2362].

(*,G) Route Entry   In PIM SM, group members join the shared RP-tree for a particular group. This tree is represented by (*,G) multicast route entries along the shortest path branches between the RP and the group members [RFC2362].

(S,G) Pair   Source S and destination group G associated with an IP packet [RFC2362].

(S,G) Route Entry   In PIM SM, (S,G) is a source-specific route entry. It may be created in response to data packets, Join/Prune messages, or asserts. The (S,G) state in routers creates a source-rooted, shortest path (or reverse shortest path) distribution tree. (S,G)RPT bit entries are source-specific entries on the shared RP-tree; these entries are used to prune particular sources off of the shared tree [RFC2362].

IP Multicast with Applications to IPTV and Mobile DVB-H   by Daniel Minoli
Copyright © 2008 John Wiley & Sons, Inc.

A la carte VoD — VoD where one pays for each item viewed (similar to pay per view). Typically the subscriber has one day to view the content [NOR200601].

Adaptation Field — An optional variable-length extension field of the fixed-length TS packet header, intended to convey clock references and timing and synchronization information as well as stuffing over an MPEG-2 multiplex [CLA200301].

ADSL (Full-Rate Asymmetric DSL) — Access technology that offers differing upload and download speeds and can be configured to deliver up to six megabits of data per second (6000 kbps) from the network to the customer. ADSL enables voice and high-speed data to be sent simultaneously over the existing telephone line. This type of DSL is the most predominant in commercial use for business and residential customers around the world. Good for general Internet access and for applications where downstream speed is most important, such as video on demand. ITU-T recommendation G.992.1 and ANSI standard T1.413-1998 specify full-rate ADSL. ITU recommendation G.992.3 specifies ADSL2, which provides advanced diagnostics, power saving functions, PSD shaping, and better performance than G.992.1. ITU recommendation G.992.5 specifies ADSL2Plus, which provides the benefits of ADSL2Plus twice the bandwidth so that bit rates as high as 20 Mbps downstream can be achieved on relatively short lines [DSL200701].

AES (Advanced Encryption Standard) — Cryptographic algorithm; NIST-approved standard. The current AES is Rijndael. It was chosen by NIST because it is considered to be both faster and smaller than its competitors. See also DES and 3DES [CON200701].

AFC — Adaptation Field Control.

Asymmetric Algorithm — Same as public key algorithm.

Asymmetric Encryption — Type of encryption in which encryption keys are different from decryption keys, and one key is computationally difficult to determine from the other. Uses an asymmetric algorithm [CON200701].

ATSC (Advanced Television Systems Committee) — A set of framework and associated standards for the transmission of video, audio, and data, using the ISO MPEG-2 standard [CLA200301].

Authentication — The process of proving the genuineness of an entity (such as a smart card) by means of a cryptographic procedure. Put simply, authentication amounts to using a fixed procedure

	to determine whether someone is actually the person he or she claims to be [CON200701].
Authorization	An authorization gives access (or legal power) to some protected service. In a CA system, the authorization gives access to encrypted services (channels, movies, etc.) [CON200701].
Bootstrap Router (BSR)	In PIM SM a BSR is a dynamically elected router within a PIM domain. It is responsible for constructing the RP-set and originating Bootstrap messages [RFC2362]. A router with multiple potential RPs; the BSRs provide mechanisms that identify RPs for various multicast groups [ROD200701].
Broadcast Environment	Environment where one system communicates to all systems.
Broadcast Interface	In CBT, any interface that supports multicast transmission [ROD200701].
CA (Conditional Access)	DVB conditional access encryption and key management scheme [CLA200301].
CableCARD	A device that consumers can plug into their DCR TV sets that permits for the descrambling of digital programming. The card works in place of a traditional STB [CON200701].
Candidate BSR (CBSR)	In PIM SM it is a router that can potentially play the role of a BSR, provided it wins an automated BSR election process [ROD200701].
Candidate RP (C-RP)	In PIM SM, a C-RP is a router configured to send periodic C-RP-Adv messages to the BSR and act as an RP when it receives Join/Prune or Register messages for the advertised group prefix [RFC2362].
CAT (Conditional Access Table)	MPEG signaling table that defines type of scrambling used and PID values of transport streams which contain the conditional access management and entitlement information (EMM)). The CAT is sent with the well-known PID value of 0x001 [FAI200101].
Center-Based Trees	Same as core-based trees.
Certificate	A digital certificate consists of three things: (1) The public-key portion of the certificate holder's public and private-key pair. (2) Information that identifies the holder of the certificate (the owner of the corresponding private key). (3) The digital signature of a trusted entity attesting to the validity of the certificate (i.e., that the key and the certificate information truly go together) [CON200701].

Cisco Group Management Protocol (CGMP)
:   A Cisco-developed group management protocol that limits the forwarding of IP multicast packets to only those ports associated with IP multicast clients. These clients automatically join and leave groups that receive IP multicast traffic, and the switch dynamically changes its forwarding behavior according to these requests.

Conditional-Access System (CAS)
:   In a DVB context, conditional access is a security technology used to control the access to broadcast content (including video and audio, interactive services, etc.) through the transmission of encrypted signals and the programmable regulation of their decryption by a system such as smart cards [CON200701].

Content Provider
:   An entity that acts as the agent for or is the prime distributor of the content.

Core-Based Tree
:   (aka center-based tree) A bidirectional shared tree where the routing state is "bidirectional," namely, packets can flow both down the tree away from the core and up the tree toward the core, depending on the location of the source in the network, and the tree is "shared" by all sources to the group. Core-based forwarding trees have a single node, for example, a router, known as the core of the tree, from which branches emanate. These branches are made up of other routers, so-called noncore routers, which form a shortest path between a member host's directly attached router and the core. A router at the end of a branch is known as a leaf router on the tree. The core need not be topologically centered between the nodes on the tree, since multicasts vary in nature, and correspondingly, so can the form of a core-based tree [BAL199301].

Core-Based Tree (CBT) Multicasting
:   A multicast routing architecture that builds a single delivery tree per group, which is shared by all of the group's senders and receivers. Most multicast algorithms build one multicast tree per sender (subnetwork), the tree being rooted at the sender's subnetwork. The primary advantage of the shared tree approach is that it typically offers more favorable scaling characteristics than all other multicast algorithms. The CBT protocol is a network layer multicast routing protocol that builds and maintains a shared delivery tree for a multicast group. The sending and receiving of multicast data by hosts on a subnetwork conform to the traditional IP multicast service model [RFC2201].

Core Router (or just "core")
:   In CBT, a "core router" is a router which acts as a "meeting point" between a sender and group receivers. The term

	"Rendezvous Point (RP)" is used equivalently in some contexts. A core router need not be configured to know it is a core router [RFC2189].
CW (Control Word)	(aka code word) The key used to encrypt the payload in a transport stream.
Datagram	Another name for an IP-level packet.
Decoding Time Stamp (DTS) or Presentation Time Stamp (PTS)	Time stamps are inserted close to the material to which they refer (normally in the PES packet header). They indicate the exact moment where a video frame or an audio frame has to be decoded or presented to the user respectively. These rely on reference time stamps for operation [FAI200101].
Dense-Mode (DM) Protocols	Multicast routing protocols designed on the assumption that the majority of routers in the network will need to distribute multicast traffic for each multicast group. DM protocols build distribution trees by initially flooding the entire network and then pruning out the (presumably small number of) paths without active receivers. The DM protocols are used in Local-Area Network (LAN) environments, where bandwidth considerations are less important, but can also be used in Wide-Area Networks (WANs) in special cases (for example where the backbone is a one-hop broadcast medium such as a satellite beam with wide geographic illumination, for example, in some IPTV applications).
DES (Data Encryption Standard)	A 64-bit block cipher, symmetric algorithm also known as Data Encryption Algorithm (DEA) by ANSI and DEA-1 by ISO. Widely used for over 20 years, adopted in 1976 as FIPS 46. See also AES and 3DES [CON200701].
Designated Router (DR)	In PIM SM, the router on a subnet that is selected to control multicast routes for the members on its directly attached subnet. When more than one PIM-capable router is located on a subnet, the selected DR is the router with the highest IP address [ROD200701]. The DR sets up multicast route entries and sends corresponding Join/Prune and Register messages on behalf of directly connected receivers and sources, respectively. The DR may or may not be the same router as the IGMP querier. The DR may or may not be the long-term, last-hop router for the group; a router on the LAN that has a lower metric route to the data source, or to the group's RP, may take over the role of sending Join/Prune messages [RFC2362].
Digital Subscriber Line Access Multiplexer (DSLAM)	Telephone carrier equipment typically residing at the central office that terminates multiple DSL lines (usually 96, 192, or 384) and multiplexes the combined output to an

	ATM, MPLS, or IP uplink. The uplink is typically an OC-3 (155 Mbps) or an OC-12 (622 Mbps).
Digital Video Broadcast—Handheld (DVB-H)	Properly a protocol. More broadly approaches and technologies to deliver commercial-grade medium-quality real-time linear and on-demand video content to handheld, battery-powered devices, such as mobile telephones and PDAs. IP multicast is typically employed.
Digital Video Recorders (DVRs)	Devices (perhaps built into the STB) that provide the ability to "time-shift" television viewing. DVRs use a hard disk to record the content. As such, they can record hundreds of hours of content, and subscribers can directly access any recording without "fast forwarding" through other programs. DVRs are integrated into the IPTV system. From the operator's Electronic Program Guide (EPG), the subscriber simply scrolls to the content to be recorded and hits a "record" button [NOR200601].
Distance Vector Multicast Routing Protocol (DVMRP)	A routing protocol, originally defined in RFC 1075, to support internetwork multicasting. DVMRP combines many of the features of RIP with the Truncated Reverse Path Broadcasting (TRPB) algorithm. DVMRP is an "interior gateway protocol," suitable for use within an autonomous system but not between different autonomous systems. The multicast forwarding algorithm requires the building of trees based on routing information. This tree building needs more state information than RIP was designed to provide, so DVMRP is much more complicated in some places than RIP [RFC1075]. DVMRP is based on RIP.
Downstream Interface (or Router)	In CBT A "downstream" interface (or router) is one which is on the path away from the group's core router with respect to this interface (or router) [RFC2189]. All interfaces that are not the upstream interface, including the router itself [RFC3973].
DRM (Digital Rights Management)	System that enables secure distribution of digital content and that prevents unauthorised access to and illegal and perfect copying of same [CON200701].
DSL (Digital Subscriber Line)	A technology that exploits unused frequencies on copper telephone lines to transmit traffic typically at multi-megabit speeds. DSL can allow voice and high-speed data to be sent simultaneously over the same line. Because the service is "always available," end users do not need to dial in or wait for call setup. Variations include: ADSL, G.lite ADSL (or simply G.lite), VDSL (ITU G.993.1), and VDSL2 (ITU G.993.2). The standard forms of ADSL

	(ITU G.992.3, G.992.5, and ANSI T1.413-Issue 2) are all built upon the same technical foundation, Discrete Multi-tone (DMT). The suite of ADSL standards facilitates interoperability between all standard forms of ADSL [DSL200701].
DSM-CC	Digital Storage Management Command and Control. A formatting defined by the ISO MPEG-2 standard, which is carried in an MPEG-2 private section [CLA200301]. A format for transmission of data and control information in an MPEG-2 private section, defined by the ISO MPEG-2 standard [FAI200501].
DTH (Direct to Home)	A generic term used to describe the overall system of signal transmissions from an earth station to a satellite and then to a home satellite dish. Generally encompasses all frequency ranges including C-band, medium- and high-power Ku-bands, and Ka-bands [CON200701].
DVB (Digital Video Broadcasting)	(aka ETSI-DVB). A set of framework and associated standards published by the European Telecommunications Standards Institute (ETSI) for the transmission of video, audio, and data using the ISO MPEG-2 standard [CLA200301]. Organization defined transmission standards for digital broadcasting systems using cable (DVB-C), satellite (DVB-S), terrestrial (DVB-T), and handheld (DVB-H) devices. See www.dvb.org [CON200701].
Dynamic Host Registration	A mechanism that informs the network that a host (receiver) is a member of a particular group (otherwise, the network would have to flood rather than multicast the transmissions for each group). For IP networks, the Internet Group Management Protocol (IGMP) serves this purpose.
Emergency Alert System (EAS)	In the United States, the government mandates that operators support the Emergency Alert System. Each operator must listen for any alerts and translate these encoded messages for presenting to viewers. An EAS receiver provides this function [NOR200601].
Encapsulator	A network device that receives PDUs (also known as SNDUs) (Ethernet frames or IP datagrams) and formats these for output as a transport stream of TS packets [NOR200601].
Encoder	A device that converts an audio or video signal to a specific streaming format, for example, MPEG-4 (or MPEG-2). The conversion typically includes compression and generation on an IP packet.
Encryption	The process of making a message unintelligible for all who do not have the proper key.

Entitlement	Access criteria authorizations.
Entitlement Control Messages (ECMs)	A conditional-access message that contains the key for decrypting transmitted programs. It is transmitted with the entitlement management message. Private conditional-access information that specifies authorization levels or the services of specific decoders. Encrypted message that contains access criteria and Control Words (CWs). The ECM is decrypted and checked against the access criteria in order to provide authorization. If authorization is granted, the CW will be released [CON200701].
Entitlement Management Messages (EMMs)	A satellite conditional access specifies customer entitlements. It is transmitted with the entitlement control message. Encrypted messages sent to the smart card or STB to authorize it for certain access criteria. The EMM contains the actual authorization data (i.e., Entitlements) [CON200701].
EPG (Electronic Program Guide)	A listing of all available TV programs covering a few days which displays on a TV screen.
ES (Elementary Stream)	A DVB/MPEG-2, raw bit stream consisting of digitized video or audio.
ETSI (European Telecommunications Standards Institute)	An independent, nonprofit organization whose mission is to produce telecommunications standards for today and for the future. See www.etsi.org.
Footprint	The geographic area of the earth on which a satellite's direct transmissions can be received by a ground-based station or home dish.
Forward Direction	The dominant direction of data transfer over a network path. Data transfer in the forward direction is called "forward transfer." Packets traveling in the forward direction follow the forward path through the IP network [CLA200301].
Forward Error Correction (FEC)	FEC is a family of well-known simplex error correction techniques that add "coding" bits to the information bits at the transmit end (encoder) that enables the decoder to determine which bits are in error and correct them (up to a limit). For example, R 5/4 FEC means 1 coding bit is added for every 4 information bits; the more coding bits the "stronger" the code (requires less transmit power or link quality to get the same performance) but more coding bits mean more bandwidth required. Because satellite transmission can attenuate the signal by up to 200 dB, FEC is critical. High coding: R 1/2; low coding: R 7/8. Typical satellite FEC is either convolutional/Viterbi with Reed–Solomon or turbo coding. Typical turbo codes provide about

	a 2-dB advantage over conventional codes. "Viterbi" soft-decision decoding has been the norm ($\sim$4.4-dB gain). "Turbo coding" advanced recently ($\sim$6.3-dB gain). "Low Density Parity Check (LDPC)" newest ($\sim$7.8-dB gain).
Free on Demand VoD	VoD where access and content are free, as stimulus to buy the overall service.
GARP Multicast Registration Protocol (GMRP)	A layer 2 network protocol defined in the IEEE 02.1D specification. It provides multicast pruning and dynamic group membership for multicast. Typically used in layer 2 switches. A switch can exchange multicast group information with other GMRP switches, prune unnecessary broadcast traffic, and dynamically create and manage multicast groups.
G.lite ADSL (or simply G.lite)	A standard that was specifically developed to meet the plug-and-play requirements of the consumer market segment. G.lite is a medium-bandwidth version of ADSL that allows Internet access at up to 30 times the speed of the fastest 56-kB analog modems—up to 1.5 Mbps downstream and up to 500 Kbps upstream. G.lite is an International Telecommunications Union (ITU) standard. G.lite has seen comparatively little use, but it did introduce the valuable concept of splitterless installation [DSL200701].
GLOP Addressing	RFC 2770 recommended that the 233.0.0.0/8 address range be reserved for statically defined addresses by organizations that already have an AS number reserved. The AS number of the domain is embedded into the second and third octets of the 233.0.0.0/8 range. GLOP is a mechanism that allocates multicast addresses to ASs (GLOP is neither an acronym nor an abbreviation.).
HDSL (High-Data-Rate DSL)	A DSL variety created in the late 1980s that delivers symmetric service at speeds up to 2.3 Mbps in both directions. Available at 1.5 or 2.3 Mbps, this symmetric fixed-rate application does not provide standard telephone service over the same line and is already standardized through the European Telecommunications Standards Institute (ETSI) and International Telecommunications Union (ITU). Seen as an economical replacement for T1 or E1, it uses one, two, or three twisted copper pairs [DSL200701].
HDSL2 (Second-Generation HDSL)	A variant of DSL that delivers 1.5-Mbps service each way, supporting voice, data, and video using either ATM (Asynchronous Transfer Mode), private-line service, or frame relay over a single copper pair. This ATIS standard (T1.418) supports a fixed 1.5-Mbps rate both up- and downstream.

	HDSL2 does not provide standard voice telephone service on the same wire pair. HSDL2 differs from HDSL in that HDSL2 uses one pair of wires to convey 1.5 Mbps whereas ANSI HDSL uses two wire pairs [DSL200701].
HDSL4	A high-data-rate DSL that is virtually the same as HDSL2 except it achieves about 30% greater distance than HDSL or HDSL2 by using two pairs of wire (thus, four conductors), whereas HDSL2 uses one pair of wires [DSL200701].
Homes Passed	Number of domiciles that are "passed" by cable plant. Alternatively, the number of homes in a defined geographic area within the footprint of satellite transmission.
IDSL (Integrated Services Digital Network DSL)	A form of DSL that supports symmetric data rates of up to 144 kbps using existing phone lines. It is unique in that it has the ability to deliver services through a DLC (Digital Loop Carrier: a remote device often placed in newer neighborhoods to simplify the distribution of cable and wiring from the phone company). While DLCs provide a means of simplifying the delivery of traditional voice services to newer neighborhoods, they also provide a unique challenge in delivering DSL into those same neighborhoods. IDSL addresses this market along with ADSL and G.lite as they are implemented directly into those DLCs. IDSL differs from its relative ISDN (Integrated Services Digital Network) in that it is an "always-available" service, but capable of using the same terminal adapter, or modem, used for ISDN [DSL200701].
IGMP Snooping	A method by which a switch can constrain multicast packets to only those ports that have requested the stream.
IGMP Snooping Switches	Local-Area network switches that do not adhere to the conceptual model that provides the strict separation of functionality between different communications layers in the ISO model and instead utilize information in the upper level protocol headers as factors to be considered in processing at the lower levels. This is analogous to the manner in which a router can act as a firewall by looking into the transport protocol's header before allowing a packet to be forwarded to its destination address. In the case of IP multicast traffic, an IGMP snooping switch provides the benefit of conserving bandwidth on those segments of the network where no node has expressed interest in receiving packets addressed to the group address. This is in contrast to normal switch behavior where multicast traffic is typically forwarded on all interfaces [RFC4541].

Incoming Interface (iif)	In PIM SM, the iif of a multicast route entry indicates the interface from which multicast data packets are accepted for forwarding. The iif is initialized when the entry is created [RFC2362].
Internet Group Management Protocol (IGMP)	The protocol used by IP Version 4 (IPv4) hosts to communicate multicast group membership states to multicast routers. IGMP is used to dynamically register individual hosts/receivers on a particular local subnet to a multicast group. IGMPv1 defined the basic mechanism. It supports a Membership Query (MQ) message and Membership Report (MR) message. Most implementations at press time employed IGMPv2; Version 2 adds Leave Group (LG) messages. Version 3 adds source awareness allowing the inclusion or exclusion of sources. IGMP allows group membership lists to be dynamically maintained. The host (user) sends an IGMP "report," or join, to the router to be included in the group. Periodically, the router sends a "query" to learn which hosts (users) are still part of a group. If a host wishes to continue its group membership, it responds to the query with a report. If the host does not send a report, the router prunes the group list to delete this host; this eliminates unnecessary network transmissions. With IGMPv2, a host may send a Leave Group message to alert the router that it is no longer participating in a multicast group; this allows the router to prune the group list to delete this host before the next query is scheduled, thereby minimizing the time period during which unneeded transmissions are forwarded to the network.
IPTV (IP-Based TV)	Approaches, technologies, or protocols to deliver commercial-grade Standard-Definition (SD) and High-Definition (HD) entertainment-quality real-time linear and on-demand video content over IP-based networks, while meeting all prerequisite quality of service, quality of experience, conditional access (security), blackout management (for sporting events), emergency alert system, closed captions, parental controls, Nielsen rating collection, secondary audio channel, picture-in-picture, and guide data requirements of the content providers and/or regulatory entities. Typically, IPTV makes use of Moving Pictures Expert Group 4 (MPEG-4) encoding to deliver 200–300 SD channels and 20–40 HD channels; viewers need to be able to switch channels within 2 s or less; also, the need exists to support multiset-top boxes/multiprogramming (say 2–4)

within a single domicile. Not to be confused with simple delivery of video over an IP network, which has been possible for over two decades; IPTV supports all business, billing, provisioning, and content protection requirements that are associated with commercial video distribution. Service needs to be comparable to that received over cable TV or direct broadcast satellite. IP multicast is typically employed.

Join List	In PIM SM, the join list is one of two lists of addresses that is included in a Join/Prune message; each address refers to a source or RP. It indicates those sources or RPs to which downstream receiver(s) wish to join [RFC2362].
Key	A digital code used to encrypt, sign, decrypt, and verify messages and files.
Key Management	Generation, distribution, storage, replacement, and destruction of keys.
Key Pair	A public key and its complementary private key. In public-key systems, each user has at least one key pair.
Last-Hop Router	In PIM SM, the last-hop router is the last router to receive multicast data packets before they are delivered to directly connected member hosts. In general the last-hop router is the DR for the LAN. However, under various conditions described in this document a parallel router connected to the same LAN may take over as the last-hop router in place of the DR [RFC2362]. It is generally the same as the DR and is responsible for forwarding packets to its directly connected members. There are some special conditions where this last-hop router is not the DR [ROD200701].
Limited-Scope Addresses (or Administratively Scoped Addresses)	The range of addresses from 239.0.0.0 through 239.255.255.255. RFC 2365 defines these addresses to be limited to a local group or organization. Routers are required to be configured with packet filters to prevent multicast traffic in this address range from flowing outside of an autonomous system (AS).
Linear Programming	Real-time TV content, including national channels, local channels, sports channels, and premium channels.
Link-Local Addresses	IP multicast addresses that have been reserved for specific functions. Addresses in the range 224.0.0.0–224.0.0.255 are reserved to be used by network protocols on a local network segment. Network protocols make use of these addresses for automatic router discovery and to communicate routing information (e.g., OSPF uses 224.0.0.5 and 224.0.0.6 to exchange link-state information). IP packets with these

	addresses are not forwarded by a router; they remain local on a particular LAN segment [they have a Time-to-Live (TTL) parameter set to 1; even if the TTL is different from 1, they still are not forwarded by the router].
MAC	Medium Access and Control of the Ethernet IEEE 802 standard of protocols [CLA200301].
MAC Header	The link-layer header of the IEEE 802.3 standard or Ethernet v2. It consists of a 6B destination address, 6B source address, and 2B type field (see also NPA) [FAI200501].
Member	In PIM SM it is the host that is to receive multicast transmissions. The protocol documentation also refers to a member as a "receiver" [ROD200701].
MPE (Multiprotocol Encapsulation)	A scheme that encapsulates PDUs, forming a DSM-CC table section. Each section is sent in a series of TS packets using a single TS logical channel [FAI200501].
MPEG-2 (Motion Picture Experts Group–2)	A set of multiplexing/encoding standards specified by the Motion Picture Experts Group (MPEG) and standardized by the International Organization for Standardization (ISO/IEC 113818-1), and ITU-T (H.220). Both MPG-2 and MPEG-4 are important for IPTV, but the recent trend is in favor of MPEG-4.
MPEG-7	An ISO/IEC standard for description and search of audio and visual content.
Multicast Address	An identifier for a group of nodes. An IP multicast address or group address, as defined in "Host Extensions for IP Multicasting," STD 5, RFC 1112, August 1989, and in "IP Version 6 Addressing Architecture," RFC 2373, July 1998. The Internet Assigned Numbers Authority (IANA) controls the assignment of IP multicast addresses. IANA has allocated what has been known as the Class D address space to be utilized for IP multicast. IP multicast group addresses are in the range 224.0.0.0–239.255.255.255.
Multicast Address Dynamic Client Allocation Protocol (MADCAP)	A protocol defined in RFC 2730 that allows hosts to request multicast addresses from multicast address allocation servers. This protocol is part of the IETF multicast address allocation architecture.
Multicast Address Set Claim Protocol (MASC)	Protocol defined in RFC 2909 that can be used for inter-domain multicast address set allocation. MASC is used by a node (typically a router) to claim and allocate one or more address prefixes to that node's domain. While a domain does not necessarily need to allocate an address

set for hosts in that domain to be able to allocate group addresses, allocating an address set to the domain does ensure that interdomain group-specific distribution trees will be locally rooted and that traffic will be sent outside the domain only when and where external receivers exist.

Multicast Environment

Environment where one system communicates to a select group of other systems.

Multicast Listener Discovery Protocol (MLDv2)

MLDv2 is a multicast listener discovery protocol that is used by an IPv6 router to discover the presence of multicast listeners on directly attached links and to discover which multicast addresses are of interest to those neighboring nodes. MLDv2 is designed to be interoperable with MLDv1. MLDv2 adds the ability for a node to report interest in listening to packets with a particular multicast address only from specific source addresses or from all sources except for specific source addresses [RFC3810]. The Internet Group Management Protocol (IGMP) (RFC1112, IGMPv2, IGMPv3) allows an IPv4 host to communicate IP multicast group membership information to its neighboring routers; IGMPv3 provides the ability for a host to selectively request or filter traffic from individual sources within a multicast group. MLD, defined in RFC 2710 (MLDv2), offers similar functionality for IPv6 hosts. MLDv2 provides the analogous "source filtering" functionality of IGMPv3 for IPv6 [RFC4604].

Multicast OSPF (MOSPF)

Protocol defined in RFC 1584 that provides enhancements to OSPF Version 2 to support IP multicast routing. With MOSPF an IP multicast packet is routed based on both the packet's source and its multicast destination (commonly referred to as source/destination routing). As it is routed, the multicast packet follows a shortest path to each multicast destination. During packet forwarding, any commonality of paths is exploited; when multiple hosts belong to a single multicast group, a multicast packet will be replicated only when the paths to the separate hosts diverge.

OSPF, a link-state routing protocol, provides a database describing the autonomous system's topology. A new OSPF link-state advertisement has been added describing the location of multicast destinations. A multicast packet's path is then calculated by building a pruned shortest path tree rooted at the packet's IP source. These trees are built on demand, and the results of the calculation are cached for use by subsequent packets [RFC1584].

Multicast Payload Forwarding	Communication mechanism to forward payload. Almost invariably this is IP based at the network layer. Typical IP multicast applications make use of User Datagram Protocol (UDP) at the Transport Layer (TA); however, Transmission Control Protocol (TCP) can also be used in the same applications.
Multicast Routing	A mechanism to build distribution trees that define a unique forwarding path between the subnet of the content source and each subnet containing members of the multicast group, specifically, receivers.
Multicast Routing Information Base (MRIB)	This is the multicast topology table, which is typically derived from the unicast routing table or from routing protocols such as MBGP that carry multicast-specific topology information. PIM DM uses the MRIB to make decisions regarding RPF interfaces [RFC3973].
Multicast Scope	A range of multicast addresses configured so that traffic sent to these addresses is limited to some subset of the internetwork. Defined in "Administratively Scoped IP Multicast," BCP 23, RFC 2365, July 1998.
Multicast Source Discovery Protocol (MSDP)	A protocol that allows multiple PIM sparse-mode domains to share information about active sources. The protocol announces active sources to MSDP peers. It is a BGP-like protocol that allows a Rendezvous Point (RP) to forward source and multicast group information to other RPs [e.g., to support redundant RPs or multidomain applications where each ISP can each have its own RP(s)] [WEL200101].
MultiCrypt	The specification of a common interface which, when installed in the set-top box or television, permits the user to switch manually between CA systems. Thus when viewers are presented with a CA system which is not installed in their box, they simply switch cards [DVB200701].
Multiple Systems Operator (MSO)	Term used to describe cable operators that own more than one franchise.
Multiprotocol Border Gateway Protocol (MP-BGP)	(also referred to by the acronym MBGP) A protocol that defines multiprotocol extensions to the Border Gateway Protocol (BGP), the unicast interdomain protocol that supports multicast-specific routing information. MP-BGP augments BGP to enable multicast routing policy and connect multicast topologies within and between BGP autonomous systems. It carries multiple instances of routes for unicast routing as well as multicast routing. Protocol that carries routing information about several protocols, including IP multicast (and also IPv6 and MPLS VPN information, among others). In IP multicast, MP-BGP

carries a separate copy of unicast routes. MP-BGP helps establish links that the PIM Join messages use, which in turn allows us to control links that the multicast traffic traverses [WEL200101].

Multiprotocol Encapsulation (MPE)

A scheme that encapsulates Ethernet frames or IP datagrams, creating a DSM-CC section. The section will be sent in a series of TS packets over a TS logical channel [CLA200301].

Multiroom

Enables simultaneous management and consumption of CA protected content on several TV sets located within the same household. The STBs must be subject to physical or logical grouping of devices. May or may not utilize a home network solution [CON200701].

Near Video on Demand (nVoD)

Service similar to PPV. While PPV service starts the movie every 2 hs, nVoD service shows the same movie on several channels, each starting as little as 15 min apart. Hence, the subscriber has a short wait time until the movie begins [NOR200601].

NIT (Network Information Table)

MPEG signaling table that contains details of the bearer network used to transmit the MPEG multiplex, including the carrier frequency (PID = 10) [FAI200101].

Nonbroadcast Networks

A network supporting the attachment of more than two stations but not supporting the delivery of a single physical datagram to multiple destinations (i.e., not supporting data-link multicast). OSPF describes these networks as nonbroadcast, multiaccess networks. An example of a nonbroadcast network is an X.25 public data network [RFC1584].

Nonmulticast Router

In the context of MOSPF, a router running OSPF Version 2 but not the multicast extensions. These routers do not forward multicast datagrams but can interoperate with MOSPF routers in the forwarding of unicast packets. Routers running the MOSPF protocol are referred to as either multicast-capable routers or MOSPF routers [RFC1584].

NPA (Network Point of Attachment)

A 6-byte destination address (resembling an IEEE MAC address) within the MPEG-2 transmission network that is used to identify individual receivers or groups of receivers [FAI200501].

NVOD (Near-Video on Demand)

Systems that deliver programming at a time acceptable to the consumer, although not instantaneous, accomplished by repeating the same programs on several channels simultaneously at frequent intervals, for example, every 15 or 30 min [CON200701].

OCAP	Defines a set of common application interfaces, data formats, and protocols for interactive cable devices, allowing cable operators, content providers, and consumer electronics manufacturers to write applications one time that will run on all OCAP-compliant devices [CON200701].
On-Tree Router	In CBT, a router that is part of a CBT distribution tree is known as an "on-tree" router. An on-tree router maintains an active state for the group [RFC2189].
OpenCable	A CableLabs project with the goal of helping the cable industry deploy interactive services over cable. See www.opencable.com.
Outgoing Interface (oif) List	In PIM SM, each multicast route entry has an oif list containing the outgoing interfaces to which multicast packets should be forwarded [RFC2362].
PAT (Program Association Table)	MPEG signaling table that lists the PIDs of tables describing each program. The PAT is sent with the well-known PID value of 0x000 [FAI200101].
Pay Per View (PPV) Programming	Services that are ordered on-the-fly (or prereserved at some point prior to a broadcast), which requires that the subscriber pay an additional fee to view specific content. Like standard television service, PPV content is broadcast at a set time [NOR200601].
Permanent Host Groups	Applications that are part of this type of group have an IP address permanently assigned by the IANA. A permanent group continues to exist even if it has no members. Membership in this type of host group is not permanent: a host (receiver) can join or leave the group as desired. An application can use DNS to obtain the IP address assigned to a permanent host group using the domain mcast.net. The application can determine the permanent group from an address by using a pointer query in the domain 224.in-addr.arpa.
PES	Program Elementary Scheme of MPEG-2 [CLA200301].
PID (Packet Identifier)	A field carried in the header of all MPEG-2 Transport Stream (TS) packets. This is used to identify the TS logical channel to which it belongs [CLA200301]. A 13-bit field carried in the header of TS packets. This is used to identify the TS logical channel to which a TS packet belongs. The TS packets forming the parts of a table section, PES, or other payload unit must all carry the same PID value. The all-ones PID value indicates a null TS packet introduced to maintain a constant bit rate of a TS multiplex. There is no required relationship between the

PID values used for TS logical channels transmitted using different TS multiplexes [FAI200501].

PIM Dense Mode
(PIM DM)

PIM DM (RFC 3973, January 2005) is a multicast routing protocol that uses the underlying unicast routing information base to flood multicast datagrams to all multicast routers. Prune messages are used to prevent future messages from propagating to routers without group membership information.

PIM Multicast Border
Router (PMBR)

In PIM SM it is a router that connects the PIM domain to other multicast routing domains. The gateway functions provided by the PMBR address the need to interoperate with other multicast routing protocols [ROD200701].

PIM Source-Specific
Multicast (SSM)

A multicast protocol where forwarding uses only source-based forwarding trees. IGMPv3 is used to support SSM. SSM mapping allows SSM routing to occur without IGMPv3 being present. SSM mapping uses statically configured tables or dynamic Domain Name System (DNS) discovery of the source address for a SSM channel.

PIM Sparse Mode
(PIM SM)

Protocol defined in RFC 2362 that uses a *pull* mechanism to deliver multicast traffic. Only subnetworks (network segments) that have active receivers that have explicitly requested the information via IGMP joins are forwarded the traffic. PIM SM makes use of a shared tree to distribute the information to active sources. The PIM SM protocol shared tree algorithm actually uses a variant of the center-based tree algorithm. PIM SM makes use of a Rendezvous Point (RP).

PKCS (Public-Key
Cryptography
Standards)

Set of standards for public-key cryptography from RSA Security Inc. See www.rsasecurity.com [CON200701].

PKI (Public-Key
Infrastructure)

System that provides public-key encryption and digital signature services.

Plaintext

Ordinary readable text before being encrypted into ciphertext or after being decrypted.

PMT (Program Map
Table)

MPEG signaling table that defines the set of PIDs associated with a program, for example, audio and video) [FAI200101].

POD (Point of
Deployment)

Obsolete name for CableCARD.

P-PPV (Prebooked
PPV)

PPV services offered in a way that the consumer has to order the service within a given time in advance.

PPT (Pay Per Time)	The consumer pays for consuming a media file once within a time limit.
PPV (Pay Per View)	Services offered in a way that the consumer will pay for the service on a PPV basis. PPV services can be offered either as prebooked (P-PPV) or impulse (I-PPV).
Pragmatic General Multicast (PGM)	A reliable multicast transport protocol for applications that require ordered, duplicate-free multicast data delivery. The protocol guarantees that a receiver in a multicast group receives all data packets from direct transmissions or via retransmissions of lost packets. PGM can detect unrecoverable data packet loss.
Premium VoD	VoD where one pays an additional monthly fee for premium content such as recent movies.
Private Key	Decryption key is often called private key in public-key systems. A private key is also used for signing a message.
Private Section	A syntactic structure used for mapping all service information (e.g., an SI table) into TS packets. A table may be divided into a number of sections. All sections of a table must be carried over a single TS (Transport Stream) logical channel [CLA200301]. A structure constructed in accordance with Table 2-30 of ISO-MPEG-2. The structure may be used to identify private information (i.e., not defined by ISO-MPEG-2) relating to one or more elementary streams, or a specific MPEG-2 program, or the entire TS. Other standards bodies, for example, ETSI and ATSC, have defined sets of table structures using the private-section structure. A private section is transmitted as a sequence of TS packets using a TS logical channel. A TS logical channel may carry sections from more than one set of tables [FAI200501].
Product Metadata	Metadata related to a media file, including product ID, category, protecting services, access modes, usage rights, pricing info, scheduling info, maturity rating, and addressing [CON200701].
Program	Television program or multimedia streams.
Program Stream	A PES packet multiplex that carries several elementary streams that were encoded using the same master clock or system time clock.
Protocol Independent Multicast (PIM)	A protocol that provides intradomain multicast forwarding for all underlying unicast routing protocols [e.g., Open Shortest Path First (OSPF) or Border Gateway Protocol (BGP)], independent from the intrinsic unicast protocol. Two modes exist: PIM Sparse Mode (PIM SM) and PIM Dense Mode (PIM DM).

Prune List	In PIM SM, the prune list is the second list of addresses that is included in a Join/Prune message. It indicates those sources or RPs from which downstream receiver(s) wish to prune [RFC2362].
PSI (Program-Specific Information)	PSI is used to convey information about services carried in a TS multiplex. It is carried in one of four specifically identified table section constructs; see also SI Table [FAI200501].
Public Key	Encryption key is often called public key in public-key systems. A public key can also be used for verification of signatures [CON200701].
Public-Key Algorithm	An algorithm where the key used for encryption is different from the key used for decryption. Furthermore, the private (decryption) key cannot be calculated from the public (encryption) key [CON200701].
Pull VoD	VoD system that stores content within the operator network. Upon request, the content is streamed to the subscriber. The advantage is that the user can select from a large, centrally stored content library. The disadvantage is that bandwidth must be allocated to each subscriber viewing VoD content [NOR200601].
Push VOD	(aka virtual VOD) A system where movies are broadcast in encrypted format and stored directly on hard disks in the STBs. A consumer can later purchase access to the movies [CON200701].
Push VoD	VoD system that automatically downloads the VoD content to the subscriber's DVR. This download is done during off-peak times or at low priority, eliminating the need for additional bandwidth. The downside is that this makes some of the DVR disk unavailable to the subscriber. As such, this approach is practical only for the latest content, which will be viewed by a relatively large number of subscribers [NOR200601].
PUSI	Payload_Unit_Start_Indicator of MPEG-2. A PUSI value of zero indicates that the TS packet does not carry the start of a new payload. The TS packet does carry the start of a new payload [CLA200301].
PVR (Personal Video Recorder)	DVR and PDR are used interchangeably with this term.
QAM (Quadrature Amplitude Modulation)	Modulation technique for cable broadcasting.
QPSK (Quaternary Phase Shift Keying)	Modulation technique for satellite broadcasting.
Querier	(also known as IGMP querier) The sender of a query message—the querier is a multicast router. A multicast

	router keeps a list of multicast group memberships and a timer for each membership; querier routers periodically send a general MQ to solicit membership information. Hosts respond to this general MQ to report their membership status for each multicast group [ITU200201].
RADSL (Rate Adaptive DSL)	A nonstandard version of ADSL. Note that standard ADSL also permits the ADSL modem to adapt speeds of data transfer [DSL200701].
Receiver	Equipment that processes the signal from a TS multiplex and performs filtering and forwarding of encapsulated PDUs to the network layer service (or bridging module when operating at the link layer) [FAI200501].
Reference Time Stamp	Time stamp providing the indication of the current time. Reference time stamps are to be found in the PES syntax (ESCR), in the program syntax (SCR), and in the transport packet adaption Program Clock Reference (PCR) field [FAI200101].
Rendezvous Point (RP)	In PIM SM, each multicast group has a shared tree via, which receivers hear of new sources and new receivers hear of all sources. The RP is the root of this per-group shared tree, called the RP-tree [RFC2362]. An RP is the root of a shared multicast distribution tree. Similar to the core router in CBT protocols.
Rendezvous Point (RP) Operation	PIM SM uses RP, a router with a special function, to support how a multicast source and receiver get connected. When a multicast source wishes to transmit multicast, it just starts sending; it is up to network routers to forward the multicast packets to the RP. In turn, the RP is aware of sources and multicasts in the network.
Reverse Direction	The direction in which feedback control messages generally flow (e.g., acknowledgments of a forward TCP transfer flow). Data transfer could also happen in this direction (and it is termed "reverse transfer") [CLA200301].
Reverse Path Forwarding (RPF)	In PIM SM, RPF is used to select the appropriate incoming interface for a multicast route entry. RPF is a multicast forwarding mode in which a data packet is accepted for forwarding only if it is received on an interface used to reach the source in unicast [RFC3973]. The RPF neighbor for an address X is the next-hop router used to forward packets toward X. The RPF interface is the interface to that RPF neighbor. In the common case this is the next hop used by the unicast routing protocol for sending unicast packets toward X. For example, in cases where unicast and multicast routes are not congruent, it can be different [RFC2362].

Route Entry	In PIM SM, a multicast route entry state is maintained in a router along the distribution tree and is created and updated based on incoming control messages. The route entry may be different from the forwarding entry; the latter is used to forward data packets in real time. Typically a forwarding entry is not created until data packets arrive, the forwarding entry's iif and oif list are copied from the route entry, and the forwarding entry may be flushed and re-created at will [RFC2362]. A route entry may include such fields as the source address, the group address, the incoming interface from which packets are accepted, the list of outgoing interfaces to which packets are sent, timers, flag bits, and so on.
Router-Port Group Management Protocol (RGMP)	A protocol that constrains IP multicast on switches that have only routers attached.
RP-Set	In PIM SM, the RP-set is a set of RP addresses constructed by the BSR based on C-RP advertisements received. The RP-set information is distributed to all PIM routers in the BSR's PIM domain [RFC2362].
Scope Zone	One multicast scope may have several instances, which are known as scope zones or zones, for short. For instance, an organization may have multiple sites. Each site might have its own site-local scope zone, each of which would be an instance of the site-local scope. However, a given interface on a given host would only ever be in at most one instance of a given scope. Messages sent by a host in a site-local scope zone to an address in the site-local scope would be limited to the site-local scope zone containing the host [RFC2730].
Scrambling	Term used for weaker encryption or controlled distortion of an analog signal. The distortion can be removed by possessing and using the descrambling equipment and proper keys [CON200701].
SDSL (Symmetric DSL)	A vendor-proprietary version of symmetric DSL that may include bit rates to and from the customer ranging from 128 kbps to 2.32 Mbps. SDSL is an umbrella term for a number of supplier-specific implementations over a single copper pair providing variable rates of symmetric service. SDSL uses 2B1Q. HDSL runs on a single pair with an Ethernet interface to the customer [DSL200701].
Session Key	A key (normally symmetric) used to encrypt each set of data on a transaction basis. A different session key is used for each communication session. The session key is normally transferred to the receiver using a key exchange mechanism

	or by encrypting the key under the receiver's public key [CON200701].
Shared Tree	A tree that uses a single common root placed at some chosen point in the network. This shared root is called a Rendezvous Point (RP) (also called core or center). All sources in the multicast group use the common shared tree. The notation (*, G) is used to represent the tree. In this case "*" is a wildcard to mean all sources.
Shared Tree (or RP-tree)	In PIM SM it is a routing tree that supports one or more multicast groups. Its architecture is essentially the same as the core-based trees we discussed last month. The RP-tree is constructed to connect all receivers to the RP [ROD200701].
SHDSL	A state-of-the-art, industry standard symmetric DSL, SHDSL equipment conforms to the ITU recommendation G.991.2, also known as G.shdsl, approved by the ITU-T in 2001. SHDSL achieves 20% better loop reach than older versions of symmetric DSL, and it causes much less cross talk into other transmission systems in the same cable. SHDSL systems may operate at many bit rates from 192 kbps to 5.7 Mbps, thereby maximizing the bit rate for each customer. G.shdsl specifies operation via one pair of wires, or for operation on longer loops, two pairs of wire may be used. For example, with two pairs of wire, 1.2 Mbps can be sent over 20,000 feet of 26 AWG wire. SHDSL is best suited to data-only applications that need high upstream bit rates. Though SHDSL does not carry voice like ADSL, new voice-over-DSL techniques may be used to convey digitized voice and data via SHDSL. SHDSL is being deployed primarily for business customers [DSL200701].
Shortest Path Tree (SPT)	In PIM SM, the shortest path tree is based on the merged shortest paths from all receivers to the multicast source. This is one of the features that distinguishes PIM SM from CBT. When appropriate, the use of the shortest path tree provides an optimal distribution network that helps to keep the multicast traffic closer to the minimum required to deliver the information to all members [ROD200701]. In PIM SM, the SPT is the multicast distribution tree created by the merger of all of the shortest paths that connect receivers to the source (as determined by unicast routing) [RFC2362].
SI Table	Service Information Table. Any table used to convey information about the service carried in a TS multiplex (e.g., ISO-MPEG). SI tables are carried in MPEG-2 private sections [CLA200301]. A table may consist of one or more table

	sections; however, all sections of a particular SI table must be carried over a single TS logical channel [FAI200501].
Signaling Tables	For a user to receive a particular transport stream, the user must first determine the PID being used and then filter packets that have a matching PID value. To help the user identify what PID corresponds to which program, a special set of streams, known as signaling tables, are transmitted with a description of each program carried within the MPEG-2 transport stream [FAI200101].
SimulCrypt	A mechanism whereby a single transport stream can contain several Conditional Access (CA) systems. This enables different CA decoder populations (potentially with different CA systems installed) to receive and correctly decode the same video and audio streams [DVB200701].
SNDU	Subnetwork Data Unit, an IPv4 or IPv6 datagram (or other subnetwork packet, for example, an arp message or bridged Ethernet frame) [CLA200301]. An encapsulated PDU sent as an MPEG-2 payload unit.
Source Tree	A tree that has its root at the multicast source and has branches forming a spanning tree over the network to the receivers. The tree uses the shortest path through the network and hence. A separate SPT exists for each individual source sending to each group. The notation (S,G) is used to describe an SPT where S is the IP address of the source and G is the multicast group address.
Source-Specific Multicast (SSM)	A form of multicast in which a receiver is required to specify both the network layer address of the source and the multicast destination address in order to receive the multicast transmission. The 232/8 IPv4 address range is currently allocated for SSM by IANA. In IPv6, the FF3x:/32 range (where x is a valid IPv6 multicast scope value) is reserved for SSM semantics, although today SSM allocations are restricted to FF3x:/96 [RFC4604].
Sparse–Dense	A Cisco alternative to choosing just dense mode or just sparse mode on a router interface. This was necessitated by a change in the paradigm for forwarding multicast traffic via PIM that became apparent during its development: it turned out that it was more efficient to choose sparse or dense on a per group basis rather than a per-router interface basis. Sparse–dense mode facilitates this ability. Network administrators can also configure the "sparse–dense" mode. This configuration option allows individual groups to be run in either sparse or dense mode depending on whether Rendezvous Point (RP) information is available

	for that group. If the router learns RP information for a particular group, it will be treated as sparse mode, otherwise that group will be treated as dense [CIS200701].
Sparse-Mode (SM) Protocols	SM is one mode of operation of a multicast protocol. PIM SM uses explicit Join/Prune messages and rendezvous points in place of dense-mode PIM's and DVMRP's broadcast and prune mechanism [RFC2362]. Multicast routing protocols designed on the assumption that only few routers in the network will need to distribute multicast traffic for each multicast group. SM protocols start out with an empty distribution tree and add drop-off branches only upon explicit requests from receivers to join the distribution. SM protocols are generally used in WAN environments, where bandwidth considerations are important.
Sparse-Mode PIM	In sparse-mode PIM only network segments with active receivers that have explicitly requested multicast data are forwarded the traffic. PIM SM relies on an explicit joining request before attempting to send multicast data to receivers of a multicast group. In a PIM SM network, sources must send their traffic to a Rendezvous Point (RP); this traffic is in turn forwarded to receivers on a shared distribution tree.
SPTS (Single Program Transport Stream)	An MPEG-2-compliant transport stream that contains a single program. Because it contains only one program, an SPTS is referenced to a single time base. The time base is encoded into the SPTS using MPEG-2 PCRs. An SPTS may contain multiple elementary streams [CON200701].
SSM-Aware Host	A host that knows the Source-Specific Multicast (SSM) address range and is capable of applying SSM semantics to it [RFC4604].
STB (Set-Top Box)	A device that enables a TV to receive and decode digital/cable/IPTV television broadcasts.
Stream Cipher	Algorithms that simply produce a keystream to be XORed with the plaintext. The same keystream is reproduced at receiver side for decryption [CON200701].
Stream Cipher Modes	Used for block cipher operation mode that operates the algorithm as a stream cipher.
STUB Multicast Routing	A mechanism that allows IGMP messages to be forwarded through a non-PIM-enabled router toward a PIM-enabled router.
Stub Network	A network having only a single OSPF router attached. A network belonging to an OSPF system is either a transit or a stub network, but never both [RFC1584].

Subscriber	A household or business that legally receives and pays for cable or pay TV services for its own use (not for retransmission).
Subscription	The consumer subscribes for some (protected) services and pays for the subscription (e.g., by invoice).
Subscription VoD	VoD where one pays a monthly fee for access to all content in the standard library.
Symmetric Encryption	Type of encryption in which encryption and decryption keys are the same key or can easily be derived from each other. In most cryptographic systems, the decryption and encryption keys are identical [CON200701].
Symmetric Flavors DSL	Symmetric variations of DSL that include: SDSL, SHDSL, HDSL, HDSL2, and IDSL. The equal speeds make symmetric DSLs useful for LAN (Local-Area Network) access, video-conferencing, and locations hosting Web sites [DSL200701].
Table Section	A payload unit carrying all or a part of an SI or PSI table.
Telco	Traditional telephone company.
Time-Shifted Viewing	An enhancement to television service that allows content to be viewed at a time which is more convenient to the subscriber [NOR200601].
Transient Host Groups	Any group that is not permanent is by definition transient. The group is available for dynamic assignment as needed. Transient groups cease to exist when the number of members drops to zero,
Transit Network	A network having two or more OSPF routers attached. These networks can forward data traffic that is neither locally originated nor locally destined. In OSPF, with the exception of point-to-point networks and virtual links, the neighborhood of each transit network is described by a network link advertisement [RFC1584].
Transport Stream (TS)	Format for transmission of DVB content. A multiplex of several program streams that are carried in packets.
Tree Information Base (TIB)	The collection of state maintained by a PIM router and created by receiving PIM messages and IGMP information from local hosts. It essentially stores the state of all multicast distribution trees at that router [RFC3973].
TS Logical Channel	Transport Stream Logical Channel. A channel identified at the MPEG-2 level; it represents level 2 of the ISO/OSI reference model. All packets sent over a channel carry the same PID value [CLA200301]. Term identifies a channel at the MPEG-2 level. This exists at level 2 of the ISO/OSI reference model. All packets sent over a TS logical channel

carry the same PID value (this value is unique within a specific TS multiplex). The term "stream" is defined in MPEG-2. This describes the content carried by a specific TS logical channel. Some PID values are reserved (by MPEG-2) for specific signalling. Other standards (e.g., ATSC, DVB) also reserve specific PID values [FAI200501].

TS Multiplex	A set of MPEG-2 Transport Stream (TS) logical channels sent over a single lower layer connection. This may be a common physical link (i.e., a transmission at a specified symbol rate, FEC setting, and transmission frequency) or an encapsulation provided by another protocol layer (e.g., Ethernet or RTP over IP). The same TS logical channel may be repeated over more than one TS multiplex (possibly associated with a different PID value), for example, to redistribute the same multicast content to two terrestrial TV transmission cells [FAI200501].
TS Packet	A fixed-length 188B unit of data sent over an MPEG-2 multiplex (ISO-MPEG); it corresponds to the cells of, for example, ATM networks and is frequently also referred to as a TS_cell. Each TS packet carries a 4B header, plus optional overhead including an adaptation field, encryption details, and time stamp information to synchronize a set of TSs [CLA200301].
TS (Transport Stream) (ISO-MPEG)	A method of transmission at the MPEG-2 level using TS packets; it represents level 2 of the ISO/OSI reference model. See also TS Logical Channel and TS Multiplex [CLA200301].
UDL (Unidirectional Link)	A one way transmission IP over DVB link, for example, a broadcast satellite link.
Unicast Environment	Environment where one system communicates directly to another system.
Upstream Interface	Interface toward the source of the datagram. Also known as the RPF Interface [RFC3973].
Upstream Interface (or Router)	In CBT, an "upstream" interface (or router) is one that is on the path toward the group's core router with respect to this interface (or router) [RFC2189].
VDSL (Very High Bit Rate DSL)	A standard for up to 26 Mbps over distances up to 50 m on short loops such as from fiber to the curb. In most cases, VDSL lines are served from neighborhood cabinets that link to a central office via optical fiber. It is useful for "campus" environments, for example, universities and business parks. VDSL is currently being introduced in market trials to deliver video services over existing phone

	lines. VDSL can also be configured in symmetric mode [DSL200701].
VDSL2 (Second-Generation VDSL)	An ITU recommendation G.993.2 specifies eight profiles that address a range of applications including up to 100-Mbps symmetric transmission on loops about 100 m long (using a bandwidth of 30 MHz), symmetric bit rates in the 10–30-Mbps range on intermediate-length loops (using a bandwidth of 12 MHz), and asymmetric operation with downstream rates in the range of 10–40-Mbps on loops of lengths ranging from 3 to 1 km (using a bandwidth of 8.5 MHz). VDSL2 includes most of the advanced feature from ADSL2. The rate/reach performance of VDSL2 is better than VDSL [DSL200701].
Video Compression	Performing a digital compression process on a video signal. Compression techniques are used to enable efficient transmission of video signals.
Video on Demand (VoD)	Service that allows the subscriber to view content whenever he or she wants from a library of stored content. VoD supports a complete set of VCR-like functions, including rewind, pause, and fast forward [NOR200601].
Watermarking	Process that lets one add hidden information in data files to prove the origin of the files.
Wildcard (WC) Multicast Route Entry	In PIM SM, wildcard multicast route entries are those entries that may be used to forward packets for any source sending to the specified group. Wildcard bots in the join list of a Join/Prune message represent either a (*,G) or (*,*,RP) join; in the prune list they represent a (*,G) prune [RFC2362].
Zone Name	A human-readable name for a scope zone. An ISO 10646 character string with an RFC 1766 language tag. One zone may have several zone names, each in a different language. For instance, a zone for use within IBM's locations in Switzerland might have the names "IBM Suisse," "IBM Switzerland," "IBM Schweiz," and "IBM Svizzera" with language tags "fr," "en," "de," and "it" [RFC2730].

REFERENCES

[BAL199301] T. Ballardie, P. Francist, J. Crowcroft, Core-Based Trees (CBT): An Architecture for Scalable InterDomain Multicast Routing, ACM SIGCOMM'93, Ithaca, NY.

[CLA200301] C. D. Horst, B. Collini-Nocker, et al., Simple Encapsulation for Transmission of IP Datagrams over MPEG-2/DVB networks, Internet Engineering Task Force, draft-unisal-ipdvb-enc-00.txt, May 2003.

[CIS200701] Cisco Systems, Internet Protocol (IP) Multicast Technology Overview, Cisco Systems, San Jose, CA.

[CON200701] Conax AS, Glossary of Terms, Oslo, Norway.

[DSL200701] DSL Forum, Fremont, CA, http://www.dslforum.org.

[DVB200701] DVB Organization, Standards, http://www.dvb.org.

[FAI200101] G. Fairhurst, MPEG-2 Digital Video, Background to Digital Video, University of Aberdeen, King's College, Dept. of Engineering, Aberdeen, UK, January 2001, http://www.erg.abdn.ac.uk/research/future-net/digital-video/mpeg2-trans.html.

[FAI200501] G. Fairhurst, M-J. Montpetit, Address Resolution for IP Datagrams over MPEG-2 Networks, Internet Draft, draft-ietf-ipdvb-ar-00.txt, June 2005.

[NOR200601] Nortel, Position Paper: Introduction to IPTV, Triangle Park, NC, 2006.

[RFC1075] RFC 1075, Distance Vector Multicast Routing Protocol, D. Waitzman, C. Partridge, S. Deering, November 1988.

[RFC1584] RFC 1584, Multicast Extensions to OSPF, J. Moy, March 1994.

[RFC2189] RFC 2189, Core-Based Trees (CBT Version 2) Multicast Routing—Protocol Specification, A. Ballardie, September 1997.

[RFC2201] RFC 2201, Core-Based Trees (CBT) Multicast Routing Architecture, A. Ballardie, September 1997.

[RFC2362] RFC 2362, Protocol Independent Multicast Sparse-Mode (PIM-SM): Protocol Specification, D. Estrin, D. Farinacci, et al., June 1998.

[RFC2730] RFC 2730, Multicast Address Dynamic Client Allocation Protocol (MADCAP), S. Hanna, B. Patel, M. Shah, December 1999.

[RFC2909] RFC 2909, The Multicast Address-Set Claim (MASC) Protocol, P. Radoslavov, D. Estrin, et al., September 2000.

[RFC3810] RFC 3810, Multicast Listener Discovery Version 2 (MLDv2) for IPv6, R. Vida, L. Costa, Editors, June 2004.

[RFC3973] RFC 3973, Protocol Independent Multicast Dense Mode (PIM DM): Protocol Specification (Revised), A. Adams, A. Nicholas, W. Siadak, January 2005.

[RFC4541] RFC 4541, Considerations for Internet Group Management Protocol (IGMP) and Multicast Listener Discovery (MLD) Snooping Switches. M. Christensen, K. Kimball, F. Solensky, May 2006 (status: informational).

[RFC4604] RFC4604, Using Internet Group Management Protocol Version 3 (IGMPv3) and Multicast Listener Discovery Protocol Version 2 (MLDv2) for Source-Specific Multicast, H. Holbrook, B. Cain, B. Haberman, August 2006.

[ROD200701] M. Rodbell, Protocol Independent Multicast Sparse Mode, CMP COMMs Design, an EE Times Community, June 3, 2007, http://www.commsdesign.com/main/9811/9811standards.htm.

[WEL200101] P. J. Welcher, The Protocols of IP Multicast, White Paper, Chesapeake NetCraftsmen, Arnold, MD.

INDEX

IP Multicast with Applications to IPTV and Mobile DVB-H   by Daniel Minoli
Copyright © 2008 John Wiley & Sons, Inc.